Religion as Relation

The Study of Religion in a Global Context

Series editors

Satoko Fujiwara
Executive Editor
University of Tokyo

Katja Triplett
Series Editor
Leipzig University

Alexandra Grieser
Managing Editor
Trinity College Dublin

The series, published in association with the International Association for the History of Religions, encourages work that is innovative in the study of religions, whether of an empirical, theoretical or methodological nature. This includes multi- or inter-disciplinary studies involving anthropology, philosophy, psychology, sociology and political studies. Volumes will examine the continuing influence of postcolonial, decolonial and intercultural dynamics, as well as contemporary responses from intersectional studies. They will also address the relevance and application of more recent approaches such as cognitivist, as well as ones concerned with aesthetic culture – art, architecture, media, performance and sound.

Published
Global Phenomenologies of Religion
An Oral History in Interviews
Edited by Satoko Fujiwara, David Thurfjel and Steven Engler

Philosophy and the End of Sacrifice
Disengaging Ritual in Ancient India, Greece and Beyond
Edited by Peter Jackson and Anna-Pya Sjödin

The Relational Dynamics of Enchantment and Sacralization
Changing the Terms of the Religion Versus Secularity Debate
Edited by Peik Ingman, Terhi Utriainen, Tuija Hovi and Måns Broo

Translocal Lives and Religion
Connections between Asia and Europe in the Late Modern World
Edited by Philippe Bornet

Forthcoming
Power and Agency in the Lives of Contemporary Tibetan Nuns
An Intersectional Study
Mitra Härkönen

Religion as Relation
Studying Religion in Context

Edited by
Peter Berger, Marjo Buitelaar and Kim Knibbe

SHEFFIELD UK   BRISTOL CT

Published by Equinox Publishing Ltd.
UK: Office 415, The Workstation, 15 Paternoster Row, Sheffield, South Yorkshire S1 2BX
USA: ISD, 70 Enterprise Drive, Bristol, CT 06010

www.equinoxpub.com

First published 2021

© Peter Berger, Marjo Buitelaar, Kim Knibbe and contributors 2021

All rights reserved. No part of this publication may be reproduced or transmitted in any form or by any means, electronic or mechanical, including photocopying, recording or any information storage or retrieval system, without prior permission in writing from the publishers.

ISBN-13 978 1 80050 069 3 (hardback)
         978 1 80050 070 9 (paperback)
         978 1 80050 071 6 (ePDF)
         978 1 80050 120 1 (ePub)

British Library Cataloguing-in-Publication Data

A catalogue record for this book is available from the British Library.

Library of Congress Cataloging-in-Publication Data

Names: Berger, Peter, 1969– editor. | Buitelaar, Marjo, editor. | Knibbe, Kim E., editor.
Title: Religion as relation : studying religion in context / edited by Peter Berger, Marjo Buitelaar, and Kim Knibbe.
Description: Bristol, CT : Equinox Publishing Ltd, 2021. | Series: The study of religion in a global context | Includes bibliographical references and index. | Summary: "Religion is studied from a multitude of approaches and methodologies: history, anthropology, philosophy, sociology, psychology and the academic study of religion. This book differs from most other introductions and handbooks in that it draws on ongoing research to show "how" researchers approach their topics. The aim is to provide orientation in this multidisciplinary context without attempting to homogenize the field. It is intended for undergraduate students studying religion as well as broader audiences interested in the study of religion" – Provided by publisher.
Identifiers: LCCN 2021017074 (print) | LCCN 2021017075 (ebook) | ISBN 9781800500693 (hardback) | ISBN 9781800500709 (paperback) | ISBN 9781800500716 (epdf) | ISBN 9781800501201 (epub)
Subjects: LCSH: Religion–Methodology.
Classification: LCC BL41 .R3634 2021 (print) | LCC BL41 (ebook) | DDC 200.72–dc23
LC record available at https://lccn.loc.gov/2021017074
LC ebook record available at https://lccn.loc.gov/2021017075

Typeset by S.J.I. Services, New Delhi, India

Contents

Acknowledgements   vii

1   Introduction: Religion as Relation
Peter Berger, Marjo Buitelaar and Kim Knibbe   1

2   Philosophy of Religion: Is Religion Universal?
Dennis Vanden Auweele   51

3   Turning the Tables: The History of Philosophy as a Field of Inquiry for Religious Studies
Christoph Jedan   70

4   Normative Pictures: The History of Christianity from a Theological Perspective
Henk van den Belt   94

5   Relations of Religion in the Graeco-Roman World: Formative Judaism and Christianity
Steve Mason   113

6   Ancient Religious Texts and Intertextuality: Plato's and Plutarch's Myths of the Afterlife
Lautaro Roig Lanzillotta   134

7   Religion as a Meaning System
Anja Visser   150

8   Religion as Attachment: A Psychological Exploration of Relational Dynamics in God Representations
Hanneke Schaap-Jonker   168

9   Bridging Inner and Outer Worlds: A Psychodynamic Approach to Meaningful Mourning
Hanneke Muthert   192

Contents

10 Dilemmas in Participant Observation in Religious Contexts
    Kim Knibbe   214

11 Away From the Centre: On the Edges and Adjacencies of
    Religious Forms
    Simon Coleman   228

12 The Importation and Generation of the Religious and the
    Sacred in Political Song
    Joram Tarusarira   242

13 Comparing Notes: The Anthropological Approach to the
    Study of Islam in Europe
    Marjo Buitelaar   261

14 Configurations of Values
    Peter Berger   275

15 Epilogue: Studying Religion in Context – Diversity and
    Commonalities in Approaches
    Peter Berger, Marjo Buitelaar and Kim Knibbe   296

Index   305

Acknowledgements

We are grateful to Lucy Spoliar for helping us in preparing the manuscript for submission and peer review, and Eavan O'Riada for creating an excellent and extensive index for this volume. Moreover, we appreciate the financial support we received from the Faculty of Theology and Religious Studies of the University of Groningen and the Groningen University Fund with regard to the workshop we organized in Groningen, out of which the idea for this volume developed and in which many of its contributors participated. Finally, we would like to acknowledge and thank our students: your questions inspired us to put together this book. We learn from you and with you. This book is dedicated to you, and the future students that we hope to orient with regard to the rich landscape of disciplines that research religion.

– 1 –

Introduction

Religion as Relation

PETER BERGER, MARJO BUITELAAR AND KIM KNIBBE

In studying religion, one encounters a multitude of approaches and methodologies: history, anthropology, philosophy, sociology, psychology and the academic study of religion (henceforth ASR).[1] With such a multitude of approaches, it can sometimes be difficult to understand the merits and limitations of each one and to compare and contrast them, let alone evaluate whether they are in fact discussing the same subject matter (what is "religion"?).

This book aims to show how these diverse ways of reflecting on religion and conducting research are manifested in particular approaches. It is intended for undergraduate students in the study of religion, or anyone who is becoming acquainted with studying religion, and is therefore written to be accessible. However, it differs from most other introductions, handbooks and manuals in that it draws on ongoing research, showing a diversity of approaches without attempting to systematize them in order to provide an overview of the "state of the art".

We asked all the authors to reflect on the following questions when writing their chapters: What is the object of your inquiry and what kind of questions can you ask of the material you study within the particular approach you adopt within your discipline? What does it take to answer

---

1. While one could argue that any scholar who studies religion engages in the academic study of religion, as we will explain later in the introduction, the "academic study of religion" can be conceived of as a discipline in its own right because of the specific trajectory that it has followed. To avoid confusion, when writing about this particular strand within the wider study of religion, we will henceforth refer to it as ASR.

these questions in a valid way? Each chapter aims to show the kinds of knowledge and insights that a particular perspective and methodology produces. Each author uses material from their own research, explicating the approach in which that material has been produced and the methodology used. This allows students to see where their own questions fit in and where they can learn more about the various methodologies and perspectives in order to ask and answer their own questions.

For example, where it may be possible to ask "who or what is God, what is the nature of God?" in some approaches, such as philosophy of religion or some strands of phenomenology of religion, these are inadequate questions in many other approaches, unless one is interested in the perspective of a particular religious tradition. An anthropologist or sociologist would immediately fire back: what do you mean by God? What about people who are polytheistic? Should we not instead be studying the diversity of ways in which people ask and answer questions such as these? And while we are deconstructing this question, why focus on ideas rather than practices? Other scholars working within the field of ASR would scoff and say: that is a theological question, we are "critics, not caretakers" (McCutcheon 2001).

Important to note here is the distinction between "religious studies" as a collection of disciplines that examine more or less the same subject matter, namely "religion", and ASR. This distinction has grown out of the different trajectories that disciplines have taken: while fields such as history, sociology, anthropology and psychology all developed subdisciplines centred around something called "religion" (variously defined), within theology faculties a field of study developed that looked at "religion beyond Christianity" in a comparative (often historically comparative) context. This book mainly contains contributions from the different disciplines that study religion, and is therefore not an introduction to ASR as it developed into a discipline distinct from theology (or the "scientific study of religion" as some prefer). Rather, as mentioned above, it is an explication of the various ways in which to study and reflect on "religion", which may not always be defined in the same way. However, these approaches do, of course, often develop in conjunction with the debates taking place in ASR, showing the importance of cross-disciplinary conversations.

We chose "religion as relation" as the loosely connecting theme for this book to highlight that for many of the approaches contributing to religious studies, religion is thought of as something "in context". Many of the authors in this book have a non-essentialist, non-reifying, contextualized notion of religion in common. This means that they see religion emerging only as "something" in relation to other things. By focusing on relationships between people's views, practices, products and the context that they live in, researching religion can become both concrete, in the sense of approaching religion as a cultural, historical and social phenomenon, and open, in that the particularities of the relationships through which religion emerges as "something" must be established in each case.

However, we have also included chapters elucidating approaches that view religion differently. Some authors specifically argue that they wish to adhere to a more essentialist, or theological, definition of religion. Nevertheless, for those employing such an approach, as in other approaches, religion is seen as a phenomenon that appears in relationship to the surrounding context (e.g. Henk van den Belt in Chapter 4). It is also important to note that there are theological, philosophical (Vanden Auweele) and psychological (Schaap, Muthert) approaches in which the study of religion is seen as encompassing the various ways that people build connections between themselves and something located in another domain, a domain that may be unpredictable and not subject to human control.

To elucidate the various ways of approaching the subject matter, this introductory chapter will first outline three different modes of defining religion. In some cultures and historical periods, the category of religion may be alien to the context that is studied. Nevertheless, the phenomenon in question is part of a body of thought and practices that is now identified as religious. How did these phenomena come to be studied as "religion" in that tradition? What is the history of such definitions? We will then address the issue of theory: what is it, and why do you need it? We will also introduce some basic distinctions in levels of analysis that we think are useful to navigate our way through the conversations across disciplinary boundaries that often take place within religious studies. Another issue that will be addressed is the relationship of the researcher to the religious context: should one be a "believer" to understand religion? Or is the category of belief itself problematic? This question is a variation of the "insider/outsider" discussion in anthropology, and our discussion will thus draw heavily on these discussions. In closing, we give an outline of the book and how the chapters relate to the central question of how religion is studied.

What is Religion? The Dilemmas and Politics of Defining

What is religion? One of the briefest and most influential definitions of religion is still that of the nineteenth-century anthropologist E.B. Tylor:

religion (in what he called its most "primitive" and basic form) is the "belief in Spiritual Beings" (Tylor 1920 [1871]: 424). Another definition is that of Mircea Eliade, also still influential in popular culture: religion is irreducible to other phenomena, an expression of the sacred that may vary in form across cultures and historical periods, but which can be studied in terms of patterns such as the dialectic between the sacred and the profane (Eliade 1959). This comes very close to current common-sense ideas of religion in most Western societies: religion is something special, something that goes beyond the mundane, beyond science, something outside the visible world that somehow gives meaning to it. If we only had the mundane world, only had science, we still would not know what it all really *means*, and that is why people turn to religion.

The European scholars who developed the category of religion in the nineteenth century assumed that all cultures across the world had some kind of belief in supernatural beings, and therefore some kind of "religion". At the time, the framework of evolutionism – the idea that you could rank societies along a ladder of development, with "Western civilization" at the top – was very influential, including in the social sciences. In some of these models, monotheism was thought to be the highest form of religion. In others (like Tylor's), science was thought to replace religion. In what he categorized as the most "primitive" societies, a more "primitive" form of religion was thought to prevail, such as animism: the belief that aspects of nature, such as a rock or stream, are imbued with spirit.

This evolutionism – with its assumption of a single unilinear development, hence culture in the singular – has since been discredited: after all, all of these types of societies have existed side by side, influencing each other. Each has a long history and may be extremely complex (and thus far from "primitive" in the sense of simpler versions of "modern society") in very different ways. However, in Tylor's definition and conceptualization, we can see three characteristics that are still often attributed to religion: it involves the supernatural, it offers a model to explain the world and may therefore come into conflict with or be discredited by science, and it involves beliefs (rather than practices).

Historically, the category of religion has emerged from European Christian encounters with other traditions and regions of the world. This brings us to the critique of the category of "religion" from in ASR. Four scholars in particular have been influential in outlining this critique, as well as in defining research agendas for the study of religion following from this critique: J.Z. Smith, Russell McCutcheon, Tomoko Masuzawa and, more recently, David Chidester. Smith succeeded the influential scholar Mircea Eliade as professor of the History of Religion at the

University of Chicago. Whereas Eliade proceeded from a "sui generis" notion of religion, taking it to be a universal dimension present in all cultures across the world, Smith turned this assumption around, showing how the category of religion is in fact a scholarly product, a second-order category to enable scholarly comparison (Smith 1982). Tellingly, the book in which he proposes this thesis is titled *Imagining Religion*. In Smith's view, it is this second-order use of religion that should be the main focus of scholars of religion.

This challenge is taken up by McCutcheon in his book *Manufacturing Religion*, which focuses more strongly on the political dimension of the "sui generis" category of religion (McCutcheon 1997), once again and more directly critiquing the work of Mircea Eliade. What does it mean to posit that religion is a "universal dimension" of human life? What effect does this have in terms of directing resources and attention in academic life? What does it mean to call the self-immolation of monks in Vietnam religious rather than political? McCutcheon famously describes his position on studying religion as erecting a crane to enable an overview, in contrast to what he calls "skyhook" theories that assume some sort of universal position that enables "objective" insight into "the human condition".

Masuzawa takes on the question of how the notion of world religions emerged in nineteenth-century Europe and the "reality effects" this paradigm has created worldwide. She argues that it initially emerged as a way of modifying and expanding the pre-existing categorization of the world in terms of Christians, "Mohammedans", Jews and "the rest", that is "pagans" and "primitives". Again, the title of her book reveals much of her argument: *The Invention of World Religion, or, how European Universalism Was Maintained in the Language of Pluralism* (Masuzawa 2005). Essentially, she argues, scholars working in the world religions paradigm refined the fourth "rest" category to include a longer list of world religions, such as Hinduism, Buddhism, Sikhism, and so on. This created a world map that looks like a puzzle, with some pieces overlapping. Without question, this way of categorizing is decidedly Eurocentric: many populations would not necessarily have recognized themselves and their practices as belonging to the world religion of "Hinduism", for example. Yet this way of categorizing has had many "reality effects" over the course of the more than a hundred years since its emergence. Thus, Masuzawa pays more attention than Smith does to the ways in which the category of religion has been appropriated in contexts of (at times anti-colonial and decolonial) struggle and has been made productive by intellectuals in colonial and postcolonial contexts. As she writes in a review of McCutcheon's book:

> much as "religion" is an imaginative invention originating in the academy, it has thoroughly permeated and saturated our quotidian (non-academic) discourses in such a way that the reality-effect of this theoretical abstraction is not in the least confined to the life of the academy. Moreover, the nearly inflationary increase in the facticity of "religion" did not result from the exclusively western academic construction having been broadcast and disseminated unilaterally to the less educated and to the non-west. Rather, as we have begun to recognise in a piecemeal fashion in recent years, the process of such a construction is much more decentralised, symbiotic, and unconcerted than previously assumed.
>
> (Masuzawa 2000: 126–127)

A similar point is made by Chidester in his book *Empire of Religion*, in which he examines how the study of religion emerged in the context of the colonial history of South Africa, not just as a product of the Western imagination encountering societies that they both subjected and tried to make sense of, but through processes of "triple mediation" by imperial, colonial and indigenous agents (Chidester 2014).

Whereas the study of the history of the term "religion" reveals many problems with this category, such as its colonial history, eurocentrism and bad fit with non-Christian formations, it has been productive in defining the subject matter for the study of religion in different ways. We distinguish broadly between the following three, which we hope students will find helpful to quickly determine what kind of "religion" in terms of subject matter a particular author may be talking about:

1. religion as a category (as analysed above) that circulates, is productive and creates facticity;
2. conceptual approaches, which define the religion in terms of abstract, sometimes functionalist terms such as sacralization, ritualization, the experience of the world as meaningful, etc; and
3. religion as the collections of practices, institutions and beliefs that refer to a domain that transcends the ordinary (sometimes referred to as substantive, such as the definitions of Tylor and Eliade referred to above).

As outlined above, we should understand the second and third approaches as emerging from the particular, mostly European and often imperial, histories of creating a universal category of religion. In what follows, we will explore the second and third approaches. In each of these approaches, there are many possible nuances and debates, which we cannot outline here, and in practice, scholars often move between the different approaches.

Many conceptual approaches to defining the subject matter go back to the work of the French scholar and founding father of sociology, Émile Durkheim. Because he uses some terms that frequently recur in the study of religion, we delve into his work a little more deeply. This is particularly important to enable a distinction between the different usages of, for example, "the sacred" in the Durkheimian sense and in Eliade's sense. While employing the same word, authors might mean something very different with it.

In many ways, Durkheim represents the opposite of Tylor's position (see Hatch 1973 for an excellent comparison). Instead of giving a substantial definition focusing on one aspect (e.g. belief), Durkheim developed a definition in which different elements relate to each other.[2] In particular, his definition included the basic distinction between the sacred and the profane; a distinction, he contends, that all societies make in one way or another. However, he did not explain this as an expression of a separate "transcendent" dimension, as Eliade later would do, but rather as the effect of social processes. Also, in his method he deviated from Tylor's "cross-cultural" analysis which compared "culture traits" across time and space to arrange them on an imagined evolutionary scale. Rather, Durkheim investigated "one case", the indigenous peoples of Australia. For Durkheim, they did not present an "origin" in a chronological sense, but a functionally simple society, in which the "workings" of religion could thus be especially well established, he assumed. With regard to Australian "totemism", Durkheim tried to show that what people actually worship is the force of "society", which becomes sacred. From this analysis, he drew conclusions with regard to the role of religion in society more generally: religion, thus, is society worshipping itself, or to be more precise, members of a community worshipping the force of society transfigured into sacred symbols.

As one of the founders of sociology, Durkheim was interested in finding out what keeps a society together (the "functional" aspect of his scholarship). By starting with the most "primitive" examples, he developed a theory of the "elementary forms of religious life", which he argued was also relevant in modern times. In Durkheim's time, French society was rapidly changing, and he was afraid that the dynamics of these changes would cause society to fall apart. Religion, in the classic sense, was thought to be declining: the Catholic Church had lost much of its credibility, and all forms of Christianity and Judaism were challenged by science and newly developing secular ideologies, such as socialism

---

2. Reference is made to "religion is society worshipping itself" in *The Elementary Forms of the Religious Life* (Durkheim 1915: 225).

and liberalism. Nevertheless, Durkheim believed that new symbols and ideas were emerging that could serve to hold together the modern society that was evolving during his time: the belief in the sacredness of the individual (Durkheim 1979).[3] In his view, what is necessarily at the basis of a society is the belief in sacred things, things set apart by society as special, symbolizing what the group values most highly and what must not be questioned. These "sacred symbols" are surrounded by rules and regulations that set them apart from the ordinary "profane" context of everyday life. These symbols do not necessarily have to refer to something "supernatural", as evidenced by his proposal of seeing the individual as sacred in modern society. There is certainly a case to be made for this: saying that the rights of the individual do not matter seems an unbearable sacrilege to most people in western societies, even though in practice human rights are very obviously not always respected, such as around the reception of refugees.

If any object, action or idea can be sacred, and therefore take on a religious character, as Durkheim argues, it follows that "religion" should not be defined by substance, that is, *what* people believe in, but by function; by what it *does*. In keeping with this line of thought, it has been suggested that football can be conceived of as religion: it brings together a whole nation, it creates effervescence – the emotional state that results from joint collective action, which is crucial for the production of sacred symbols (see Berger 2016) – and the behaviour of fans certainly suggests that they attribute sacredness to the football field, the shirts of certain players, or other objects associated with football. While it may be pushing Durkheim's argument a bit far, it can be useful to look at a great many phenomena in this way: what is held sacred in a society? What, for example, are symbols of unity for a society, a nation state? What are the rules surrounding their use and manipulation? What kind of emotions and responses does the destruction of certain symbols provoke, what kinds of laws are made against the desacralization of such symbols, such as flag-burning? The sociologist Robert Bellah developed this type of analysis under the rubric of "civil religion" (Bellah 1967).

Drawing on Durkheim, as well as on the work of historians and anthropologists, other more conceptual approaches to defining the subject matter for the study of religion have focused on ritual (see Bell 1992; see also Bell 1997 for excellent overviews of the debates and histories), and

---

3. See "Individualism and the Intellectuals" (Durkheim 1973), where Durkheim makes the argument that individualism is a strong cohesive value in modern society, even positing it as a "religion".

on "meaning-making": the search for a meaningful life based on psychological and philosophical theories.

Such conceptual ways of defining religion run the obvious risk of including everything in their definition and thus becoming unhelpful in distinguishing religion from other phenomena. Therefore, the search for a more satisfactory definition of religion that would specify something about what people "believe" in or refer to in practices that are deemed religious continued.

This brings us to the third approach: substantive understandings of the subject matter. A pragmatic and influential approach to the subject matter of religion was formulated by the religious studies scholar Ninian Smart, who distinguishes seven dimensions without exactly "defining" religion: doctrinal, mythological, ethical, ritual, experiential, institutional and material. The seven dimensions Smart distinguishes clearly suggest a certain subject matter that fits with the "world religions" paradigm discussed above. In the introduction to his book *Dimensions of the Sacred* (1999), for example, he offers the following description of the subject matter of religious studies:

> That aspect of human life, experience and institutions in which we as human beings interact thoughtfully with the cosmos and express the exigencies of our own nature and existence.
> (Smart 1999: 1)

Thus, Smart broadens the subject matter somewhat to not only include "world religions" but also "ideologies", "worldviews", and "spiritualities". While pointing in a certain direction of what constitutes the subject matter for religious studies, Smart's description is fuzzy and not well bounded. Note the reference to "the cosmos": since Tyler and Eliade, the notion of the supernatural, the sacred as a universal dimension of human experience has been criticized, as has the notion of the transcendent. Yet the urge to retain a "theological" dimension appears to be persistent.

This fuzziness of subject matter impelled the anthropologist Clifford Geertz to come up with another definition, which also became quite influential. Like Smart, he does not refer explicitly to the transcendent, but to a "general order of existence", comparable to Smart's "cosmos":

> Religion is defined as (1) a system of symbols which acts to (2) establish powerful, pervasive, and long-lasting moods and motivations in men by (3) formulating conceptions of a general order of existence and (4) clothing these conceptions with such an aura of factuality that (5) the moods and motivations seem uniquely realistic.
> (Geertz 1993: 90)

Religion, in this view, is difficult to distinguish from culture more broadly. Nevertheless, Geertz attempts to do so by defining culture in more general terms: "a historically transmitted pattern of meanings embodied in symbols, a system of inherited conceptions expressed in symbolic forms by means of which men communicate, perpetuate, and develop their knowledge about and attitudes toward life" (ibid.: 89).

Geertz's definitions of religion and culture belong to the *interpretative tradition* in sociology and anthropology as pioneered by Max Weber, another "founding father" in the social sciences and the study of religion. This tradition proceeds from the understanding that people's behaviours are informed by systems of meaning leading to a certain understanding of the world. What is new in Geertz's definition of religion, is that it highlights people's own conceptions and experiences of the world, the history of these conceptions and the link to lifestyle. Yet, in an influential dissection of Geertz's definition of religion, Talal Asad has criticized it as being too firmly based on a Christian view of religion that presupposes some sort of "essence" of religion in the sense of a particular, distinguishable set of practices and ideas, which should be seen as distinct from the essence of, most crucially, politics. Concerning Islam, for example, Asad points out, it does not make sense to detach religion from issues of power. Furthermore, Geertz's definition does not consider the historicity of religious systems. Therefore, Asad argues, a universal definition of religion cannot exist, because both the constituent elements – their relations and the definition itself – are the historical product of discursive processes (Asad 2002: 116).

Thus, we return to the first approach to religion: religion as a category that is historically variable but does "act" in the world, creates "facts on the ground" as it were – not least the existence of the study of religion. From this perspective, conceptual and substantive approaches to religion appear to be attempts to generalize from a mostly Christian heritage about what religion is, what it should be and what it is not. Indeed, Asad has called for an "anthropology of the secular", shifting attention from what religion is and does to how "religion" is distinguished from the rest of our social and cultural world and how it is then circumscribed and regulated, but also how "the secular" is in fact informed by religion (Asad 2003). This call, as well as developments in other fields, such as political science and cultural sociology, has been taken up and has resulted in very fruitful new research lines concerning the variations of secularism on different levels: political, societal, cultural (e.g. Wohlrab-Sahr and Burchardt 2012; Mahmood 2015). Furthermore, as several scholars have argued, the burdened histories of the concept of religion does not imply that we should remain bogged down in endlessly criticizing this concept, but should instead critically reform and build on the approaches developed through these histories (Vásquez 2012: 39; Chidester 2020).

So, what can we conclude from this – admittedly very brief – overview of the problems of defining the subject matter for religious studies? First, conceptual definitions run into the problem that they are too inclusive and are often linked to particular functionalist views of psychology and society. Second, substantive definitions encounter the problem that they cannot be universal. Third, all these ways of defining the subject matter may have histories and current effects that are ethically problematic (colonial, imperial, excluding, creating racialized and gendered hierarchies) and which conceptually hamper our understandings: if religion is assumed to be separate from politics, for example, this directs the scholarly gaze away from an analysis in terms of power; if religion is assumed to be antithetical to modernity, it always remains the "rest" category in need of explanation rather than understood as intrinsic to it (Vásquez 2012).

Yet undeniably "religion as a category" is out there in the world (Von Stuckrad and Wijsen 2016). People use it, even if they do not always mean the same thing by it, and this has many implications. For example, particular rights relating to "freedom of religion and belief" legislation have consequences in terms of legal exemptions from paying taxes, state subsidies for training clergy, as well as conflicts with legislation with regard to sexual health and reproductive rights, the rights of sexual minorities, and tax status (see e.g. Sullivan 2005; Hurd 2015; McIvor 2020). Thus, the category of religion is not only a "plaything of the scholarly imagination" as Smith argued, but is embedded within numerous semantic fields, in particular histories of knowledge formation (Von Stuckrad 2010) and domination and resistance. Here too, it is important to study "religion" in context, to understand the implications of the existence and use of this category.

It is important to note that in practice, most scholars do not fit neatly into one of these categories in their approach. An example is the "media turn" in studying religion, exemplified in the work of Birgit Meyer, Irene Stengs, David Morgan, Matthew Engelke and several others. The meaning of the concept "media" in this approach goes beyond understandings in common parlance in terms of telecommunication devices or social media. Rather, the concept draws attention to the ways in which all religious experiences are mediated. In the words of Engelke, in this work "religion" is often understood as the set of practices, objects, and ideas that manifest the relationship between the known and visible world of humans and the unknown and invisible world of spirits and the divine"

(Engelke 2010: 374). The focus of academic enquiry, therefore, is on the materiality of mediating devices to both effect and shape the ways humans link with the divine, spiritual or transcendental (Meyer 2011: 27–28).

In its reference to an "invisible world" and the divine the media turn seems to fall within the approach that views religion in substantive terms. However, this approach has also been fruitfully employed to understand processes of sacralization that do not necessarily reference the divine or spirits, such as heritage making, the sacralization of kings, music idols and the nation state (see e.g. Meyer and de Witte 2015; Balkenhol, van den Hemel and Stengs 2020). Thus, a focus on media and aesthetics goes beyond the "substantive" understanding of religion and also develops as a conceptual approach. Furthermore, it incorporates the understanding of religion as a category in examining how "indigenous" practices are sometimes celebrated as heritage, sometimes as religion, sometimes as both.

The authors of the various chapters in this volume have all made particular choices with regard to these dilemmas of defining their subject matter, and they explain these choices in their chapters. Often, these choices do not fit neatly into one or other of the three approaches outlined above, illustrating that distinguishing them is of heuristic value first and foremost, a way to situate the approach, rather than offering a neat classification of closed categories. Thus, while many contributions in the volume do not provide explicit deliberations on what religion "is", several chapters reflect on the "edges and adjacencies" as Simon Coleman calls them to ask where do we assume religion to be, and where do we assume it to be absent? Similarly, Kim Knibbe reflects on a scholar's own (non)-religiosity in researching religion; where does it begin and end in the practice of participant observation?

The Practice of Theorizing

As outlined above, we invited the authors to reflect on and demonstrate how they studied religion. Part of this "how" are the conceptual frameworks that they as scholars bring to their subject matter, in other words, the theories they bring to bear on the material they investigate. These theories may be explicitly discussed or remain implicit but there is no way around having a point of view, looking at religion in a certain way and reflecting on the concepts we use to organize what we see (and hear etc.). Recognizing something as "religion" already implies a theoretical operation, as we saw in the above discussion on defining religion. But what is theory and why do we need it?

For the study of religion, Aaron W. Hughes (2013: 2f) distinguished "theory" from "method" (and "by extension "methodology"", as he says), as the former refers to "frameworks", while the latter signifies "scholarly practices". In contrast, Tim Ingold argued, with regard to anthropology, that "theory consists, in the first place, not in an inventory of ready-made structures or representations [read: frameworks], to be picked up and used as it suits our analytic purposes, but in an *ongoing process of argumentation*. In this sense, theory is an activity, something we do" (Ingold 1996: 3, original emphasis). To Ingold, then, theory is also a practice. This may be surprising for students, who might be inclined to regard theory as something abstract and remote.

We propose that when studying religion, and when employing the different perspectives represented in this book, it is helpful to understand theory not as a pre-existing framework but as a practice. Thus, in the title of this section we used the verb "theorizing" and not the noun "theory". In this way, the dichotomy of thought/mind (theory) and action/body (method) is less pronounced and the status difference between theory (grand reflections) and practice (mere "data collection") is questioned (cf. Ingold 1996: 2). Particularly in the social sciences, theorizing and data collection are intimately intertwined. However, such a "down-to-earth" approach to theorizing is not shared by all the disciplines present in this volume. In philosophy, for instance, "theory" is regularly understood as a high-level systematization of considered judgments (Rawls 2005: 48–51) and in this philosophical sense, it combines what social scientists would refer to as models, conceptual schemes and general presuppositions.

Moreover, it is clear that some disciplines and scholars find theorizing more important than others. While the social sciences seem to be continually concerned with building and refuting theories, historians in the humanist tradition, for example, may be much less dedicated to such efforts. Steve Mason, author of Chapter 5 of this volume, argues that as a historian investigating human actions in the past and reconstructing bygone life-worlds, he is first of all concerned with his material (personal communication). To him, making sense of new material is like trying to understand a person one meets for the first time; it requires imagination, curiosity and openness. Having a theory could interfere with this process and alienate the researcher from their material, which is then downgraded to a "case study" to serve theory testing. Many anthropologists would agree. Obviously, this does not imply that the researcher engages with the material as a *tabula rasa*. In the dialogue between scholar and material, predispositions and conceptualizations are made explicit, and assumptions are weighed. Thus, no explicit theory is at stake here, but instead a dialectical process of understanding and reasoning.

In psychology, an emphasis on theorizing is relatively recent, an exception being psycho-dynamic approaches that early on stressed the importance of a wide range of analytical concepts; for example Winnicott's famous theory about transitional objects that support people in connecting their inner psychic world with their cultural (religious) and social contexts (Winnicott 1971), or a psychological theory of thinking (Bion 1967: 110–119). Strands of psychology that emerged after the Second World War, such as personality psychology, health psychology, cognitive science, initially engaged mainly with micro-range theories to determine correlations of religion with other behaviours, for example, on the question of whether people who attend church regularly report less depression. Although such questions are still asked, Anja Visser, author of Chapter 7 of this volume, identifies a shift towards attempts to assemble and embed these micro-range theories into broader accounts of behaviour that help to understand the mechanisms and motivations behind more specific thoughts, acts and feelings (personal communication). Terror management theory (Greenberg, Pyszczynski and Solomon 1986), for example, is used to predict and explain religious and spiritual beliefs and activities, health risk behaviours, and our self-understanding. Over the past decade, Anja Visser notes, this shift has expressed itself in the requirement by psychology journals to place study hypotheses in the framework of higher-level theories to show their theoretical relevance.

Aside from "theory" it may be useful to distinguish between "method" and "methodology", although the terms are often used interchangeably. "Method" refers to concrete techniques that are used to study a phenomenon (e.g. how to conduct an interview). In "methodology", the "-ology" is important as it indicates another level, the study of how research is done, for example, reflecting on how interviewing relates to normative dimensions of social life in particular. Or, as the *Concise Dictionary of Sociology* (Marshall 1996: 326) puts it: "the study of how, in practice, sociologists and others go about their work, how they conduct investigations and assess evidence, how they decide what is true and false". The same dictionary (ibid.: 532) understands theory as "an account of the world which goes beyond what we can see and measure. It embraces a set of interrelated definitions and relationships that organizes our concepts and understanding of the empirical world in a systematic way". Note that this latter definition also seems to stress the intellectual process, unless one adds that "an account of the world" is given and constructed by someone. Moreover, and this takes us back to Ingold's view, this "account-giving" is not a solitary mental operation but it occurs in relation and in contrast to other people: it is an exchange, and thus an activity.

Students may not think of themselves as theorists, an honorary title usually reserved for the deep thinkers in the discipline. However, in a general sense, *theorizing* is something that all of us do all of the time. It has to do with the way humans generate knowledge. Perception, description, abstraction, interpretation and generalization are some of the key processes involved in producing knowledge, be it academic or everyday knowledge (cf. Joas and Knöbel 2004: 18). For example, if someone notices a sensation somewhere in their belly, they might wonder if this is just an ordinary rumble or perhaps the beginnings of "pain". A process of reflection then usually sets in, generalizing this particular instance, comparing it with other such experiences in the past, relating it to certain kinds of activities (e.g. food that has been eaten, recent contact with a neighbour with stomach flu), and contemplating the possibility of a particular cause; in other words, certain hypotheses are considered and tested. They might even check the internet to identify their condition as a certain category of illness (perhaps "irritable bowel syndrome"). Ultimately, they may go to see a doctor to talk about the "stomach pain", thereby already giving an interpretation of this particular sensation. When asked to describe the pain, they will notice how difficult it is to translate uncertain sensations into precise words. If the doctor is a classic biomedical type, certain kinds of interpretations and subsequent actions will follow. The same sensation would be seen very differently from an alternative practitioner's viewpoint. In the highlands of Central India, where Peter Berger works, stomach pain is often associated with attacks of "spirits of the deceased" and a person would go to a healer to find out what has happened and what to do about it. In other words, the process of enquiry is similar but the frameworks within which the actors abstract, generalize and explain are different. But theorizing is certainly involved here since an "account of the world" is given in relation to other actors (neighbours, doctors, internet authors, healers).

Theory thus consists of operations that are part of everyday life. Most actions involved – translation, generalization, abstraction – make it quite evident that something is added. As authors we are creators (the literal meaning of author), and, therefore, automatically theorists. Of the operations mentioned above, "description" may appear to be the most passive or self-evident activity, a case of reproduction in which phenomena are identified that are out "there". However, a little experiment, such as asking people what they see in a painting, will quickly reveal that we tend to see what we know and overlook what we are unfamiliar with. In other words, perception and description are highly selective processes informed by the observer's historical and cultural conditions as well as by their strategies and intentions. Male scholars have tended to overlook (ignore?) the role of women and their perspectives on the phenomena they study. British administrators in nineteenth-century India described supposedly "spontaneous insurgencies" by their colonial subjects, thereby camouflaging in their accounts the organized and intentional practice of rebellion against British rule (Guha 1988). Although not all descriptions are so obviously politically motivated as those of the colonial administrators, there are no innocent descriptions; all are necessarily selective and biased, "partial truths" at best (Clifford 1986).

The consequence of this, then, is to recognize every author as a creator and as an "authority", as someone in the condition ("-ity") of power to make statements about something. This means that understanding the conditions of this author(ity) is crucial in contextualizing the production of knowledge. This is not new: in 1965 one important voice in the anthropology of religion wrote this about the authors on "primitive religion": "If one is to understand the interpretations of primitive mentality they [the scholars under discussion] put forward, one has to know their own mentality, broadly where they stood; to enter into their way of looking at things, a way of their class, sex, and period" (Evans-Pritchard 1965: 14).

As in anthropology, reflexivity about the connection between knowledge and power and locations of knowledge has developed in psychology in the course of its history as well. Earlier (roughly before the 1960s), it was simply assumed that experts "have knowledge". A more diverse view on knowledge did not develop until later, such as the recovery approach (Lukoff 2007), which stresses the individual potential for convalescence and gives a voice to diverse actors, such as patients, family members or different clinicians.

Thomas Kuhn in *The Structure of Scientific Revolutions* (1970) and Bruno Latour and Steve Woolgar in *Laboratory Life* (1986) have put forward forceful arguments about the historical and social embeddedness of theories and theorizers.[4] The latter work shows in detail how "facts" are constructed through microsocial processes in a social space of negotiation, persuasion and dispute (called "agonistic field"), which actually disguises the process of their production: "The result of the construction of a fact is that it appears unconstructed by anyone" (Latour and Woolgar 1986: 240). The history of science, Kuhn argues, is not the regular and cumulative production of knowledge based on logic and increasing insights alone, but proceeds in leaps and through ruptures that are

---

4. For a summary and contextualization of their arguments see Rosenberg (2011, esp. chapters 12 and 14); for a criticism see Boghossian (2010).

also socially and historically mediated. At any moment in a "normal phase", a certain paradigm prevails (i.e. accepted assumptions, values, techniques, standards and models of scientific practice), which enables the community of scientists to "see" certain things and not others (cf. Kuhn 1970: 176f). What does not fit is integrated as a theoretical "anomaly". But science also goes through revolutionary paradigm shifts and as paradigms function like worldviews, nothing seems the same as before, "as if the professional community had been suddenly transported to another planet where familiar objects are seen in a different light and are joined by unfamiliar ones as well" (ibid.: 111). Or, as Alex Rosenberg puts it: "When allegiance is transferred from one paradigm to another, the process is more like a religious conversion than a rational belief shift supported by relevant evidence" (Rosenberg 2011: 230). Referring to natural science, Kuhn describes these paradigms as incommensurable, as mutually exclusive.

What are the "paradigms" in the study of religion and what could paradigm shifts mean in this context? For ASR, competing paradigms can often be related to the three approaches to religion as outlined above, where the debate is frequently between those who see religion as *sui generis* (something that cannot be reduced to its constituent parts, with some kind of "essence" that can be traced across history and cultures)[5] and those who see religion as a category that emerged from a particular history and whose boundaries may shift. Below, we provide two other examples of disciplines that study religion – namely, anthropology and psychology – and look at how paradigms shaped their assumptions about religion.

In anthropology paradigms are more fundamental than analytical concepts and more encompassing than specific theories; they are not only a way to see the world but they constitute an assemblage of basic assumptions, questions, concepts and methods that each rely on and reinforce one another.[6] "Evolution", mentioned above, was a paradigm

---

5. Note that the notion of something *sui generis* may be understood in different ways. It may refer to the assumption that a phenomenon (e.g. religion) can or even should be studied in isolation. However, it is also used by sociologists and anthropologists to argue that a "culture" or a "society" has a reality of its own, transcending the constitutive parts (e.g. individuals) and thus cannot purely be explained by the properties of those parts. This view that something is *sui generis* (literally "of its own kind") because it is more than the sum of its parts goes back to Durkheim (1982: 39f, 54, 144) and does not necessarily entail that the phenomenon in question exists in isolation and should be studied accordingly.
6. For an example of how paradigms changed over decades in a certain subfield of anthropology –namely the anthropology of India – and how theorizing related to

that fundamentally framed the questions that scholars of religion asked in the second half of the nineteenth century and the methods they thought would be appropriate. Like many others of his time, E.B. Tylor assumed the unilineal evolution of humankind and a progression from simple to complex forms of "culture" (cf. Tylor 1920 [1871]; Stocking 1968). Thus, questions asked often referred to the "origin" of phenomena. For example, was "animism" considered to be the earliest and simplest form of religion? Assuming that all human groups progress through the same stages of development and taking the psychic unity of humankind (the so-called uniformitarian view) for granted, the "comparative method" seemed appropriate. This included grouping elements – marriage customs, objects, forms of sacrifice – on an imagined scale of progress, across space and time and decontextualizing them in the process. If an element did not fit well with the period in which it was found, it was considered a "survival" from an earlier phase. A matrilineal form of descent, for example, was taken to point to an earlier state of "matriarchy". Moreover, because humans are understood as always thinking in the same way (something that returns in the work of Lévi-Strauss), introspection was considered an appropriate tool. Tylor thus pondered the question of how "primitive man" could come up with the idea of a soul and deduced a plausible explanation based on what he himself would have thought were he a "primitive" man (e.g. the appearance of deceased persons in dreams suggests the idea of a "soul"). Finally, considering the paradigm of evolution, the historical and political context of the colonial era has to be considered along with its fantasies of superiority.

The fact that the next generation of anthropologists discarded the paradigm of evolution along with all its concomitants and implications was directly related to a new way of collecting data and therefore a new kind of data (Kuper 1996). Anthropologists stopped being armchair scholars and started engaging in long-term ethnographic fieldwork, a method that produced a completely different set of questions. A further consequence was that earlier assumptions appeared to have been completely misplaced. Again, it was political circumstances that made this method possible. The general point here is that theory development is a consequence of engaging with a certain kind of data (historical, empirical or other) and this dialogue between data and theoretical reflection is highly creative and productive. New theories developed as anthropologists moved from the desk to the field and later when moving from Africa to Papua New Guinea and Amazonia.

---

ethnography in this particular case, see the extended critical discussion by Peter Berger (2012).

Evolution was replaced by the paradigm of function in the 1920s, which dominated British social anthropology in particular until the 1960s. However, the earlier questions about the origin of religion were not solved; rather, they were no longer considered relevant and were regarded as unresearchable: as conjectural history. Rather than answering old questions, scholars posed new ones and started to look at old problems from a new perspective. Magic was no longer considered as the phase preceding religion. Instead, the function of magic was studied in relation to other social institutions. Confirming Marshall Sahlins' dictum that we will all ultimately be not only dead but also wrong (Sahlins 2002: 2), the functionalists, in turn, were also regarded as mistaken by the next generation, for example in their assumption of a general balance, or equilibrium, between the institutions of a society. Therefore, while a specific paradigm seems to make perfect sense to scholars for a time, a later generation, operating in a different historical context and engaging with new material, wonders what made their ancestors believe in all this. In an increasingly diversified academic field, more paradigms (structure, meaning, power) followed, and were dismissed.[7]

Yet, paradigms are usually not completely dismissed and cannot strictly be regarded as incommensurable. First, paradigms have revivals. For example, evolution was replaced by function, but was revived as "neo-evolutionism" by American anthropologists such as Leslie White in the 1950s. Second, different paradigms can be found to be co-present even in a single author. Émile Durkheim, for one, wrote in a language that relied heavily on biological metaphors and narratives of evolution, especially in his early work, while much of his interest focused on mechanisms of social and religious life, a rather "functionalist" concern. Yet, in many ways his work can also be regarded as structuralism *avant la lettre*, investigating the relationships between cultural ideas (see Chapter 14, this volume).

The paradigms of function, evolution and meaning were (and are) also important in psychology, as questions of a person's socio-emotional development and the integration of personality dimensions and processes of signification have remained pertinent. However, in contrast to anthropology, paradigm shifts in psychology seem to have been less connected to innovations in data and methods. The evolutionary paradigm, for example, continued to be relevant, even though the kinds of data psychologists were dealing with changed substantially from

---

7. For further critical summaries and discussion of key paradigms in anthropology (of religion), see Hackett (2005) and Moore and Sanders (2006). For the sociology of religion, see Davie (2013), Dillon (2012) and Beckford and Demerath (2007).

introspection about personal experience and observation of behaviour to laboratory experiments. What makes psychology special in relation to all other approaches discussed in this volume is its relationship to medical studies and ultimately its ambition to improve health and well-being. This orientation makes psychology particularly disposed to a functional outlook. However, as ideas about what constitutes a functioning personality change, it could be argued that, rather than innovations in data and methods, social and political transformations in how people and their functioning are valued have led to paradigm shifts in this discipline. An example of this would be how religion is valued within psychology. Influential early psychologists, such as Freud (1856–1939), considered religion mainly as a threat to health, because it inhibited people's progression from instinct-driven children to rational adults (an evolutionary perspective). In the wake of emancipation movements, later psychologists, such as Erikson (1902–1994), viewed religion more positively because they believed that it assisted in socio-emotional development through the transference of social support, social norms and values (emphasizing meaning). Nevertheless, several of Erikson's contemporaries (e.g. Maslow, 1908–1970) also felt that this normative role of religion inhibited people's ability to make the transition towards self-fulfilment and autonomy, thus viewing it as a negative factor for health and well-being.

These changing views over the decades about the use and abuse of religion in the field of psychology take us back to Tim Ingold's understanding of theory as an ongoing process of argumentation. As mentioned above, theory-making is not a solitary endeavour; it always involves teamwork. Further, this process occurs in different arenas, such as conferences, (online) classrooms or field sites, and the participants in this debate are scholars, students and interlocutors alike. There should be no privileged place for these dialogues, nor are there privileged actors (cf. Ingold 1996: 3f). Moreover, these dialogues cut across time, engaging the ideas of scholars of different times and ages.

This section started by stating that everyone is engaged in theory-building. But what are the particular characteristics of academic theories in contrast to folk theories or common sense, which are also systems of knowledge? Perhaps there is no principled difference and some scholars would criticize the hegemony of Western scientific discourse (see the discussion on Ewing and the "problem of belief" below), doubting the privileged place of "science" among other knowledge frameworks, and finding "rationality", supposedly a hallmark of science, to be just another folk category (cf. Geertz 1984; Ingold 1996; Sahlins 1996; Kapferer 2002). That being said, there are a few criteria that one can point to as important features of academic theories (cf. Joas and Knöbel 2004). Academic theories should, somewhat idealistically, be consistent, not contradictory; they should involve sound argumentation based on evidence produced by transparent methods, and systematically build hypotheses that, if they cannot be verified, should at least be falsifiable, following Karl Popper. As scholars of religion do not usually engage in laboratory experiments (although some do), our conceptual apparatus gains a special importance. While students may experience it as a cumbersome and unnecessary complication – and at times terminology seems to obstruct more than it reveals – theories construct meta-languages and concepts in order to refine the arguments they make and the debates they engage in. To once again quote Tim Ingold, who argues – for anthropology in particular but this holds for other disciplines as well – that the apparent fuzz of words has crucial importance for theory-building:

> Every word carries, compressed within it, a history of past usage, and it is only by unravelling such histories that we can gauge the appropriateness of particular words for current or projected purposes. ... The process of theory ... is tantamount to the fashioning of an anthropological language dedicated to establishing the commensurability of radically contrasting forms of knowledge and experience.
>
> (Ingold 1996: 4)

Most importantly, perhaps, academic theory-building as an ongoing process of argumentation should involve radical self-reflection. In principle, everything can be questioned. There should be no protected areas behind which any point of departure can be hidden, thereby excluding itself from critical investigation. This applies not only to particular theories but to the general conditions of academic knowledge production.

Levels of Analysis

"Analysing" means taking apart or disassembling a complex phenomenon. It is one of those procedures that are part of theorizing and thus of the "ongoing process of argumentation" we have discussed above. It is necessarily also part of doing research and even of critically reading the work of other scholars. As mentioned earlier, religion as relation necessarily means that religion is nothing on its own. Certainly, religion is embedded in culture and society. But what, then, do these terms mean and how are we going to deal with them?

As with religion, the terms "society" and "culture" have been understood in many different ways. Depending on different academic traditions, one term is seen as more encompassing, and as including the other. These debates do not concern us here. Instead, we want to provide students of religion with an analytical tool to "take apart" and apprehend the complexity of either society or culture, and with it, religion. Three levels of society or of social life can be distinguished (one could say the same for culture, but we will refer to society here): categories, rules and behaviour.[8] The fact that these distinctions are "analytical" means that they do not exist "out there" but are scholarly constructs that have a heuristic purpose: they help us understand.

Behaviour may be regarded as the most obvious term of the three. Human beings do things, they act. It is important to distinguish social action from behaviour in its simplest form. If someone stumbles over a stone because they are not walking carefully, they are behaving in a certain way, but not acting socially. Social action, as Max Weber pointed out, has subjective meaning for the individual but it is significantly oriented towards others and this social orientation has an influence on the course of action (Weber 1964: 88). This makes the matter much more complex. Usually, we are dealing with behaviour in this sense of social action. What is crucial and what distinguishes behaviour in principle from the other two terms of rules and categories is that it can be observed. In the empirical study of religion, we pay attention to what people do, for example how they worship. We see movements across space, the treatment of objects, we hear what they say, sing, shout or chant. Obviously, not all disciplines that study religion have material that gives direct access to this level of social life. Archaeologists, for example, deal with objects, sometimes texts, and they have to infer from their material what people actually did.

Rules, on the other hand, are not about what actors actually do, but what they are supposed to do; the term norm also refers to this level of social life.[9] Obviously, rules inform what we do, but we do not follow rules all the time. This is already a crucial point to investigate in any

---

8. See Rodney Needham (1973: 171f) and Barnard and Good (1984: 9f) on this distinction with regard to the study of kinship, and Heidemann (2011: 28f) with regard to culture in general.
9. Rules that state an appropriate or desired behaviour are discussed in the following. Such rules often have an explicitly moral component; they entail what is "good" or "bad". Statistical norms, on the other hand, simply indicate what people actually do on average, as in the statement: "20% of adult Europeans are smokers". This provides an idea about average behaviour but has no ethical implications and does not suggest whether adults should or should not smoke.

particular context – the relationships between a rule and actual practice. When do actors follow rules, and when do they bend or ignore them? To take the example of worship again, there may be explicit rules about how to go about it. For example, the participants may need to have fasted for one day, they should be married, and men and women should perform in separate places. While we observe that these rules are strictly followed in some situations, some or all rules are ignored in others. This may signify that the two contexts are not of equal value for the participants. But there may be a host of other reasons and it would be up to the researcher to investigate the various factors involved to account for deviance or compliance.

Some rules are written on paper, perhaps even carved in stone, but most aspects of our daily lives are not regulated by such explicit norms, but rather by implicit agreements about what constitutes "proper" practice. People who are socialized in a particular environment often take such rules for granted; they become embodied patterns, which Bourdieu (1990) calls habitus. Precisely because of these often tacit rules, it is difficult to enter a completely new social context, as one's "common sense" no longer works and the rules that should be followed cannot simply be checked beforehand in some encyclopaedia or on the internet. Take the example of greeting. Germans seem to shake hands all the time, while in the Netherlands, people of opposite sexes greet one another with three kisses on the cheek. However, as anyone who has visited either of these countries knows, the situation is much more complex, as considerations of gender, age, subculture, place, formal and informal contexts all inform whether or not a handshake or kisses are appropriate. A newcomer would have to learn the rules of the game, most likely through observation and participation, including trial and error.

However, there are mechanisms, and in particular sanctions, that point towards rules or even enforce compliance with them. As with rules, sanctions can be formal or informal. The penal law quite explicitly states what kind of sanction follows a particular act regarded as a "crime". The enforcement of sanctions – as Émile Durkheim (1984) in particular pointed out – strengthens the rule. A rule that is never enforced becomes meaningless. Such old-fashioned laws that have not been applied for a long time but lead a dormant life are regularly removed from the law books. This happened just recently with the German law concerning the defamation of leaders and representatives of foreign states, colloquially called "Majestätsbeleidigungsgesetz" (which translates roughly as "majesty defamation law"). After being the target of a German comedian, the Turkish President Erdogan filed a case against the comedian under §103 of the German penal law, which stipulates a punishment of up to five years" imprisonment. This law had not been applied for many years and, as it is now considered anachronistic, has been abolished.[10] Similarly, the Dutch law against blasphemy (established in 1886) was abolished in 2014. However, it is again mainly informal sanctions that are relevant for our everyday lives and that regulate behaviour in often subtle ways. There are a host of different forms to sanction behaviour that is considered inappropriate, from subtle irony, to gossip and outright violence. It is mainly through such sanctions that the rules of social life become explicit, understandable for the newcomer and researchable for the scholar.

Teaching experience shows that of the three terms discussed here, "category" is usually considered the most difficult for students to grasp. As understood here, a category is a mental entity. Categories are culturally received ideas that people have, which Durkheim (1995) called "collective representations", as he wanted to stress their social nature. Categories organize the diversity of perception and are crucial in our attempts to make sense of the world. As such, they are elements of abstract thought structures and in contrast to behaviour we cannot directly observe categories. But we can infer them as they are manifested in manifold ways, through behaviour and rules; more specifically through language, art, architecture, music, poetry, science and, not least of all, religious practices, objects and texts. To return to the examples mentioned above: a certain practice of worship may signify the ideas of "devotion" and "love"; a handshake may refer to the notion of "friendship", but it may also invoke the idea of "contract". From an isolated observation alone, it would be difficult to infer what the action "means" and in actual practice actors may try to convey different kinds of messages or ambiguous ones. This becomes evident when we look at handshakes between politicians in the public sphere. What do they do with their left hand? Keep it in the pocket? Clap the other person's shoulder paternalistically and thus involving a dimension of hierarchy where the official message should be one of "equality"?

This last example shows that while the three levels can be distinguished analytically, they are closely related. The rule that politicians who meet should shake their (right!) hand does not say anything about the left hand. In other words, in actual practice, there are numerous ways in which such a rule can be acted out, and the actors involved can add different meanings and signify different ideas. However, while the levels are related, there is no direct correspondence, let alone determinism

---

10. See www.bundesregierung.de/Content/DE/Artikel/2017/01/2017-0
1-25-abschaffung-paragraf-103-stgb.html, accessed 27 June 2017.

involved. Rules say something about behaviour that might be expected, but they do not determine behaviour directly. This aspect is also related to the difference in constancy. Of the three levels, behaviour is the most volatile: it shows the most variations and it changes more quickly than rules and categories. The latter do change as well, of course. New ideas are formed in the social and historical process and old ones are transformed, but this usually happens more slowly. Fortunately, we might add, because if our mental frameworks were to change from one week to the next, social life would be virtually impossible.

Doing research and reading scholarly texts with this simple and necessarily provisional analytical scheme concerning behaviour, rules, and categories in mind will enable students, we hope, to "see" better and in a more nuanced way and help them formulate new questions in their study of religion. When looking at the chapters in this book through the lenses of this analytical tool, students will also notice that priority is often given to a certain dimension of religious life. Philosophy (see Chapter 2, this volume) is mainly concerned with thought and thus with the level of categories, although the history of philosophy is also concerned with the philosophers in their social contexts, in which case the other two levels might become relevant as well. As the term indicates, a history of ideas is mainly concerned with the development of representations. However, historians usually seek to learn about the actual behaviour of actors and the normative frameworks that informed their lives (see Chapter 5, this volume). The term "behaviourism", a branch of psychology, already indicates that this school does not pay much attention to ideas – which are put into the "black box" – but focuses on environmental stimuli and responses from the individual (see Skinner 1938). As for anthropology, there are different strands, stressing either behaviour ("interactionism") or ideas (see Chapter 14, this volume) – revealing very different notions of "society". However, in general, it is acknowledged that a thorough understanding of humans as social creatures requires an investigation of all levels, insofar as the material at hand allows this. Moreover, many scholars have tried to overcome the dichotomy of thought and action theoretically. Bourdieu's notion of "habitus", mentioned above, is just one example of this (other scholars are Giddens or Sahlins, for example). This reminds us that the distinction between behaviour, rules and categories may be a useful tool to understand complex social realities, but this model should not itself become normative in how we understand religion, culture and society. In many non-Western societies, the categorical distinctions we cherish and which are the result of our specific history (thought/action, subject/object) do not have the same currency at all. This brings us to an issue that is specific to the study of religion as it is (or was) lived: the problem of belief.

The Problem of Belief

One aspect of scholarly self-reflection that deserves particular attention in the study of religion that was already alluded to in the first section but that we will further reflect on here, concerns the "problem of belief". Should scholars of religion be religious themselves, or rather the opposite? Should they be objective, and what could that mean? What should their attitude be towards the religious traditions they study? Should they even believe in these traditions? These questions are particularly relevant to the ethnographic study of "lived religion", where scholars do not rely on texts or artefacts but on engaging with people who may have very different notions about what is real, the nature of things (e.g. stones may have spirits) and what kinds of beings populate the world. Should a scholar then proceed from the assumption that these people are simply wrong, and try to explain how they have come to have such a wrong understanding? Or should a scholar allow for the possibility that their interlocutors' views of the world are just as valid and true as their own, simply different? Below, we summarize some of the debates concerning this issue and the positions espoused by different ethnographers.

In the second half of the nineteenth century, when the above-mentioned paradigm of evolution predominated, scholars of religion regularly described indigenous belief systems as "superstition" or "flawed" thinking. However, the same scholars, such as Tylor or Frazer, were not very sympathetic to Christian religion either, certainly not in its institutional form. Enlightenment ideas about the primacy of rationality and a strong belief in progress partly explain this situation. The dogmatic attitude of church authorities that restricted scholarly work also added to the aversion to religion and Christianity in particular. In 1881, for example, the Bible scholar William Robertson Smith was accused of heresy and removed from his chair in Aberdeen (cf. Evans-Pritchard 1962).

The standard position that gradually developed was one of neutrality. In the study of religion, Edmund Husserl proposed the notion of *epoché*, which asked to "bracket" and temporarily suspend value judgements and judgments about what is real about the phenomenon under investigation, and to study them as they appear (cf. Knibbe and Versteeg 2008). This position is reflected, for example, in the comments of two anthropologists of religion. Evans-Pritchard (1965: 17, original emphasis) writes:

> What I have said does not imply that the anthropologist *has* to have a religion of his own, and I think we should be clear on this point at the outset. He is not concerned, *qua* anthropologist, with the truth or falsity of religious thought. As I understand the matter, there is no possibility of his *knowing* whether the spiritual beings of primitive religions or of any others have any existence or not, and since that is the case he cannot take the question into consideration. The beliefs are for him sociological facts, not theological facts, and his sole concern is with their relation to each other and to other social facts.

A year later, in 1966, Geertz wrote:

> One of the main methodological problems in writing about religion scientifically is to put aside at once the tone of the village atheist and that of the village preacher ... so that the social and psychological implications of particular religious beliefs can emerge in a clear and neutral light.
> (Geertz 1973: 123)

This position, which focuses on the "empirically available", has been called "*methodological* atheism" by sociologist Peter L. Berger (1967: 100, original emphasis); the religious studies scholar Smart subsequently suggested the term "methodological agnosticism" as this would not rule out the possibility of the existence of "gods" or "spirits" (Smart 1973).

To the novice in the study of religion, this stance might appear to make perfect sense because it seems undogmatic and open to the investigation of other people's religious ideas and practices without judging them as good or bad, right or wrong. However, methodological agnosticism has been criticized from different angles, and we want to briefly summarize four critical reactions to the position of neutrality, which we gloss as positivism, belief as method, positionality and ethnographic experience (cf. Bowie 2006; Cox 2003; Engelke 2002).

A positivist position is convinced that facts can be established beyond doubt. Often, it also involves causal explanations and aims to uncover laws, not merely regularities, something which many scholars of religion would say is difficult to establish for their field. Although probably a minority among scholars of religion, these voices can be found, for example, in the cognitive anthropology of religion (e.g. Boyer 1993). A very straightforward position is also espoused by James Lett (1999). In his view, religion and science are diametrically opposed to one another: science is rational as scientific statements can be falsified, whereas religious statements involve claims to supernatural forces that have either already been proven wrong or cannot be falsified. They are thus not scientific but irrational. Lett's conclusion: the "simple fact of the matter is that every religious belief in every culture in the world is demonstrably untrue" (ibid.: 111). He goes further, saying that it is the ethical responsibility of scholars to call nonsense by its name because otherwise their intellectual integrity, credibility and scientific progress would suffer: "It seems to me that the obligation to expose religious beliefs as nonsensical is an ethical one incumbent upon every anthropological scientist for the simple reason that the essential ethos of science lies in an unwavering dedication to truth" (ibid.).

We do not want to discuss this position here in detail, but some criticisms are quite obvious. Lett basically dismisses religion using the yardstick of science, but why should these criteria apply to religion in the first place? As mentioned above, many scholars would see commonalities between science and other systems of knowledge, including religion. Also, how legitimate is it to dismiss religion as "wrong" if it has personal meaning for many and also fulfils social functions, and how does it help? Should scholars of religion not instead try to understand religion rather than simply regard it as untrue, even a "vice" (Lett 1999: 114)? While many scholars of religion would be highly critical of Lett's position on these and other grounds, we should be grateful to him for putting it so bluntly because it makes explicit assumptions and claims that often only lurk in the background. Also, as we discussed above, the historical and political context of scholars is crucial. In Lett's case, the political landscape in the USA, including Christian fundamentalisms and Creationists' claims, might be a relevant point to consider.

Whereas Lett's position is a kind of negative theology (Evans-Pritchard 1965: 17) that sees the acceptance of religion by scientists as a vice, the opposite position holds that those scholars who are themselves religious have an advantage in understanding religion, or at least certain of its dimensions (cf. Engelke 2002). We quoted Evans-Pritchard above, who said that scholars of religion do not have to be religious themselves. However, in the final paragraphs of the same book we also find statements to the contrary. Here he indicates that an understanding of religious experience is possible only for the religious anthropologist: "The non-believer seeks for some theory – biological, psychological, or sociological – which will explain the illusion; the believer seeks rather to understand the manner in which a people conceives of a reality and their relations to it", and he goes on to quote Pater Wilhelm Schmidt's dictum that a non-believer will talk about religion "as a blind man might of colours" (Evans-Pritchard 1965: 121).

Again without wishing to discuss this position at length, two comments may be apposite. The first hinges on the question of whether it really is similarity that has epistemological priority – that is, whether we understand better what we know. Moreover, does it then follow that what is different is difficult to understand? Anthropology and its ethnographic method have shown, by contrast, that through a sustained effort of engaging in another life-world the path to (partial) understanding leads across the many bridges of difference; difference is a bridge, not a border. Rather than having a self-evident "faith in the familiar" (to borrow the title of Kim's book; Knibbe 2013), it is *understanding through difference* that characterizes the ethnographic method.

The second, related point is that an assumed similarity of religious experience can be quite misleading. How can we be sure that such experiences and emotions are indeed the same? Renato Rosaldo (1989: 1–24) even declared in a famous article that only after the death of his wife in the field did he understand the emotions of the Ilongot headhunters, even the practice of headhunting as a whole, and derived general methodological conclusions from it. Regarding this claim, Berger argued elsewhere that "to deduce explanations from subjective emotional experience can lead to serious distortions and trivial understanding of cultural phenomena" (Berger 2010: 136). The dictum that "I know what religious experience means and therefore I understand what their religious experience means" seems just another variant of the method of introspection that Evans-Pritchard himself so vehemently rejects as the "if I were a horse" fallacy (1965: 24, 43).

Evans-Pritchard (1965) ultimately dismisses all theories of "primitive religion" that he discusses in his book. "Do they help me understand my own religiosity?" he asks himself, and answers the question in the negative; then why should they help understand other people's religion (ibid.: 120)? This clearly illustrates the similarity assumption mentioned above. Evans-Pritchard's conversion to Catholicism during the Second World War, and this is the final point, clearly shows his shift in bias, from a sociological and structural to an experiential and "insider" understanding of religion. His famous analysis of Azande witchcraft (Evans-Pritchard 1976) was among the first ethnographies of indigenous religions that showed the inherent logic and consistency of their beliefs and practices. If you accept a few basic assumptions, Evans-Pritchard wrote, this system makes perfect sense. After his conversion, however, his view of religion seemed to have changed, from religion as a social fact (also stressed in the quote above) to religion as personal experience. His book on the Nuer political system (Evans-Pritchard 1940) has been celebrated as a sociological study that actually anticipated structural analysis. In his book *Nuer Religion* (Evans-Pritchard 1956), by contrast, he ultimately considers the relationship between believer and God as the most important dimension. Collective aspects of religion would tell us something about the social structure, but nothing about religion "in itself"; this we learn from the "personal expression" of religion (ibid.: 320). He concludes (ibid.: 322): "Nuer religion is ultimately an interior state". If that state can be grasped at all, then it will be grasped by people who also believe. However, at "this point the theologian takes over from the anthropologist", which is the last sentence of the book. For Mathew Engelke, who discusses the "problem of belief" with regard to Evans-Pritchard and Victor Turner, "their writings suggest that belief is an element in their methods. Religious conviction became a tool in their anthropological projects, a way of bridging the distance between themselves and "the other" (Engelke 2002: 8).

A third position that can be glossed with "positionality" would first of all radically dismiss Geertz's statement quoted above that anything can be represented in a "clear and neutral light". From this perspective such an endeavour would appear naïve. Rather, it would stress that any statement or interpretation is mediated and influenced by the social and historical context the actor finds themselves in, including the locations by age, gender, creed or class. This position is closely related to the demand for radical self-reflection by scholars that is mentioned in the previous section. It also originated about the same time, in the 1980s, when "reflexive anthropology" became popular, as well as postcolonial approaches. Both the positivist and the belief-as-method strand would be criticized for not attempting to unearth the conditions of the production of their theories, for not finding this necessary. As such, the claim of neutrality would be regarded not only as naïve but as dangerous as well. Significantly, "power" is an important explanatory tool in these approaches, perhaps even a paradigm as discussed above. A scholar who represents this approach is Asad, who became famous for criticizing Geertz's theory of religion precisely on these grounds, for not reflecting on the conditions and genealogy of his own theory. The crucial place Geertz gives to meaning Asad sees as taking the standpoint of theology (Asad 1983: 245): "let us [rather] begin by asking what are the historical conditions (movements, classes, institutions, ideologies) necessary for the existence of particular religious practices and discourses. In other words, let us ask: how does power create religion?" (ibid.: 252). It should be clear that for Asad, this pertains not only to religions but to definitions and scholarly accounts about religion as well (cf. Chapter 11, in this volume). From that perspective, it does not matter whether a scholar of religion is an atheist or a Christian (or Buddhist etc.) as every scholar is necessarily positioned and biased. The responsibility is to critically investigate these positions and biases and to reflect on and perhaps adjust the concepts and methods we use to understand our subject matter.

While the positions outlined can be found in any study of religion, irrespective of the methods applied or the kind of material, the last strand to be discussed here mainly (though not solely) refers to the long-term empirical study of religion, which is based on ethnographic fieldwork. The main argument here is that regardless of the scholar's initial attitude (atheist, agnostic, religious), the very nature of the fieldwork process entails a blurring of the boundaries of "my (un)belief" and "their religion". We have already mentioned Evans-Pritchard with regard to two positions (neutrality and belief-as-method). However, to some extent, he also pioneered the position that emphasizes ethnographic experience because he stressed the relevance of "context". Belief is not an absolute matter, but is contingent on the shifting situations and (socio-cultural) environments that actors find themselves in.

As such, Evans-Pritchard (1976: V) described in the beginning of his book on Azande religion his only personal acquaintance with witchcraft. He knew that witchcraft is supposed to be visible, that it is a bright light and "like a fire". On his usual nocturnal stroll before going to sleep, he saw a bright light moving towards the homestead of a man called Tupoi, close to his own hut. The next morning the ethnographer enquired about possible causes of the light but could not find any. People assured him that this must have been witchcraft. A little later on the same day, a relative of Tupoi who was staying in this homestead at the time, died. He never found out the true reason for the light, Evans-Pritchard writes, but the Azande's ideas about witchcraft would be a very adequate explanation in this context. He leaves open the question of whether he himself thought that it might have been witchcraft after all (cf. Engelke 2002: 5).

Such moments of immersion and ambiguity that often occur in emotionally intense situations (cf. Berger 2010) have been described by numerous anthropologists. One particularly vivid case is presented by Michael Kearney in his short chapter "A very bad disease of the arms" (Kearney 2004). This text forcefully brings home the contextual nature of beliefs or worldviews mentioned above. The event occurred in the 1960s when Kearney was doing doctoral research in a Mexican town. Rather aptly, his research concerned the local worldview, in which witchcraft was again a key component. Kearney's own attitude towards the local beliefs was "scientific and materialist" (ibid.: 41). The anthropologist had an intellectual curiosity and scholarly concern, but nothing more than that: "it never occurred to me that their fantastic worldview might have anything more than a certain metaphoric validity. ... My complacence was soon to be shattered" (ibid.: 42). Kearney carefully describes the different ingredients of the situation, including the aesthetic scenario that helped to create an "aura of factuality" (Geertz 1973: 109f). He had been in the field for six months – enough time to absorb some basic patterns and ideas – when he became entangled in the object he was studying. He agreed to administer medicine to a woman with a bad skin disease, who happened to be the sister-in-law of one of the two most feared witches in town. From his Western perspective, his treatment was a great success but a friend then told him that it was a very stupid thing to have done, namely interfering in a witchcraft war, thereby reversing the power relationships that had been established before he had cured the woman; "you better be very careful", his friend advised. Still firmly located in his own worldview, he laughed at his friend, asking him "You don't believe in those superstitions, do you?" – "not very much", his friend replied (Kearney 2004: 45). Note the ambiguity again.

After another incident that added to the build-up to the pivotal moment (an autopsy of a traffic victim using crude metal instruments), Kearney found himself working alone in his house one night when he sensed an itching on one of his arms. When he pulled up his sleeve to inspect the cause he saw "large angry welts" and fell into "a state of stark terror" (ibid.: 47), fearing for his life as never before. Kearney describes how his former rationality temporarily disintegrated completely and was superseded by the worldview he was studying, localizing the "skin disease" in the witchcraft context he had now involuntarily become a part of. With respect to the former section, we can say that in generalizing and understanding this phenomenon on his arms, the *theory* of witchcraft seemed to accord with the "facts" much better than any "scientific" explanation. After a few moments (he did not know how long it actually lasted), his former worldview returned and the process of scientifically rationalizing the incident set in. Later, Kearney realized that this was an instance of "extreme cognitive dissonance. Reality was all askew. I had the most intense sense of being suspended between two different worlds" (ibid.: 48). Significantly, this experience had a long-term effect on the anthropologist, for whom witchcraft was no longer merely a topic of intellectual curiosity. He had experienced the depths, intensity and reality of what it means to be part of this world; he had learned to appreciate the worldview (ibid.: 49).

Some anthropologists have reported similar experiences but have drawn quite radical conclusions from them. With reference to her experience working with Sufi saints in Pakistan, for example, Katherine Ewing (1994) has argued that while the position of neutrality we discussed above has by now been thoroughly critiqued in theory, the practice of anthropology still demands such a position. This taboo of "going native" leads to an "epistemological abyss", which is a radical distinction between how "we" can know the world and how "they" can know it. It amounts to "a refusal to acknowledge that the subjects of one's research might actually know something about the human condition that is personally valid for the anthropologist: it is a refusal to believe" (Ewing 1994: 571). Ewing even goes a step further, identifying a power asymmetry: "This refusal constitutes a hegemonic act, an implicit insistence that the relationship between anthropologist and 'informant' be shaped by the parameters of Western discourse" (ibid.: 571). She thus formulates a claim regarding how anthropologists should approach other belief systems, acknowledging that their relevance is on a par with the anthropologist's own worldview. In a way, Ewing's position is the inverse of Lett's. While the latter states that all religions are untrue and that scholars of religion have the ethical responsibility to say so, Ewing argues that the refusal of belief is ethically untenable and that other people's worldviews are as valid as one's own and as valid as science.

Whether or not we want to follow Ewing in her claims about anthropological hegemony, the important point generally shared by all scholars taking such a stand is that the ethnographic endeavour facilitates the temporal merging of worldviews and thus of (situational) belief. Ewing articulates this more strongly still:

> It is impossible for ethnographers not to become part of the society in which they spend a significant part of their lives. Ethnographers are drawn, often involuntarily, into the nets of significance cast by the people among whom they conduct research and are thrust into their discourse and debates.
>
> (Ewing 1994: 578)

Susan Harding comes to a similar conclusion after doing research with born-again Christians in the USA. Whether it be Evans-Pritchard's witchcraft lights, the welts on Kearney's arm or Ewing's "dreams from a saint" (which we have not discussed here), all these examples confirm Harding's view that when doing fieldwork, the "membrane between disbelief and belief is much thinner than we think" and that "this space between belief and disbelief, or rather the paradoxical space of overlap, is also the space of ethnography. We must enter it to do our work" (Harding 1987: 178). This position is in line with the proposal of methodological ludism developed by André Droogers, who argues that engaging with a religious worldview ethnographically could be compared to "serious play": one engages with another way of ordering reality "as if" it were true (the subjunctive mode). However, as Knibbe and Droogers explore in a co-written article, this position runs into the problem that, during long-term research, the subjunctive mode either becomes the reality, or the ethnographer chooses to dismiss this reality and "return" – albeit changed – to their own ways of understanding the world (Knibbe and Droogers 2011). Thus, this proposal does not really solve the question of the hegemonic relationship of "science" in relation to religion that Ewing identified.

In sum, it is clear that each scholar of religion employing ethnographic methods has to find their own way of dealing with "the problem of belief", on a theoretical level and in actual research practice. In her contribution to this volume (Chapter 10), Knibbe focuses on a variation of this dilemma: when to and why (not) participate in religious practices. What is no longer possible, however, is to ignore the importance of these questions for our work on religion.

The Contributions to this Volume

In the first contribution to the volume following this Introduction, Dennis Vanden Auweele (Chapter 2) addresses the question of how philosophers of religion approach the question what religion is, thus continuing the discussion in the first part of this chapter, but confining himself to the debates that have been taking place in philosophy. He focuses on the work of three influential scholars to give an overview of how philosophers of religion have been thinking about the universality and timelessness of religion since the eighteenth century. Vanden Auweele describes a development from thinking about what unites religions to appreciating what differentiates them. He first discusses Kant, who saw the essence of religion in its function to cultivate the mind and motivate people to act in a morally good way. He then moves on to Hegel, who argued that the essence of religion can only be grasped in its historical instantiation of progressive symbolic attempts to represent reason. Hegel compared religion with art and philosophy, which respectively represent the more sensuous and abstract dimensions of reason's growing self-consciousness. Schelling, the third scholar that Vanden Auweele discusses, contended that all people are united in a latent memory of mythic consciousness of a first, all-encompassing God. Schelling explained the existence of diverging religions as emerging from the development of language, as a result of which groups speaking different languages gave different names to this first bond with God. In Schelling's view, people may ultimately be united again in accepting Jesus Christ as the revelation of God. In the last section of the chapter, Vanden Auweele takes stock by discussing postmodern philosophy, which criticizes the Christian bias in previous thinking about religion and rejects the very possibility of "grand narratives" or comprehensive stories to explain reality or reveal truth. He concludes by noting that, contrary to what we might expect, deconstructing grand narratives does not mean that all postmodern philosophers deny an essence of religion; one strand in postmodern philosophy of religion acknowledges the experience of divine transcendence, but argues that this experience cannot be grasped by superimposing rational concepts on it.

The philosophy of religion is one of the oldest and therefore most classical approaches to the study of religion. Acknowledging that religious studies owe a lot to philosophy, Chapter 3 by Christoph Jedan is an attempt at reversing a long-standing trend of importing concepts and methods established in other disciplines. Jedan's chapter embarks on the opposite reflection that religious studies actually have a lot to offer other disciplines. In this vein, Jedan suggests that the historiography of philosophy could profit immensely from taking its cue from the terminology and research interests of religious studies. Using Stoicism as a central case study, Jedan explores *inter alia* the analytical usefulness of Smart's early differentiation of six dimensions of religion and of the concept of lived religion (adding a seventh one only later on). Finally, the author reflects on what ASR stands to gain by engaging with the history of philosophy.

For theologians, as Henk van den Belt explains in Chapter 4, it is not enough to experience and believe in divine transcendence without rationally thinking it through (the strand within modern philosophy discussed by Vanden Auweele according to which no rational concepts should be superimposed on religious experiences): theologians continue where other religious studies scholars leave off, by aiming to arrive at a more satisfactory approximation of the ultimate knowledge of existence that they believe rests with God. In his chapter, Van den Belt reflects on the nature of a theological perspective in religious studies by drawing on his own study of the woodcut illustrations in Martin Luther's catechisms. He argues that although the research question concerning the meaning of the woodcuts as such is not necessarily theological, several specific characteristics of a theological approach can be identified in his research project. Van den Belt distinguishes three levels of analysis of the woodcuts in which specific theological issues play a role. The first concerns the object of research: theological expertise in the history of Christian doctrines and practices is important for understanding the message of the pictures. On a second, methodological level, Van den Belt observes a tension between the perspectives of theology and religious studies: a theological interpretation assesses the sources from the perspective of a shared belief. This means that the research question concerning the woodcuts is no longer confined to an analysis of the pictures, but is subsequently related to the theological presuppositions of Christianity, or in this case of (Lutheran) Protestantism. Finally, on an epistemological level, theologians are critically aware of and acknowledge the worldview in which they connect all knowledge to their basic convictions and beliefs regarding God's relationship to the world. Van den Belt concludes his contribution by arguing that although this third epistemological and confessional level should not influence the results of the academic study, it should not be denied or excluded either. Assuming a position that resembles the argument concerning "positionality" above, Van den Belt instead holds that theologians and other researchers alike should reflect on and account for their own presuppositions.

Contrary to presupposing a divine essence and cause, as scholars such as Van den Belt do in the theological approach, historian Steve Mason (Chapter 5) exemplifies a constructivist historical approach to religion. Mason analyses how people in the Graeco-Roman world (c.300 BCE to 300 CE) framed Jews and Christians. In line with Asad's critique that much research in religious studies builds on conceptions that are specifically Christian rather than universal, Mason argues that the label "religion" obfuscates more than it illuminates when describing the ancient past of these two major traditions. To substantiate this claim, he begins by surveying what "shell categories" residents in the Graeco-Roman world used to communicate with each other and order their knowledge of the world. Informed by both ancient textual and material sources, Mason argues that a diverse and vibrant Judaean culture, with its own famed mother-city, law-giver and customs, temple, priesthood, sacrificial system, and a larger expatriate community was "freeze-dried" by later Christians and reduced to "Juda-ism" as a belief system. "Christianity" looked altogether different: Christians were small bands of men and women meeting secretly in members" houses to worship Christ. They refrained from animal sacrifices, and some expected imminent evacuation from the world. Mason concludes by considering how a historical understanding of these very different phenomena of a Judaean "ethnos" and what began as a kind of Christian "club" can help to explain such puzzles as the Christian polemic against and simultaneous attraction to "Judaism", the "persecution" of Christians but not Jews, and "conversion" to Judaism or Christianity.

Like Mason, Lautaro Roig Lanzillotta (Chapter 6) takes a constructivist historical approach in his case to explain how the study of intertextuality can enhance our understanding of the continuous process of how texts are reread and rewritten in order to create new meanings, or to adapt old ones to their new, ever-changing contexts. The study of intertextuality is described as an approach that ponders the way texts live in other texts in order to determine if and how texts reflect, reshape, or transform one another. The author points out how, in recent decades, influenced by the work of Julia Kristeva, Roland Barthes and Gérard Genette, the notion of intertext as a "new tissue of past citations," or "dense web of allusion" has been applied beyond the literary world and extended to photography, movie, music, painting and even architecture. After providing an overview of intertextuality and its wide applicability when conceived in this comprehensive and encompassing way, Roig Lanzillotta exemplifies an intertextual approach to the study of the myths of the Afterlife as developed by Plato and Plutarch of Chaeronea. After comparing Plato's myth of Er and Plutarch's myths in On the Sign of Socrates, On the Delays of Divine Vengeance and Concerning the Face Which Appears in the Orb of the Moon, he applies Genette's approach to intertextuality in order to both assess Plutarch's textual transformations and show how they generate new meanings more suited to the expectations of authors and readers of the first centuries CE.

The chapter "Religion as a Meaning System" by Anja Visser (Chapter 7) is the first of three chapters that focus on particular psychological approaches to the study of religion. The wider field of psychology is primarily interested in cognitive approaches that study how people consciously or subconsciously process and interpret the information that reaches the nervous system through the senses. In her chapter, Visser discusses a strand of the cognitive approach that focuses on largely conscious, individual and cognitive (thought) processes – the study of religion as a meaning system. Approaching religion as a meaning system has gained popularity in the psychological study of religion during the past decade, particularly in studies on the relationship between religion and health or well-being.

Visser explains how in this approach, a meaning system is conceived of as a personal collection of what the approach identifies as norms, values, beliefs and attitudes that each person develops through socialization in their sociocultural context and through their personal experiences. This meaning system influences a person's identity, the meaning they ascribe to life and to life events, and their sense of certainty. The point of departure in this approach is that when confronted with new situations that do not fit within their existing meaning system, a person will experience emotional distress and search for ways to realign the two levels of meaning. Visser argues that approaching religion as a meaning system can help us to understand how religious beliefs, practices and experiences can be both a cause of and a solution to distress. She illustrates this approach by discussing her research project in which she combines quantitative and qualitative data collection and analysis to study the relationship between religion and well-being in the context of cancer. Assessing the merits and limitations of such an approach to the study of religion, she points out that the main challenge in this line of research relates to the enormous variety in the content of religion and the meanings that individuals attach to religion in different domains, phases and situations in their lives. Visser concludes that while quantitative research into religion as a meaning system can produce important, measurable results that sketch overall patterns, there is a need for qualitative research to gain a better understanding of specific embodied experiences and meaning-making that these correlations refer to in the personal lives of the research participants.

The need to contextualize the meaning of religion in the lives of individuals comes even more prominently to the fore in the relational approach to the psychology of religion adopted by Hanneke Schaap-Jonker (Chapter 8) and Hanneke Muthert (Chapter 9). Exploring religion from the perspective of attachment theory, Schaap-Jonker addresses how people's conceptions of God are informed by early attachment processes (i.e. the development of a close emotional bond between a child and an attachment figure, usually the parents). This relational psychological approach therefore examines religion in the context of experiences in early interactions and their mental representations, conscious and subconscious relational dynamics, and attachment styles.

Schaap-Jonker first presents attachment theory. Starting with the development of infants, she explains the concepts of attachment styles, internal working models and the mentalizing process. She then discusses the theory of God representations as core aspects of religiousness from an attachment approach. She does so by building on the work of Lee Kirkpatrick, one of the first researchers in this field. Stating that a God representation can function as an attachment figure, Kirkpatrick formulated two hypotheses – correspondence and compensation – to explain the psychological function of religion in a person's life. Schaap-Jonker illustrates the relation between attachment processes and God representations by discussing the results of quantitative and qualitative research on God representations. She concludes by discussing the strengths and weaknesses of conceptualizing religion as attachment, the most important limitation being that attachment theory alone can obviously not explain the function of all God representations.

To understand what different functions God representations and other dimensions of religion may have is further elaborated in the chapter by Hanneke Muthert, who, like Schaap-Jonker, adopts a relational approach to the psychology of religion to discuss how religion may feature for people in precarious situations who have to cope with loss. For psychologists of religion and spiritual counsellors, such an exploration of "relational space" is valuable because it is precisely in the space where a person's inner world and the outside world overlap that religious meaning can be experienced. In order to clarify the added value of concentrating on this relational space in studying bereavement, Muthert suggests combining various theories that all proceed, each with their own focus, from the assumption that mourning is essentially relational, and which understand mourning as making sense of loss; a good match between the social context and individual mourning capacities appears to be crucial for "healthy" or effective mourning. Central to the theoretical framework Muthert presents is a psychodynamic theory model that distinguishes three different psychological structures, "modes of being" that each have their own specific mourning capabilities. She argues that religion has the potential to fit well with all three modes of being, but that good matches are not always obvious. The chapter ends with a discussion in which the author reflects on the implementation and limitations of the theoretical framework presented in her chapter in counselling practices. Despite certain limitations, the theoretical framework developed by Muthert constitutes an important contribution to current mourning theories and practices by bridging people's inner and outer worlds, and taking into account different modes of being that grieving people may find themselves in.

In principle, the theories and methods that characterize the psychological approaches to religion discussed by Visser, Schaap-Jonker and Muthert are open to adaptation to the study of religion in non-Western contexts. In practice, however, psychological theories are predominantly developed, tested and applied in Western contexts. While some of their case studies are also located in the West, the authors of the remaining chapters in this book reflect on cultural specificities by taking a qualitative, ethnographic perspective to contextualize religious practices and meanings. Taking up the "problem of belief" discussed in this introduction, but now from a more practical perspective, Kim Knibbe (Chapter 10) reflects on the dilemmas of conducting participant observation in religious contexts. She asks how, as a researcher, one navigates the ways in which religious ways of explaining, interpreting and making sense of the world may compete or clash with academic ones. Traditionally, there seem to be roughly three options available to the researcher: methodological atheism, methodological theism or methodological agnosticism. Knibbe demonstrates that each of these positions create their own problems in ethnographic fieldwork, particularly in terms of the relationship between the researcher and the "researched". Drawing on her fieldwork among people who call themselves "spiritual" in the Dutch context, she discusses how developing and maintaining rapport involves negotiating not only issues of differences in cognitive frameworks, but also differences in embodiment, emotion and affect. By summarizing some of the literature and drawing on her personal experiences, Knibbe explores how views on dealing with the dilemmas discussed relate to different ideas about what "research" entails. In a very concrete way, then, the chapter by Knibbe exemplifies the kind of reflection on their own positionality and presuppositions that Van den Belt in his contribution argues all researchers should engage in.

Like Knibbe, Simon Coleman (Chapter 11) addresses in his contribution the issue of how to study religion in the field. Rather than contemplating the method of participant observation as such, Coleman focuses on the question of where the researcher should look for religion when conducting participant observation. His chapter opens with the paradoxical observation that despite their commitment to focusing on everyday social relations, anthropologists studying ritual tend to focus on sites and contexts of ritual density and commitment – fieldwork situations occupied by more engaged believers and religious specialists. Drawing on his work among Pentecostals in Sweden, shrine pilgrims in England, and the numerous and unpredictable visitors to English cathedrals, Coleman explores the methodological and theoretical issues involved in studying ritual peripheries, penumbras and edges. He explores both the difficulties and opportunities in carrying out such work, and considers the usefulness of a number of different metaphorical and analytical frames for analysing ritual action and engagement that take place away from the centres of performance, including ideas of "vicarious", "lateral", "adjacent" and "alienated" participation. He points out that ritual and religion emerge as deeply relational in such analyses, but often also as inchoate and under-determined.

The relevance of studying the "edges" or "adjacencies" of religion is further demonstrated in Chapter 12 by Joram Tarusarisa, who investigates the impact of religious resonances in "Nora", a Zimbabwean political song. His analysis demonstrates that what is said to be religious and/or sacred is not cast in stone but is the result of practices, discourses and narratives woven around what gets defined as such. He discusses how the song sets apart the ruling party, the Zimbabwe African National Union – Patriotic Front (ZANU-PF), and its former leader Robert Mugabe and turns them into representations of the religious and/or sacred. Tarusarira's analysis casts light on how the song's narratives and discourses created a numinous vision and version of Zimbabwe that was to be delivered by the then President Mugabe, who was said to be "anointed" to guide his followers and deliver them from the land of Egypt (coloniality) to the

Promised Land (independence and sovereignty). He demonstrates that the song has an explanatory dimension by which it claims to provide answers to questions of ultimate meaning in times of political instability and conflict that characterized Zimbabwe at the time when the song was composed. In doing so, it provides a theodicy, a narrative that answers ultimate questions concerning life and people's (Zimbabweans') place in the universe. Tarusarira's analysis of the song and its performances is thus a concrete example of how the study of "religion" does not involve the study of a "thing" in itself, but an enquiry into how particular actors and institutions weave particular ideas, discourses and narratives, using a particular language which reflects their subjectivities and interests, to create the religious and/or sacred. The author concludes by stating that the proffered definitions of religion tell us more about those offering them than what they claim to be telling us about religion.

The political implications of framing religion in specific ways, as addressed by Tarusarira, and the need to also look for religion in places other than situations of ritual density, as argued by Coleman, are the two main themes addressed by Marjo Buitelaar in Chapter 13, who focuses in her contribution on the study of Islam. The author starts by observing that, in response to the present situation in which "Islam" and "the West" are increasingly pitted against each other in public discourse and violent attacks are carried out in the name of Islam, there is a trend in academic research projects and educational programmes of focusing increasingly on the relation between religion, politics and conflict. Buitelaar argues that by singling out situations in which Islam is a foreground presence, particularly ones in which conflicts are framed in terms of existing between Muslims and non-Muslims, we run the risk of reducing Muslims to their "Muslimness" and producing too one-sided a knowledge about the meaning of Islam in the daily lives of Muslims. To demonstrate how this one-sidedness can be avoided by looking at instances in which Islam is only a background presence, the author discusses, for example, images circulating in social media of the ritualized expressions of grief shared by Muslim and non-Muslim fans at the fate of Ajax footballer Abdelhaq Nouri, who was in a coma for years after collapsing during a game. She points to the "normalizing" effect of the casual or background presence of Islam in these images in which the Muslim identification of the Nouri family is neither highlighted nor neglected. Buitelaar argues that the collective expressions of grief demonstrate the power of shared, immediate experiences to acknowledge both commonalities and differences between actors of different cultural and religious backgrounds. In turn, this acknowledgement enables productive communication and interaction that cuts across diverse ways of being in the world; it is concrete, shared experiences that create common ground and space for "comparing notes" in the sense of opening up to the perspectives of others and scrutinizing our own in order to recognize, assess and learn from both commonalities and specificities. Buitelaar concludes by stating that taking an intersectionality approach allows anthropologists to compare notes more effectively and thus produce richer insights into the meaning of religion in the lives of individuals. In turn, sharing stories with the larger public that demonstrate both commonalities and specificities between Muslims and non-Muslims in a certain cultural context can contribute to de-exceptionalizing Muslims and creating a platform for a more productive comparing of notes between citizens of different cultural backgrounds.

Central to public debates about commonalities and differences between citizens of different religious and cultural backgrounds is the compatibility of cultural values and the norms through which these values are actualized. Values, and changes in value systems, are the central theme in Chapter 14 of this volume, in which Peter Berger discusses a specific strand of structural anthropology that he emphasizes can be useful in the analysis of both empirical and historical data: the theory of value as developed by Louis Dumont, which has its roots in Durkheim's sociology of religion. Berger begins by contextualizing Dumont's theory in the history of the discipline of anthropology by outlining the main features of Dumont's analytical framework and how it has been developed by Joel Robbins. He sketches how Dumont, informed by his Indological and anthropological research on the Hindu caste system, developed a general theory of hierarchy, the latter being just the other side of the coin of value (as posing a value introduces hierarchy). While Lévi-Strauss was mainly concerned with binary oppositions in cultural structures, Dumont argued that relationships between ideas are hierarchical. Left and right, for instance, are not simply opposites but stand in a hierarchical relation. When taking an oath or shaking hands after making an agreement, only the right hand is appropriate because it stands for the whole person. Dumont discussed the various properties of value and added the concepts of "context" and "level" in order to account for a dynamic relationship between ideas and values within a certain framework he called ideology. Joel Robbins further developed the dynamic potential in Dumont's theory in explaining processes of change and globalization. In line with Mason's argument that the label of "religion" as a universal cultural category often obfuscates more than it illuminates outside the Western world, the author demonstrates that the theory of value as developed by Dumont and Robbins provides an important perspective from which to study religion, precisely because it does not depend on "religion" as a privileged analytical concept or domain.

Folllowing these individual contributions, the book closes with an epilogue discussing some of the commonalities and specificities of the various approaches presented in the book.

In Closing

Students of religion may experience the various approaches presented here as bewildering diversity. Indeed this book is meant as an invitation to engage with this diversity of approaches and as an encouragement to think about certain phenomena from a variety of theoretical and methodological vantage points. With this introduction we have aimed to provide students with an overview of some key dimensions to consider when studying religion and selecting the appropriate approach. The following questions may serve as a guideline in navigating this diversity of approaches:

1. What understanding of religion does a scholar depart from?
2. What concepts are used and what kind of theorizing do they make possible?
3. What level of analysis is addressed?
4. Is there any consideration of the "the problem of belief"?

We invite our readers to explore the rich territory of religious studies presented in this volume.

Acknowledgements

We wish to thank the anonymous reviewers, the editors of this series Morny Joy and Katja Tripplett, as well as colleagues Christoph Jedan, Steve Mason, Hanneke Muthert, Dennis Vanden Auweele and Anja Visser for their very helpful comments on this introduction. We, of course, are responsible for any errors or shortcomings.

About the Authors

Peter Berger (PhD 2004, FU Berlin) is associate professor of Indian religions and the anthropology of religion at the University of Groningen. His areas of interest include the anthropology of religion, indigenous religions (esp. in India), theory and history of anthropology and the anthropology of India. His books include *Feeding, Sharing and Devouring: Ritual and Society in Highland Odisha, India* (De Gruyter, 2015), and he coedited *Godroads: Modalities of Conversion in India* (Cambridge University Press, 2020), *Ultimate Ambiguities: Investigating Death and Liminality* (Berghahn, 2016), *The Modern Anthropology of India* (Routledge, 2013) and *The Anthropology of Values* (Pearson, 2010).

Marjo Buitelaar is professor of contemporary Islam from an anthropological perspective at the University of Groningen. Her research interests concern Islam in everyday life and narrative identity construction in a post-migration context. Buitelaar is presently programme-leader of a research project on "Modern Articulations of Pilgrimage to Mecca" (NWO grant 360-25-150). Her most recent co-edited books in English are *Religious Voices in Self-Narratives* (2013); *Hajj, Global Interactions through Pilgrimage* (2015); and *Muslim Women's Pilgrimage to Mecca and Beyond: Reconfiguring Gender, Religion and Mobility* (2021).

Kim Knibbe is associate professor of anthropology and sociology of religion at Groningen University. She is currently directing the project "Sexuality, Religion and Secularism" with Rachel Spronk (funded by NWO). Previous research focused on Catholicism and spirituality in the Netherlands and on Nigerian Pentecostalism in Europe and the Netherlands. She has also published a series of theoretical and methodological reflections on studying religion. Her most recent co-edited books and special issues are *Secular Societies, Spiritual Selves?* (with Anna Fedele, 2020) and "Theorizing Lived Religion" (with Helena Kupari, *Journal of Contemporary Religion*, 2020).

References

Asad, Talal. 1983. "Anthropological Conceptions of Religion: Reflections on Geertz." *Man* 18(2): 237–259. https://doi.org/10.2307/2801433

Asad, Talal. 2002. "The Construction of Religion as an Anthropological Category." In *A Reader in the Anthropology of Religion*, edited by Michael Lambek, pp. 114–132. Blackwell Anthologies in Social and Cultural Anthropology. Malden, MA: Blackwell Publishing.

Asad, Talal. 2003. *Formations of the Secular: Christianity, Islam, Modernity*. Stanford, CA: Stanford University Press.

Balkenhol, Markus, Ernst van den Hemel and Irene Stengs. 2020. "Introduction: Emotional Entanglements of Sacrality and Secularity – Engaging the Paradox." In *The Secular Sacred*, 1–18. New York: Springer. https://doi.org/10.1007/978-3-030-38050-2_1

Barnard, Alan and Anthony Good. 1984. *Research Practices in the Study of Kinship.* Asa Research Methods in Social Anthropology, no. 2. London: Academic Press for the Association of Social Anthropologists.

Beckford, James A. and Nicholas Jay Demerath. 2007. *The Sage Handbook of the Sociology of Religion.* Oxford: Sage.

Bell, Catherine. 1992. *Ritual Theory, Ritual Practice.* Oxford: Oxford University Press.

Bell, Catherine M. 1997. *Ritual: Perspectives and Dimensions.* Oxford: Oxford University Press.

Bellah, Robert Neelly. 1967. "Civil Religion in America." *Daedalus* 96(1): 1–21.

Berger, Peter L. 1967. *The Sacred Canopy.* Garden City, NY: Doubleday & Company.

Berger, Peter. 2010. "Assessing the Relevance and Effects of "Key Emotional Episodes" for the Fieldwork Process." In *Anthropological Fieldwork: A Relational Process*, edited by D. Spencer and J. Davies, pp. 119–143. Newcastle upon Tyne: Cambridge Scholars Publishing.

Berger, Peter. 2012. "Theory and Ethnography in the Modern Anthropology of India." *HAU: Journal of Ethnographic Theory* 2(2): 325–357. https://doi.org/10.14318/hau2.2.017

Berger, Peter. 2016. "Death, Ritual, and Effervescence." In *Ultimate Ambiguities. Investigating Death and Liminality*, edited by P. Berger and J. Kroesen, pp. 147–183. New York: Berghahn.

Bion, Wilfred R. 1967 [1962]. "A Theory of Thinking." In *Second Thoughts*, pp. 110–119. London: Karnac. https://doi.org/10.1016/B978-1-4831-9866-8.50011-4

Boghossian, Paul Artin. 2010 [2006]. *Fear of Knowledge: Against Relativism and Constructivism.* Oxford: Clarendon.

Bourdieu, Pierre. 1990. *The Logic of Practice.* Cambridge: Polity Press.

Bowie, Fiona. 2006. *The Anthropology of Religion: An Introduction.* Oxford: Blackwell.

Boyer, Pascal. 1993. *Cognitive Aspects of Religious Symbolism.* Cambridge: Cambridge University Press. https://doi.org/10.1017/CBO9780511896866

Chidester, David. 2014. *Empire of Religion: Imperialism and Comparative Religion.* Chicago, IL: University of Chicago Press. https://doi.org/10.7208/chicago/9780226117577.001.0001

Chidester, David. 2020. "Already There: Categories, Formations, and Circulations in the Future of the Study of Religion." *Religion* 50(1): 40–45. https://doi.org/10.1080/0048721X.2019.1681084

Clifford, James. 1986. "Introduction: Partial Truths." In *Writing Culture: The Poetics and Politics of Ethnography*, edited by James Clifford and George E. Marcus, pp. 1–26. Berkeley, CA: University of California Press.

Cox, James L. 2003. "Religion without God: Methodological Agnosticism and the Future of Religious Studies." Retrieved from www.scribd.com/document/164402875/Religion-Without-God-Methodological-Agnosticism-Hibbert-lecture-2003 (accessed 29 June 2017).

Davie, Grace. 2013. *The Sociology of Religion: A Critical Agenda*. Oxford: Sage.

Dillon, Michele (ed.). 2012. *Handbook of the Sociology of Religion*. Cambridge etc.: Cambridge University Press.

Durkheim, Émile. 1915 [1912]. *The Elementary Forms of the Religious Life*, translated by J.W. Swain. London: George, Allen & Unwin.

Durkheim, Émile. 1973. *Émile Durkheim on Morality and Society: Selected Writings*, edited by Robert N. Bellah. Chicago, IL: University of Chicago Press.

Durkheim, Émile. 1979 [1898]. "Individualism and the Intellectuals." In *Durkheim on Religion*, edited by W.S.F. Pickering, pp. 59–73. Cambridge: James Clarke & Co.

Durkheim, Émile. 1982 [1895]. *The Rules of the Sociological Method*. Translated by W.D. Halls. New York: The Free Press.

Durkheim, Émile. 1984. *The Division of Labour in Society*. Basingstoke: Macmillan. https://doi.org/10.1007/978-1-349-17729-5

Durkheim, Émile. 1995 [1912]. *The Elementary Forms of Religious Life*. Translated by Karen E. Fields. New York: The Free Press.

Eliade, Mircea. 1959. *The Sacred and the Profane: The Nature of Religion*. New York: Houghton Mifflin Harcourt.

Engelke, Matthew. 2002. "The Problem of Belief: Evans-Pritchard and Victor Turner on 'the Inner Life'." *Anthropology Today* 18(6): 3–8. https://doi.org/10.1111/1467-8322.00146

Engelke, Matthew. 2010. "Religion and the Media Turn: A Review Essay." *American Ethnologist* 37(2): 371–379. https://doi.org/10.1111/j.1548-1425.2010.01261.x

Evans-Pritchard, Edward E. 1940. *The Nuer: A Description of the Modes of Livelihood and Political Institutions of a Nilotic People*. Oxford: Clarendon Press.

Evans-Pritchard, Edward E. 1956. *Nuer Religion*. Oxford: Clarendon Press.

Evans-Pritchard, Edward E. 1962. *Essays in Social Anthropology*. London: Faber and Faber.

Evans-Pritchard, Edward E. 1965. *Theories of Primitive Religion*. Oxford: Clarendon Press.

Evans-Pritchard, Edward E. 1976. *Witchcraft, Oracles, and Magic among the Azande*. Oxford: Clarendon Press.

Ewing, K.P. 1994. "Dreams from a Saint: Anthropological Atheism and the Temptation to Believe." *American Anthropologist* 96(3): 571–583. https://doi.org/10.1525/aa.1994.96.3.02a00080

Geertz, Clifford. 1973. *The Interpretation of Cultures*. New York: Basic Books.

Geertz, Clifford. 1984. "Anti Anti-relativism." *American Anthropologist* 86(2): 263–278. https://doi.org/10.1525/aa.1984.86.2.02a00030

Geertz, Clifford. 1993. *The Interpretation of Cultures: Selected Essays*. London: Fontana Press.

Greenberg, Jeff, Tom Pyszczynski and Sheldon Solomon. 1986. "The Causes and Consequences of a Need for Self-esteem: A Terror Management Theory." In *Public Self and Private Self*, edited by Roy F. Baumeister, pp. 189–212. New York: Springer. https://doi.org/10.1007/978-1-4613-9564-5_10

Guha, Ranajit. 1988. The Prose of Counter-Insurgency. In *Selected Subaltern Studies*, edited by Ranajit Guha and Gayatri Chakravorty Spivak, pp. 45–84. Oxford: Oxford University Press.

Hackett, Rosalind I.J. 2005. "Anthropology of Religion." In *The Routledge Companion to the Study of Religion*, edited by John R. Hinnels, pp. 144–163. London: Routledge.

Harding, Susan F. 1987. "Convicted by the Holy Spirit: The Rhetoric of Fundamental Baptist Conversion." *American Ethnologist* 14(1): 167–181. https://doi.org/10.1525/ae.1987.14.1.02a00100

Hatch, Elvin. 1973. *Theories of Man and Culture*. New York: Columbia University Press.

Heidemann, Frank. 2011. *Ethnologie*. Göttingen: Vandenhoeck & Ruprecht.

Hughes, Aaron W. 2013. "Theory and Method in the Study of Religion: Twenty-five Years On." In *Theory and Method in the Study of Religion: Twenty-five years on*, edited by A.W. Hughes, pp. 1–17. Leiden: Brill. https://doi.org/10.1163/9789004257573_002

Hurd, Elizabeth Shakman. 2015. *Beyond Religious Freedom: The New Global Politics of Religion*. Princeton, NJ: Princeton University Press. https://doi.org/10.23943/princeton/9780691166094.001.0001

Ingold, Tim. 1996. "General Introduction." In *Key Debates in Anthropology*, edited by T. Ingold, pp. 1–13. London: Routledge.

Joas, Hans and Wolfgang Knöbel. 2004. "Was ist Theorie?" In *Sozialtheorie: Zwanzig einführende Vorlesungen*, edited by H. Joas and W. Knöbel, pp. 13–28. Fanrkfurt/M: Suhrkamp.

Kapferer, Bruce. 2002. "Introduction: Outside All Reason – Magic, Sorcery and Epistemology in Anthropology." In *Beyond Rationalism: Rethinking Magic, Witchcraft and Sorcery*, edited by B. Kapferer, pp. 1–30. New York: Berghahn. https://doi.org/10.3167/015597702782409310

Kearney, Michael. 2004. "A Very Bad Disease of the Arms." In *Changing Fields of Anthropology: From Local to Global*, pp. 41–50. Lanham, MD: Rowman and Littlefield.

Knibbe, Kim. 2013. *Faith in the Familiar: Religion, Spirituality and Place in the South of the Netherlands*. Leiden: Brill. https://doi.org/10.1163/9789004214934

Knibbe, Kim, and André Droogers. 2011. "Methodological Ludism and the Study of Religion." *Method and Theory in the Study of Religion* 23: 285–305. https://doi.org/10.1163/157006811X608395

Knibbe, Kim, and Peter Versteeg. 2008. "Assessing Phenomenology in Anthropology." *Critique of Anthropology* 28(1): 47–62. https://doi.org/10.1177/0308275X07086557

Kuhn, Thomas. 1970 [1962]. *The Structure of Scientific Revolutions*. Chicago, IL: The University of Chicago Press.

Kuper, Adam. 1996. *Anthropology and Anthropologists: The Modern British School*. London: Routledge & Kegan Paul.

Latour, Bruno and Steve Woolgar. 1986 [1979]. *Laboratory Life: The Construction of Scientific Facts*. Princeton, NJ: Princeton University Press. https://doi.org/10.1515/9781400820412

Lett, James. 1999. "Science, Religion, and Anthropology." In *Anthropology of Religion: A Handbook*, edited by S.D. Glazier, pp. 103–120. Westport, CT: Greenwood.

Lukoff, David. 2007. "Spirituality in the Recovery from Persistent Mental Disorders." *Southern Medical Journal* 100(6): 642–646. https://doi.org/10.1097/SMJ.0b013e3180600ce2

Mahmood, Saba. 2015. *Religious Difference in a Secular Age: A Minority Report*. Princeton, NJ: Princeton University Press. https://doi.org/10.2307/j.ctvc77k82

Marshall, Gordon (ed.). 1996. *Concise Dictionary of Sociology*. Oxford. Oxford University Press.

Masuzawa, Tomoko. 2000. "The Production of 'Religion' and the Task of the Scholar: Russell McCutcheon among the Smiths." *Culture and Religion* 1(1): 123–130. https://doi.org/10.1080/01438300008567146

Masuzawa, Tomoko. 2005. *The Invention of World Religions: Or, How European Universalism Was Preserved in the Language of Pluralism*. Chicago, IL: University of Chicago Press.
https://doi.org/10.7208/chicago/9780226922621.001.0001

McCutcheon, Russell T. 1997. *Manufacturing Religion: The Discourse on Sui Generis Religion and the Politics of Nostalgia*. Oxford: Oxford University Press.

McCutcheon, Russell T. 2001. *Critics Not Caretakers*. Albany, NY: State University of New York Press.

McIvor, Méadhbh. 2020. *Representing God*. Princeton, NJ: Princeton University Press.

Meyer, Birgit. 2011. "Mediation and Immediacy: Sensational Forms, Semiotic Ideologies and the Question of the Medium." *Social Anthropology/Anthropologie Sociale* 19(1): 23–39.
https://doi.org/10.1111/j.1469-8676.2010.00137.x

Meyer, Birgit, and Marleen de Witte. 2013. "Heritage and the Sacred: Introduction." *Material Religion* 9(3): 274–280.
https://doi.org/10.2752/175183413X13730330868870

Moore, Henrietta L. and Todd Sanders. 2005. "Anthropology and Epistemology." In *Anthropology in Theory: Issues in Epistemology*, edited by H.L. Moore and T. Sanders, pp. 1–21. Malden, MA: Blackwell.

Needham, Rodney. 1973. "Prescription." *Oceania* 43(3): 166–181.
https://doi.org/10.1002/j.1834-4461.1973.tb01207.x

Rawls, John. 2005 [1971]. *A Theory of Justice*. Cambridge, MA: Belknap Press.

Rosaldo, Renato. 1989. *Culture and Truth: The Remaking of Social Analysis*. Boston, MA: Beacon Press.

Rosenberg, Alex. 2011. *Philosophy of Science: A Contemporary Introduction*, 3rd edn. Hoboken, NJ: Taylor & Francis. https://doi.org/10.4324/9780203807514

Sahlins, Marshall. 1996. "The Sadness of Sweetness: The Native Anthropology of Western Cosmology." *Current Anthropology* 37(3): 395–415.
https://doi.org/10.1086/204503

Sahlins, Marshall. 2002. *Waiting for Foucault, Still*. Chicago, IL: Prickly Paradigm Press.

Skinner, B.F. 1938. *The Behavior of Organisms: An Experimental Analysis*. New York: Appleton-Century.

Smart, Ninian. 1973. *The Science of Religion and the Sociology of Knowledge: Some Methodological Questions*. Princeton, NJ: Princeton University Press.

Smart, Ninian. 1999. *Dimensions of the Sacred: An Anatomy of the World's Beliefs*. Berkeley, CA: University of California Press.

Smith, Jonathan Z. 1982. *Imagining Religion: From Babylon to Jonestown*. Chicago, IL: University of Chicago Press.

Stocking, George W. Jr. 1968. "Edward Burnett Tylor." *International Encyclopedia of the Social Sciences*. New York: Macmillan.

Sullivan, Winnifred Fallers. 2005. *The Impossibility of Religious Freedom*. Princeton, NJ: Princeton University Press.

Tylor, Edward B. 1920 [1871]. *Primitive Culture: Researches into the Development of Mythology, Philosophy, religion, Language, Art, and Custom, Volume I*. London: John Murray.

Vásquez, Manuel. 2012. "Grappling with the Legacy of Modernity: Implications for the Sociology of Religion." In *Religion on the Edge: De-Centering and Re-Centering the Sociology of Religion*, edited by Courtney Bender, Wendy Cadge, Peggy Levitt, and David Smilde, pp. 23–42. Oxford: Oxford University Press. https://doi.org/10.1093/acprof:oso/9780199938629.003.0002

Von Stuckrad, Kocku. 2010. *Locations of Knowledge in Medieval and Early Modern Europe: Esoteric Discourse and Western Identities*. Leiden: Brill. https://doi.org/10.1163/ej.9789004184220.i-240

Von Stuckrad, Kocku, and Frans Jozef Servaas Wijsen, eds. 2016. *Making Religion: Theory and Practice in the Discursive Study of Religion*. Leiden: Brill.

Weber, Max. 1964. *The Theory of Social and Economic Organization*. New York: The Free Press.

Winnicott, Donald W. 1971. *Playing and Reality*. London: Tavistock/Routledge.

Wohlrab-Sahr, Monika, and Marian Burchardt. 2012. "Multiple Secularities: Toward a Cultural Sociology of Secular Modernities." *Comparative Sociology* 11(6): 875–909. https://doi.org/10.1163/15691330-12341249

– 2 –

Philosophy of Religion

Is Religion Universal?

DENNIS VANDEN AUWEELE

Philosophers tend to ask questions that are by their nature near impossible to answer conclusively. These highly unique and difficult questions sought traditionally to gain insight into the timeless essence of concepts such as "the good", "the human being", "God" and many more. The history of philosophy is filled with thinkers who have been at odds on these issues. Many have disputed among themselves on the essence of goodness, humanity and divinity; others have cautioned that such knowledge is beyond the reach of human beings; and others have even emphasized that such knowledge does not exist at all. Can human beings really look at things from God's perspective? Can we look *sub specie aeternitatis* – from the perspective of eternity? Traditionally, philosophical questioning by its very nature has sought to understand the timeless, non-contingent or universal essence of things but ever since a number of innovations that started in the nineteenth century, the task of philosophy seems to have shifted from thinking about what unites things to appreciating what sets things apart: from thinking unity to thinking difference. In particular, philosophy is now tasked to unsettle those who comfortably have their neatly structured worldview.

In this contribution, I would like to address the trajectory from the one to the other perspective on the nature of philosophy – one seeking unity, the other difference – with regard to my own field of study, namely (Continental) philosophy of religion. There are two main approaches

---

Keywords: philosophy of religion, universal religion, Kant, Schelling, Hegel, postmodernity

in philosophy of religion which are usually called "Analytic" and "Continental" – traditionally these overlapped with the Anglo-Saxon islands and the European mainland respectively, but things are no longer as clear. In the Analytic approach, there is a general tendency to use logical argumentation, probability schemes and inferential reasoning in order to argue in favour of or against certain tenets of religious belief. Questions such as the following are then raised: Do we have rational ground to assume that there is a divine creator of the universe? Can miracles happen? Could human beings have evolved from a less complex organism? This is not my field of study. In my view, debates in this line of thought miss the essential innovations that have been made in Continental philosophy of religion since the late eighteenth century, the most important of which is that determinate and secure knowledge of transcendent things is beyond the reach of human reason. Rather than focusing on specific religious objects in order to assess their rational validity, Continental philosophers are more interested in what exactly religion attempts to express and in what way this impacts particular human agents.

My own research has predominantly been historical: I have tracked the development of Continental philosophy of religion from the late eighteenth century to the end of the nineteenth century. With this historical knowledge, one is able to understand and even assess better those discussions in contemporary Continental philosophy of religion (which sometimes has a culpable lack of historical awareness). Most of my publications have addressed the philosophical perspectives on religion and religious topics in the philosophy of Immanuel Kant, Arthur Schopenhauer, Friedrich Wilhelm Joseph von Schelling and Friedrich Nietzsche. In that respect, I have opted to deal antagonistically with the topic of this volume by showing that religion is not merely to be thought of as "relation" but that many thinkers in the philosophical canon have pointed out certain universal elements germane to religion that exceed the differences between various faiths. To clarify this, I will start by detailing the nature of philosophical thought; then proceed to clarify how this applies to philosophy of religion; then to address the philosophy of religion of Kant's moral religion; then to address how Hegel emphasized the importance of history for a proper understanding of religion; then to detail Schelling's counterargument to the Hegelians who believed that religion was at its end; then to deal with some contemporary discussions on the presuppositions of universal religion; finally to discuss some of the exciting debates in contemporary Continental philosophy of religion.

The Nature of Philosophical Thought

Perhaps a word of caution at the outset: those who come to philosophy with answers at the ready will find their worldview profoundly challenged; and those who come to philosophy looking for answers will most likely find only more questions. Philosophy is a terrible burden to those who suffer from insecurities. But the immense boon of a philosophical training is an intellectual discipline to suspend easy answers so as to engage appropriately with very profound questions in an open dialogue without dogmatism or narrow-mindedness.

This is not to say that all satisfaction is postponed indefinitely. I would be surprised if there is any philosopher that does not retain the hope that, one day, philosophy might receive a glimpse of the true essence of reality. The Greek philosopher Plato - writer of dialogues and a founding father of Western philosophy - conjured up a wonderful image to illustrate just this aspect of doing philosophy (further reading: Annas 2003 and Fraenkel 2012). In his dialogue entitled *Phaedrus*, he proposes the following analogy: "Let us then liken the soul to the natural union of a team of winged horses and their charioteer" (Plato 1997: 524). One of the horses is beautiful and good, the other is the very opposite. In the human being's quest to climb up to the Heavens, "the heaviness of the bad horse drags its charioteer towards the earth and weighs him down if he has failed to train it well, and this causes the most extreme toil and struggle that a soul will face" (ibid.: 525). The bad horse is a metaphor for the human body that constantly distracts human beings from philosophical contemplation. Imagine sitting down to read a good book and not quite getting into a good reading position. But some so-called Immortals (Greek heroes that become demi-gods) are so fortunate that they reach the top of the Heavens because they have disciplined their horses well. Most mortal men will not reach the Heavens, but some might get a brief glimpse of highest reality, but "just barely. Another soul rises at one time and falls at another, and because its horses pull it violently in different directions, it sees some real things and misses others" making the whole effort "terribly noisy, very sweaty, and disorderly" (ibid.: 526). This is why a *philosopher's mind wants to grow wings*, namely to rise above the disorderly, sweaty ruckus of normal life and transcend to the very heavens.

Not unlike the other sciences (most of which have gradually developed and separated from philosophy), the steady accumulation of insight gave cause to divide philosophy up into a number of disciplines. In order to address some of these philosophical questions in a more specialized way, philosophy has split up into a number of interrelated disciplines such as ethics, epistemology, political philosophy and philosophy of religion. In this contribution, I would outline the content of one of these – philosophy of religion – and then engage one contemporary discussion in this field briefly, namely *whether or not there is such a thing as a universal religion*. This is a very relevant question – both for historical and contemporary reasons – because it investigates whether the various cultural practices that we call religions have in fact a common essence, which allows one to establish criteria for calling something a religion (and something not a religion). What makes a cultural practice into a religion? And how liberal exactly are we supposed to be on this subject? Is everything that is said to be a religion, really a religion? Surely, Christianity, Islam, Judaism, Hinduism and Buddhism are religions, but can the same be said of Scientology, Jediism, the Church of the Flying Spaghetti Monster or even of atheism? And for what reasons exactly?

What is Philosophy of Religion?

Continental philosophy of religion can be defined as the radically critical reflection on religion as a socio-cultural phenomenon that starts only from the simple fact that there is religion and infers from this towards its ground or rationale. The primary subject under scrutiny is therefore religion as a set of practices, and not the proportional content of any religious faith (such as the existence of God). Philosophy of religion does not overtly make any theological presuppositions, which is why it differs from its related fields of study such as systematic theology (the philosophical attempt to structure intelligibly the doctrine of Christian faith), rational and natural theology (the philosophical attempt to prove the veracity of certain religious doctrines through respectively rational or empirical argumentation) and political theology (the philosophical study of religious topics and their pertinence for politics, economics and society).[1]

This way of reflecting on religion without any theological bias only came to real prominence in the eighteenth century. This relatively late birth of philosophy of religion can be explained by the historical fact that reflection on religion was traditionally considered to be subservient to theology. This means that reflections on the nature and function of

---

1. There are some who would define philosophy of religion more generally, in which case it can encompass all the fields mentioned above. In my definition, philosophy of religion is a relatively young subdomain of philosophy since it only came to its prominence somewhere in the eighteenth century and rose to notoriety mainly in German and English philosophy, and to a lesser extent in French, Italian and Eastern European philosophy.

religion tended to take shape within a comprehensive theology, which modelled in many ways the perspectives one was allowed to entertain with regard to religion. But since, traditionally, religion had given shape to virtually any aspect of human existence, this meant that philosophy was highly limited in its critical potential. It should then come as no surprise that the ideological founder of Communism, Karl Marx, had said that the criticism of religion is the mother of all criticism. Insofar as the nature, function and purpose of religion were defined from the perspective of theological or philosophical reflection on God, one was not really critically engaging religion. Thomas Aquinas – perhaps the most important philosopher in this tradition – wrote an enormous reflection on God, human beings and religion, which is called *Summa Theologiae* (written somewhere between 1265 and 1274). He starts this philosophical investigation with a reflection on the nature of God, then he reflects on the nature and ethics of human beings, and finally he investigates how human beings can transcend to God through religion and Christ. This means that religion and faith are understood from within the framework of a previously established understanding of God. If this is the case, philosophical reflection can only help to understand religion and not add its own critical reflection. This is why this way of doing philosophy was called, after Anselm of Canterbury, faith seeking understanding (*fides quaerens intellectum*).

The situation changed, however, throughout modern philosophy (which roughly started in the sixteenth to seventeenth centuries), when serious doubts were expressed with regard to the viability of a philosophical theology that builds primarily from the concept of God. Traditionally, it was held that human reason was capable of understanding the nature and agency of God through rational inquiry. But what if it is shown that God exceeds human understanding? How are we to think of religion then if we can no longer work our way down from God? This new way of thinking came to expression most powerfully by the increasing critique of the traditional topics of natural and rational theology, namely the proofs for the existence of God. These proofs for the existence of God sought to provide certainty about the existence of God (and, at times, also about the reasonableness of Scripture). Throughout the Ancient and Medieval tradition, there have accordingly been developed a great number of proofs for the existence of God. These were summarized numerous times by philosophers, most famously by the German philosopher Immanuel Kant (1724–1804). Kant suggested that there are three traditional proofs for the existence of God: the ontological proof, the cosmological proof and the physico-teleological proof (although one can easily add many more, such as the proof from miracles, the moral proof, etc. – further reading: Nagasawa 2011).

The *ontological proof* for the existence of God, likely first developed by the British theologian Anselm of Canterbury, suggests that God is that-which-a-greater-cannot-be-thought. This means that God necessarily possesses all possible predicates to the highest extent. As such, God must also possess the predicate "existence" to the highest possible extent, otherwise one would be able to think something greater than God. But since God is that-which-a-greater-cannot-be-thought, this line of thought is self-defeating and God must necessarily exist.

The *cosmological proof* for the existence of God points out that everything that exists has a cause for its existence. This means that the world, even the universe, must have a cause for its existence. But if this line of thought goes on infinitely or *ad infinitum*, there would be an infinite amount of causes. There cannot be an actual infinity of things (which is literally impossible to imagine) and so there has to be a first cause that is itself uncaused. That first cause is what people generally call God.

The *physico-teleological proof* for the existence of God points out that the world appears to have some form of purpose or design. All things seem to have a certain level of perfection that allows them to achieve their function. When one notes such design in an object (for instance, in a clock) one automatically assumes that this object has been designed by someone (like a clockmaker). Now, since human beings, animals and the world equally appear to have a purpose and design, they have to be designed by something more than mere chance and accident. This designer is what people generally call God.

While other proofs for the existence of God have also been elaborated (such as the proof from miracles or the moral argument), these three are the most debated proofs for the existence of God. Throughout the eighteenth century, these gradually became less and less convincing up until the point that few philosophers would engage them seriously.[2]

---

2. These proofs for the existence of God they have become particularly controversial in contemporary discussions. For instance, the cosmological argument is attacked by theoretical physics and the *Big Bang*-hypothesis and the physico-teleological argument is attacked by evolutionary biology and the Darwinian theory of natural selection. Certain atheist philosophers – such as Richard Dawkins and Daniel Dennett – are keen to poke holes in the argumentative structure of these proofs. A proper grasp of the history of philosophy of religion will show, however, that these contemporary attacks on these arguments usually attack heavily simplified versions of these arguments. Long before these twenty-first-century interventions, philosophers with a more thorough understanding of history did already start to lose faith in these arguments. For an example of these discussions, see Dennett and Plantinga (2011).

From this dearth – namely the impossibility to engage rationally with the concept of God – the field of philosophy of religion was born. David Hume is an important precursor to the field of philosophy of religion because he had prepared for the demolition of the abovementioned arguments. Hume would never attack an argument directly, but would raise a number of sceptical concerns that render these arguments less credible. For instance, some people justify their belief in the existence of God by claiming to have witnessed a miracle. Hume carefully points out that anyone who gives a testimony to have observed a miracle can never meet even the simplest requirements of persuasiveness. In Hume's view, it will under any circumstance always be more rational to believe that such an individual is delusional or lying rather than to believe that he or she has actually observed a miracle. The strength of Hume's attacks on the proofs for the existence of God derived mainly from the fact that the proofs themselves were rendered incredible rather than trying overtly to disprove these proofs. The vanguard of the assault on traditional theology was not atheism but scepticism (further reading: Gaskin 1988).

In the later eighteenth century (especially in France) and the nineteenth century (in Germany and the United Kingdom), these attacks became more direct. Many philosophers would even simply dismiss the arguments for the existence of God without argument. Discarding out of hand or simply ignoring is probably the most vicious attack anyone can give to any idea. The famous atheist philosophers Arthur Schopenhauer and Friedrich Nietzsche devote little time to disproving these arguments and simply analyse psychologically what makes human beings desire to prove the existence of God. In a way, this is their engagement with philosophy of religion: they study the cultural phenomenon and discover its ground to be in human weakness and not divine revelation. Even more disparaging is Schopenhauer's point that by attending to these arguments, one gives far too much credit to theism. Theistic philosophy has the burden of proof on its side, and the atheistic naturalism of Schopenhauer is really the default position: "Proof is incumbent upon the person who makes a claim, whereas the so-called atheism possesses the right of first occupancy and first has to be driven from the field by theism. I venture here the remark that human beings come into the world uncircumcised and consequently not as Jews" (Schopenhauer 2014: 105).

One somewhat unforeseen consequence of the decrease in cogency of the proofs of God was that philosophical reflection on religious themes could no longer work *top-down*, so to speak, but must happen *bottom-up*. This means that philosophers who wanted to investigate religion, faith and their related concepts would have to take their cues from the socio-cultural fact of religion. And so, the field of philosophy of religion

– or *Religionsphilosophie*, *godsdienstfilosofie* or *philosophie religieuse* – was born. Since then, some of the most interesting philosophical authors in the nineteenth and twentieth century have delved into this domain. Their conversation partner was mostly the Judeo-Christian tradition, but gradually the West opened up towards the East. In the early days, some have taken up philosophy of religion in order to justify Christian orthodoxy, others have been critical of Christianity but open towards a renewal of Christian religion and others still have expressed serious hesitations towards religion altogether. Unburdened of demands for Christian orthodoxy and with no authority beside reason herself, these philosophers have claimed the freedom to investigate everything concerning religion with a critical eye.

Universal Religion: Kant and Rational Religion

When one starts to reflect philosophically on the nature of religion, one of the most obvious questions to ask is the following: What is the essential function of religion? Is there a timeless essence to religion that she attempts to complete throughout her historical permutations? This question hopes to bypass all historical contingencies that became associated with religion and seeks to understand the inner essence of religion as such. Throughout the nineteenth century, this was the issue that was most prominently addressed in philosophy of religion. To rephrase the question in terms that anticipate certain twentieth-century interventions in this debate: Is there such a thing as an underlying essence to all socio-cultural practices that are generally called religions or are these simply highly diverse practices that share some functional similarities? Throughout the nineteenth century, there were lively debates on the essence of religion that underlies all different historical religions. While there was no consensus on what exactly formed the essence of religion, there did seem to be a consensus that there was such a thing as an essence to religion. In the twentieth century, this consensus was challenged by innovations, which often had their origin in the sociology and anthropology of religion.

Immanuel Kant was among the first to suggest a view of a universal essence that underlies religion in the newly established field of philosophy of religion (further reading: Wood 1970) – his reflections were preceded in a less systematic way by a number of, especially English, authors such as Hume, Clarke, Toland and Locke. Kant was a famous philosopher who spent the entirety of his life in the Prussian town of Königsberg, now Kaliningrad. He was one of the foremost proponents of the German

Enlightenment (*Aufklärung*), which is a philosophical ideology that prioritizes autonomy and critical reflection over tradition and dogma. From this basic premise, he famously built a view of metaphysics, epistemology and ethics that centred on the idea of rational autonomy. And from this perspective, no philosopher could have expected that – after being revolutionary in all these fields – Kant would decide to engage positively with the topic of religion. Is not religion the exact opposite of autonomy that should be discarded together with any and all forms of illegitimate, oppressive authority? Indeed, Kant recognizes that "morality ... is in need neither of the idea of another being above him in order that he recognize his duty, nor, that he observe it, of an incentive other than the law itself" (Kant 1996: 57). But Kant is quick to add that certain particular characteristics of human beings necessitate a turn to religion.

Kant's recourse to religion can then be understood best from that aspect of human nature that makes human beings congenial to religion. This has to do with the fact that human beings are not naturally well-disposed towards what they morally ought to do or, as Kant calls it, human beings are not inclined to the moral law or categorical imperative (which provides the content of our moral duties). In fact, Kant argued that human beings even have a strong propensity to abuse their autonomy in the pursuit of egoist inclinations. This is what Kant calls the propensity to evil or the *Hang zum Böse*. Human beings have a natural propensity to make very poor use of their autonomy. This proposition sounds so strikingly Christian that the famous poet Goethe exclaimed that Kant "had criminally smeared his philosopher's cloak with the shameful stain of radical evil, after it had taken him a long human life to cleanse it from many a dirty prejudice, so that Christians too might yet be enticed to kiss its hem" (quoted in Barth 1969: 178).

What Kant is trying to point out is that human beings are not very responsive to abstract argumentation. This is an experience that any parent or educator might find relatable: one can give good reasons to someone for a certain course of action, such arguments only have a minimal effect on the behaviour of human beings. We need something more than abstract argumentation such as the lure of reward, the fear of punishment or the heroic awesomeness of stories. Especially this latter aspect is what enthralled Kant: human beings are often awe-struck by stories, such as of great magnanimity or passionate devotion. In ways, most historical faiths have repeated stories of certain heroes that rise above themselves. The sublime attraction of these heroes can help motivate human beings to act in a morally good way.

With this, Kant believes he has stumbled upon the universal essence of religion. Historical faiths are supposed to provide narratives, practices and symbols that appeal to fragile, embodied human beings. To put things slightly provocatively, historical faiths are to become a form of assistance to practical morality. While in the tradition before Kant, philosophy was believed to be the *handmaiden of theology* (*ancilla theologiae*), Kant reverses this by arguing that historical faiths should be at the beck and call of morality. While this is the timeless essence of religion as such, different historical faiths (Christianity, Islam, Buddhism, Hinduism, etc.) have provided content to this basic function in different ways. Kant believes that some faiths, such as Judaism and Islam, have strayed from their purpose. They have elevated their historical clothing over the universal, ahistorical moral message of religion. In other words, these religions are about completing certain practices (such as rituals) in order to become blessed, while Christianity – in Kant's view at least – is about developing a proper morality. Kant attributes the waywardness of Judaism and Islam to the fact that human beings generally prefer to be a "favourite" than a good "servant": rather than putting in all the hard work of being a good moral person, they look for transcendent election. Some versions of Christianity have fallen prey to the same error. In response to improper traditions and problematic practices, Kant proposes to reform historical faiths in such a way that they are more in tune with their inner essence.

Bringing in History: Hegel

Kant's philosophy of religion establishes that the timeless essence of religion is moral education, namely to cultivate a frame of mind that might be conducive to moral activity. This means that whatever historical garments a religion wears are always subservient to their universal, ahistorical message. But have historical faiths not changed dramatically throughout the ages? Does this really mean nothing? Are the different shapes and sizes of historical faith but different instantiations (some better than others) of the moving face of eternity? Shortly after Kant, many philosophers tried to incorporate history as a more positive element of religion.

Georg Wilhelm Friedrich Hegel (1770–1831) was a German philosopher in Berlin and for all intents and purposes destined to succeed and improve upon Immanuel Kant. He believed that the Kantian dualism between historical faith and universal religion was ultimately untenable. One can only know the essence of religion by grappling with its historical instantiation. There is no direct knowledge of something's timeless essence that does not pass through its empirical and historical instantiation. This means that, if one wants to know what religion is, one has to oversee the whole of the historical development of religion: only the whole is true (*das Wahre is das Ganze*). This has a number of impressive consequences for understanding religion.

First, any attempts to fix the truth of religion in any historical instantiation will always be wrong since this provides but a temporary and fractured perspective on religion. Hegel notes how religion has historically evolved from natural mythological religions, to religions of the book, to revealed religion. In that process, one is slowly coming to grips with the essence of religion. Second, the development of religion throughout history is teleological. This means that its development has a certain aim (the Greek for purpose/aim is *telos*) in mind, namely to come to self-understand the essence of religion. Those who stand at the proverbial end of history will be able to ascertain finally what religion really is. Hegel believed himself to stand at the end of history, and so was able to come to understand the essence of religion. Third, the teleological development of history takes place slowly, which means that certain aspects of religion's history that many find deplorable (religious wars, the Inquisition, the Crusades, etc.) are necessary steps in coming to terms with what religion is. Without these more negative elements, history could not move forward since any determinate system of thought can only evolve if it is challenged by its opposite. The whole slaughter bench of history, as Hegel calls it, is ultimately justified and necessary from the point of view of the historical development of religion. The proper endpoint of religion could only be realized by going through the monstrosity (*Ungeheure*) of religion's historical incarnations.

What is then the conclusion of Hegel's philosophy of religion? For Hegel, religion is one way, next to art and philosophy, by which history comes to realize that it is a purposive process that works towards the self-realization of *Geist*. Spirit or *Geist* is an enigmatic term in Hegel's philosophy that is closely related to reason. The history of art, religion and philosophy is a teleological development towards the most reasonable point of view. Art attempts to represent reason sensuously; religion attempts to represent reason symbolically; and philosophy attempts to represent reason abstractly. While all of these practices have done so with limited success initially, throughout their historical development they have become more self-conscious. This ultimately found its apotheosis in Hegel's philosophy where art, religion and philosophy are understood as ways by which reason comes to know itself (further reading: Hodgson 2005).

Dennis Vanden Auweele

Is Religion at its End? Schelling on Mythology and Revelation

While Hegel was applauded by many of his contemporaries for bringing history into the debate on the essence of philosophy of religion, soon a powerful polemic emerged on what this means exactly for religion after Hegel. Is religion something that should have come to an end? And why has it not done so already? Conservative readers of Hegel read him as someone who could reconcile reason with Christianity but more progressive readers read him as someone who inaugurated the end of religion. Some of those who provided a leftist interpretation of Hegel (most famously Karl Marx) believed that religion is not so much a means by which history moves forward, but something that impedes or even halts the progress of history. Marx famously believed that religion was opium of the people, which made their lives under conditions of exploitation more bearable but at the same time occluded their vision of the sources of their oppression. Perhaps when religion was taken away, then the revolution of the proletarian masses might begin which brings capitalism and oppressive tyranny to an end; or perhaps religion would fade away when the workers had become aware of their miserable lot and revolted against their oppressors?

There were, however, more charitable engagements with religion. Friedrich Wilhelm Joseph Schelling (1775-1854) shared a room with Hegel at the *Tubinger Stift*, which was a prominent Evangelical college of residence and study. After enjoying brief notoriety in the 1790s and 1800s, he would fade into anonymity when Hegel took to the stage. After Hegel's death in 1831, Schelling made his re-entry in Berlin and delivered some much-anticipated lectures, which were expected to remedy the difficulties with Hegel's *Religionsphilosophie*. Many attended these lectures, and most of these were disappointed (for instance Marx's compatriot Engels and the famous existentialist philosopher Kierkegaard). Schelling had been brooding on his philosophy of religion at least since the 1810s, and now he finally lectured (he did not publish anything in fear of plagiarism) and chose the topics of mythology and revelation.

The lectures on mythology were delivered a number of times. Schelling wonders what the original foundry or birthing place of mythology really is. Most Christian philosophers believed that mythology was nothing but a poetic or artistic invention by certain mythological authors, such as Homer and Hesiod. This was then thought of as a faulty, bad religion that was set right by Christianity, the revealed religion. Schelling spent a number of decades reading and investigating the different world mythologies and he was struck by the deep, inner similarities between these mythologies. How can one explain these similarities if mythology was nothing but a poetic invention?

In response, some philosophers have proposed the view that mythological stories are allegories. They represent a physical, historical, ethical or scientific truth by means of stories and parables. This would explain the similarities between different mythologies, since these stories all attempt to communicate a rational truth. Schelling hesitates with regard to this view, and proposes numerous arguments to oppose it. The most powerful of these arguments is simply the factual realization that everywhere mythology precedes philosophy. How can there be philosophy and reason in mythology if philosophy proceeds from and does not precede mythology?

This means that the origin of mythology must lie beyond poetics and philosophy. Philosophy and poetry are "two equally possible – not beginnings but – exits from mythology" (Schelling 2007: 36). The only possible explanation of mythology can be found by tracing mythology back to its origin. Before mythological stories were written down, they were part of an oral culture that kept these stories alive in a certain people. And prior to developing speech, these mythic stories were intimately and closely experienced by that people. Indeed, mythology is derived from a primal, mythic consciousness that lives through the myth rather than narrates it. In fact, it is through the addition of *logos* (reason, speech) to the *mythos* that a people gradually starts to distance itself from mythic consciousness. It is through adding distance by orally transmitting these stories and finally writing them down that these stories are altered and rendered more reasonable. The original mythic consciousness is more immediate, more intimate, but less clear.

The only way that one can then gain insight into this mythic consciousness is by looking into what this mythic consciousness left behind, namely mythological stories. While Schelling was exceptionally knowledgeable about the great world mythologies of his time, his view of mythology is, for our standards, relatively meagre and his investigation likely biased. He found that in all mythologies there is a primal unity in a first all-encompassing God (Uranos, Elohim, Brahma), which is broken by a second, usually female, principle (Gaia, Jahwe, Vishnu). In that struggle, there is usually a multiplicity of gods who take over in a successive and ultimately structural polytheism. In Greek mythology, this was how Uranos was overthrown by Kronos who, in turn, was overcome by Zeus, Hades and Poseidon. This means that all mythologies exhibit a move from a primal unity towards greater and greater diversity.

Schelling believed that these mythological stories are the latent memory of the self-development of the world as the historical revelation of God. Practically, this means that humanity was at one point a people intimately but ambiguously united in the same mythic consciousness. In developing language, human beings started to give a name to this mythic unity. Through this, different peoples were born who all relate to the same first principle (or God) but choose to name this principle differently. It is language that splits humanity up in different peoples (cf. the Biblical story of Babel). Through further developing and refining language, these mythologies develop into successive and structural forms of polytheism. And then the whole world is divided because of different names we give to the same God.

But this great division has a purpose: it serves to cultivate the maturation of the human race. Through developing language, human beings become responsible, free and knowledgeable creatures. The first, intimate bond with God was unchosen, involuntary and unknown. Human beings were like animals. Through refining their skills, human beings have come to a point of great diversity where they are offered the chance to freely submit to the true God. This becomes possible because God reveals Himself in history through his Son, Jesus Christ. This is the subject matter of Schelling's lectures on revelation.

For Schelling, mythology and revealed religion are the motor of history. Mythology has separated humanity into different peoples who can work, once again, to unity by accepting Jesus Christ as the revelation of God. Religion is the way human beings come to know God, first involuntarily in mythic consciousness and mythologies, later voluntarily in revealed religion.

Universal Religion as Christian Bias

What should be very clear is that these philosophers who have investigated the supposedly universal essence of religion, all clearly have a bias towards Christianity. This rightly causes suspicion: why is Christianity the religion that most powerfully and clearly expresses the universal truth of religion?

Through anthropological and sociological research into different cultures, the deep similarities that were initially detected between different faiths became problematic. One particularly difficult issue was the relegation of the ritualistic in religion. From a philosophical point of view, ritual seems of less importance than the cognitive content of religion. This becomes very obvious in Hegel and Schelling who see in religion the symbolical representation of transcendence. It could be argued that such a relegation of ritual to cognition is only true for (a specific form of) Christianity, namely Protestant Christianity. This bias towards cognition in philosophy of religion became very apparent in a certain discussion between Clifford Geertz and Talad Asad. Geertz provided a very influential definition of religion as "a system of symbols which acts to establish powerful, pervasive, and long-lasting moods in men by formulating conceptions of a general order of existence and clothing those conceptions with such an aura of factuality that the moods and motivations seem uniquely realistic" (Geertz 1973: 90). He was challenged for his view of religion that perpetuated the relegation of ritual to cognition. By following Geertz, one is enabled to provide a fairly rational definition of religion; if one privileges ritual over cognition, however, this becomes vastly more difficult. The central problem was then not so much that he misidentified what religion was, but that the very attempt to provide a universal definition of religion is a typically Christian perspective that privileges the cognitive and symbolical over the ritual elements of religion. It was mainly Talal Asad that had argued extensively that a universal definition of religion will always exclude certain things (Asad 1993).

One of the most impressive interventions of Asad was to point out how the idea of a "universal religion", or a universal essence to everything religious, has a certain genealogy. It stems from the time of the religious wars between Catholics and Protestants, in an attempt to provide oecumenical unity. When one is able to provide a foundation of similarities between different faiths, one is given the opportunity to see beyond the minor differences. This means that the "universal essence" of religion is not reached through objective, philosophical investigation but was a *desideratum stemming from particular needs* (see also Vial 2016).

While Asad's argument appears cogent, his argument does not conclusively caution against universal definitions of religion. In short, Asad has merely pointed out that the venture of providing a universal definition of religion has a history, which should make us wary of the outcomes of that investigation. But everything has a history, and some histories are more questionable than others. For instance, Nietzsche has shown that most systems of morality originate in profound cruelty. Does this invalidate morality altogether? Surely not! This means that the result of Asad's argument should be that one ought to investigate the possibility and content of the universal essence of religion carefully, being very conscious of one's own background and personal preferences.

Dennis Vanden Auweele

Philosophy of Religion Today

Philosophers have reluctantly taken to heart that the erstwhile hope for finding a sense of the true essence of religion cannot simply ignore historical and ritual practices. What religion does is of more relevance than what content religion claims to have. This has given rise to a new trajectory in philosophy of religion, which is usually called postmodern philosophy of religion.

Postmodern philosophy is generally thought of to begin around the turn of the nineteenth to the twentieth century. This way of philosophizing is notoriously difficult to define, for one because it has a tendency to unnerve easy definitions of any topic. Be that as it may, there are three elements that are generally thought of as central to postmodern philosophy. First, the end has come for what Jean-François Lyotard has called "great narratives": comprehensive stories that could fully and exhaustively detail the whole range of reality. One immediately thinks of Christianity, but postmodern philosophers are equally sceptical of the modern story of rationality or the contemporary hegemony of positive science. No one narrative can explain everything. Second, since postmodern philosophy objects to a general, common narrative, it must also reject the traditional way to think about truth. Human beings are not simply rational embodied beings who are capable of making objective statements. Instead, human beings always judge situations subjectively in accordance with their own perspectives and values. Postmodernity then generally eschews any absolute truths in favour of relativist perspectivism (although surely not all postmodern philosophers take this to extremes). Third, philosophy as a discipline should shift focus from thinking about what unites different things into one great system towards showing how any ideology is to be both oppressive and exclusive (this is particularly pertinent for such fields as gender studies, feminist philosophy, race studies, colonial studies, etc.).

How can one productively engage in philosophy of religion given the presupposition of postmodern philosophy? Some philosophers speak of a turn to the theological in philosophy since the later twentieth century (see especially Janicaud 1991). By this, they mean that philosophy has once again taken revelation seriously, but not in the sense prior to philosophy of religion. Before modern philosophy, systematic theology would use philosophy to clarify its given topics. In the twentieth century, philosophers take seriously again the idea that there might be a revelation of transcendence which exceeds their powers of understanding (see particularly Jean-Luc Marion, Michel Henry, Jack Caputo and Richard Kearney). The proper response to such a revelation is not to impose rational concepts upon the irrational, but to cultivate a receptivity to such remarkable events.

From this perspective, they propose to rethink religion as itself a response to the intimate revelation of transcendence (not a historical project such as, for instance, for Hegel). The problem then with traditional religion has been that it has superimposed philosophical concepts upon the hyperbolic revelation of divinity. They have systematized that which objects to any systematization. Religion is not to be a strong theology (as Luther called it a *Theologia Gloriae*) but a weak theology (or *Theologia Crucis*). Whenever one uses rational concepts to understand that which happens in divine revelation, one immediately creates a wedge between the divine and oneself. The only acceptable stance towards such revelation is prayer.

One debate that has recently become particularly prominent is how this new development makes any religious encounter with God into a mystifying trauma. If one cannot use concepts, ideas or thoughts in order to understand God, then there is no way to gently mediate the experience of divine transcendence with our finite intellects. But has religion not always been a great treasure trove of narratives on how to mediate between finite humanity and the infinite? Is religion by itself then not something that clears the way for an authentic experience of transcendence? For many postmodern philosophers, the specific ideas and rituals of any religion are really an obstacle to a proper experience of transcendence. But can these practices not serve so as to render more palpable the piercing gaze of the infinite?

Conclusion

Philosophy of religion investigates all questions relating to religious topics from the perspective of the socio-cultural fact of religion. Ideally without any partisan bias and thoroughly self-conscious of their own background, philosophers then engage with questions that might never be answered conclusively. One of these questions is the essence of religion. While many faiths might express this essence differently, there is something that clearly links all faiths to one another. Historically, this investigation was likely biased towards Christianity and furthermore towards a fairly cognitive interpretation of Christianity. By this, the ritualistic and practical dimension were at worst obscured by or at best relegated to the propositional, cognitive content of religion. Is one then to throw away any and all cognitive elements of religion so as to come to a proper, unclouded experience of pure religion? Or can these elements play a role in shaping our understanding of that which transcends the immanent world?

About the Author

Dennis Vanden Auweele is lecturer in philosophy at KU Leuven (University of Leuven). His main research interest is in modern philosophy, with a focus on nineteenth-century German philosophy of religion. He has published the following monographs: *Exceeding Reason: Freedom and Religion in Schelling and Nietzsche* (de Gruyter, 2020); *Pessimism in Kant's Ethics and Rational Religion* (Lexington, 2019); *The Kantian Foundation of Schopenhauer's Pessimism* (Routledge, 2017). He has edited, among others, the following books: *Past to Present of Political Theology* (co-edited with Miklos Vassanyi, Routledge, 2020); *Thinking Metaxologically: William Desmond's Philosophy between Metaphysics, Religion, Ethics and Aesthetics* (Palgrave Macmillan, 2018).

References

Annas, Julia. 2003. *Plato: A Very Short Introduction*. Oxford: Oxford University Press. https://doi.org/10.1093/actrade/9780192802163.001.0001

Asad, Talal. 1993. *Genealogies of Religion*. Baltimore, MD: Johns Hopkins University Press.

Barth, Karl. 1969. *Protestant Thought from Rousseau to Ritschl*, translated by Brian Cozens. New York: Simon and Schuster.

Dennett, Daniel C. and Alvin Plantinga. 2011. *Science and Religion. Are They Compatible?* Oxford: Oxford University Press.

Fraenkel, Carlos. 2012. *Philosophical Religions from Plato to Spinoza: Reason, Religion, and Autonomy*. Cambridge: Cambridge University Press. https://doi.org/10.1017/CBO9781139043052

Gaskin, J.C.A. 1988. *Hume's Philosophy of Religion*. London: Macmillan. https://doi.org/10.1007/978-1-349-18936-6

Geertz, Clifford. 1973. "Religion as a Cultural System." In *The Interpretation of Cultures*. New York: Basic Books.

Hodgson, Peter. 2005. *Hegel and Christian Theology. A Reading of the Lectures on the Philosophy of Religion*. Oxford: Clarendon Press.

Janicaud, Dominique. 1991. *Le tournant théologique de la phénoménologie française*. Paris: Editions de l'Eclat.

Kant, Immanuel. 1996. *Religion and Rational Theology*, edited by Allen Wood and George di Giovanni. Cambridge: Cambridge University Press. https://doi.org/10.1017/CBO9780511814433

Nagasawa, Yujin. 2011. *The Existence of God. A Philosophical Introduction.* New York: Routledge. https://doi.org/10.4324/9780203818626

Plato. 1997. "Phaedrus." In *Plato: Complete Works*, edited by John M. Cooper, translated by Paul Woodruff and Alexander Nehamas. Indianapolis, IN: Hackett Publishing.

Schelling, F.W.J. 2007. *Historical-Critical Introduction to the Philosophy of Mythology*, translated by Mason Richey and Markus Zisselsberger. New York: SUNY Press.

Schopenhauer, Arthur. 2014. *Parerga and Paralipomena: Volume 1*, translated and edited by Christopher Janaway and Sabine Roehr. Cambridge: Cambridge University Press.

Vial, Theodore. 2016. *Modern Religion, Modern Race.* Oxford: Oxford University Press. https://doi.org/10.1093/acprof:oso/9780190212551.001.0001

Wood, Allen. 1970. *Kant's Moral Religion.* Ithaca, NY: Cornell University Press.

– 3 –

Turning the Tables

The History of Philosophy as a Field of Inquiry for Religious Studies

CHRISTOPH JEDAN

Introduction

In recent decades, practitioners of the scholarly study of religion have worried about the identity of their discipline. Their uneasiness is understandable, given the situation of religious studies where diverse scholarly methods are applied to continually expanding fields of enquiry.

I do not want to pretend even for a moment that the diversity of methods and fields of inquiry is not real, neither do I wish to deny that it can have a temporarily blinding effect upon its spectators. However, my argument is premised on the perception that such a diversity of methods can also be a key strength, and that the study of religion embodies concepts and research themes which can fruitfully be applied to other disciplines. Specifically, it might be surprising that scholars of religion have hardly ever made the history of philosophy an object of study by applying the concepts and methods of their own discipline.[1] In this chapter I shall conceptualize and defend such a religious studies approach to the historiography of philosophy. The structure of my

---

1. An important exception is Lewis (2015). However, he envisages a more limited conversation between religious studies and the philosophy of religion. I shall refer below to Lewis's important comments on the role of normativity in religious studies.

Keywords: historiography of philosophy, Ninian Smart, lived religion, Stoicism, parity argument

contribution is as follows: I shall first conceptualize an approach to the history of philosophy from the point of view of religious studies. Then I shall address a possible objection, namely that a religious studies approach is the prime example of an anachronistic and thus methodologically inadequate strategy of interpretation. Afterwards, I shall discuss a case study: Stoicism, a philosophical school with origins in the Hellenistic era. Stoicism has been influential throughout Western cultural history and is now subject to numerous revivals and popularizations. Finally, I offer a few pointers towards what the scholarly study of religion stands to gain from research into the history of philosophy.

Conceptualizing a Religious Studies Approach to the History of Philosophy

What would a religious studies approach to the history of philosophy be like? Our discussion ought to begin with a modicum of "expectation management". In order to conceptualize this approach, we need no hard-and-fast definitions of what religion and religious studies "really are". Not only are the terms "essentially contested", which means that conclusive definitions cannot be provided, but there is no need of definitions in the present context. Neither is there a need to deny (implausibly) that religious studies form a conglomerate of very different research traditions. It is sufficient that we can reach a pragmatic agreement about the richness of such approaches as can be found where academic religious studies are researched and taught. Nor do we have to claim (again, implausibly), for a religious studies approach to be possible, either that philosophy always took place in strong institutional settings whose inner workings could be compared to those of a church or, indeed, that philosophizing is essentially a "theological" mode of thought. Even if I myself have previously emphasized theological aspects in the history of philosophy (see e.g. Jedan 2009, 2010, 2014, 2017) – a reduction to such concepts would leave untapped the full benefit of a religious studies approach to the history of philosophy. The logic behind the trend in religious studies towards looser characterizations of religion, and away from essentializing definitions that narrow down religion to Christian templates of church-focused faiths, has been to align thinking about religion with developments in philosophical thinking about definitions; these notions of "family resemblances" were introduced by Wittgenstein. The upshot has been that phenomena such as apparently "secular" worldviews could become a fertile field of inquiry in the study of religion.[2] Among such "broader" characterizations of that field of inquiry, Ninian Smart's pioneering proposal of initially six and subsequently seven "dimensions" of religion deserves pride of place (1968, 1969, 1989, 1996). Smart argues that the dimensions are characteristic of religious studies" field of study and constitute, at the same time, the field of what *can* be studied as religion.[3] They are (see Smart 1968: 15–19):

1. A *doctrinal dimension*: religions (typically) teach doctrines.
2. A *mythological dimension*: here Smart points to the narrative dimension of religions that tell stories to interpret the emergence of the world, the life of an important teacher, and so on. It is clear that the mythological dimension is closely related to the doctrinal dimension.
3. An *ethical dimension*. Together, these three dimensions constitute what Smart calls the "worldview" of religions.
4. Religions also have a *ritual dimension* that becomes tangible in practices of worship, prayer, contemplation or meditation.
5. Religions have an *experiential dimension* that affects the inner life: initiation, enlightenment and conversion experiences are typical examples.
6. Religions have an important *social aspect*, the institutional or simply community framework, which gives the other five elements their social place.
7. A seventh aspect, the *material dimension* of religion, the physical forms in which religions are embodied, is added in Smart's publications from 1969 onwards.

The use of such a list would enhance the historiography of philosophy by extending its analytical focus. Traditionally, this historiography has concentrated on what could be characterized, in Smart's model, as the *worldviews* of specific philosophers. Characteristically, its focus has been even more limited, since the historiography of philosophy has prioritized its "doctrinal" and "ethical" dimensions. Where the mythological aspect has not been ignored completely, it has come into focus as a *problem* that needs to be explained away, for how could a rational and argumentatively

---

2. See Smart (1989: 21–25; 1996: 8–14). Smart's broad version of the subject area of religious studies makes the use of his dimensions (below) appear particularly fitting and attractive.
3. However, it is worth stating that Smart did not intend his list to be a fixed description of necessary conditions. The dimensions need not be instantiated to the same degree; it would even be conceivable that a dimension is not instantiated at all or that researchers lack material to judge whether or how a dimension is instantiated.

inventive philosopher such as *x* be content with introducing myths into their work? Was *x* serious in this? Could mythological digressions – for that is how the mythological production of philosophy is looked upon in the academic historiography of philosophy – be understood as a nod to less enlightened readers? Do such digressions ultimately serve to convey a serious message? The list of questions could be continued. Substitute the name "Plato" for "*x*" and one could generate a substantial bibliography that would illustrate my point.

From the perspective of religious studies it hardly needs to be emphasized that a reduction to the two dimensions of doctrine and ethics – and the misconstruction of the mythological dimension – is harmful, because it prevents us from understanding to a fuller extent how and why philosophies *mattered* in individual biographies, in communities, and as broader cultural trends. To gain a full appreciation of how and why philosophies can be cultural and social forces it would be essential to study the mythological and other dimensions of Smart's model.

Of course, an emphasis on philosophy's mythological, ritual, experiential, social and material dimensions would mean that the history of philosophy needs to enrich its research methods. Today, the academic philosophical landscape is dominated by "analytical philosophy", as it is known, a practice of philosophy originating in the Anglo-Saxon world, with a strong emphasis on language, logic and argument, conceiving of philosophy in earnest conversation with the natural sciences. The historiography of philosophy has followed suit. Its dominant style is analytical: historians of philosophy analyse whether or not a specific author *x* was "right" from today's perspective and succeeds in addressing, if not solving, problems with which analytical philosophers still grapple. It is significant, however, that even from analytical historians of philosophy there has been a call to pay close attention to cultural context. The question is thus transformed from whether or not *x* was right into the question of whether or not it is understandable that *x* would hold a specific position given their own cultural context (see below).

This is still a far cry from asking what ought to be done if a religious studies approach were to enrich the historiography of philosophy – to expand the realm of inquiry to embrace questions such as: In what sense did the views of *x* gain traction in society? How did those views circulate, and how did they inform the lives of others? Did others regard *x* as an authoritative figure and, if so, how was the life and the work of *x* remembered and celebrated? In what sense can we say that *x* was not a unique figure but a typical representative of their time? Did the realization that *x* was not a unique figure, but perhaps the member of a larger body of opinion or a philosophical "school" reflect on the legitimacy and attractiveness of *x*'s philosophy? What communities were created and fostered? What role did they play in the day-to-day lives of their members?

Such questions would also necessitate the use of research methods other than the typical "normative" argument exemplified by philosophical historiography even in its attenuated, modernized, context-aware version. By approaching the history of philosophy from the angle of Smart's dimensions we need to expand the philosophical historiographer's focus, which has hitherto been obsessed with normative argument. The material to be considered by the philosophical historiographer must also expand. Quantitative and qualitative data, personal documents, letters and newspaper reports then come into focus, at the expense of philosophy's implausibly elitist and ultimately unsustainable focus on a few high-profile authors as unique agents of cultural change. Instead, the philosophical historiographer's field of inquiry must be a broader social and cultural history, in which the lives, the views and the impact, both of philosophers and of the communities surrounding them, are to be located.

During such inquiries, concepts first developed in the scholarly study of religion can play a key role. In the present context, I shall restrict myself to a single example: the concept of "lived religion". The phrase "lived religion" has flourished in Anglo-American research since the last decade of the twentieth century. The phrase itself, however, derives from the older concept of a *religion vécue* in the French sociology of religion (Hall 1997: vii) and denotes an important – but for a long while insufficiently analysed – aspect of religiosity. Whereas earlier interpretations focused on "official" religion as "defined" and "prescribed" by religious institutions and religious elites, the concrete, lived experience of religious people had attracted less attention. As Meredith B. McGuire (2008: 11–12) explains:

> Many scholars of religion have assumed that individuals practice a single religion, exclusive of other religious options; for example, if they take the Presbyterian option, supposedly they cannot also be Catholic and Buddhist. Unfortunately, that concept of individual commitment and belonging has been based, uncritically, on narrow Western (particularly Protestant) norms. I refer to these concepts of "religion" and religious "commitment" as normative, because they take for granted ideas about how adherents ought to be committed and about what consonance ought to exist between individuals' beliefs and practices and the proclaimed teachings of their chosen religion. The historically Protestant assumptions linked to these norms include voluntarism (i.e. the idea that the individuals, rather than family, tribe, or other relationships, ought to be the relevant unit for

making such choices). Because Western scholars' concepts of religion and religious commitment developed out of the European crucible of religious contests, however, our conceptual apparatus has simply failed to question the image of religious membership and individual religious practice built on mutually exclusive, indeed antagonistic, categories. Those assumptions clearly fail to describe adequately how individuals engage in their religions in their everyday lives.

Sociologists who turned to "lived religion" then observed a surprising religious creativity that expressed itself, for example, in how everyday experiences affect religious practice and how aspects of supposedly incompatible religions are combined in religion-as-lived. It is clear that these findings gainsay widespread expectations of consistency. Once more, McGuire (2008: 15):

> Because religion-as-lived is based more on ... religious practices than on religious ideas or beliefs, it is not necessarily logically coherent. Rather it requires a practical coherence: It needs to make sense in one's everyday life, and it needs to be effective, to "work", in the sense of accomplishing some desired end (such as healing, improving one's relationship with a loved one, or harvesting enough food to last the winter). This practical coherence explains the reasoning underlying much popular religion, which may otherwise appear to be irrational and superstitious.

While the concept of lived religion is influenced by its original context of discovery, and exhibits a strong – arguably, a too strong – contrast between practices and texts,[4] it can serve as a useful corrective for the historiography of philosophy. I highlight the following questions by way of example: Is not the question of school membership exaggerated in the historiography of philosophy? Are not historians of philosophy obsessed with interpreting school membership in a Protestant sense as the acceptance of specific beliefs which the author in question must then repeat in their work and put into practice in their life? How much tolerance do we have for inconsistencies in philosophical texts? Do historians of philosophy suffer from an exaggerated expectation of consistency, which stimulates them to explain away inconsistencies in a highly speculative way? Are not inconsistencies, the coexistence of different traditions and thoughts, the norm even among an intellectual elite? Are not inconsistencies better explained by the practical function that philosophical texts also and undeniably have, as well as by the context in which they were written?

---

4. More on this below.

Perhaps we should coin the concept of a "lived philosophy" in order to capture a research agenda that is stimulated by taking seriously a religious studies approach in the historiography of philosophy.[5]

Defending a Religious Studies Approach to the History of Philosophy

I have argued that a religious studies approach to the history of philosophy can open up new perspectives and can avoid problems arising from the dominant analytical-philosophical approach to, and its focus on, classical philosophical texts. Now it is time to dispel a pressing concern: How can a rigorous historiography use concepts and themes taken *from the outside*, not only from outside the texts that are studied, but even from a different discipline? How could such an approach not be guilty of *anachronism*, in the sense that the religious studies approach advocated here might be seen as undertaking to write the prehistories of questions and problems that had not yet been formulated?[6]

My response consists in a *parity argument.*[7] Epistemic fairness requires that we do not expect an approach to fulfil standards that are more stringent than those to which other similarly placed disciplines and approaches adhere. Thus, if it can be shown that the interpretative strategies and concepts that a religious studies approach brings to bear on the history of philosophy are on a par with other historiographical

---

5. While I have still to defend and flesh out the promise of a religious studies approach to the historiography of philosophy, I want to point out right off the bat that such an approach should not be conflated with the concept of (ancient) philosophy as an art of living, spearheaded by the French historian of philosophy Pierre Hadot (e.g. Hadot 1995; important forerunner: I. Hadot 1969). Hadot's concept of philosophy as an art of living is right in speculating about the way in which philosophies impact on the lives of their adherents. However, Hadot's concept focuses on philosophical schools that are depicted as on the whole rather "Protestant", voluntaristic communities focused on the maintenance of doctrinal orthodoxy. Hadot's approach could thus best be characterized as an exploration of what philosophical orthodoxy could mean for the lives of its followers. That is a far cry from what a "lived philosophy" approach stimulated by religious studies aspires to achieve: (1) it stimulates the search for more concrete practical functions of philosophy, and (2) it focuses more on a "practical coherence" that is behind seemingly inconsistent teachings.
6. For highly influential formulations of such concerns see Collingwood (1978) and Skinner (1969).
7. Parity arguments are widespread in today's analytical philosophy of religion. They typically serve to deflate critiques of religion from an allegedly "natural science" perspective (see e.g. Quinn 1991).

approaches to philosophy that are "established" in the sense that they are widely accepted or even considered exemplary, then a religious studies approach to the history of philosophy can be thought justified.

It should be clear that this argument provides only a *relatively* weak form of justification: the method to be justified (A) is just as trustworthy as another already established one (B). Those who distrust B do not receive an independent explanation as to why A should be accepted. This relatively weak form of justification should not be seen as a deficiency, since it is difficult to see what an ultimate justification of historiographical approaches could look like. At any rate, the current stalemate between historiographies with "idiographic" ambitions, which have their foundation in nineteenth-century historicism, and the postmodern devaluation of the significance of sources in favour of later appropriations, gives little reason to hope for such a justification (see also Bevir 1999).

Specifically, I propose to use as a point of comparison the methodological reflections of professional historians of philosophy who engage with the nowadays dominant analytical-philosophical historiography of philosophy. The classic anthology in the field is *Philosophy in History: Essays in the Historiography of Philosophy* (Rorty, Schneewind and Skinner 1984). In their preface, the authors distance themselves from an approach to the history of philosophy that is all too common in Anglo-Saxon analytical philosophy:

> Analytic philosophers have seen no need to situate themselves within Gadamer's "conversation which we are" because they take themselves to be the first to have understood what philosophy is, what questions are the genuinely philosophical ones. The result of having this self-image has been an attempt to tease out the "genuinely philosophical elements" in the work of past figures, putting aside as irrelevant their "religious" or "scientific" or "literary" or "political" or "ideological" concerns. ... Such an attitude produces a history of philosophy which eschews continuous narrative, but is more like a collection of anecdotes – anecdotes about people who stumbled upon the "real" philosophical questions but did not realize what they had discovered. It is hard to make a sequence of such anecdotes mesh with the sort of narratives intellectual historians construct. So it is inevitable that such narratives should strike analytic philosophers as "not getting at the *philosophical* point" and that intellectual historians should see analytic philosophers as "anachronistically" reading current interests back into the past.
>
> (Rorty, Schneewind and Skinner 1984: 11–12)

This quotation illustrates the opposition perceived by Rorty, Schneewind and Skinner between intellectual history and a widespread form of analytical philosophical historiography. As they see it, analytical philosophers bring external concepts and questions to bear on the historical material, concepts and questions deriving from today's analytical-philosophical discourse, with the result that the history of philosophy becomes a chain of precursors to today's debates. A little later in their book, they suggest that analytical philosophy is too much directed towards the natural sciences and has thus made productive connections to the other humanities, and indeed to culture as a whole, more difficult to achieve.

It should be noted, however, that these authors do not criticize the analytical philosophical historiographers" approach for bringing *external* categories and concepts to bear on the historical material. To them, such an approach appears inevitable. They reject ideas of a "pure" past, a past that would be, as it were, "uncontaminated" by today's perspectives and interests, and informed by an illusory, romantic ideal of purity (Rorty et al. 1984: 8). They compare the work of a philosophical historian with that of an ethnographer who also had to use *etic* concepts and categories in order to study *emic* ones (ibid.: 6–7). Nor do they take issue with the analytical historiography of philosophy for its having a strong "presentist" aspect (i.e. focused on today's questions and problems); that they regard as inevitable. What they actually charge analytical historians of philosophy with is *too narrow* a construction of today's concerns. In this situation they formulate a single general rule: "There is, in our view, nothing general to be said in answer to the question 'How should the history of philosophy be written?' except 'As self-consciously as one can – in as full awareness as possible of the *variety of* contemporary concerns to which a past figure may be relevant'" (ibid.: 11).

The dual acknowledgement of an unavoidable presentism of all philosophical historiography with a simultaneous opening to a diversity of perspectives can be regarded as the *de facto* standard in philosophers' current reflections on the historiography of their discipline. It would be a wholly different matter for us to ascertain to what extent that methodological standard is actually realized in specific studies of the history of philosophy, or to what extent it is practised "on the ground". Given anecdotal evidence, there is little reason for being sanguine on that point.[8] Such an inquiry, however, would not only be outside the scope of this chapter, such an inquiry is not needed for our envisaged parity argument.

This parity argument points out that the religious studies approach I have been proposing cannot be rejected as methodologically unsound

---

8. John Cottingham (2005), for example, states that his academic peers regularly ignore such methodological reflections in an academic system focusing on "publish or perish" conveyor-belt production.

since it does not violate the methodological standard laid down by Rorty and colleagues, which is a *de facto* standard in the field when it comes to methodological reflection. The fact that a religious studies approach to the history of philosophy interrogates its sources with etic concepts and categories (which the dimensions formulated by Smart or the concepts of lived religion or lived philosophy clearly are) cannot be held against it. Methodologically, therefore, a religious studies approach to the history of philosophy and the approach advertised by Rorty and colleagues are on a par.

Arguably, we could go even further and suggest that a religious studies approach to the history of philosophy stimulates the opening of perspectives as advocated by Rorty and colleagues in a far better and far more comprehensive way than any of the traditional philosophical approaches. The reason for this is that religious studies, with its characteristic disciplinary range, has during the course of its history not only been in a critical conversation with (reductive) interpretations from the natural sciences, but has also been able to take on board a wide repertoire of social scientific research traditions as well as humanities approaches. That repertoire includes philosophical approaches, but, as illustrated by the variety of disciplinary approaches represented in this volume it goes much further, to include, for instance, philology, cultural history, cultural anthropology as well as quantitative and qualitative methods employed in the psychology and sociology of religion.[9] This makes an approach inspired by religious studies more suitable than any other for exploring the rich and productive connections between the history of philosophy and culture as a whole.

Although our parity argument shows that there is no reason in principle to distrust a religious studies approach to the history of philosophy, the *specific* interpretations obtained by it would have to satisfy widely accepted standards for the evaluation of historical explanations. Such standards ought to align with best practices in, for instance, the academic study of intellectual history. In this respect, the intellectual historian Mark Bevir has formulated six fundamental criteria worthy of mention (Bevir 1999: 102–106),[10] namely:

---

9. See the overviews in Diem-Lane (2014) and Chitakure (2016).
10. It should be noted that Bevir's model focuses on competition between networks of historical theories from the perspective of historical holism. A theory network deserves our support precisely when it fulfils the six criteria to a greater degree than competing networks fulfil them. My assertion is, of course, not that Bevir's holism and his attempt to mediate between objectivity and the scepticism that gives rise to his theory are undisputed in the philosophy of history. Rather, I

1. *accuracy* (how close is a historical explanation to the facts supporting it);
2. *comprehensiveness* (how great is the variety of facts covered by an explanation);
3. *consistency* (a theory network should be, so far as possible, without internal contradictions);[11]
4. *progressiveness* (a network of theories should contain new theories that allow new predictions);
5. *fruitfulness* (those new predictions should be supported by facts); and
6. *openness* (the network of theories consists of clearly defined statements that facilitate criticism).

While Bevir's criteria capture in an exemplary manner the evaluation of competing theories within the same already-established discipline, we should also allow for the peculiarity that a religious studies approach to the history of philosophy stands to compete with interpretations of the same texts in *another* discipline, so that a religious studies approach will have to prove itself. In this situation, a further criterion ought to be fulfilled by specific interpretations: those obtained through a religious studies approach to the history of philosophy ought to succeed in taking up previous findings of the (analytical-philosophical) historiography productively and in re-contextualizing them. In other words, a *convergence criterion will* play an important role in assessing specific interpretations.

A Case Study: The Stoic School

After presenting a broad-brush sketch of a religious studies approach to the history of philosophy, and after defending the approach against general methodological objections, we ought to illustrate its promise with an example. But to what extent can such an approach take up existing research, in the sense of fulfilling the convergence criterion, and what novel suggestions for future research can it produce?

---

contend that his criteria reflect a broad consensus among academic intellectual historians in the evaluation of concrete historical works.

11. This does not contradict my remarks about a concept of lived philosophy inspired by religious studies. The concept aims to explain apparent contradictions in philosophical texts from the second-order perspective of "practical coherence" instead of focusing on a simplistic, first-order ideal of consistency that invites unwarranted speculation.

In this context I want to focus on the Stoic tradition. Founded in Athens at the beginning of the third century BCE by Zeno, a tradesman from Cyprus, Stoicism is notable for claiming (1) that virtue is the only ingredient of happiness (*eudaimonia*) and (2) that many of the benefits deemed important by contemporary philosophers (health, family situation, income, reputation, even the duration of one's life) are irrelevant for one's *eudaimonia*. Moreover, (3) Stoicism is characterized by the idea that human beings can derive the principles of virtue by observing nature, since nature is the realization of a divine principle ("natural law"). (4) There tends to be a stark contrast between virtue and vice, the latter being the result of ignorance of the principles exhibited in nature. (5) The possession of virtue tends to be regarded as exceptional, and the Stoics tend to discuss practical ethics by reflecting on what the ideal Stoic, namely the sage, would do in the circumstances.

Stoicism is an attractive choice for a case study, since it has been a long-term force in European culture, from its foundation in Athens in the Hellenistic period to becoming, for instance, an important worldview among the Roman elite in the late Republic and early Empire. Many researchers have speculated about influences on the authors of the New Testament and upon subsequent Christian theology. Moreover, Stoicism has been credited with stimulating new social "imaginaries" that have helped to usher in our modern, secular world. Most recently, Stoicism has been claimed as a decisive influence behind certain cognitive styles of behavioural therapy. Thus, there has clearly been broad and varied attention to Stoicism and its role in Western culture, and enough to make the fulfilment of the convergence criterion a legitimate topic of inquiry.

More specifically, much of the previous research on Stoicism has focused on what are categorized in Smart's schema as doctrinal and ethical dimensions. Where a religious studies approach comes into its own is in stimulating comparative work. Undeniably, some of that work was carried out in the earlier research on the Stoic tradition. For instance, in the late nineteenth and early twentieth centuries comparisons were made in attempts to present Stoicism as a precursor of early Christianity (e.g. Farrar 1868; Bonhöffer 1894; Alston 1906). Those attempts have since found their detractors (e.g. Sellars 2006), and with some reason: all-too-easy comparisons that simply subscribe the Stoics to a Christian worldview lack much-needed historiographic sophistication. However, it can hardly be denied that Stoic philosophy incorporates sustained theological discussions (e.g. Sedley 1999, 2007; Algra 2003; Sedley 2007; Meijer 2007; Vogt 2008; Jedan 2009; Pià Comella 2016). While this makes for attractive comparisons to other theologies, a religious studies approach would prompt further enquiry: comparisons should be extended to worldviews that do not so overtly fit the mould of Christian theology. Treatises from the Confucian and Buddhist traditions, for instance, could serve as excellent points of comparison. Both Stoic authors and the Confucian tradition appear to present very similar depictions of their holy man, the sage. Both traditions share the conviction that the sage's virtue represents cosmic harmony and by its mere existence makes the world "right".

It is worth pointing out that these suggestions tie in with a rising academic interest in "comparative philosophy". However, it should also be noted that comparative philosophy is a nascent field, currently focused on building bridges between African or Asiatic philosophies on the one hand and Western traditions of academic philosophy on the other. Arguably, comparative philosophy lacks the long-standing practice and the evident sophistication of methodological discussions in the field of comparative religion, particularly when it comes to balancing historical contextualization and the abstraction needed for comparison. In other words, this is yet another area in which the history of philosophy could learn much from the scholarly study of religion.[12] Moreover, since Alasdair MacIntyre's publications, the concept of "tradition" has become more important for historians of philosophy. This concept, however, is based on shared presuppositions and remains within the remit of a long-established history of philosophy with its focus on texts and the reconstruction of arguments. Again, philosophers can learn a lot from a broader concept of tradition utilized in the study of religion.[13]

So far as the mythological dimension is concerned, research to date has shown that the Stoics adopted a critical stance towards the traditional "polytheistic" myths of the Greco-Roman culture around them. They reinterpreted, for instance, the names of the gods in such a way that those names could be regarded as reminders of Stoic theology (e.g. Mansfeld 1999; Algra 2003, 2007). Nevertheless, we should not be content with this finding, since it prepares the ground for separating the Stoics from their culture. From this perspective, culture merely "surrounds" the Stoics; it would not have a true influence on their views. Such separations make it all too easy for philosophers to celebrate their intellectual heroes as being unaccountably more advanced, more "modern" than the world around them. However, heroes thus understood have ceased to be

---

12. See, for instance, the overview in Stausberg (2011); exemplary monographs are those by Sharma (2005) and, most recently, Freiberger (2019).
13. See, for instance, MacIntyre (1981, 1991). While MacIntyre has certainly been influential in the study of religion (see e.g. Stout 2004), a larger array of phenomena has been taken into consideration (following e.g. Shils 1981). For a short introduction, see Satlow (2012).

real figures in a real cultural context. To put it differently, traditional philosophical historiographies make it all too easy to build up a dichotomy, in which the allegedly more refined, quasi-scientific insights of the Stoics are played out against an allegedly crude, polytheistic mythology.

The danger lurking behind such a procedure is the promotion of an understanding of myth as untruthful, as a matter of irrational faith, and as opposed to methodical truth-finding. A religious studies approach to the history of philosophy should invite us to analyse in greater detail how the Stoics themselves were mythologically *productive*. The numerous descriptions of the ideal figure of the sage or the cosmic city, for instance, should be examined more closely; not, as has been the case, after having undergone analytical-philosophical "purification" and reduction to their presentist explanatory power (e.g. Vogt 2008; Brouwer 2014), but as narrative products, which in turn should be compared with narrative structures in other philosophical schools and religions.

With the next three dimensions identified by Ninian Smart – ritual, experiential and social – we further expand the focus of a traditional history of philosophy. The ritual dimension of Stoic philosophy has generated the greatest interest so far. Historians of philosophy have analysed texts in which the Stoics expound their views on prayer (e.g. Pià Comella 2014, 2016; McDowell 2017) as well as Cleanthes's famous *Hymn to Zeus* (e.g. Thom 2005; Asmis 2007). In the context of a "philosophy as art of living" approach, they have also analysed the later Stoa, in particular Marcus Aurelius's *To Himself* (edition: Haines 1930) as prescribing "spiritual exercises" that are comparable to current psycho-therapeutic and meditation techniques (e.g. Hadot 1992; Sellars 2009; Robertson 2016). Such attempts, however, are still a far cry from analysing the practices of Stoic philosophers as rituals.

The experiential dimension of Stoicism has generated much less interest. This is an area in which the impact of a religious studies approach to the history of philosophy could result in a fundamental shifting of the goal posts of academic discourse. A religious studies approach would focus on philosophy as experienced in the lives of its practitioners. This is an aspect that has been systematically disregarded by the traditional historiography of philosophy, even if lip-service is being paid to philosophy as an "art of living". By and large, the traditional analytical-philosophical approach to the history of philosophy has yet to acknowledge that there are academically valid and societally relevant questions to be asked in this regard, and academic philosophy has so far been content to relegate potentially relevant sources to philological discussions concerning the transmission of texts.

Christoph Jedan

I offer three examples. First, it has been noted that a Stoic disciple's reaching the most advanced level of the Stoic curriculum is referred to – in a later summary – as an "initiation" (e.g. Babut 1974; Mansfeld 1999; Algra 2003; Jedan 2009). The dimension of lived experience invoked by this terminology, however, has received scarce attention.

The same holds for descriptions of reaching the goal of *eudaimonia*, which we find, for instance, in the fifth book of Cicero's *Tusculan Disputations* (edition: Kirfel 1997). Traditional history of philosophy has paid most attention to Cicero's sources. Furthermore, the same curious neglect of the experiential dimension characterizes conventional historiographies of philosophy in relation to a whole body of Stoic literature: consolations. We gather from a remark in Cicero's *Tusculan Disputations* (3.81) that there must have been a considerable output of philosophical treatises trying to assuage grief on all sorts of loss (exile, blindness, illnesses, death, and so on.). Most of those texts are lost, but among those that are preserved, Stoic treatises on death and exile occupy an important place. In the traditional analytical-philosophical historiography such texts have attracted little interest, leaving the field to philological discussions of the use of sources and speculative reconstructions of a lost source, a third-century BCE treatise *On Grief* by the Platonist philosopher Crantor (see e.g. Kassel 1958; Johann 1968). Even philologists have been largely critical of those consolatory writings, as drawing heavily on traditional locutions about grief and loss and as exhibiting a non-partisan stance by quoting and making use of insights by rival philosophical schools (see e.g. the contributions in Baltussen 2013). A religious studies approach to the history of philosophy would note the curious neglect of such treatises by otherwise well-studied authors – most notably, perhaps, Seneca – and the neglect of a whole tradition of philosophical teaching and writing. Such neglect is based (a) on the unacknowledged obsession with delineating strict school identities and orthodoxies (e.g. what author x, being a Stoic, must have thought and written) as well as (b) on unexamined preconceptions about philosophy as an academic scholarly enterprise. Moreover, (c) there are largely unexamined preconceptions at work about the general trend in our culture: philosophical consolations must have petered out with the Enlightenment, reinforcing ideas that philosophy is primarily a specialized academic affair and has no role to play in our everyday lives.

Such obsessions and preconceptions stand to be challenged by a religious studies approach that stimulates researchers to cast their nets wider and seek fresh fields of research rather than to assume *a priori* that such fields cannot exist or cannot be of any interest. One example of this would be a decided focus on philosophers as authors of letters and as public speakers, addressing fellow human beings in very different walks of life. It would be a promising opportunity to analyse these interventions comparatively: for instance, when speakers at a funeral address mourners who are highly diverse in terms of worldview and life experience, to what common denominators do they seek to appeal? And how does this observation, together with the ways in which those speakers try to bridge differences in worldview and experience, contribute to our analysis of that aspect of the philosophers' activities?

The social dimension in the history of philosophy has been all but totally ignored. It is clear that Stoicism as a tradition was sufficiently visible for later stoics to identify themselves as Stoics and to distance themselves from the teachings of other traditions, even if the concept of lived philosophy should serve as a powerful reminder that identities are always relational and should therefore not be essentialized and overemphasized. To assume that a key factor in a school's visibility and continuity lies in its doctrines and, in the case of Stoicism, in its theological doctrines in particular (Jedan 2009) is perhaps not mistaken, but it is a far cry from a full appreciation of the social dimension. Any appreciation of the full extent of philosophy's social dimension will have to engage with philosophy-as-lived.

In this regard there is a curious blind spot among traditional historians of philosophy when it comes to today's revival of Stoicism (or "modern Stoicism"). Since the turn of the millennium or thereabouts there has been a clear trend towards making ancient Stoicism usable as a way of life for people today (pioneering: Becker 1998). This movement has elicited hardly any scholarly interest, even if it is widely acknowledged that Stoicism constitutes a tradition that extends to the present day (see e.g. Strange and Zupko 2004; Sellars 2016).

A religious studies approach, on the other hand, would inevitably seize on this new development and would not be content with staid comparisons between modern Stoic doctrines and those of the ancient Stoics to measure, as it were, modern Stoicism's "orthodoxy". A religious studies approach would instead spearhead comparative studies in relation to a broad array of contemporary phenomena. Already in its layout, a book such as *The Daily Stoic* (Holiday and Hanselman 2016) is reminiscent of the Herrnhuter or Neukirchner calendars (for each day, a Stoic quotation is paired with a short meditation). Texts such as *How to be a Stoic* (Pigliucci 2017), *Stoicism: Introduction to the Stoic Way of Life* (Gale 2017) or *Stoicism: Full Life Mastery* (Gale 2018) are quite comparable with Christian self-help books, and Evangelical self-help books in particular. Book series such as the *Stoic Six Pack* (Anon. 2014, 2017) offer clear attempts at a canonization of Stoic texts. Questions suggesting themselves include how such calendars and books are used in everyday Stoic life today. A religious studies approach would come into its own by providing a thorough knowledge of quantitative and qualitative empirical research methods that allow us to formulate and answer such questions.

A different field of inquiry is suggested by the existence of online forums such as the blog *Modern Stoicism* (formerly *Stoicism Today*, modernstoicism.com) and accompanying online courses (*Stoic Mindfulness and Resilience Training*, learn.modernstoicism.com/p/smrt), which purport to teach a modern life based on Stoic principles. Are they comparable, for instance, to Islamic sermons and fatwahs circulating on the Internet? What authority do the recipients attribute to their teachers and their teachers' statements? One could also compare "event formats" such as the international *Stoic Week* to larger-scale religious events. What do modern Stoics seek (and find) in these events and what influence does this have on their daily lives? Do these new Stoics "evangelize" their contemporaries, or do they find evangelism inappropriate in a secular cultural climate?

Another modern phenomenon, the website "Daily Stoic – Ancient Wisdom for Everyday Life" (https://dailystoic.com) affords a glimpse of the importance of applying the seventh Smartian dimension, the material aspect, in an analysis of philosophy. In addition to offering short articles and videos, the website hosts a web shop in which aspiring Stoics can purchase a "*memento mori* signet ring" ($245), an "*amor fati* pendant" ($99) or indeed a "*premeditatio malorum* medallion" (a bargain at $26). While it is tempting to poke fun at this commercialization of philosophy, the more serious aspect should not be ignored: how important is materiality to philosophy? How central are meeting places, books, leaders and so on for communities and individuals who are studying and practising philosophy? Analyses of historical movements such as the Stoics have insufficiently focused on attachments to school buildings, the importance of libraries and books, clothing, physical mementos and so forth. Attention to those aspects could build on and improve existing research (see e.g. Sedley 1989).

So, clearly, the answers to those and similar questions are interesting not only because they shed light on the contemporary history of Stoicism; they might also fulfil a *heuristic* function. Just as historians of science have turned in recent years to the replication of historical experiments in the hope of gaining a greater sensitivity to historical sources (e.g. Höttecke 2000), so historians of philosophy can expect studies of modern Stoicism to provide inspiration for research into the motives, experiences and so on of the ancient Stoa.

In the context of this chapter I cannot even begin to answer those questions. I hope, however, that my brief remarks show, by the example of Stoic philosophy, that a religious studies approach suggests an innovative and enriching research agenda.

Benefits for Religious Studies

So far I have proposed, defended and begun to develop a religious studies approach to the history of philosophy. The emphasis has inevitably been on perceived shortcomings in the currently dominant historiography of philosophy. However, this should not be taken to imply that a conversation between philosophy and the study of religion would be anything other than two-sided. Bringing a religious studies perspective to bear on the history of philosophy means at the same time an expansion of the research focus of religious studies. This is bound to have reverberations for future research. If philosophy turns out to be a way of world-making that is highly comparable to religion, then the study of philosophy will help us to put religion(s) into relief and to better understand the place of religion(s) in culture(s). In addition to conferring benefit by providing new material, however, the conversation between religious studies and philosophy could also help at a conceptual level. I indicate just two examples of this assistance:

1 The concept of "lived religion" has been influenced too strongly by its context of discovery, in particular the reaction against "Protestant" understandings of religion. One of the topics that have received insufficient attention is the role played by *texts* in the everyday lives of religionists of all stripes. Research into the history of philosophy, where texts indisputably play a key role, can serve as a helpful reminder of the importance of those texts and their varied and creative uses in lived religion. In all likelihood, the analytical and close reading skills exhibited in the historiography of philosophy could help practitioners of the study of religion to extend and enhance their conceptual apparatus.
2 In the picture drawn of their discipline by many practitioners of the study of religion, "normativity" is a deeply problematic notion. Some go even so far as to tie the existence of religious studies to a marked resistance towards philosophical and theological modes of

thought since the latter are perceived as explicitly normative.[14] While that resistance is entirely understandable from the history of the discipline, and above all from the permanent attempt to distinguish itself from theology, the question must be raised about whether or not the perpetuation of that resistance is counterproductive. In this vein, Thomas A. Lewis (2012, 2015) has shown that an exaggerated critique of normativity tends to set religion against *reason* (as *reason's other*) and thus characterizes religion as a refuge for those seeking indefensible securities of faith. Moreover, an antagonism towards normative discourse does not correspond to what actually happens on the ground in the study of religion. Instead, as Lewis argues, it should be recognized that the normative dimension is inescapable. The normative dimension is evident, for example, in the selection of a topic, in judgments about "what a thing is really all about" (Lewis 2015: 50), and in the fact that, by providing critical information, religious studies can undermine reasons for someone to act in a way they would have acted in the absence of adequate information (ibid.: 52). In short, if questions of normativity are inescapable, religious studies had better seek out the best available methods of addressing them.

In conclusion: The research on the history and contemporary developments of philosophy, particularly philosophy-as-lived, are likely to result in upping the game not only for philosophy, but also for religious studies. Scholars of religion receive not only new material to contextualize religious phenomena sensitively; they also receive help in sharpening their tools. Is this too good to be true? Let us make it come true.

---

14. A good example of this tendency is the German Wikipedia entry on religious studies, see https://de.wikipedia.org/wiki/Religionswissenschaft. In effect, that tendency can be traced back to the "phenomenological" strand of religious studies, which created a niche for religious studies by emphasizing its focus on the human side of religion. The Groningen scholar Gerardus van der Leeuw's dictum is well-known, that science can only talk about human beings in relation to the divine – it knows nothing about God's agency ("In der Religion ist Gott der Agens in der Beziehung zum Menschen, die Wissenschaft weiß nur vom Tun des Menschen in der Beziehung zu Gott, nichts vom Tun Gottes zu erzählen"; van der Leeuw 1956: 3). The phenomenology of religion's descriptive effort stood in marked contrast to "normative" concerns with ultimate truths, goodness and the like. It should be noted that Ninian Smart, who can be categorized as a phenomenologist, maintained a highly nuanced understanding of the role of normativity in religious studies (see e.g. Smart 1968: 14–15). It is probable that the way forward for religious studies would be a more relaxed attitude towards theology, while theology would also profit from taking insights of religious studies on board, but this is far beyond the scope of the present chapter (see e.g. Helmer 2012).

About the Author

Christoph Jedan is professor of ethics and philosophy of religion at the Faculty of Theology and Religious Studies, University of Groningen. His research interests include Ancient Greek and Roman philosophy, the intersections of religion and philosophy today (religion and politics, postsecularism), and the history and continuing relevance of consolation for death and loss. He has (co-)authored and (co-)edited a dozen books and special journal issues, inter alia *Stoic Virtues: Chrysippus and the Religious Character of Stoic Ethics* (Continuum, 2009) and (with Avril Maddrell and Eric Venbrux) *Consolationscapes in the Face of Loss: Grief and Consolation in Space and Time* (Routledge, 2019).

References

Algra, K. 2003. "Stoic Theology." In *The Cambridge Companion to the Stoics*, edited by B. Inwood, pp. 153–178. Cambridge: Cambridge University Press. https://doi.org/10.1017/CCOL052177005X.007

Algra, K. 2007. *Conceptions and Images: Hellenistic Philosophical Theology and Traditional Religion*. Amsterdam: KNAW.

Alston, L. 1906. *Stoic and Christian in the Second Century: A Comparison of the Ethical Teaching of Marcus Aurelius with that of the Contemporary and Antecedent Christianity*. London: Longmans.

Anon. (ed.). 2014. *Stoic Six Pack: Meditations of Marcus Aurelius and More*. n.p.: Enhanced Media.

Anon. (ed.). 2017. *Stoic Six 2: By Musonius Rufus et al.* n.p.: Enhanced Media.

Asmis, E. 2007. "Myth and Philosophy in Cleanthes' *Hymn to Zeus*." *Greek, Roman, and Byzantine Studies* 47: 413–429.

Babut, D. 1974. *La religion des philosophes grecs: De Thales aux Stoïciens*. Paris: Presses Universitaires de France.

Baltussen, H. (ed.). 2013. *Greek and Roman Consolations: Eight Studies of a Tradition and Its Afterlife*. Swansea: Classical Press of Wales. https://doi.org/10.2307/j.ctvvnbhx

Becker, L.C. 1998. *A New Stoicism*. Princeton, NJ: Princeton University Press.

Bevir, M. 1999. *The Logic of the History of Ideas*. New York: Cambridge University Press.

Bonhöffer, A.F. 1894. *Die Ethik des Stoikers Epictet*. Stuttgart: Enke.

Brouwer, R. 2014. *The Stoic Sage: The Early Stoics on Wisdom, Sagehood and Socrates*. Cambridge: Cambridge University Press. https://doi.org/10.1017/CBO9781139162487

Chitakure, J. 2016. *The Pursuit of the Sacred: An Introduction to Religious Studies*. Eugene, OR: Wipf & Stock.

Collingwood, R.G. 1978. *An Autobiography*. Oxford: Oxford University Press.

Cottingham, J. 2005. "Why Should Analytic Philosophers Do History of Philosophy?" In *Analytic Philosophy and History of Philosophy*, edited by T. Sorell, and G.A.J. Rogers, pp. 25–41. Oxford: Oxford University Press.

Diem-Lane, A. 2014. *How to Study the Sacred: An Introduction to Religious Studies*. Walnut, CA: MSAC Philosophy Group.

Farrar, F.W. 1868. *Seekers after God*. London: Macmillan.

Freiberger, O. 2019. *Considering Comparison: A Method for Religious Studies*. Oxford: Oxford University Press. https://doi.org/10.1093/oso/9780199965007.001.0001

Gale, J. 2017. *Stoicism: Introduction to the Stoic Way of Life: Beginners Guide to Mastery*. Wroclaw: Amazon Fulfillment.

Gale, J. 2018. *Stoicism: Full Life mastery: Mastering the Stoic Way of Living and Emotions*. Leipzig: Amazon Distribution.

Hadot, I. 1969. *Seneca und die griechisch-römische Tradition der Seelenleitung*. Berlin: De Gruyter. https://doi.org/10.1515/9783110840933

Hadot, P. 1992. *La citadelle intérieure: Introduction aux "Pensées" de Marc Aurèle*. Paris: Fayard.

Hadot, P. 1995. *Qu'est-ce que la philosophie antique?* Paris: Gallimard.

Haines, C.R. (ed., trans.) 1930. *Marcus Aurelius*. Cambridge, MA: Harvard University Press.

Hall, D.D. (ed.). 1997. *Lived Religion in America: Toward a Theory of Practice*. Princeton, NJ: Princeton University Press.

Helmer, C. 2012. "Theology and the Study of Religion: A Relationship." In *The Cambridge Companion to Religious Studies*, edited by R.A. Orsi, pp. 230–254. Cambridge: Cambridge University Press. https://doi.org/10.1017/CCOL9780521883917.013

Holiday, R. and S. Hanselman. 2016. *The Daily Stoic: 366 Meditations on Wisdom, Perseverance, and the Art of Living*. London: Profile.

Höttecke, D. 2000. "How and What Can We Learn from Replicating Historical Experiments? A Case Study." *Science and Education* 9: 343–362. https://doi.org/10.1023/A:1008621908029

Jedan, C. 2009. *Stoic Virtues: Chrysippus and the Religious Character of Stoic Ethics*. New York: Continuum.

Jedan, C. 2010. Göttliches und menschliches Handeln in der frühen Stoa." In *Wille und Handlung in der Philosophie der Kaiserzeit und Spätantike*, edited by J. Müller and Hofmeister R. Pich, pp. 25-44. New York: De Gruyter.

Jedan, C. 2014. "Troost door argumenten: Herwaardering van een filosofische en christelijke traditie." *Nederlands Theologisch Tijdschrift* 68: 7-22. https://doi.org/10.5117/NTT2014.68.007.JEDA

Jedan, C. 2017. "The Rapprochement of Religion and Philosophy in Ancient Consolation: Seneca, Paul, and Beyond." In *Religio-Philosophical Discourses in the Mediterranean World: From Plato, through Jesus, to Late Antiquity*, edited by G.H. Van Kooten and A. Klostergaard Petersen, pp. 159-184. Leiden: Brill. https://doi.org/10.1163/9789004323131_009

Johann, H.-T. 1968. *Trauer und Trost: Eine quellen- und strukturanalytische Untersuchung der philosophischen Trostschriften über den Tod*. Munich: Fink.

Kassel, R. 1958. *Untersuchungen zur griechischen und römischen Konsolationsliteratur*. Munich: Beck.

Kirfel, E.A. 1997. *Tusculanae disputationes - Gespräche in Tusculum*. Trans. and ed. by E.A. Kirfel. Stuttgart: Reclam.

Lewis, T.A. 2012. "On the Role of Normativity in Religious Studies." In *The Cambridge Companion to Religious Studies*, edited by R.A. Orsi, pp. 168-185. Cambridge: Cambridge University Press. https://doi.org/10.1017/CCOL9780521883917.010

Lewis, T.A. 2015. *Why Philosophy Matters for the Study of Religion - and vice versa*. Oxford: Oxford University Press. https://doi.org/10.1093/acprof:oso/9780198744740.001.0001

MacIntyre, A. 1981. *After Virtue: A Study in Moral Theory*. Notre Dame, IN: University of Notre Dame Press.

MacIntyre, A. 1991. *Three Rival Versions of Moral Enquiry: Encyclopaedia, Genealogy, and Tradition*. Notre Dame, IN: University of Notre Dame Press.

Mansfeld, J. 1999. "Theology." In *The Cambridge History of Hellenistic Philosophy*, edited by K. Algra et al., pp. 452-478. Cambridge: Cambridge University Press. https://doi.org/10.1017/CHOL9780521250283.014

McDowell, M. 2017. *Prayer in the Ancient Stoic Tradition: A Preliminary Study with Comparisons to Prayer in the New Testament*. London: Sulis.

McGuire, M.B. 2008. *Lived Religion: Faith and Practice in Everyday Life*. Oxford: Oxford University Press.

Meijer, P.A. 2007. *Stoic Theology: Proofs for the Existence of the Cosmic God and of the Traditional Gods*. Delft: Eburon.

Pià Comella, J. 2014. *Une piété de la raison: Philosophie et religion dans le stoïcisme imperial.* Turnhout: Brepols. https://doi.org/10.1484/M.PHR-EB.5.112497

Pià Comella, J. 2016. Prière et "appropriation" des dogmes dans le stoïcisme impérial romain." *Revue de Philologie, de litterature et d'histoire anciennes* 90: 139–164. https://doi.org/10.3917/phil.901.0139

Pigliucci, M. 2017. *How to Be a Stoic: Ancient Wisdom for Modern Living.* London: Rider.

Quinn, P.L. 1991. "Epistemic Parity and Religious Argument." *Philosophical Perspectives* 5: 317–341. https://doi.org/10.2307/2214099

Robertson, D.J. 2016. "The Stoic Influence on Modern Psychotherapy." *The Routledge Handbook of the Stoic Tradition*, edited by J. Sellars. New York: Routledge.

Rorty, R., J.B. Schneewind and Q. Skinner (eds). 1984. *Philosophy in History: Essays in the Historiography of Philosophy.* Cambridge: Cambridge University Press. https://doi.org/10.1017/CBO9780511625534

Satlow, M.L. 2012. "Tradition: The Power of Constraint." In *The Cambridge Companion to Religious Studies*, edited by R.A. Orsi, 130–150. New York: Cambridge University Press.
https://doi.org/10.1017/CCOL9780521883917.008

Sedley, D.N. 1989. "Philosophical Allegiance in the Greco-Roman World." In *Philosophia Togata: Essays on Philosophy and Roman Society*, edited by M.T. Griffin and J. Barnes, pp. 97–119. Oxford: Oxford University Press.

Sedley, D.N. 1999. "Hellenistic Physics and Metaphysics." In *The Cambridge Companion to Hellenistic Philosophy*, edited by K. Algra et al., pp. 355–411. Cambridge: Cambridge University Press.
https://doi.org/10.1017/CHOL9780521250283.012

Sedley, D.N. 2007. *Creationism and Its Critics in Antiquity.* Berkeley, CA: University of California Press. https://doi.org/10.1525/9780520934368

Sellars, J. 2006. *Stoicism.* Berkeley, CA: University of California Press.

Sellars, J. 2009. *The Art of Living: The Stoics on the Nature and Function of Philosophy*, 2nd edition. London: Bristol Classical Press.

Sellars, J. (ed.). 2016. *The Routledge Handbook of the Stoic Tradition.* New York: Routledge. https://doi.org/10.4324/9781315771588

Sharma, A. 2005. *Religious Studies and Comparative Methodology: The Case for Reciprocal Illumination.* Albany, NY: State University of New York Press.

Shils, E. 1981. *Tradition.* Chicago, IL: University of Chicago Press.

Skinner, Q. 1969. "Meaning and Understanding in the History of Ideas." *History and Theory* 8: 3–53. https://doi.org/10.2307/2504188

Smart, N. 1968. *Secular Education and the Logic of Religion*. London: Faber and Faber.

Smart, N. 1969. *The Religious Experience of Mankind*. New York: Scribner.

Smart, N. 1989. *The World's Religions: Old Traditions and Modern Transformations*. Cambridge: Cambridge University Press.

Smart, N. 1996. *Dimensions of the Sacred: An Anatomy of the World's Beliefs*. London: HarperCollins.

Stausberg, M. 2011. "Comparison." In *The Routledge Handbook of Research Methods in the Study of Religion*, edited by M. Stausberg and S. Engler, pp. 21–39. New York: Routledge.

Stout, J. 2004. *Democracy and Tradition*. Princeton, NJ: Princeton University Press.

Strange, S.K. and J. Zupko. 2004. *Stoicism: Traditions and Transformations*. Cambridge: Cambridge University Press. https://doi.org/10.1017/CBO9780511498374

Thom, J.C. 2005. *Cleanthes' Hymn to Zeus: Text, Translation, and Commentary*. Tübingen: Mohr Siebeck.

van der Leeuw, G. 1956. *Phänomenologie der Religion*, 2nd, revised and expanded edition. Tübingen: Mohr Siebeck.

Vogt, K.M. 2008. *Law, Reason, and the Cosmic City: Political Philosophy in the Early Stoa*. New York: Oxford University Press.

– 4 –

Normative Pictures

The History of Christianity from a Theological Perspective

HENK VAN DEN BELT

The fact that theology relates religion to God makes its position problematic in an academic context where the study of religions is determined by an empirical approach to reality. Can theology meet the requirements of "methodological atheism" or "methodological agnosticism" without committing suicide? The answer to this question not only depends on the definition of theology, but also on the way in which neutrality in studying religion is understood. Defining neutrality in a positivistic way clearly excludes theology from academic discourse. An awareness of any researcher's "positionality", however, puts the theologian more on a par with the anthropologist, sociologist and historian of religion.

This chapter first investigates why theology's relationship with religious studies is complicated and tense. Then the question regarding theology's proper limitations and object is answered from one of the classic theological traditions: scholasticism. Next, it reflects on the issue of whether a theological perspective makes any difference for historical research. This will be illustrated from the analysis of some woodcuts from the period of the Reformation. The section finally explains what a theological perspective can add to the general understanding of the history of Christianity and how this perspective relates to a comprehensive worldview.

Keywords: theological method, revelation, scholasticism, Aristotelian causes, historical theology

From the perspective of religious studies, the limitations of theology seem to be obvious. Theology presupposes the existence of God or the divine and refers to revelation as a source of knowledge. It does not take a contextualized notion of religion for granted but contests that notion, departing from an essentialist definition of religion. Its main limitation, therefore, is the belief of the scholar in revelation that excludes communication of the scholarly results with non-believers, even when the positionality of every researcher is taken into account. Even in the field of anthropology, however, some assert that the membrane between belief and disbelief is rather thin. Therefore, this section seeks to explain how the scholarly results and conclusions of theology can be communicable within an academic context and how theological reflection can take place in the arena of the public academy.

Theology and Religious Studies

Historically speaking, theology is a core business of the university. Until the eighteenth century, basically all the universities in Western Europe had theological faculties and theology was seen by many as the queen of the sciences. In the context of modernity, theology, however, has become a stepdaughter of the university. Of course, that has everything to do with the claim that theology is about God and with the conviction that it is impossible to say anything academically about the divine, because God does not belong to empirical reality. Faith in God is fine, it is religion, and it can be studied, but God himself – if he exists – is beyond the reach of the human intellect, therefore theology as "discourse about God" is improper at the academy.

If a theological faculty is maintained at a public university, this is mostly out of respect for the historical tradition. More often theology is studied in the context of seminaries or divinity schools, sometimes closely related to a broader public university, but mostly separated from them institutionally. The study of theology takes a distinct approach – either called "confessional" or labelled as an "inside-perspective" – that is not appropriate at the public university. Theology is taught in a close affiliation with churches serving the education of their professionals.

In practice, theology at a public university is restricted to the study of the empirical reality of a given religion – Christianity in the Western context – and the study of this religion is subject to the common academic methodological principles of the humanities. As a result, there is hardly any difference in academic practice between theology and religious studies, albeit that religious studies often – though not necessarily

– compares diverse religions, whereas theology studies one religious tradition. The discipline of religious studies – historically a daughter of theology – has emancipated itself from and even swallowed its mother.

The Problem of Revelation

One of the first professors of the Groningen faculty of theology, the Reformed theologian Franciscus Gomarus (1563–1641), defined theology as *sermo de Deo*, discourse about God: "Theology, derived from the word *theologos*, according to its origin and use in Greek, does not properly mean "discourse of God," but "discourse about God"" (Gomarus 1644: 3:1). An etymological definition of theology is still popular today, as Kelly M. Kapic's excellent short introduction to the study of theology *A Little Book for New Theologians* illustrates: "The term "theology" means a word (*logos*) about God (*theos*), so when anyone speaks about God ... he or she is engaged in theology" (Kapic 2012: 15).

In the seventeenth century, theology was generally defined as discourse about God, although Gomarus's definition reveals some hesitance: Is God himself speaking in theology or are we speaking about God? Although he did not choose the discourse *of* God – "revelation" in theological terms – as a proper definition of theology, still revelation was the presupposition of all human discourse about God. After four centuries this has not changed: theology presupposes the existence of the divine and the possibility to say something about the divine that makes sense and therefore is founded upon something that has been "revealed". So today many theologians will still agree with Gomarus's definition of theology as God-talk (*sermo de Deo*).

What has changed fundamentally, however, is the modern idea of science, as principally pertaining to empirical reality. Therefore the most fundamental problem for theology as an academic discipline is the notion of revelation. Claims about God or about what God reveals can neither be empirically verified nor falsified, which in the modern context is an essential condition for any scholarly or scientific claim.

Any theological claim seems to rest necessarily on "esoteric" knowledge that may be fine for the church or the seminary, but is not allowed as a source for knowledge in a (public) university, because it is inaccessible for those who reject the general possibility – or a specific claim – of revelation.

A solution for this problem might be the restriction of theology to the study of that what is said about God by human beings. In that case it concerns neither a discourse of God, divine revelation, nor a discourse about God, reflection on divine revelation. Rather, theology then pertains to an analysis of what is, properly or improperly, said about God. In such an approach, the object of theology is not God, but "God" between quotation marks. The academic theologian refrains from normative statements, but critically relates himself to what other people believe or claim to believe about God. Theology, then, is rather the analysis of God-talk than God-talk itself.

This "solution", however, leads to two problems. First of all, how can a theologian in this case decide whether the analysed discourse of others about God is proper? This seems to be impossible without actually making at least implicit normative statements about the divine. Secondly, if the theologian deliberately decides to refrain from normative statements his analysis does not differ from psychological, sociological, or anthropological perspectives. The Gordian knot of theology is that it either, by definition, exceeds the limits of empirical reality or it does not differ from religious studies.

Pilgrim Theology

In the premodern context, scholastic theologians already had nuanced ideas about revelation and our knowledge based on it. We will not dig into the historical details and complexities of the philosophy that dominated academic theology from its beginning at the first universities of the twelfth century until the rise of the early Enlightenment in the seventeenth century, and which can be labelled as "Christian Aristotelianism" (Muller 1998). This system of thought offered the basic technical tools and the fundamental structure for scholastic theology, covering a range of positions from medieval academic theology to the variety of Lutheran, Reformed and Roman Catholic theologies after the Reformation.

Two elements in the self-understanding of scholastic theology are useful for the understanding of academic theology today. The first one regards the limitations of theology. Scholastic theology was careful to make a distinction between divine truth and human knowledge of that truth and held a nuanced view of what can and what cannot be said concerning God.

In protestant scholasticism, the distinction between divine truth and our knowledge of it was expressed by differentiating between archetypal theology – the knowledge that God has of himself – and ectypal theology – the knowledge that creatures can have of God. In a very instructive application of this scholastic distinction, John Webster summarizes: "Archetypal theology is God's self-knowledge; ectypal theology is the knowledge of God possible for finite rational creatures. The former is God's simple, eternal intelligence of himself, the latter can be described in its temporal unfolding" (Webster 2009: 62).

This temporal creaturely knowledge of the divine was again subdivided into several sorts, for instance the knowledge of angels or of saints in heaven. The weakest sort of knowledge was called *theologia viatorum* or pilgrim theology, the knowledge about God that sinful human beings can derive from God's revelation (Van Asselt 2002). This knowledge is imperfect because human beings are mere creatures and because their intellect is fallible, still it is trustworthy as far as it is in agreement with revelation.

The nuanced scholastic distinction is rooted in an awareness of God's transcendence. He could be known because he had revealed himself, but he was also greater than his revelation, because he was hidden in and behind it. Although theology was defined as a discourse about God, based on a discourse of God, it was nevertheless always viewed as tentative and provisional. This implies a principal caution in scholastic theology grounded in the distinction between Creator and creature; the gap between both could only be bridged as far as it pleased the Creator to reveal himself and even then human knowledge was partial and provisional per se. To be honest, the fierce debates between theologians about the theological truths – based on the revealed knowledge – often contradict this principal caution.

Theology today can learn from scholasticism to be modest in its claims about God, not in the first place because of modern scepticism about revelation and postmodern relativism, but for intrinsic theological reasons. Theological modesty – any discourse about God is provisional and partial – is rooted in the first article of the Christian creed, in the faith in God who as Creator differs essentially from his creatures. Theologians today are often very modest in their claims and therefore discussion about the academic status of theology is not helped by the caricature that theologians can claim anything about the divine with an appeal to the esoteric category of revelation.

God as First Cause and Final Destination

Next to the scholastic reflections on theology, the scholastic view of the diverse aspects of reality, based on the Aristotelian concept of the four causes, is still helpful to define the relation and distinction between theology and religious studies. In his *Physics* II, 3 and *Metaphysics* V, 2, Aristotle distinguishes between four causes: the material cause, the matter out of which something exists, the formal cause, the form in which it exists, the efficient cause, the reason why it has come into being, and the final cause, the goal or end for the sake of which it exists.

All things (1) are affected by something else, (2) exist of material, (3) have a form, and (4) exist for a purpose. Take, for example, a boy who is building a tower. The boy is (1) the efficient cause, but he cannot build without blocks, (2) the material cause. To build a tower, however, he must have some perhaps unconscious idea in his mind of what a tower is, (3) the formal cause. In the case of this example the ultimate joy of throwing everything down is perhaps (4) the final cause of the existence of the tower.

Scholastic theologians used the Aristotelian causes to organize their theological texts, presuming that everything that exists has these four causes or four different aspects. They mostly structured a discussion of a particular theological topic starting with (1) the efficient cause, next they discussed (2) the matter and (3) form, and lastly, the (4) final cause.

In distinction from ancient philosophy, Christian theology did not understand the four causes as ontological categories that determined the nature of reality. According to ancient philosophy form and matter constituted the individual existence of the things. According to the theologians, however, form and matter were only aspects of reality that was constituted or created by God.

In scholasticism, God was seen as the ultimate efficient cause of all that existed. He stood somewhere behind the visible and intelligible world of matter and form – that was not eternal or self-constitutive – and constituted and sustained all things. This did not imply an immediate causal relationship between God and everything that existed, for the term *causa* in scholasticism referred to an aspect of reality rather than to a cause with an immediate effect. Scholastic theology introduced the concept of instrumental or secondary causes – you could number them as (1b) in the scheme – to explain how God's rule over all related to human responsibility. That God, for instance was the efficient cause of every newborn baby, did not exclude human secondary or instrumental causes. This distinction was important to understand the existence of evil in combination with the belief in God's omnipotence and perfect goodness. God was not held responsible for evil. Evil was not seen an independent substance, it was literally a no-thing; it was a parasite of the good creation and existed only as the holes in a cheese exist.

Nevertheless, God was seen as somewhere behind the scenes of all created things and therefore he was the first cause, because nothing could come into being or remain in existence, except for God's creation and sustenance.

At the same time God was seen as the final cause or goal of all things that exist. The glory of God is the world's final end, though things may, of course, also have other sub ultimate goals. These are sometimes called proximate final causes – which you could number (4a) in the scheme – as opposed to the ultimate final cause – number (4b) – which is God. Prayer, for instance, might serve to comfort believers and this comfort is one of the final causes of prayer, but the ultimate final cause is God, because prayer ultimately aims at communication with God. In sum, according to scholastic theology, we can discern six causes or aspects:

1a the efficient cause (*causa efficiens*);
1b the secondary or instrumental cause (*causa instrumentalis*);
2   the matter or material cause (*causa materialis*);
3   the form or formal cause (*causa formalis*);
4a the sub-ultimate final cause (*causa finalis proxima*); and
4b the ultimate final cause (*causa finalis ultima*).

The Objects of Theology and Religious Studies

This scholastic understanding of the divine as the first cause and final destination of all that exists can still be helpful today to explain the difference between theology and religious studies, especially with regards to their objects. Theology relates to the ultimate questions of where things come from and what they are meant for. Although these questions do not belong to the field of empirical research, this does not imply that they are irrelevant or should be excluded from academic reflection. Philosophy – as far as it is more than the study of the history of thought – shares this interest in ultimate questions with theology.

The object of theological reflection transcends the object of religious studies, since it not only analyses phenomena and intends to explain them intrinsically, but also faces the question of why religion exists after all and what its ultimate goal might be. Of course, it is also possible to answer these questions on the intrinsic level of the instrumental, formal and material causes of the rituals and creeds, or even to explain religion as such as a functional aspect of the evolutionary development of humankind. Theology, however, does not exclude the possibility of the reality of God and of divine revelation in advance, but intends to understand religious phenomena also from the perspective of their first cause and final destination.

Yet, theological reflection also has much in common with the other humanities and especially with religious studies. In scholastic terms, theology and religious studies have the (1b) instrumental, (2) material, (3) formal, and (4a) proximate final causes or aspects of religion as their common research object. For (1b) the instrumental aspects, one might think of important historical events or of the transmission of religious beliefs and practices in a certain tradition. The (2) material aspects of religion, of course, are not restricted to material artefacts as such, but also include texts and the thoughts expressed by them. The (3) formal aspects of religion comprise rituals and any other forms of religious expression. A (4a) proximate final goal of a religious practice might be comfort or social cohesion.

Prayer, for instance is (1) part of a tradition, (2) has a certain content, (3) includes a form of words and gestures, and (4) is practised for certain purposes. Theology and religious studies both deal with the same questions. Where does prayer come from, what is it, how do you practice it and what does it do? Theology, however, also relates prayer to God as its source and ultimate goal. Theology and religious studies assess these four groups of aspects of religion with similar empirical and historical methods. Only theology, however, reflects on the (1a) efficient and (4b) ultimate final causes or aspects of religion with a specific theological method. In order to do so it presupposes the existence of God and the possibility of revelation. These presuppositions, of course, may also influence the answers given to questions related to the four aspects that theology has in common with religious studies, but that is due to the positionality of the researcher.

Respecting Religious Claims

The exclusion of these aspects from academic reflection merely because of the impossibility to study them empirically leads to an understanding that fundamentally differs from the self-understanding of the religions, a self-understanding with which theology seeks to be positively – though not uncritically – engaged. Theology presupposes a certain acceptance of the religious claims about the existence of God – as first cause and final destination of religion – and about the possibility of revelation. The extra theological dimension or the specific theological perspective does not discern things that are totally different from those researched from the perspective of religious studies, but it intends to understand that same reality – consisting of instrumental causes, matter, forms and proximate goals – in a different way.

According to the scholastic understanding of theology as "pilgrim theology", theologians should always be cautious with respect to bold truth-claims about the divine. If these claims are made, they refer to aspects of reality that are principally behind the scenes of the visible and tangible world. Religious claims intend to answer ultimate questions about the origin and purpose of what exists. It is essential for religion to offer answers to such ultimate questions.

These questions by nature go beyond what is commonly understood as the proper object of scientific or academic study. It is not necessary or even desirable, however, to exclude a discussion of these questions – including a possible clash of answers – completely and dogmatically from the academic debate. Otherwise, non-religious ways of dealing with these questions in philosophy and ethics would also have to be excluded. Ultimately, such an exclusion would lead to a taboo on any normative statements in academia, because these statements always presuppose a certain religious or secular worldview or perspective. Theology is a modest and careful way of dealing with religion, including its self-definition and self-understanding as a relevant reference to God or the divine.

On the other hand, it is important to note that theology has much in common with the other humanities and especially with religious studies, not only with respect to the common object of research, but also methodologically. Practical theology, for instance, reflects on the practices of the church and uses the same tools for the empirical study of these practices as anthropologists or sociologists. Biblical studies use the same techniques for reconstructing the text from the manuscripts and interpreting the possible intentions of the human authors as any other study of ancient texts would do, even when the scholar, as a theologian, is convinced that the text contains divine revelation.

Only that part of theology which is mostly called "systematic theology" or the sub discipline of "dogmatics", has a specific object in God and in revelation that exceeds the limits of what other academic disciplines – including religious studies – are able to study. Systematic theology reflects immediately on the divine and on revelation, by facing questions regarding the existence and character of God and regarding the truth of revelation, for instance with respect to the resurrection of Christ. Therefore systematic theology is the most difficult discipline to maintain in the present academic context.

Not all theology consists of dogmatics, however, and if systematic theology maintains its caution as pilgrim theology, its reflection on the first cause and final goal of religion should not be excluded from academic discourse. In the meantime, the other theological subdisciplines that focus on the history, the sources, and practices of a religion are also theological insofar as they intend to relate these objects of research to their first cause and final goal. In sum, religious studies and theology have partially common research objects. But they look at these objects from different perspectives, religious studies do not and theology does reflect on the possible relationship of the research object with the divine. The similarity and the difference in methods will now be illustrated for historical theological research from the period of the Reformation.

Woodcuts as an Example

A theological perspective on the history of the church and of theology approaches the sources by primarily using historical methods, focusing on the instrumental, material, formal and proximate final aspects of the history of religion. All historians strive or should strive for objectivity or at least transparency in their research, although "objectivity in historical study does not, and cannot, exist if it is defined as an absence of involvement with or opinion about the materials" (Bradley and Muller 2016: 47–48). Therefore it is important for any historian, and especially – though not exclusively – for historians who take a theological perspective, to be aware of and open about their own position regarding the sources.

Theologians should express their intention to relate the historical material to the theological questions and distinguish carefully between the historical results of their research and the theological reflections on them. A specific example from my historical research serves to illustrate what a theological perspective on the history of religion has in common with other perspectives and in which respects it differs from them.

An interesting aspect of the material heritage of the Reformation consists of the woodcut illustrations in early catechisms. Martin Luther included woodcuts in his *Deudsch Catechismus* to illustrate the main topics of the creed, the Lord's Prayer, and the Ten Commandments (Luther 1529). These woodcuts became very influential in the Lutheran catechetical tradition. The specific illustrations and texts and the authorial intentions – as far as they can be reconstructed – do not necessarily beg for a theological perspective. In scholastic terms, the matter and form are common ground for anyone who would want to research them.

Some years ago I published an article on these woodcuts (Van den Belt 2017). My historical research question regarded the authorial intention of the woodcuts in their relation to the text of the catechism. This is, of course, not necessarily a theological question. My analysis intended to be transparent, communicable, and verifiable for anyone else.

From the perspective of art, the woodcuts are not very impressive. The illustration of the third commandment – remember the Sabbath day – pictures a preacher, probably Martin Luther, on the pulpit with the congregation listening to him. The scene, however, seems to be an open-air preaching, because the background shows someone who is collecting wood. The reference is to a story related in the Bible (Numbers 15, 32-36), where someone is punished for collecting wood on the Sabbath.

In her study of the Ten Commandments in paintings and other illustrations in the late medieval and early modern periods, Veronika Thum shows that the picture was originally a woodcut of a preacher and a congregation, with the crucifix in the middle and the preacher pointing to it. For the illustration of the third commandment the crucifix was simply cut out of the woodblock and replaced by the scene of the wood collector; the remains of the loincloth are still visible (Thum 2006: 84).

In Luther's *Enchiridion* or *Kleine Catechismus* the illustrations are only accompanied by the text of the commandment and one short question and answer, for instance: "The first commandment. You shall have no other gods. What does that mean? Answer: We must fear, love and trust God above everything."[1] The answers that explain the other commandments all start with the phrase that we must fear and love God. The ninth commandment, for instance, means that "We must fear and love God, lest we craftily seek to get our neighbour's inheritance or house, and obtain it by a show of justice, etc., but help and serve him to keep it."[2]

Melanchthon

To answer the question about authorial intention it is important to know that the woodcuts were made by the Wittenberg artist Lucas Cranach and that they were not intended for the catechisms, but for large placards or posters (Luther WA 30/1:561, cf. Thum 2006: 80). Most probably all of the woodcuts for the Ten Commandments were printed on one broadsheet together with the text of the commandments. The illustrations were chosen by Phillip Melanchthon who wanted to use them for his own catechism. Ultimately only a fragment of that catechism was printed,

---

1. "Das Erste gebot. Du solt nicht ander Götter haben. Was ist das? Antwort. Wir sollen Gott vber alle ding fürchten / lieben / vnd vertrawen" (Luther, WA 30/1:354). The translation is mine.
2. "Wir sollen Gott fürchten vnd lieben / Daß wir vnserm Nehesten nicht mit liste nach seinem Erbe oder Hause stehen / vnd mit einem schein des Rechtens an vns bringen / etc. Sondern jhm dasselbige zu behalten / fürderlich vnd dienstlich seyn" (Luther, WA 30/1:361). The translation is mine.

because Melanchthon decided not to compete with Luther's catechisms. The illustrations developed over the years, with various printers and artists, but remarkably enough, the chosen stories from the bible always are the same, though there is no reference to these stories in the catechism texts.

In sum, Melanchthon asked Cranach to make woodcuts for his catechism; they were first printed as posters to illustrate the texts of the Law, the Creed and the Lord's Prayer; later they found their way to Luther's *Deudsch Catechismus*, and, finally, the pictures of the biblical stories became standard illustrations in the Lutheran catechetical tradition. This narrows the research question after the intention for the woodcuts down to the question why Melanchthon chose these bible stories to illustrate the commandments. The accompanying texts of his only fragmentarily published catechism show that the original intention of the pictures was to warn and admonish potential sinners to obey the commandments in the belief that God is the hidden witness and judge of all human actions.

The text accompanying the woodcut on the third commandment, for instance, says: "Sanctify the Holy Day. That means that you should sanctify the Holy Day by learning and hearing God's word. Such disobedience is found to be punished in Numbers 15 to the person who gathered wood on the Sabbath."[3] Thus far, the analysis shares common ground with a general historical approach. So what makes the difference if the same material is assessed from a theological perspective and how can the intentions of Melanchthon be evaluated theologically?

Law and Gospel

Some specific aspects of the woodcuts seem to be important for a correct theological understanding. In the first place, Melanchthon chooses stories from the Bible to illustrate the commandments. Medieval illustrations of the Ten Commandments in churches mostly do not refer to the Bible and even Martin Luther's explanations of the Ten Commandments that were printed prior to his catechisms use illustrations from everyday life rather than the Bible. The sixth commandment, for instance, was illustrated by a man and women in bed and the seventh by a pickpocket (Luther 1520). Melanchthon's shift to Scripture is remarkable.

---

3. "Du solt den feiertag heiligen. Das heist heiligen den feiertag, das man Gottes wort leret und höret. Solchen ungehorsam aber findet man gestrafft *Numeri* am. xv. an dem, der holtz las am Sabbath" (Melanchthon 1915: 74).

It is also important to note that the illustrations are exclusively chosen from the Old Testament. This can hardly be coincidental, considering that the illustrations of the petitions in the Lord's Prayer are exclusively from the New Testament. All the Old Testament stories to which the illustrations for the Ten Commandments refer, emphasize that transgression of the commandment is punished. The only positive example is Joseph who refuses to have sex with Potiphar's wife and whose obedience to the tenth commandment is tested and ultimately blessed.

Theologically the choice for the Old Testament corresponds with the Lutheran emphasis on the pedagogical function of the law. The law confronts us with sin and its consequences in order to lead us to Christ. To quote Luther's *Short Form of the Ten Commandments, the Creed, and the Lord's Prayer* (1520), an early predecessor of the catechisms: "The commandments teach man to recognize his sickness, enabling him to perceive what he must do or refrain from doing, consent to or refuse, and so he will recognize himself to be a sinful and wicked person."[4] The goal of the law is to teach people that they are ill. Next, the Gospel, summarized in the Apostle's Creed, teaches where to find the medicine of grace, namely in Christ.

Thirdly, to understand their theological meaning, it is important to realize that the woodcuts originally were intended to speak for themselves in the education of children and other illiterate people by referring to the biblical stories as illustrations of the commandments. The woodcuts, just like the images in Lutheran churches, functioned as books for the laity.

Finally, the catechisms and the illustrations originated within the context of the visitations in Saxony between 1528 and about 1531, initiated because of concern for the chaotic conditions in the Lutheran parishes. In 1527 Melanchthon drafted the *Instructions for the Visitors of Parish Pastors*. He stresses that the law must be preached in order that the hearers repent from their sins and fear God. "Therefore they shall often and diligently preach, explain and apply the Ten Commandments, and not only the commandments, but also how God will punish those who do not keep them, as God has often inflicted such temporal punishment. For such examples are written in order to be presented to the people."[5]

---

4. Also lehren die Gebote den Menschen seine Krankheit erkennen, daß er stehet und empfindet, was er thun und nicht thun, lassen und nicht lassen kann; und erkennet sich einen Sünder und bösen Menschen (Luther, *WA* 7, 204); the English translation is from Lyle Bierma (2013: 22).
5. "Darumb sollen sie die zehen gebot offt und vleyssig predigen, und die auslegen und anzeigen, nicht allein die gebot, sondern auch wie Gott straffen wird die, so sie nicht halten, wie auch Got solche offt Zeitlich gestrafft hat. Denn solche exempel

In sum, I concluded from my research that the illustrations were meant to correct the ignorance among the common people in the villages and to amend wrong inferences from the message of the Reformation. In this case Luther and Melanchthon were especially concerned about the opinion drawn from the gospel of grace that Christians can ignore the commandments. The woodcuts underline that God as the witness and judge of human actions punishes sin and blesses obedience. This emphasis, in turn, intends to evoke an interest in the gospel of the grace of Christ.

Theological Reflection on a Material Level

All these conclusions can still be shared by theology and religious and historical studies in general. Obviously, good historical research by a theologian concerning the church or the doctrines of the church meets the requirements of the historical methodologies. To define the specific theological contribution to this kind of research, one can distinguish between three levels.

First of all, theological expertise is essential to understand the message of Melanchthon's pictures. Theology focuses on the doctrines and practices of one specific religion – in this case Christianity and specifically Lutheran Protestantism. Whereas the comparative study of religion might study practices and doctrines as religious rites and theories, theology tries to understand and interpret these practices and doctrines from within the framework of a specific religion.

On this material level, theology can be defined as an approach in which the final object of reflection is human thought about and claims regarding God, either the God of Judaism, Christianity or Islam. On this level, however, the difference with religious studies only regards the focus of theology on one religion. It is possible to be an expert in the history of Protestantism without being a theologian. On the other hand, no one will deny that theological expertise – in the sense of knowledge about the thought about God – is important for the right understanding of religious phenomena. In any case, it is important to remember that theology does not necessarily entail systematic theology or a normative discourse about God. In the terms of scholasticism, theology can deliberately stick to the material and formal causes or aspects of religion and join the debate with religious studies, without adding anything specifically theological. On the material level, theology applies the same

---

sind geschriben, das man sie den leuten für halte" (Melanchthon, CR 26, 52). The translation is mine.

methodologies as the humanities, for instance, historical methodology. On this level there is no principal difference between theology and history or religious studies, though there might be a specific theological expertise in the way in which the material is dealt with.

Theological Reflection on a Methodological Level

On a second level, which I call methodological, there is more tension between a theological and a mere historical approach. Here, theology turns to a normative evaluation of the religious phenomena that transcends the field of religious studies or history. For that reason, theology is sometimes defined as an "inside perspective", a perspective from a specific and often normative or confessional point of view, in which the shared confessional tradition is presupposed as the basis for an engaged discussion.

This "inside perspective" should not be understood as prejudiced or biased by definition, in contradistinction with a so-called "outside perspective". Post-modern understandings of the philosophy of science acknowledge that all researchers have their inside perspectives, because no one is objective. All scholars should be aware of and transparent about their presuppositions rather than deny that they have them. Everyone has an inside perspective and a public university is an arena for the debate about these perspectives and not a place where certain perspectives are excluded in advance.

In the example of the woodcuts, on the methodological level, the research question is not which message Melanchthon intended to communicate, but rather how this message relates to his confessional presuppositions. This question is not asked in a general way – then it could be a historical question – but theologically by a researcher who shares these presuppositions. Of course, a theologian can also reject these specific presuppositions from his own understanding of God and revelation. In that case he will bring his own view into a critical discussion with the results of the research on the first and material level.

This second level is "methodological" because it implies the use of a specific theological method, namely that of the critical theological discussion on the normative basis of a shared or contested confessional identity. Religious studies can analyse a religious practice by comparing it to practices in other religions. A theological interpretation, however, understands and assesses the practice from a confessional perspective. Normative theological statements can only be made on the basis of belief in God and divine revelation. This approach does not necessarily imply a defence of the shared theological position, for one can also be critical of the particular approach. According to Melanchthon, for instance, obedience is blessed and disobedience punished, but this emphasis can be manipulative and lead to fear for God instead of obedience out of love.

A question like "What do you think about Melanchthon's interpretation and why do you think so?" should not be excluded from the academic discourse, because of its normativity. Historical theology answers these kinds of questions from shared confessional presuppositions. Of course, there are other possible normative assessments of Melanchthon's illustrations. His authorial intentions can be appreciated or rejected on other grounds than the shared Protestant or even Christian belief in the Christian revelation. An absolute prohibition of normativity in humanities is untenable. That would leave the historical discipline, for instance, with the two options of a reproduction of the facts of history or an endless deconstruction and reconstruction of the historical narrative. The humanities need ultimate perspectives and some of them might be theological rather than philosophical. In any case, it is more fruitful to be transparent regarding these perspectives than to deny having any.

Theological Reflection on an Epistemological Level

Any normative valuation of history – or of contemporary religious phenomena – implies a perspective that goes beyond the limits of empirical research. This perspective is either immanent, non-religious, or transcendent and religious. If it is religious it interprets reality from the ultimate efficient and final causes beyond matter, form and empirical causality.

According to Alvin Plantinga (2010: 676), "belief in God is perfectly proper and rational, perfectly justified and in order, even if it is not accepted on the basis of [scientific] arguments." Belief in God as the incomprehensible Creator and as the first cause and final goal of all that exists, offers a comprehending perspective not only for theology but for knowledge in general. Too often theologians have reserved the idea of revelation for something special, for the work of Christ or for the Bible.

I have learned from the theologian Herman Bavinck (2003: 233) to see the world as the embodiment of God's thoughts; it looks like a book that we can read. When we gain knowledge, we are, in fact, re-thinking and re-considering the thoughts of the Creator embodied in creation. If this is the case, then all knowledge rests in revelation, although this is, of course, a theological interpretation of knowledge.

This epistemological level, however, is only relevant in an academic sense as far as academia is the arena where the debate about diverse worldviews and perspectives of reality takes place. If discourse about the possible foundations of our knowledge and about the ultimate presuppositions of our normative statements is excluded from academia, where on earth will it then be possible to discuss these issues?

Although, as a historian, the theologian is primarily interested in the sources of Christianity and does not want to be bothered too much by philosophical presuppositions, as a theologian, the historian is critically aware of his worldview in which he connects all knowledge to his basic convictions and beliefs regarding God's relationship to the world and its history.

This epistemological level should not influence the results of the academic study as such, as far as they regard matter, form and empirical causality of the historical religious phenomena. However, neither should it be dogmatically excluded from academia, given the fact that all researchers have to be aware of and reflect on their own presuppositions and positionality.

Religion Related to God

The fact that theology relates religion to God is less problematic than it might seem to be. As we have seen, theology is limited and cautious of too bold claims, not because of methodological atheism or agnosticism but for very theological reasons. Although some theological statements are not generally communicable because of presupposed belief in God and revelation, theological reflection has much in common with religious studies. The scholastic distinction of several causes or aspects of reality is helpful in showing both where theology and religious studies overlap and where they differ. The ultimate questions regarding the source and ultimate goal of religion are not always at stake and the theological approach of the matter, form and empirical causality of religion is just one of the many perspectives of religion.

This theological approach or perspective is limited because it relates religion to divine revelation. Therefore, it is important to discern the different levels on which theology plays a role. On the material level the expertise of the theologian regarding one specific religious tradition adds to the more comparative approach of the anthropologist, sociologist or historian and on this level there is no principal difference with religious or historical studies. On the methodological level there is more tension, because theology turns to a normative evaluation of religion from a belief or confessional tradition. The use of the theological method of critical evaluation on the normative basis of a shared or contested confessional identity, however, does not principally differ from other normative assessments of religion that are rather inescapable not only in religious studies but in the humanities in general.

Theological reflection on the epistemological level relates the study of religion, and of reality as such to basic pre-scientific convictions and beliefs regarding God's relationship to the world and its history, that is to one's worldview. On this level theology is not just a weird and tolerable species of religious studies. It is the other way around. The comparative study of religion studies human religious behaviour as a small part of God's world. Theology claims that religious studies, – together with all the sciences – are rethinking the thought of God. On the epistemological level, theology is not one of the forms of religious studies, but religious studies contributes to theology, because it studies a part of reality that from a theological perspective also tells us something about God. Religious studies – together with all other sciences – reflect on God's world and thus contribute to the *sermo de Deo*.

About the Author

Henk van den Belt (PhD 2006, Leiden University) is professor of systematic theology at the VU University, Amsterdam and director of the Herman Bavinck Center for Reformed and Evangelical Theology. He is currently working on a research project concerning the development of the doctrine of divine providence in Reformed theology. He is the author of *The Authority of Scripture in Reformed Theology: Truth and Trust* (Brill, 2008) and of several articles on Reformed Orthodoxy and on neo-Calvinism; he edited *Restoration through Redemption: John Calvin Revisited* (Brill, 2013) and the second volume of the *Synopsis of Purer Theology* (Brill, 2016).

References

Bavinck, Herman. 2003. *Reformed Dogmatics: Prolegomena*, volume 1, edited by John Bolt. Grand Rapids, MI: Baker Academic.

Bierma, Lyle D. 2013. *The Theology of the Heidelberg Catechism: A Reformation Synthesis*. Louisville, KY: Westminster John Knox Press.

Bradley, James E. and Richard A. Muller. 2016. *Church History: An Introduction to Research Methods and Resources*, 2nd edition. Grand Rapids, MI: William B. Eerdmans Publishing Company.

Gomarus, Franciscus. 1644. *Opera theologica omnia* (3 volumes). Amsterdam: Joannis Janssonius.

Kapic, Kelly M. 2012. *A Little Book for New Theologians: Why and How to Study Theology*. Downers Grove, IL: IVP Academic.

Luther, Martin. 1520. *Der .x. gebot ein nutzliche erklerung*. Basel: Adam Petri.

Luther, Martin. 1529. *Deudsch Catechismus: Gemehret mit einer newen vnterricht vnd vermanung zu der Beicht*. Wittenberg: Georg Rhau.

Luther, Martin. 1530. *Deudsch Catechismus: Gemehret mit einer newen Vorrhede und vermanunge zu der Beicht*. Wittenberg: Georg Rhau.

Luther, Martin. 1883-2009. [= Luther WA] *D. Martin Luthers Werke: Kritische Gesamtausgabe*, edited by Ulrich Köpf and others (127 volumes). Weimar: Böhlau.

Melanchthon, Philipp. 1834-1860. [= Melanchthon CR] *Opera quae supersunt Omnia*, series *Corpus Reformatorum*, edited by C.G. Bretschneider and H.E. Bindseil. Halle: Braunschweig.

Melanchthon, Philipp. 1915. *Supplementa Melanchthoniana* [Schriften zur praktischen Theologie, vol. 1, Katechetische Schriften], edited by Ferdinand Cohrs and Paul Drews. Leipzig: Haupt.

Muller, Richard A. 1998. "Scholasticism, Reformation, Orthodoxy, and the Persistence of Christian Aristotelianism." *Trinity Journal* 19(1): 81-96.

Plantinga, Alvin. 2010. "Reformed Epistemology." In *A Companion to Philosophy of Religion*, Blackwell Companions to Philosophy, no. 9, 2nd edition, edited by Charles Taliaferro, Paul Draper and Philip L. Quinn, pp. 674-680. Oxford: Blackwell. https://doi.org/10.1002/9781444320152.ch79

Thum, Veronika. 2006. *Die Zehn Gebote für die ungelehrten Leut: Der Dekalog in der Graphik des späten Mittelalters und der frühen Neuzeit*. Munich: Deutscher Kunstverlag.

Van Asselt, Willem J. 2002. "The Fundamental Meaning of Theology: Archetypal and Ectypal Theology in Seventeenth-century Reformed Thought." *Westminster Theological Journal* 64(3): 319-335.

Van den Belt, Henk. 2017. "The Law Illuminated: Biblical Illustrations of the Commandments in Lutheran Catechisms." In *The Ten Commandments in Medieval and Early Modern Culture*, edited by Walter Melion, Jürgen Pieters and Youri Desplenter, pp. 196-218. Leiden: Brill. https://doi.org/10.1163/9789004325777_012

Webster, John. 2009. "Principles of Systematic Theology." *International Journal of Systematic Theology* 11(1): 56-71. https://doi.org/10.1111/j.1468-2400.2008.00423.x

– 5 –

Relations of Religion in the Graeco-Roman World

Formative Judaism and Christianity

STEVE MASON

In modern research on the Graeco-Roman world, religion features prominently. At least, there are countless books ostensibly on ancient religion, although the reader soon discovers that they unfold their subject matter as myths, gods, temples, altars, priests, and animal sacrifices (Burkert 1985: 8; Baumgarten 2002; Scheid 2003: 18–29; Johnston 2004: 3–153; Rives 2007: 13–53). They do not claim that a category comparable to our religion was current in antiquity. Religion is a resistant category, however, no doubt because of its convenience: it covers the most obvious bits of a society's "God-stuff".

The problem arises when we treat the category as real, for example when we characterize Judaism and Christianity as the only two surviving *religions* from antiquity.[1] This assumes that there were many such religions. The common story is that, in the fourth century, the small and vulnerable religion of Christianity managed to consume its rival religions, closing their temples, altars, and social functions. Only Judaism was

---

1. E.g. Parkes (1934: 33): "two religious organisations"; Sanders (1977): *A Comparison of Patterns of Religion*; Segal (1986: 1): "[T]he time of Jesus marks the beginning of not one but two great religions of the West"; Finn (1997: 91): "Out of the innumerable religions and religious movements of the Greco-Roman world, only two ... outlasted the Roman Empire"; Schäfer (2012: 1): "This is a book about ... boundaries within religions".

Keywords: Graeco-Roman world, ancient history, ancient Judaism, early Christianity, ancient religion

indigestible. Christians felt obligated to preserve this religion, Judaism, because they believed that both scriptural prophecy and the unhappy state of the Jews validated Christian truth. Christians *needed* Jews, albeit for an abusive relationship (Ruether 1974).

Justin Martyr's *Dialogue with Trypho - a Jew* (c.140 CE) shows these two dynamics working in symbiosis. According to the Christian philosopher Justin, God stripped everything of value from the old ship of the Jews as he put it in dry-dock, and gave it to the newly christened fellowship of Christus-believers, to preserve as a vestigial heritage. Now without metaphors: when Roman armies destroyed the Judaean capital Jerusalem (70 CE), and especially when Hadrian built Aelia Capitolina on the same site and forbade Jews from entering (135 CE), Christians found the proof they needed of a divine salvage-and-transfer operation. To explain God's retiring of his flagship, they accused all Jews of having lynched God's son, Jesus, in Jerusalem.[2] In Justin's *Dialogue*, the character Trypho has fled the second conflict in Judaea, which saw the building of Aelia and banishment of Jews. Justin explains these events as retribution for the murder of Christ (*Dial.* 1: 16). He devotes most of his work to arguing that Jewish scripture finds its fulfilment in Christian devotion. For the fifteen centuries following Christianity's ascent, where Jewish minorities were allowed to remain in Europe's Christian cities[3] they were subjected to sermons aimed at converting them to Christ (Mason 2016a: 43–57).

This is the usual explanation of how a *mother religion*, Judaism, gave birth to a *daughter religion*, Christianity. By and large, it makes sense of the evidence. The catch is *religion*: a magic blanket that can make a fellowship look like an actual ship. But to ancient eyes, Jews and Christians were different sorts of groups.

We find it difficult to untangle this because the category religion is so familiar and appealing, but we forget that it was a Christian creation. Having had no secure place in the classical social-political lexicon (below), as their influence grew in the third century Christians began to rewrite that hostile lexicon. To do so, they repurposed the Latin word *religio*, which had formerly meant any sort of solemn obligation, as a category uniquely suited for their creed-based world-view, "Christian-ism"

---

2. Matt 22.1-14; Luke 19.41-44; Acts 3.14-15; Melito, *Pasch.* 94–99; Tertullian, *Apol.* 21; Eusebius, *H.E.* 1.1; 3.7.1; documents for Christianity and the Jews are in Marcus and Saperstein (2015).
3. Jews were expelled from Christian France between 1185 and 1394, England and Wales in 1290, German states in 1348, 1510, and 1528, Spain in 1492, Portugal in 1497, parts of Italy in 1389, 1544, and 1594. Martin Luther's bitter 1543 essay, *The Jews and their Lies*, cited Titus's destruction of the temple as "sufficient evidence that they assuredly have erred".

(Boyarin 2004; Mason 2007). After the emperor Constantine's endorsement of Christianity in the fourth century, their model began to nudge out the classical lexicon. Each culture that had left the Christians rootless was now inverted and reduced to an *-ism*, a belief system contrastable with Christian faith: Juda-ism, Samaritan-ism, Hellen-ism, or pagan-ism.

By the seventeenth century, after 1200 years of Christian civilization and the rise of Islam, since the seventh century, the Christian religious landscape comfortably comprised "Christianity, Mohametanism [Islam], Judaism and Idolatry" (Smith 1998: 271). That fourth body, idolatry, was experiencing rapid cell-division, however, as the West more seriously encountered the East. It soon included Hindu-ism, Buddh-ism, Confucian-ism, and Dao-ism – all supposed belief systems, in fact freeze-dried reductions of vibrant civilizations.

Every student of religion learns that no definition of religion works for all cases. But that is because the category was imposed by Christians on very different cultures. The strongest criticisms of religion as covering category have come from experts in India, China, and Japan (Fung 1948: 1–6; Smith 1963: 28: 61–64; Masuzawa 2005; Josephson 2012; cf. Smith 1998: 269–270). I propose here that abstracting Juda-ism from ancient Judaean society, to create a religion comparable to Christianity, creates no fewer problems. Before the rise of Christianity, no one saw these as two species of the same genus.

Background and Method

Studying the human past unavoidably makes us think about history as a method. Let us ponder each of these words for a moment: method and history. From its earliest Greek occurrences, method (Greek *methodos*) has had two senses: (a) a technique or procedure for doing something (extracting natural gas, learning piano) and (b) the whole way of thinking that characterizes a discipline (the scientific method). For history, the former meaning would include specialist understanding of archaeology, inscriptions, coins, papyri, and text production. We see the latter meaning in such famous book titles as *The Historian's Craft* (Bloch 1941), *What is History?* (Carr 1961), *The Idea of History* (Collingwood 1994), or *In Defence of History* (Evans 2000). These assume that historians (should) share a philosophy, rationale, and logic – method in the holistic sense.

What constitutes this method? Herodotus (fifth century BCE) was known in antiquity as "the father of history" because he first applied the method of "inquiry", or *historia* in Greek, to the human past. In its root meaning, that is, *historia* had nothing to do with the past. It meant *research*. Before Herodotus, it was mainly used of investigating nature. He created "history" by explicitly calling for a similar methodical care in studying the past – rather than merely recycling stories and comforting traditions. He himself would scour the world in the search for evidence about the recent Persian–Greek wars too easily ignored by his fellow Greeks. Herodotus's effort was so successful that his slogan *historia* would become fully identified with the human past. Still today, most practitioners would at least agree that historians need to undertake methodical investigation of something. Of what?

This is not the place for a history of history. It is enough to observe that, during the nineteenth century, as universities threw off centuries of church imposition and embraced scientific knowledge (albeit in the service of new nation-states), history's place in the academy became an awkward question. Until then it had been mainly written by amateurs, whether philosophers or statesmen in retirement. Could it be a worthy companion in the common room with professional scientists? Historians responded to the challenge by breaking in opposite directions (Beiser 2011). Some found the heart of the scientific spirit in precise, careful observation and cautious induction: getting the particulars right (Ranke 2011; Droysen 1893; Carlyle 1900–1901). Applied to history, this meant putting aside grand narratives to focus on one piece of evidence: a text, biography, or event. "Historicizing" everything (German *Historismus*) meant breaking it into discrete elements for contextual analysis, without assuming similarity or coherence.

Other scholars, on the contrary, found the essence of science in aggregation, generalization, covering laws, and prediction. They dismissed particulars, especially the royals and generals who had previously dominated history books, as trivial aberrations. Like the medical doctor – or veterinarian – who judges a swollen elbow or rash by comparison with general norms, not caring much what you think about it, these historians were interested only in what was typical. In order to qualify as science, they thought, history had to generate laws: when people are in situation X, they behave in way Y. This approach moved history out of its ageing home in the humanities to the shiny suburbs of social science (Comte 1830–1842, 1896; Buckle 1857: 1.2–7; Mason 2016b: 19–41). This basic tension has not gone away. Both streams are found in history departments today.

The study of ancient religion most often lives in religious studies departments, which have their own version of the same bifurcation. A social scientist might define religion according to a provisional ("heuristic") model, then go looking for its markers. Many things existed in antiquity without names, the logic is: the earth's turning on its axis and revolving around the sun, obviously, but also diseases such as malaria – and human power-relations or economic constraints. Most researchers within the social sciences, as the label suggests, focus on trans-local and generalizable experience. A scholar in the humanistic stream of history will instead turn to particular texts, events, and situations.

Although each side has vilified the other, in principle there is no need to choose. We are free to pose any questions we like of the past. Some are aggregative by nature; others deal with particulars. I, for example, lean on the work of social historians for the ancient economy, demography, and family relations, but gravitate towards investigating particular events, writers and texts, lives, and conflicts (e.g. Mason 2016a). Even in this humanistic branch of history, however, we cannot hope to understand particulars if we have no sense of their shared values, language, and categories of communication: how they ordered knowledge of their world. Today we have a shared lexical bank, or public script. Without thinking about it, we can readily talk with foreigners about education or health systems, legislatures, courts, police, religion, citizenship. In the ancient world, they could not have recognized these terms, but they had their own counterparts. They are the focus of this chapter: What shell categories did residents of the Graeco-Roman world use to communicate with each other? Let us measure them against our "religion". Agreeing with some recent studies that they did not know a comparable category (Nongbri 2013; Barton and Boyarin 2016), I shall spell out some consequences of the categories they did use for our understanding of ancient Judaism and Christianity.

Ancient Categories

Are you religious? What is your religious background? How do you see the relationship between religion and science, or between religion and the state? Do you consider religion beneficial or harmful? These questions make sense to us because religion is a known category. We can study it in school or university, or read the religion section in some newspapers. Individuals are free to make their religion central in their lives, we agree, but that is a private matter. In our public script, religion is a voluntary pursuit detached from others. That is, we would consider it a glaring infringement of our norms if medical procedures, business meetings, or football games began with hymns and prayers – let alone animal sacrifices to a deity.

In antiquity things were different. There was no way to formulate the questions above in Greek, Latin, or Hebrew (Boyarin 2004: 202–25; Mason

2016b: 175–220). Both domestic and public life were, to be sure, saturated with elements we recognize as religious, but there was no way to extrude them into a distinct domain matching our "religion". Sacrifices were enmeshed in civic, political, military, and family life, but sacrifices do not figure in our conception of religion anyway, and they were not a distinct sphere of life. This matters because it means that there were no *religions*, and because religion – if it was not a thing – could also not have been a distinct motive in human action, as in "I am acting for my religion". One could act from zeal for the god of Jerusalem, Carthage, or Rome, for example, but that was all entangled with other aspects of social-political belonging in those places.

What were the ancient categories, then? As the Romans expanded their empire eastward, into the heartland of the Jews and the birthplace of Christianity, during the first century BCE, they took over Greek ways of ordering knowledge and supplied Latin equivalents. Greek discourse featured two root categories, which appear frequently in texts and inscriptions: *ethnos* and *polis*.[4] Along with related terms for laws, ancestral customs, and piety, these two terms covered much of what we could call religion, but also a great deal more fused together.

The fourth-century BCE author we call Pseudo-Skylax gives a vivid impression of the centrality of *ethnos* and *polis*, using them 369 times in his brief 114-paragraph tour of the Mediterranean. Here is a taste (*Per.* 104–106):

> After Cilicia comes an *ethnos*: the Syrians. In Syria the Phoenicians, an *ethnos*, live along the sea. … A *polis* of the Tyrians is Sarapta; another *polis* is Tyre, having a harbour within its walls. This is the royal island of the Tyrians. … Ake [Acco], a *polis*. … Arad, a *polis* of the Sidonians. Ioppe [Jaffa], a *polis*. … Ascalon, a *polis* – and a royal one, of the Tyrians. This is the limit of Coele-Syria. … After Syria [eastward] are the Arabs – an *ethnos* of horse-riding nomads.

This language assumes that everyone ever born belongs to an *ethnos* (near-synonym *genos*). They have no choice: this is the origin-group that shapes their upbringing and customs (Jones 1996). We are not speaking of a scientific, hierarchical taxonomy. *Ethnos* was a convenient word because it was so elastic: it meant a bunch or group of any size. All Syrians constituted an *ethnos*, but so did small groups such as Phoenicians, Gazans, Azotans, or Idumaeans.[5]

---

4. Herodotus 611 times, Diodorus Siculus 3,368, Strabo 1,913, Philo of Alexandria 911, Josephus 2,416, Plutarch 3,774, Dio of Prusa 878, Pausanias 851.
5. E.g. Strabo, *Geog.* 8.1; 16.2.2; Pausanias 7.16.10; Josephus, *A.J.* 1.122–139.

Most of the world's *ethnē* (plural) were thought to have derived from just a few major sources.⁶ The Egyptians were one prime source, being thought to have spawned many eastern *ethnē* – including the Jews-Judaeans, who had migrated from Egypt to southern Syria and fashioned a new identity. Environment was assumed to be a crucial factor in defining any *ethnos*: the quality and temperature of its air, nature of its terrain, and availability of water. Mountainous country thus nurtured a hardy *ethnos*, whereas plains, marshes, and deserts created a weaker population. These nature-informed predispositions were tempered by an *ethnos*'s formative experiences: wars won or lost, further migrations or absorption of migrants, great lawgivers (Sparta's Lycurgus or Judaea's Moses), relations with neighbours, and forms of worship. That is why ancient writers, when describing the character of a foreign *ethnos* at the present time, and no matter where they live, tend to return to their origins and formative experiences in the homeland (e.g. Tacitus, *Hist.* 5.1-13; cf. *Germania* – with Latin *gens* for *ethnos*).

What, then, was a *polis*? The Greek countryside made it possible for populations living fairly close to each other, as the crow flies, to maintain distinct cultures, because mountains or expanses of water separated them. They built walls to protect their core institutions – markets, shops, assembly and council halls, courts, *gymnasia*, temples, and a few residences – usually in a space of just 1 or 2 square kilometres. This area constituted the *polis* proper, or *astu*. The walled compound anchored a much larger hinterland (*chōra*). The countryside provided farmsteads, herding, fishing, and in some cases mining. Its villages were smaller nodes of communal life, though all were dependent on the *astu* for governance and justice. The size of the walled *polis* was limited by practical constraints, whereas the dependent territory could range from a few to thousands of square kilometres. It could also expand or shrink dramatically as a result of conflict. Although the majority of people lived in the countryside, civilized life meant having a *polis* structure of laws and customs. If your people lacked a *polis*, as the Arabian nomads above, they were an *ethnos* only. Otherwise, your *polis* belonged to an *ethnos*, as above Tyre, Sarapta, and Ascalon are *poleis* (plural) of the Tyrian *ethnos*.

This Greek way of ordering society spread eastward with the rapid conquests of Alexander the Great and the rule of his successors (320s BCE). It was not merely a discourse overlaid on reality, however. It was a scheme that also created the material world. That is, the Hellenistic monarchs and the Romans after them established new *poleis*, often where an unaffiliated village had stood before. In Syria, these new *poleis*

---

6. See Herodotus 7.91 on the diverse origins of Cypriots.

fused Greek culture – with such characteristic institutions as *gymnasia* (educational-athletic institutions), assembly and council halls, markets, and classical architecture and statuary – with the Semitic traditions that had been around for centuries. Local deities such as Baal, Astarte, and Atargatis were assimilated to Greek Zeus, Artemis, and Tychē (Kaizer 2008).

By the first century BCE, southern Syria – including Judaea – thus had numerous distinct population centres configured as *poleis*: Gaza, Ascalon, Tyre, Sidon, and Berytus along the coast; Scythopolis, Hippos, Gadara and Gerasa inland. Jerusalem was a *polis* with an unusually large territory, Judaea (*Ioudaia*). Its inhabitants were first of all Judaeans (*Ioudaioi*) – the same word we normally translate "Jews". In ethnographic discourse, that was the place where Judaean laws, customs, calendar, and worship were normative. When Judaeans lived abroad, even for generations, like Syrians or Egyptians abroad they remained a tolerated foreign minority, called metics (Latin *incolae*), who had to find a way to get along with the local *polis*'s laws and customs.

A "mother-*polis*" – the original meaning of Greek *mētropolis* – was one that had dispatched colonies (*apoikiai*) abroad. Greeks and Phoenicians, and later the Romans, established colonies around the Mediterranean. Each colony gradually forged a new character by mixing the mother-*polis* culture with the local environment. Judaeans came late to the colonizing party, but during the Hasmonean expansion (140s–70s BCE), they too imposed Judaean colonies on much of southern Syria, before the Romans arrived in the 60s and returned them to their earlier inhabitants. The 1st-century authors Philo and Josephus use the language of mother-*polis* and colony for Judaean minorities abroad (Philo, *Conf.* 78; *Flacc.* 46; *Legat.* 281–82; Josephus, *Apion* 2.38) – rather than the less cheerful modern term *Diaspora*.

One can hardly overstate the importance of *polis*-belonging in antiquity, as the source of one's first identity and pride. Not only did each *polis* worship its own gods, observing their holy days and sacrificial demands, but each also had its own way of counting time – years, months, weeks, days, or holidays. Each had its own Year 1 and Day 1, month names, and divisions (Samuel 1972). Each *polis* carefully guarded its citizenship, which was usually available only to the children of citizens. A person's original *polis* was the only place in the world where they truly felt at home, where the laws were *the* law. Foreign groups, even of long residence, remained vulnerable to that citizen body. Although usually tolerated, they could face hostility and abuse in times of crisis.

Roman imperial rule, far from eradicating the old Greek *poleis*, re-energized them. That is because the Romans innovated a model of empire according to which proud *polis* leaders would help them govern and share fully in the empire's interests, partly because some were granted Roman citizenship. Roman governors would spend much of the year visiting each *polis* in their province, to maintain good relations with leaders and populace. As far as possible, the governor was happy to leave internal affairs to local leaders.

Between them, the categories of *ethnos* and *polis* included much of what we would label religion. The example of Jews-Judaeans shows, however, why we cannot extricate "religious" from other elements. The Judaeans were an *ethnos* (Hebrew `am) with a famous homeland in Jerusalem-Judaea, an ancient lawgiver (Moses), and distinctive laws covering civil and criminal law, calendar, diet, purity rules, and proper worship of their ancestral god. But these were all of a piece. They did not separate some laws as "religious" and others not, or separate religious from other civic activities.

One of the hardest aspects of ancient life for us to grasp is the usual ancient form of worship. Our sanitized category "religion" obscures the bloody, smoky, and smelly nature of ancient worship. People worshiped mainly by offering their deity the meal that he or she desired. A meat sacrifice required elaborate ritual slaughter. The sacrificer had to be careful because the offering could be rejected, if it was not offered the right way (Baumgarten 2002; Knust and Varhelyi 2011; Naiden 2013). Every *polis* had holy or sanctified zones, which only those who had purified themselves could enter (Parker 1983). These included the shrine of the deity and altars where sacrifices were conducted. Some of these were massive, such as the building-size altar of Pergamum now in a Berlin museum; others were thigh-high stones. The best animals were selected, dressed with garlands, and roasted, accompanied by chants and prayers and offerings of wine, grain, and oil, which might also be offered on their own. Ancient priests, accordingly, were not theologically trained teachers and counsellors, comparable to modern clergy, but specialists in performing sacrificial rituals. Calling those activities the heart of ancient religion, as if this category matched what we call religion, requires us to bleach out the gore of sacrifice, while ignoring many ancient activities that more closely resembled those of modern religion.

For along with this triad of more or less given identity markers – *ethnos*, *polis*, and sacrificial cult – people could usually choose to join a group or club (*thiasos*, *hetairia*, Latin *collegium*), with others who shared their interests. Because these voluntary associations were largely ignored by elite writers, unless they created trouble, evidence comes mainly from inscriptions (Kloppenborg and Wilson 1996; Arnaoutoglou 2002, 2005; Harland 2003; Kloppenborg, Ascough and Harland 2011; Ascough,

Harland and Kloppenborg 2012). Some were clubs for members of a guild, such as bakers, metal- or leather-workers, but a voluntary association could become the most prominent feature of one's identity. Some were local chapters of international societies, devoted worshippers of Isis or Mithras – or Christus – or those committed to pursuing a disciplined, philosophical life together (see Lucian, *Philosophies for Sale*). Such groups had a defined membership, initiation procedures, a code of behaviour, and regular meetings. They often worshipped a patron deity, and they cared for members who became ill or died – in the absence of state welfare or private insurance.

If *ethnos* and *polis* life, including (sacrificial) worship, included many elements of what we call religion – attention to gods, public ritual, a calendar of holy days – many other typical activities in modern houses of worship were better paralleled in ancient philosophical schools: study of authoritative texts, discussion of the nature of the divine and the soul, virtue, and the afterlife. That is because ancient Christians were a voluntary association resembling philosophical schools in some respects, and they had the largest role in shaping the concept of a religion. We turn now to compare ancient Jews and Christians in terms of ancient categories.

Ancient Judaism and Religion? Conversion as a Test Case

Jews-Judaeans fit the *ethnos-polis-colony* scheme well, and they were discussed precisely that way by insiders and outsiders.[7] The Jewish authors Philo and Josephus use "the *ethnos* of the Judaeans" as a default phrase, because this was the obvious category for Judaeans, Syrians, Romans, or others.[8] The great geographer Pliny considered the Judaeans'

---

7. E.g. the *ethnos Ioudaiōn* statue base from Aphrodisias (Smith 1988: 57 and Plate VIII); Plutarch, *Pomp.* 45.1-2 (listing Judaeans among eastern *genē* conquered by Pompey); an inscription from the Circus Maximus honouring Titus for conquering *gentem Iudaeorum* (*Corpus Inscriptionum Latinarum* 6.944); a vast range of Jewish and early Christian literature (1 Macc. 8.23-27; 10.25; 11.30-33; 12.3, 6; 2 Macc 4.35; 10.8; Greek *Jub.* 1.1; in Matt 21.43; Luke 7.5; 23.2; John 11.48-52 (4 times); 18.35; Acts 10.22; 24.3, 10, 17; 26.4; 28.19); in Latin literature generally (Cicero, *Prov. Cons.* 10.3; Columella, *Rust.* 3.8; Pliny, *H.N.* 5.66-67 [with 7.97-98; 13.47]; Tacitus, *Hist.* 5.8).
8. E.g., Philo, *Mos.* 1.7, 34; *Dec.* 96; *Spec.* 2.163, 166; 4.179, 224; *Virt.* 212, 226; *Prob.* 75; *Flacc.* 1, 45, 179, 191; *Legat.* 117, 160, 184, 194, 207, 210, 256, 373; *Hypoth.* 6.10; Josephus, *War* 1.1; 2.197, 202-283; 6.17, 330, 342; 7.423; *Ant.* 7.456; 11.123, 184-185, 270, 272, 285, 303, 323, 340; 12.6-7, 135, 141, 357, 412, 417-418; 13.1, 48, 126-127, 143, 166; 14.196, 212, 248, 306, 320; 15.15, 179, 383; 16.56, 158, 162; 17.174, 330; 18.378; 19.278, 284-285, 309; 20.11l; *Apion* 1.137; 2.43.

mother-*polis*, Jerusalem, the jewel of the Orient (*H. N.* 5.70). When they discussed Judaeans anywhere in the world, ancient writers predictably cited their origins, homeland, lawgiver, and mother-*polis* to explain the *ethnos* (Stern 1974). Judaeans also met the expectation that an *ethnos* worshipped its god(s) by sacrificing animals. Until 70 CE, Jerusalem housed the only temple and altar available to Judaeans worldwide (the small shrine in Leontopolis, Egypt, remaining a puzzle to historians). Judaeans abroad would make the long pilgrimage to Jerusalem to offer sacrifice in their world-famous sacred compound.

Before we contrast the Christians, I must anticipate a possible objection: What about conversion? Since we read about people *converting to Judaism*, surely that, at least, makes Jews comparable to Christians – as religions (for want of a better word) to which people could convert? I raise this point because it has been advocated by prominent scholars. Jewish conversion practices, which entail immersion in a ritual bath (*miqveh*) and circumcision for males, are nowadays called *religious* rites. Since they are traceable to antiquity, were they not religious then too? Some historians of ancient Judaism have proposed that a major change occurred in antiquity, when Judaeans – originally an *ethnos* propagating itself by natural succession – began to attract converts. Assuming conversion to be a property of religion, these scholars argue that provision for converts marked "the beginnings of Jewishness" – or of Judaism as a religion (Cohen 1999: 136–137; Schwartz 2005: 68–78).

In respectful disagreement, I would point out that attraction to, and adoption of, foreign laws and customs was a known issue within the *ethnos-polis*-cult triad, without the need for religion – a category not invoked by ancient writers. Consider the question from three vantage points.

First, the Bible already makes provision for foreigners who adopt the laws of Moses (later: Judaean law), on the assumption that they live in the land. In fact, the Hebrew and Greek terms that would later be used for "religious" converts, *ger* and *prosēlytos* [proselyte], in the Hebrew Bible and its Greek translation the Septuagint, referred to a foreigner who has "come over" to live under our laws (Exod 12.48-49). The parade example was Ruth, a Moabite who insisted on moving with her late husband's mother to Bethlehem near Jerusalem, there to live under biblical law. She famously declared to Naomi, "Your people shall be my people, and your god my god" (Ruth 1.16). This idea of coming in, to change one's identity so comprehensively as to live by a new calendar, law, and rhythm of life, would remain as a model throughout the Graeco-Roman world, even for foreigners who joined Judaean communities abroad. Those who did so abandoned their family traditions to embrace the laws of Moses and Judaean customs.

Second, attraction to foreign ways and constitutions was familiar elsewhere in antiquity, though not common because it invited the accusation of disloyalty to one's people. Herodotus tells a story about a Scythian royal attracted to Greek customs, for example, who paid with his life for his new enthusiasm (4.76–80). His people would not tolerate such betrayal. Spartans attracted huge numbers of admirers, and periodically expelled foreigners who threatened to dilute their admired traditions. Conversely, a Spartan general was condemned for adopting Persian ways (Thucydides 1.130–132). The seductiveness of both Egyptian and Judaean customs reportedly led the emperor Tiberius to expel these groups from Rome, along with Romans "infected" by them (Tacitus, *Ann.* 2.85). Judaeans were thus fully part of this picture. No one could object if they maintained their ancestral customs. But if they seemed to encourage foreigners to reject their own traditions, indignant criticism followed (Tacitus, *Hist.* 5.5; Celsus in Origen, *C. Cels.* 5.41).

Third, Philo and Josephus, the Judaean authors most fully engaged with the ambient culture, discussed attraction to Judaean law in precisely these established terms, without needing to invoke a new category. Philo, celebrating the humanity of Moses's laws, indicates that his provision for those who "come in" to share them still holds good in first-century Alexandria:

> Having legislated for fellow-members of the *ethnos*, he [Moses] holds that newcomers [or "those who have come over"] must be deemed worthy of every privilege, because they have left behind blood-affiliation, homeland, customs, sacred rites and temples of the gods, the gifts and honours too, having undertaken *a noble migration*. ... He directs those of the [Judaean] *ethnos* to love the newcomers, not only as friends and relatives, but as their own selves in body and soul.
>
> (*Virt.* 102–103)

Josephus makes the same move, treating the biblical welcome of foreigners who "wish to live under the same laws with us" as still in force and insisting that Moses did not consider familial bonds a result of ancestry alone, but also a shared life choice. Like Spartans, Judaeans do not allow the dilution of their laws, but (unlike Spartans) they welcome those who resolve to come and live under them (*Apion* 2.210, 261; generally, 2.255–286). He even furnishes a recent example. At the climax of his *Antiquities*, a twenty-volume exposition of Judaea's peerless laws (*A.J.* 1.7–14, 20–26), he tells the dramatic story of the royal family from Adiabene (modern Iraq), which becomes enamoured of Jerusalem's laws (*A.J.* 20.17–96). This puts them in mortal peril because their local nobles will not tolerate *foreign* allegiance and defection from Adiabenian customs (nothing about religion here). The royal family opts to identify so closely with Jerusalem that many of its members move there, build palaces, and take leading roles in the Judaean War. Their burial chambers can still be seen today.

"Conversion to Judaism", then, although considered a religious experience in modern terms, in antiquity meant a highly visible change to join a foreign *ethnos* and live under its laws – somewhat (not quite) like a change of citizenship for us. Let us now consider where the early Christians fit (or not) in the same social-political scene.

Ancient Christians and Religion

To put it simply, nothing we have said about the Judaeans applies to early followers of Christus. If Judaeans ticked all the boxes of an *ethnos*, Christians ticked none. As Christians, they had no homeland, ancient laws and customs, temples, priesthood, or sacrificial cult. They were a different kind of group, made up of voluntary associations in the existing *poleis* and towns of the eastern Mediterranean. Their members – male citizens, women, and slaves (Matthews 2001) – were raised in the customs of those *poleis*, but pointedly gave that up to worship a Judaean man crucified by a Roman governor. Christus-followers were a single-issue salvation circle, united by their allegiance to Christus and an idea of salvation from him – not by their *ethnos* or *polis*, ancestral traditions, or citizenship.

The earliest Christian texts we possess are Paul's letters from about 40 CE. They provide a vivid picture of these realities. Paul's first known lines reveal that he has been entrusted with what he calls *The Special Announcement* (*to euangelion* – usually "gospel"). Its content is that "those who trust" must prepare themselves for evacuation when Christus returns from heaven (1 Thess. 1.4-10). They prepare for this by leading blameless lives, to ease the transition to spiritual ascent (4.9-17; 5.21-23). Their withdrawal from the world's practices will enable them alone to escape the divine wrath that is about to fall on humanity.[9] As they hold themselves apart from *polis* activities, they should expect hostility from neighbours who consider them mad, bad, or both. Paul himself recounts his traditional background as a Judaean only to say that he now considers it so much excrement, in contrast to Christ-belonging (Phil. 3.3-16). Naturally, he faces hostility everywhere, not least from fellow-Judaeans

---

9. 1 Thess. 2.17–3.13; 4.13-21; 5.1-11, 23; 1 Cor. 1.7-9; 7.25-35; 15.12-57; Gal 1.4.

and in the towns he visits, and advises his followers to expect the same, but persevere to the end (1 Thess. 1.6, 2; 2.2, 14–16). His letters show him often in custody or facing beatings,[10] as he goes about denouncing a world that is disintegrating before "the day of Jesus Christ" (1 Cor. 1.7-8; 1.17–2.5; 3.13; 7.31; 15.12-58). To those who would tell him to get a life and participate in *polis* affairs, he is scathing (Phil. 3.2-11): "*Our* political community is in the heavens, from where we await a saviour, the Lord Jesus Christ" (Phil. 3.20).

We are fortunate to have surviving correspondence between a Roman governor, Pliny ("the Younger"), and the emperor Trajan in the early second century CE (*Ep.* 10.96, *c.*110 CE). Although this comes from two generations after Paul, it is close enough to suggest how others viewed the Christians. Pliny seems a very decent man (Wilken 2003). But as the emperor's emissary to the troublesome province of Pontus-Bithynia (north-western Turkey today), he is concerned about a fast-growing Christus fellowship. Certain that they are up to no good, but unsure how, and seeing the socio-economic harm they are creating, he arrests and interrogates a number of purported Christians, as well as ex-members who say they left the group as much as a quarter-century earlier (*c.*85 CE). Pliny assumes that they engage in the gross immorality mentioned in other ancient texts: orgiastic sex, incest, and eating infants (cf. Minucius Felix, *Oct.* 8.5–11.1; Tertullian, *Apol.* 2). He is determined to stem this "contagion". His dual approach is, first, to use Trajan's ban on all clubs to stop Christian meetings (they obviously fell in this category), and second, to persuade the Christians he encounters to return to their senses and traditional customs. Trajan agrees (*Ep.* 10.97) that the *Christiani* must be given every chance to "rethink" their foolish choice, facing execution only if they persist.

Pliny's letter brings us to the nub of the issue in this chapter. Christians were not a religion for him, but another club, comparable to firefighters or any other group that defined itself by initiation and membership. They were completely different in kind from Judaeans, who were such by ancestry. It was possible to become a Judaean, as we have seen, but this was a life-decision about primary *ethnos*-affiliation, which would involve either a move to Judaea or, within a *polis*, joining the *ethnos* community there to live by its calendar, laws, and festivals – and be buried in its cemetery (Mason 2007: 477). We do not know how many people moved to Judaea, though funerary inscriptions in the Jerusalem area attest some (Avni, Greenhut and Ilan 1994). Christian "conversion" was similar in what was being rejected – the world's other cultures – but altogether

---

10. Phlm 8-23; 1 Cor. 4.9-13; Phil. 1.13-26; 2 Cor. 11.23-27.

different in what one joined. When Jews-Judaeans (or other *ethnē*) fell into conflict with the citizen population in a *polis*, the only real option was their expulsion. When Christians became a problem for *polis* officials, there was nowhere to expel them to because they belonged there, in theory. Short of expelling them to heaven, their claimed homeland, the only remedy was to persuade or compel them to give up this choice and return to their traditions.

The most obvious parallel in ancient discourse to "Christian conversion" was therefore not joining another *ethnos*, but choosing a philosophical life. Various texts speak of discovering philosophy in quasi-evangelical language. People who were once blind now see! Awakened to new life, they renounce the world's values of money, power, and sex for inner peace and virtue (*Nigr.* 1, 35–38; Epictetus in Arrian, *Diatr.* 3.21–23; Diogenes Laertius 4.16). Philosophers, like Christians, were ridiculed for being so at odds with common values. Roman officials considered high-status philosophers a particular nuisance because of their willingness to criticize monarchical regimes, even at the cost of death (Nock 1933: 164–253; Macmullen 1966: 46–94). Emperors never forgot that the senators who murdered Julius Caesar had philosophical pretensions. When people consider themselves answerable to a higher law, who knows what they might do? Converts to Christianity, though they included more women and slaves than a philosophical school, looked somewhat the same: smug critics of worldly values willing (sometimes) to die rather than give up their commitment.

Along with the implicit contrasts we have seen between the Christian Paul and the Jewish Philo or Josephus, outside observers also realized that Christians rejected allegiance to traditional laws and customs, including Judaean. First, consider two Christians writing around 200 CE. Clement of Alexandria's *Exhortation to the Greeks* is a frontal attack on *ethnos* identity, on the ground that Christian truth is infinitely older than anything considered ancient among the *ethnē* (*Protr.* chs. 10–11). All these gods are late-comers, who "fell on *poleis* and *ethnē* like plagues" (3.1). His closing exhortation declares (12.1): "Let us then steer clear of custom! ... Custom is a snare, a trap, a pit, an evil treat." Tertullian of Carthage ridicules "these oh-so-pious champions and avengers of laws and ancestral institutions" (*Apol.* 5–6). He makes Christian weirdness, in relation to traditional *ethnos*-allegiance, a virtue. The Christians are a *secta* (group, faction), it is true. They date only from the time of Tiberius (21.1) and bear only the name of a man, not of an *ethnos* (3.6; 21.26). But they should not be harassed, just as philosophers are not when they reject common values (*Apol.* 46). While awaiting their heavenly departure, after all, Christians lead disciplined lives and pose no threat (*Apol.* 38–39).

Some observers made the same points from the outside, but championing *ethnos*-allegiance. None of them thought Judaean culture superior to Greek,[11] but they agreed that Judaeans were an established *ethnos* admirably loyal to its laws, whereas Christians were a danger to social order. In the early second century Tacitus, a friend of Pliny, mentions Judaea throughout his narrative and, when he is about to describe Jerusalem's destruction in war, relates the origin of the Judaean *gens* and its homeland (*Hist.* 5.2–5). Christians, in stark contrast, Tacitus mentions just once as a "mob despised for their shameful acts". They take their name from a mere man, Christus – a criminal executed by a Roman governor, whose death generated a "deadly superstition" (*Ann.* 15.44). In a similar way, the neo-Platonist Porphyry (late third century) would include Judaeans alongside Egyptians, Syrians, and others as examples "by *ethnos*" of the disciplined life (*Abst.* 4.2), whereas he was unsparing in his mockery of Christian beliefs, which he had studied, concerning the return of Christ and heavenly ascent (above).[12]

The second-century philosopher Celsus made the same contrast between Jews and Christians. According to the Christian writer who preserved his fragments, he celebrated the customs of all *ethnē*. Citing Pindar's maxim that "*nomos* (custom/law) is king of all", he expected each *ethnos* to cherish its own laws (*C. Cels.* 5.35, 40). He criticized Judaean exclusiveness (1.14, 22–23, 26; 5.41–42), but respected Jews as such an *ethnos* (5.25). He had no time for Christians, however, because they adhered neither to the traditions of their upbringing nor to those of the Judaeans. They had no place in the world (5.33). The emperor Julian (ruled 361–363 CE) made the same points even more forcefully. He was raised as a Christian but turned against the new faith. When he became emperor, he tried to undo the measures his uncle Constantine had set in motion and rescue classical society. He even planned to rebuild Jerusalem's temple so that the Judaean *ethnos* could practise their traditions fully – and the Christian claim to have superseded them would crumble (*C. Gal.* 351d, 324c–d).[13] Julian relished the diversity of *ethnē* (*C. Gal.* 116a–141d) and found no place for Christians. They must either return to their native Greek laws or, having chosen to follow a Judaean, follow Judaean laws (*C. Gal.* 42e–43b, 305d). Julian could not understand life outside an

---

11. Julian, *C. Gal.* 116a–b, 131b–d, 168b–c, 171a, d–e, 176a–c, 184b–c, 198b.
12. Fragments of Porphyry are in Harnack (1916; cf. Hoffmann 1994).
13. I follow the Loeb numbering in Wright (1923: 3.319–428).

ethnos. Christians had concocted a strange brew, he thought, of the worst aspects of Judaean and Greek societies, while missing the crucial need for *ethnos* affiliation (209d, 238a–b, 253a–291a).

Conclusions

Whereas we usually regard Judaism and Christianity as two species of the same genus, religion, historical thinking creates problems for this scheme. Being members of a famous *ethnos* with a homeland, laws, and temple, as the Jews were in the Graeco-Roman period, was a different thing – indeed opposite – from abandoning one's *ethnos-polis* traditions to join a saviour-based fellowship or club. This is not to deny points of intersection or partial similarity. But belonging to an ancestral *ethnos* and joining new "brothers and sisters" in worshipping Christus and awaiting his return were basically different kinds of experience, not a matter of belonging to one of "two religions".

About the Author

Steve Mason (BA, MA McMaster; PhD University of St Michael's College, Toronto) is professor emeritus of ancient Mediterranean religions and cultures at the University of Groningen. He edits the international series Flavius Josephus: Translation and Commentary (Brill, 2000–), to which he has also contributed *Life of Josephus* (2001) and *Judean War 2* (2008); he is now working on *Judean War 4*. His first monograph was *Flavius Josephus on the Pharisees* (Brill, 1991); most recent are *A History of the Jewish War, A.D. 66–74* (Cambridge University Press, 2016) and *Orientation to the History of Roman Judaea* (Wipf & Stock, 2016).

References

Arnaoutoglou, Ilias N. 2002. "Roman Law and *Collegia* in Asia Minor." *Revue internationale des droits l'antiquité* 49: 27–44.

Arnaoutoglou, Ilias N. 2005. "*Collegia* in the Province of Egypt in the First Century CE." *Ancient Society* 35: 197–216. https://doi.org/10.2143/AS.35.0.2003849

Ascough, Richard S., Philip A. Harland, and John S. Kloppenborg. 2012. *Associations in the Greco-Roman World: A Sourcebook*. Waco, TX: Baylor University Press.

Avni, Gideon, Zvi Greenhut, and Tal Ilan. 1994. "Three new Burial Caves of the Second Temple Period in Aceldama (Kidron Valley)." In *Ancient Jerusalem*

Revealed, edited by Hillel Geva, pp. 206–218. Jerusalem: Israel Exploration Society.

Barton, Carlin A. and Daniel Boyarin. 2016. *Imagine No Religion: How Modern Abstractions Hide Ancient Realities*. New York: Fordham University Press. https://doi.org/10.1515/9780823271221

Baumgarten, Albert I. (ed.). 2002. *Sacrifice in Religious Experience*. Leiden: Brill. https://doi.org/10.1163/9789004379169

Beiser, Frederick. 2011. *The German Historicist Tradition*. Oxford: Oxford University Press. https://doi.org/10.1093/acprof:oso/9780199691555.001.0001

Boyarin, Daniel. 2004. *Border Lines: The Partition of Judaeo-Christianity*. Philadelphia, PA: University of Pennsylvania Press. https://doi.org/10.9783/9780812203844

Buckle, Henry T. 1857. *History of Civilization in England*. 3 vols. London: Henry Frowde. https://doi.org/10.2307/25527645

Burkert, Walter. 1985. *Greek Religion*, translated by J. Raffan. Cambridge, MA: Harvard University Press.

Carlyle, Thomas. 1900–1901. *Critical and Miscellaneous Essays* (5 vols). New York: Scribner.

Cohen, S. J. D. 1999. *The Beginnings of Jewishness: Boundaries, Varieties, Uncertainties*. Berkeley, CA: University of California Press.

Comte, Auguste. 1830–1842. *Cours de Philosophie Positive* (6 vols). Paris: Bachelier.

Comte, Auguste. 1896. Th*e Positive Philosophy of Auguste Comte* (3 vols), translated and condensed by Harriet Martineau. London: Bell & Sons.

Dindorf[ius], Ludwig [Ludovicus]. 1870–1871. *Historici Graeci Minores* (2 vols). Leipzig: Teubner.

Droysen, Johann G. 1893. *Outline of the Principles of History*, translated by E. B. Andrews. Boston: Ginn & Company.

Finn, Thomas M. 1997. *From Death to Rebirth: Ritual and Conversion in Antiquity*. Mahwah: Paulist.

Fung, Yu-Lan. 1948. *A Short History of Chinese Philosophy*, edited and translated by Derk Bodde. New York: Macmillan.

Harland, Philip A. 2003. *Associations, Synagogues, and Congregations: Claiming a Place in Ancient Mediterranean Society*. Minneapolis, MN: Fortress Press.

Harnack, Adolf von. 1916. *Porphyrius: Gegen die Christen*. Berlin: Reimer.

Hoffmann, Richard J. 1994. *Porphyry's Against the Christians: The Literary Remains*. New York: Prometheus.

Johnston, Sarah Iles (ed.). 2004. *Religions of the Ancient World: A Guide*. Cambridge, MA: Harvard University Press. https://doi.org/10.2307/j.ctv1n3x1dt

Jones, Christopher P. 1996. "ἔθνος and γένος in Herodotus." *Classical Quarterly* 46: 315–320. https://doi.org/10.1093/cq/46.2.315

Josephson, Jason A. 2012. *The Invention of Religion in Japan*. Chicago, IL: University of Chicago Press.

Kaizer, Ted. 2008. *The Variety of Local Religious Life in the Near East in the Hellenistic and Roman Periods*. Leiden: Brill. https://doi.org/10.1163/ej.9789004167353.i-396

Kloppenborg, John S., Richard S. Ascough and Philip A. Harland. 2011. *Greco-Roman Associations: Texts, Translations, and Commentary*. Berlin: De Gruyter.

Kloppenborg, John S. and Stephen G. Wilson (eds). 1996. *Voluntary Associations in the Graeco-Roman World*. London: Routledge.

Knust, Jennifer Wright and Zsuzsanna Varhelyi (eds). 2011. *Ancient Mediterranean Sacrifice*. Oxford: Oxford University Press. https://doi.org/10.1093/acprof:oso/9780199738960.001.0001

Macmullen, Ramsay. 1966. *Enemies of the Roman Order. Treason, Unrest, and Alienation in the Empire*. London: Routledge. https://doi.org/10.4159/harvard.9780674864962

Marcus, Jacob R. and Marc Saperstein. 2015. *The Jews in Christian Europe: A Source Book, 315-1791*. Pittsburgh, PA: Hebrew Union College Press; University of Pittsburgh Press. https://doi.org/10.2307/j.ctt1f89t1n

Mason, Steve. 2007. "Jews, Judaeans, Judaizing, Judaism: Problems of Categorization in Ancient History." *Journal for the Study of Judaism* 38: 457–512. https://doi.org/10.1163/156851507X193108

Mason, Steve. 2016a. *A History of the Jewish War, AD 66-74*. New York: Cambridge University Press. https://doi.org/10.1017/CBO9781139020718

Mason, Steve. 2016b. *Orientation to the History of Roman Judaea*. Eugene, OR: Wipf & Stock.

Masuzawa, Tomoko. 2005. *The Invention of World Religions, or, How European Universalism Was Preserved in the Language of Pluralism*. Chicago, IL: University of Chicago Press. https://doi.org/10.7208/chicago/9780226922621.001.0001

Matthews, Shelly. 2001. *First Converts: Rich Pagan Women and the Rhetoric of Mission in Early Judaism and Christianity*. Stanford, CA: Stanford University Press.

Naiden, F.S. 2013. *Smoke Signals for the Gods: Ancient Greek Sacrifice from the Archaic through Roman Periods*. Oxford: Oxford University Press. https://doi.org/10.1093/acprof:oso/9780199916405.001.0001

Nock, Arthur Darby. 1933. *Conversion: The Old and the New in in Religion from Alexander the Great to Augustine.* London: Oxford University Press.

Nongbri, Brent. 2013. *Before Religion: A History of a Modern Concept.* New Haven, CT: Yale University Press.
https://doi.org/10.12987/yale/9780300154160.001.0001

Parker, Robert. 1983. *Miasma: Pollution and Purification in Early Greek Religion.* Oxford: Clarendon.

Parkes, James. 1934. *The Conflict of the Church and the Synagogue: A Study in the Origins of Antisemitism.* Philadelphia, PA: Jewish Publication Society of America.

Ranke, Leopold von. 2011 [texts from the nineteenth century]. *The Theory and Practice of History*, edited by Georg G. Iggers. London: Routledge.

Rives, James. 2007. *Religion in the Roman Empire.* Oxford: Blackwell.

Ruether, Rosemary R. 1974. *Faith and Fratricide: The Theological Roots of Anti-Semitism.* New York: Seabury.

Samuel, Alan E. 1972. *Greek and Roman Chronology: Calendars and Years in Classical Antiquity.* Munich: Beck.

Sanders, E.P. 1977. *Paul and Palestinian Judaism: A Comparison of Patterns of Religion.* London: SCM.

Schäfer, Peter. 2012. *The Jewish Jesus: How Judaism and Christianity Shaped Each Other.* Princeton, NJ: Princeton University Press.
https://doi.org/10.23943/princeton/9780691153902.001.0001

Scheid, John. 2003. *An Introduction to Roman Religion*, translated by Janet Lloyd. Bloomington, IN: Indiana University Press.

Schwartz, Daniel R. 2005. "Herodians and *Ioudaioi* in Flavian Rome." In *Flavius Josephus and Flavian Rome*, edited by Jonathan Edmondson, Steve Mason and James Rives, pp. 63–78. Oxford: Oxford University Press.
https://doi.org/10.1093/acprof:oso/9780199262120.003.0004

Segal, Alan F. 1986. *Rebecca's Children: Judaism and Christianity in the Roman World.* Cambridge, MA: Harvard University Press.

Smith, Jonathan Z. 1998. "Religion, Religions, Religious." In *Critical Terms for Religious Studies*, edited by M.C. Taylor, pp. 269–284. Chicago, IL: University of Chicago Press.

Smith, R.R.R. 1988. "*Simulacrum Gentium*: The *Ethne* from the Sebasteion at Aphrodisias." *Journal of Roman Studies* 78: 50–77.
https://doi.org/10.2307/301450

Smith, Wilfred Cantwell. 1963. *The Meaning and End of Religion: A New Approach to the Religious Traditions of Mankind.* New York: Macmillan.

Stern, Menahem. 1974. *Greek and Latin Authors on Jews and Judaism* (3 vols). Jerusalem: Israel Academy of Sciences.

Wilken, Robert L. 2003. *The Christians as the Romans saw Them*, 2nd edition. New Haven, CT: Yale University Press.

Wright, Wilmer Cave (ed.). 1923. *The Works of the Emperor Julian* (3 vols). London: W. Heinemann.

– 6 –

Ancient Religious Texts and Intertextuality
Plato's and Plutarch's Myths of the Afterlife

LAUTARO ROIG LANZILLOTTA

Introduction

Up to not so long ago texts were approached with rather rigid traditional literary methods in which author, text, and reader were envisaged in a fixed and unidirectional chronological sequence. In their quest for meaning readers were constrained by the notions of originality, uniqueness, singularity and autonomy of both author and text. A good example of this approach is the historical method applied to the study of ancient religious texts, the primary goal of which is to try to understand as closely as possible the author's original meaning and their intended audience or readership (DeConick 2016: 383).

Intertextuality challenges traditional notions of writing, text and reading. Based on a new vision of meaning, it rejects the idea that the production of meaning is unidirectional, stemming from the author who instils into the text and reaching the reader as its final decoder. In fact, in the intertextual approach the interest moves away from the author, who is to a certain extent dispensable, in order to focus preferably on the reader. Not only is the author dispensable (Barthes 1968); also the notions of uniqueness and originality of texts are questionable. Appealing to the etymological sense of the term "text" as "a tissue, a woven fabric" (Barthes 1977: 159), intertextuality claims that a text does not exist in isolation, but is rather at the same time result of previous

---

Keywords: intertextuality, Plutarch of Chaeronea, Plato, Gerard Génette

texts and beginning of future ones, the so-called *intertext*.¹ In the words of a well-known scholar, "it is not true that works are created by their authors. Works are created by works, texts are created by texts, all together they speak to each other independently of the intention of their authors" (Eco 1986: 199).

Intertextuality

The origins of Intertextuality go back to the twentieth century and more specifically to the studies of the Swiss linguist Ferdinand de Saussure (1857–1913) and the Russian philosopher and literary critic Michail M. Bakhtin (1895–1975). While the former established the relational nature of meaning and thus of texts by pointing to the systematic features of language, the latter introduced the notion of dialogic works of literature, namely texts that are in a continuous dialogue with other texts.² This dialogue is not unidirectional and extends both into the past and into the future: modern texts may in fact affect and alter the meaning of past ones in the same way that works from the past affect modern ones.³

The term intertextuality,⁴ however, was first coined by Julia Kristeva (1967) in an article on Bakhtin, in which, combining Saussurean and Bakhtinian theories of language and literature, she provided the first

---

1. Plett (1991: 5): "A *text* may be regarded as an autonomous sign structure, delimited and coherent. Its boundaries are indicated by its beginning, middle and end, its coherence by the deliberately interrelated conjunction of its constituents. An *intertext*, on the other hand, is characterized by attributes that exceed it. It is not delimited, but de-limited, for its constituents refer to constituents of one or several other texts. Therefore it has a twofold coherence: an intratextual one which guarantees the immanent integrity of the text, and an intertextual one which creates structural relations between itself and other texts. This twofold coherence makes for the richness and complexity of the intertext, but also for its problematical status."
2. Kristeva (1980: 68): "Bakhtinian dialogism identifies writing as both subjectivity and communication, or better, as intertextuality. Confronted with this dialogism, the notion of a 'person-subject of writing' becomes blurred, yielding to that of 'ambivalence of writing'."
3. Allen (2000: 211): "Dialogic refers to the idea that all utterances respond to previous utterances and are always addressed to other potential speakers, rather than occurring independently or in isolation. Language always occurs in specific social situations between specific human agents. Words always contain a dialogic quality, embodying a dialogue between different meanings and applications. Bakhtin's dialogism undermines any argument for final and unquestionable positions, since every position within language is a space of dialogic forces rather than monologic truth."
4. Kristeva (1980: 15): the French term *intertextualité* "was originally introduced by Kristeva and met with immediate success; it has since been much used and abused

articulation of intertextual theory. The interconnectedness and interdependence of modern life makes the intertextual method especially appealing today due to the central place allotted in it to the notion of relationality. This relationality may be viewed from different perspectives such as semasiology (or analysis of the sign), semiotics (the relation between signs, texts and the cultural context), literary theory (relation between texts and the literary system), and reception studies (the transformative relation between text A and text B) (Allen 2000: 6).[5]

Intertextuality knows two rather different approaches (Plett 1991: 3-4). On the one hand, progressives (post-structuralists, deconstructionists, modernists) such as Kristeva, Barthes, or Derrida see intertexuality as a way to disrupt notions of meaning, claiming the triumph of plurality and the freedom of the reader in order to proclaim the "death of the author" (Barthes 1968). On the other hand, traditionalists (genre, translation, and media structuralist theorists) such as Genette and Riffaterre attempt rather to create and stabilize meaning (Morgan 1985: 9). They retain "a belief in criticism's ability to locate, describe and thus stabilize a text's significance, even if that significance concerns an intertextual relation between a text and other texts" (Allen 2000: 97).

The Goal of Intertextuality

It should be clear by now that the goal of intertextuality is not the study of the sources of a given text or writer. From this latter, rather rigid perspective, research stops once an author's sources have been assessed. Once a link between two texts has been firmly established, or the presence of text A in text B has been identified the scope of the investigation has been fulfilled. Admittedly, such a study could also be amplified in order to determine When, How, and Why text A was used by B; and

---

on both sides of the Atlantic. The concept, however, has been generally misunderstood. It has nothing to do with matters of influence by one writer upon another, or with the sources of a literary work; it does, on the other hand, involve the components of a textual system such as the novel, for instance, is defined in *La Revolution du langage poetique* as the transposition of one or more systems of signs into another, accompanied by a new articulation of the enunciative and denotative position. Any signifying practice is a field (in the sense of space traversed by lines of force) in which various signifying systems undergo such a transposition."

5. Allen (2000: 221): "intertextual processes have nothing to do with traditional notions concerning 'influence'. Far from an author-to-author transmission of ideas and styles, Kristeva argues that intertextuality, or what she renames transposition, concerns the way in which one 'sign system' is incorporated into another 'sign system' and the semiotic changes this transposition entails."

perhaps it may also raise the question as to whether and if so to what extent text B deviates from text A. However, the main point of interest in such an analysis is always the source, in a quest for the original, for the model that helped a given writer to shape his or her thought and work. Terms such as eclecticism or syncretism (of sources) are frequent in such studies and properly reflect the exclusive concern with the sources I am referring to (Donini 1988).

The intertextual perspective, differently, does not establish a hierarchical relationship between Hypo and Hypertext; nor does it necessarily pay more attention to the source than to the target text. Rather it considers both texts A and B as equally important and interesting, seeing them more as conversation partners that create meaning by the very exchange they establish with one another. The point is that, as Gerald Prince states, "any text is a hypertext, grafting itself onto a hypotext, an earlier text that it imitates or transforms; any writing is rewriting; and literature is always in the second degree. Now though all literary texts are hypertextual, some are more hypertextual than others, more massively and explicitly palimpsestuous" (Genette 1997a: IX). If one can agree with Jorge Luis Borges (1971) when he writes that "writing is the act of re-reading previous texts", or that the history of literature ponders the "the diverse intonation of a few metaphors" (Borges 1964), then it seems logical to assume that the goal of intertextuality will be the analysis of these diverse intonations resulting from this rereading or rewriting previous texts. In this sense, more important than linking two texts is determining the kind of relationship mediating between them. Intertextuality, consequently, is mainly interested in understanding the continuous process of rereading and rewriting texts in order to create new meanings, or to adjust old ones to their new, always changing contexts.

The Method: Gérard Genette's Approach to Intertextuality

From the two intertextual factions sketched above, progressive and traditionalist, I will be focusing on the second one, since by applying the intertextual method my intention is not deconstructing either authorship, writing or reading, but rather assessing textual transformations in ancient religious and philosophical texts. I will use Genette's methodology, as developed in his trilogy *The Architext* (1992), *Palimpsests* (1997a) and *Paratexts* (1997b), a trilogy in which, according to Allen "Genette pushes the practice of structuralist poetics into an arena which can be termed intertextual. In so doing, Genette not only makes major revisions in the practice of poetics, he also produces a coherent theory and map of what he terms "transtextuality'" (Allen 2000: 98). Based on a thorough analysis of the transformation of texts in the bulk of Western literature, Genette thinks it is possible to determine how, why and to what end texts transform. By applying Genette's method to the analysis of Plato's and Plutarch's myths, my intention will be both to assess Plutarch's textual transformations and to show how they generate new meanings more suited to the expectations of authors and readers of the first centuries CE. At the same time, this brief analysis will illuminate how ancients understood literature, tradition, and innovation, and a whole set of closely related issues such as authorship, text, reading, model, quotation, and imitation.

Let us now pay attention to the five modes of transtextuality as distinguished by Gérard Genette.[6] In his terminology what we all call intertextuality is called hypertextuality; "Intertextuality " in Genette's terminology rather concerns the use of quotations, allusions or plagiarism in a text; while "Paratextuality" deals with all those issues that, even if closely related to the text, are not strictly speaking the text, namely title, subtitle, notes, and so on. "Metatextuality" in turn describes the commentaries on a given text; and "Architextuality" the modes of discourse, of enunciation and the literary genre (Genette 1997a: 1-7). These "various forms of transtextuality are indeed aspects of any textuality, but they are also potentially, and to varying degrees, textual categories" (ibid.: 8).

"Hypertextuality", consequently, is the subcategory that deals with the appearance and transformations of a given text A, or hypotext, in another text B, or hypertext.[7] Besides the transformations in which the hypotext is transformed by means of imitation (satirical or not), most of Western literature transforms the texts by other means, the so-called *transposition* (ibid.: 24-30).

---

6. According to Genette (1997a: 1), transtextuality is "the textual transcendence of the text, which I have already defined roughly as 'all that sets the text in a relationship, whether obvious or concealed, with other texts'".
7. Genette (1997a: 5): "By hypertextuality I mean any relationship uniting a text B (which I shall call the hypertext) to an earlier text A (I shall, of course, call it the hypotext), upon which it is grafted in a manner that is not that of commentary."

Plutarch of Chaeronea's Hypertextual Strategies and His Transformation of Plato's Myths

Plutarch of Chaeronea (46–120) is an important writer for our knowledge of the ancient philosophical and religious world. On the one hand, his works are enormously relevant to the history of ancient philosophy, since they allow us to understand the development of Platonism in the first centuries of the era, but also provide crucial information on the Presocratics, the Cyrenaeans, the Stoa and Epicureanism. On the other hand, Plutarch is an important aid for the assessment of ancient religiosity, since his writings illuminate numerous general and particular religious issues (Roig Lanzillotta 2012: 2–13; 13–21).

However, Plutarch is especially significant for our understanding of the way Plato (424–348) was read in the first centuries CE. Always oscillating between tradition and innovation, in his close and complex relationship to Plato, Plutarch of Chaeronea appears to have applied the five categories of transtextuality distinguished by Genette. Intertextually, Plutarch often quotes from and alludes to Plato's texts;[8] Paratextually he many a time comments and adds notes to the masters' works; Metatextually he wrote commentaries, such as *On the Generation of the Soul in the Timaeus*;[9] and Architextually he toyed and experimented with the nature and function of different modes of discourse used by Plato. In this chapter, however, I am interested in his hypertextual relationship to Plato and intend to apply Genette's method to the study of Plutarch's myths of the afterlife included in three works by Plutarch, *On the Sign of Socrates*, *On the Delays of the Divine Vengeance* and *Concerning the Face Which Appears in the Orb of the Moon*. In this analysis my goal is not to unveil their dependence on Plato's model but rather to show how Plutarch's intertextual strategies in adapting and reworking of Plato's myths allow him to create artifacts more suited to his and his audience's philosophical and religious needs. The comparison between Plutarch's source and his creative transformation thereof in his *Moralia* will provide I hope a nice example of *transposition* according to Gérard Genette's terminology.[10] Given the space allotted I won't be able to provide here a full analysis of all three

---

8. See, for example, Plutarch, *On Isis and Osiris* 361 in reference to Plato, *Laws* 717A.
9. See also Plutarch's *Platonicae Quaestiones*.
10. Genette (1997: 198): "Now the thematically unfaithful continuation extends beyond the category of serious imitation to that of transposition, actually a very marked, at times very aggressive, variant of transposition (i.e. thematic correction, or even refutation). I shall not go into a full discussion of that practice here, but it stands to reason that one can just as easily reverse the significance of a text by giving it a sequel that refutes it as by modifying its setting, its tone, or its plot."

myths. I hope, however, to preliminarily convince the readership by delving into one case study, Timarchus's myth in *On the Sign of Socrates*, and leaving the analysis of the other two cases for future studies.

Plutarch's Imitation of Plato's Myth of Er

The Myth of Er is perhaps one of Plato's most famous literary creations and has had a huge impact on later religious and philosophical thought. It is included in the tenth book of Plato's *Republic* (614–621), where Socrates introduces it as an example of the results of justice and injustice. We have incisive and deep-going analyses by Richardson (1926), Annas (1982), Thayer (1988) and Ferrari (2009) just to mention but a few. The myth tells the story of Er, a man who apparently died on a battlefield but returned to life nine days later. In his account of the world hereafter, Er describes the cosmos, the rewards of the just in heaven and the punishment of the wicked in the underworld. He also describes how souls are reborn into a new body and a new life, and how the type of life souls choose depends on the rewards and punishments received after death.

Despite some attempts to downplay the influence of Plato's Myth of Er on Plutarch's use of myths, by pointing to other dialogues by Plato or to various (mostly Oriental) influences, my intention is to uncover how the Myth of Er reverberates in Plutarch's myths in *On the Sign*, *On the Delays* and *Concerning the Face*. To begin with, in all three Plutarchan writings different individuals also narrate stories disclosing important features of the cosmos and afterlife. In two of them, the protagonists even undergo similar near-to-death experiences as that of Er, in which they receive their special knowledge about the Beyond. In *On the Sign* Timarchus enters the cave of the Oracle of Trophonius (Hamilton 1934b; Hani 1975) and after a blow on his head, the sutures of his skull get open and release the soul. This is the beginning of his vision in the afterlife, in which he gets to know about the destiny of the soul after death and the influence of *daimons* on human life (590B–592F; Verniere 1977). Similarly, *On the Delays* describes the experience of Thespesius; whose consciousness gets out of his body after falling on his neck. This marks the beginning of his travel in the hereafter (563E–568A), since differently than Timarchus, who does not seem to change his location (Deuse 2010), Thespesius's soul is said to move quickly and easily in every direction (563F). Guided by a relative, he visits diverse locations of the Beyond, such as the abyss of Lethe or "Oblivion" and the Mixing Bowl of Dreams, before seeing the terrible punishments of the wicked (Pérez Jiménez 2001). Only in *Concerning the Face* the myth is not result of accidental alterations of the individual's consciousness, but rather of the Stranger's initiation into the mysteries of Cronos by his servitors (942C). The contents of the myths, however, are rather similar (Hamilton 1934a; Teodorsson 2010).

The proximity between Plato's and Plutarch's myths is obvious and can be seen on the basis of their equivalent function, literary form, composition and contents. To begin with from a functional perspective Plato's and Plutarch's myths seem to serve similar purposes. Lévi-Strauss argued that the function of myths in traditional societies was to fill the gap between ideal and real worlds. Given that humans build by means of language the ideal world in which they live, Lévi-Strauss affirms, contradictions arising when we face a world made of matter and not of ideas are softened by the use of myths (Lévi-Strauss 1967). By playfully combining elements from both worlds myths do not solve the contradictions, but building a bridge between both realities make them bearable. Plato's and Plutarch's mythical creations or recreations, differently, intend to fill no gap: in both cases their myths rather dispose of the tangible world altogether, prolonging the ideal one with the creation of a parallel reality that better suits their ideal views of justice, theodicy, cosmology, anthropology and ethics. In both cases, rather than bridging both worlds, myths are intended to lend support, reinforcing it, their ideal view of reality (Roig Lanzillotta forthcoming).

From a literary perspective, also, the points of contact seem to be too many not to admit literary dependence. In two of the three cases under scrutiny, Plutarch's myths occupy in his works exactly the same position as the Myth of Er does in the *Republic*. Placed at the end of the writing, the myths provide a sound closure to the previous philosophical enquiry. Whether appropriate or not from a conceptual or argumentative angle, the fact is that the myths put a halt to the dialogue, condensing in their narratives the problems, questions and tensions of the previous discussion. The exemplary function of the mythical story allows the reader to wrap up the argument without the need of reaching a rational answer to all the queries raised by the interlocutors. If the previous case shows a functional parallelism in Plutarch's conception of myth, Genette would describe the current one as *stylistic imitation*, which indicates that we are dealing with "serious imitation" or *forgery*, as opposed to satirical imitation of *caricature* (French, *charge*).[11]

And, of course, this already points to a similar conception of myth as a means of conveying philosophical messages, albeit in a different mode of argumentation. *Mythos* in Plutarch is also used and presented as

---

11. Genette (1997: 85): "forgery is an imitation in a serious mode whose dominant function is the pursuit or the extension of a pre-existing literary achievement".

complementary mode of restating previous points, of summarizing what has been said by means of *logos*.¹² In the same way that the Myth of Er in the *Republic* closes ten books of rational argument on the superiority of justice, Plutarch's myths wrap up the previous rational arguments of *On the Sign*, *On the Delays* and *Concerning the Face*. The position at the end of the treatises shows that myths are intended to be accepted at face value and not for discussion. In the only case that the myth does not appear at the end of the treatise, *On the Sign*, Plutarch notably lets one of the interlocutors claim that Timarchus's story should be considered "as sacred and not to be profaned, [and] should be dedicated to the god" (593A), which seems to imply that it should not be interpreted or further discussed upon, but simply accepted as it is.

Plato's influence on Plutarch can also be seen from a compositional perspective. Interestingly, none of the stories included by Plutarch are told in direct speech. Myths in all three treatises are always presented as stories of a third person and are therefore characterized by *oratio obliqua*, as is also the case in the Myth of Er. From a rhetorical perspective, of course, this strategy lends persuasiveness to the story, since it is not an argument by the interlocutor, but a story by a more credible legendary figure: together with Er the Pamphylian, the protagonist of Plato's myth, Timarchus in *On the Sign*, Thespesius in *On the Delays* and the Stranger in *Concerning the Face* also belong so to say to the "mythical" past of their stories. It is precisely the attribution of the tale to a third person that shows that Plutarch depends for his myths on Plato's Myth of Er and not on another myth of the afterlife in Plato, all of them told by Socrates in direct speech. Once again, serious imitation or *continuation* according to Genette can be seen in the use of the same stylistic instrument (Genette 1997a: 111).¹³

But it is from the point of view of contents that Plutarch's dependence on Plato's myth is most visible. As already *Apology* (40C–41C) and *Phraedrus* (249A–C) in a short fashion or the lengthier versions in *Gorgias* (523A–527A) or *Phaedo* (107D–114E) do, the Myth of Er in the *Republic* (614B–621D) displays in front of the reader a view of the afterlife that we

---

12. On the binary *mythos/logos* in Greek thought, see Gerard Naddaf in Brisson et al. (1998: vii–liii).
13. Genette (1997a: 162): "Continuation is not like other imitations, since it must abide by a certain number of additional constraints: first, naturally – given that any satirical caricature is prohibited – imitation here must be absolutely faithful and serious, which rarely happens in usual pastiche. But above all, the hypertext must constantly remain continuous with its hypotext, which it must merely bring to its prescribed or appropriate conclusion while observing the congruity of places, chronological sequence, character consistency, etc."

also find in the three myths included in Plutarch's works. The destiny of the souls after death, their whereabouts before and after judgment, their punishment and reward are located in a very developed eschatological landscape, the description of which spares no efforts in the construction of such lively literary creation that arguably explains its huge impact on later literature: Cicero, Plutarch, the Chaldean Oracles, the Corpus Hermeticum, Nag Hammadi library, Macrobius, just to name a few, all build on Plato's model. With Genette, we can class all these cases as *homodiegetic*, in so far as they retake the same mythological subject (Genette 1997a: 296–299).[14] As we will see in the next subsection, however, Plutarch's hypertextual relationship to the Myth of Er is visible not only in his *pragmatic continuation* of Plato, but especially in his textual transformation of his model.

Plutarch's Rereading and Transformation of the Myth of Er

Being the most developed of all his versions of the afterlife, Plato's Myth of Er combines many of the elements scattered through Plato's works. Accordingly, it can be divided into three large sections covering diverse aspects of the afterlife. The first section (614C–616A) develops the theme touched upon by Plato in many different dialogues and central to his view of justice: theodicy and immortality of the soul. The second section (616B–617C) provides a sound cosmological framework to these views, describing the places of judgment, punishment and reward, and giving them a location in the cosmic whole. The third section (617D–621B), finally, retakes the ideas developed in the first part, since the notions of reward and punishment are intrinsically connected to personal choice in the way of life and subsequently to the theme of reincarnation. It is my contention that Plutarch's myths in the *On the Sign*, *On the Delays*, and *Concerning the Face* are conceived to develop, respectively, one of the sections of Plato's Myth of Er.

This is not to say to they are exclusively devoted to one of these themes. In the same way as the Myth of Er, Plutarch's myths are conceived as integral overviews of the afterlife. In the specific framework of the particular texts all three myths include references to eschatological judgment, its cosmological setting, and to anthropological aspects related to ethics and eschatology. Significantly, however, each of Plutarch's myths does seem gravitate around a main theme. In what

---

14. Genette (1997a: 296): "Whatever the mode of its functioning, a transformation may or may not touch upon the diegetic framework of a text. We must therefore distinguish between **homodiegetic and heterodiegetic** transformations."

regards *On the Delays*, it is undeniable that Plato's first subject, theodicy, is its main concern: Punishment and reward, being instrumental to the fulfilment of divine justice, receive the main focus. As far as *On the Sign* is concerned, even if apparently focused on Socrates's sign (590A), beside some rudiments of anthropology and daimonology, cosmology is arguably the main subject of the revelation granted to Timarchus (below). When we come to *Concerning the Face* things look similar, since cosmology, anthropology and ethics seem to serve the central theme: the eschatology of the human being after the first and (eventually) the second death, together with reincarnation, daemonology and so on. If my analysis is correct, Plutarch's three hypertexts transform their models by means of *excision* and *transfocalization* to such an extent that with Genette we need to assess the *transmotivation* in the hypertext (Genette 1997a: 287). With an eye at space allotted, a couple of examples from Timarchus's myth in *On the Sign* will suffice to highlight these changes.

Despite the fact that Plutarch, as stated, is loyal to his model's use of indirect speech, the beginning of the myth already shows the first transformation, since the story is told by a different person. This *transvocalization* not only means an alteration in the narrative voice (Genette 1997a: 289), however.[15] More importantly, it also introduces a change in the circumstances of the protagonist, since Timarchus's vision is no more due to an accidental catalepsy resulting from a blow in battle, but rather from a voluntary action: As a matter of fact, the *transmotivation* I was referring to before has to do with the fact that the vision loses its casual nature and is presented as the result of initiation (*On the Sign* 590A).[16]

---

15. Genette (1997a: 289): "In both cases, then, we have something more than transfocalization; we have a shift in the narrative voice (from Ulysses to Elpenor, from Des Grieux to the anonymous narrator)-i.e. a transvocalization. Transvocalization is, among other things, one of the means or one of the prerequisites of transfocalization; Tiberge's viewpoint could not very well be adopted if Des Grieux were to be left in charge of the narrative. But that is no reason for confusing the two notions."
16. See Plutarch, *On the Sign* 590A, where Timarchus is presented as "a high-spirited young initiate in philosophy". On transmotivation, see Genette (1997a: 324): "The substitution of a motive, or transmotivation, is one of the major procedures of semantic transformation. Like others that have been previously discussed, it can take three aspects, the third being merely the combination of the first two. The first is positive; it consists of introducing a motive where the hypotext offered, or at least stated, none. This is motivation in its simplest state, and we have seen it operate in amplification: e.g., in Joseph in Egypt, the volume in Joseph and His Brothers which Thomas Mann said was an answer to the question "why?" (why does Mrs Potiphar provoke Joseph, and why does Joseph turn her down?). The second aspect is purely negative; it consists in suppressing or eliding an original

As was to be expected in this context, we find *elliptic continuation* by means of expansion: Plato's succinct introduction of Er's account "when his soul went from his body"[17] is replaced by the long description of the transformation Timarchus's soul experiences. Addition and correction are also at play, since *On the Sign*'s account of the "soul becoming bigger and billowing out like a sail" (590C) allows the reader to assume that revelation in the context of the initiation involves no intellect, as was the case of Er. The description of Timarchus's experience in terms of seeing and hearing reinforces this assumption: the combination of both senses seems to point to the soul's participation in sensual perception highlighting the sensorial nature of this revelation. Once he is granted the hearing and seeing of what he experiences, a voice (whose speaker, Timarchus, is never able to see) also interprets what he sees and hears, which emphasizes both the passivity of the protagonist and his role as spectator in the revelation (Roig Lanzillotta 2020).

But the *transmotivation* at work in *On the Sign* necessarily implies a wider expansion of the model, by means of the so-called *narrativization* that materializes in a *transmodalization* of the text.[18] The following pages further enrich, correcting it, Plato's model, launching us by means of Timarchus's quasi-psychedelic vision into the cosmological re-elaboration of the Myth of Er, its most important restructuration being the transposition of Hades to the celestial region (Verniere 1977: 163–194). As a matter of fact, almost three full Loeb-pages of Greek text revisiting Plato's cosmological model pass by before we first hear the voice addressing Timarchus, whose cosmological teaching still fills another two pages before delving into a rudiment of *daemonology*, the seeming goal of the revelation: the position of the Styx, the Four Principles of all things, the order and function of Fates, and the role of the Moon are all one by one reinterpreted.

---

motivation. This is demotivation, such as we have glimpsed in Herodias, where the innocent reader no longer quite understands why Salome is demanding Jokanaan's head. The third operates by way of a wholesale substitution – i.e. by a double process of demotivation and (re)motivation (by a new motive): "demotivation + remotivation = transmotivation."

17. Plato, *Republic* 614C: "Ἔφη δέ, ἐπειδὴ οὗ ἐκβῆναι, τὴν ψυχὴν πορεύεσθαι μετὰ πολλῶν."
18. Genette (1997: 277): "I designate as transmodalization, less ambitiously, a transformation bearing on what has been termed, since Plato and Aristotle, the mode of presentation of a work of fiction, which can be *narrative* or *dramatic*. Modal transformation can, on the face of it, be one of two sorts: *intermodal* (involving a shift from one mode to another) or *intramodal* (involving changes within the internal functioning of the mode)."

Similar hypertextual changes can also be found in the focalized myths of *On the Delays* and *Concerning the Face*, which develop the other two sections of the Myth of Er, with which I will deal perhaps in future studies.

Concluding Remarks

In his relationship vis-à-vis Plato, Plutarch at the same imitates (*continues* in Genette's terminology) and transforms (*transposes*) his Platonic model. By imitating and developing Plato's conception of myths, literary function, compositional technique and contents, Plutarch creates a stable Platonic context in which he positions himself firmly within Platonic philosophical and literary tradition. Once so far, reinterpretation, development, and correction of Plato's model, however, indicate that his intention is not to slavishly repeat Plato's views and conceptions. His creative re-elaboration rather shows that reinterpretation and adaption of Plato's eschatological model was one of the core goals of his texts.

An intertextual approach to *On the Sign*, *On the Delays* and *Concerning the Face* and their comparison with the *Republic* show not only that Plutarch transforms his source. The analysis of his hypertextual strategies also allows us to understand the intention and goal of these changes. By excising and transfocalizing his model in his three treatises, Plutarch not only focuses on one of the sections of the Myth of Er at the time; he is also able to expand, correct or complement, adapting Plato's views to the new cultural context in which he lived. In Plutarch's time we are far removed from the idealized context of the *polis* in which Socrates dialogued with Glauco. On the one hand, the pressing cultural context and the interschool polemics demand a more specific conception of the human being, one which moreover squares with a consistent cosmological framework. On the other, the more demanding ethics of the time required a credible theodicy, one which also rhymes with the widespread eschatological patterns of ascent and descent. By revisiting Plato's precedent, in my view, Plutarch's three myths in *On the Sign*, *On the Delays* and *Concerning the Face* were intended as complementary chapters in a new eschatological discourse that consciously facelifted Plato's views, adapting them to the new spirit of the times.

About the Author

Lautaro Roig Lanzillotta (Dr. litt. 1997; theol. 2004) is professor of New Testament and early Christianity at the Faculty of Theology and Religious

Studies of the University of Groningen. He has published extensively on Plutarch of Chaeronea, early Christian apocrypha, and the Nag Hammadi library and gnosticism. He is editor in chief of *Gnosis: Journal of Gnostic Studies* and of the *Nag Hammadi Bibliography Online*. His most recent books are *A Man of Many Interests: Plutarch on Religion, Myth, and Magic* (2019), edited with D.F. Leão; and *Plutarch's Religious Landscapes* (Leiden 2020), edited with R. Hirsch-Luipold. Together with Jacques van der Vliet, he just finished his forthcoming monograph: *The Apocalypse of Paul. Edition, English Translation and Commentary of the Coptic version of the text*.

References

Allen, Graham. 2000. *Intertextuality*. London: Routledge. https://doi.org/10.4324/9780203131039

Annas, Julia. 1982. "Plato's Myths of Judgement." *Phronesis* 27(2): 119–143. https://doi.org/10.1163/156852882X00096

Barthes, Roland. 1968. "La mort de l'auteur." *Manteia* 5: 12–17. English translation: "The Death of the Author." In *Image - Music - Text*, edited by Stephen Heath, pp. 142–148. Glasgow: Fontana.

Barthes, Roland. 1977. *Image - Music - Text*, translated by Stephen Heath. London: Fontana.

Borges, Jorge L. 1964. *Otras Inquisiciones* (1937–1952). Buenos Aires: SUR, 1952. English translation: *Other Inquisitions* 1937–1952, translated by R.C.L. Simms. Austin, TX: University of Texas Press.

Borges, Jorge L. 1971. "Pierre Menard, autor del *Quijote*." In *Ficciones*, pp. 47–59. Madrid: Alianza. English translation: "Pierre Menard, Author of *Quixote*." In *Labyrinths*, pp. 62–71. Harmondsworth: Penguin, 1970.

Brisson, Luc, et al. 1998. *Plato the Myth Maker*. Chicago, IL: University of Chicago Press.

DeConick, April D. 2016. "Criticisms, Debates, Futures: The Historical Method and Cognitive Historicism." In *Religion: Social Religion*, pp. 383–406. Macmillan Interdisciplinary Handbooks. New York: Gale Cengage Learning.

Deuse, Werner. 2010. "Plutarch's Eschatological Myths." In *On the Daimonion of Socrates: Human Liberation, Divine Guidance and Philosophy*, edited by Heinz-Günther Nesselrath, pp. 169–197. Mohr Siebeck.

Donini, Pierluigi. 1988. "The History of the Concept of Eclecticism." In *The Question of Eclecticism*, edited by John Dillon and A.A. Long, pp. 15–33. Berkeley, CA: University of California Press. https://doi.org/10.1525/9780520317611-006

Eco, Umberto. 1986 [1984]. "Casablanca: Cult Movies and Intertextual Collage." In *Travels in Hyperreality: Essays*, pp. 197–211. New York: Harcourt Brace Jovanovich.

Ferrari, G.R.F. 2009. "Glaucon's Reward, Philosophy's Debt: the Myth of Er." In *Plato's Myths*, edited by Catalin Partenie, pp. 116–133. Cambridge: Cambridge University Press.

Genette, Gérard. 1992. *The Architext: An Introduction*, translated by Jane E. Lewin. Berkeley CA: University of California Press.

Genette, Gérard. 1997a [1982]. *Palimpsests: Literature in the Second Degree*, translated by Channa Newman & Claude Doubinsky and foreword by Gerald Prince. Lincoln and London: University of Nebraska Press.

Genette, Gérard. 1997b. *Paratexts: Thresholds of Interpretation*, translated by Jane E. Lewin and foreword by Richard Macksey. Cambridge: Cambridge University Press. https://doi.org/10.1017/CBO9780511549373

Hamilton, W. 1934a. "The Myth in Plutarch's *De Facie* (940F–945D)." *The Classical Quarterly* 28: 24–30. https://doi.org/10.1017/S0009838800009915

Hamilton, W. 1934b. "The Myth in Plutarch's *De Genio* (589F–592E)." *The Classical Quarterly* 28: 175–182. https://doi.org/10.1017/S0009838800020000

Hani, Jean. 1975. "Le mythe de Timarque chez Plutarque et la structure de l'extase." *Revue des Études Grecques* 88: 105–120. https://doi.org/10.3406/reg.1975.4060

Kristeva, Julia. 1967. "Bakhtine, le mot, le dialogue et le roman." *Critique* 33(239): 438–465.

Kristeva, Julia. 1980. "Word, Dialogue and Novel." In *Desire in Language: A Semiotic Approach to Literature and Art*, edited by Leon S. Roudiez, pp. 64–91. New York: Columbia University Press.

Lévi-Strauss, Claude. 1967. *Structural Anthropology*. Garden City, NY: Anchor.

Morgan, Thaïs. 1985. "Is there an Intertext in this Text? Literary and Interdisciplinary Approaches to Intertextuality." *American Journal of Semiotics* 3(4): 1–40. https://doi.org/10.5840/ajs1985342

Pérez Jiménez, Aurelio. 1993. "El viaje sidéreo de las almas: origen y fortuna de un tema clásico en Occidente." *Fortunatae* 5: 101–123.

Pérez Jiménez, Aurelio. 2001. "Plutarco Versus Platón: Espacios Místicos en el Mito de Tespesio." In *Estudios sobre Plutarco: Misticismo y Religiones Mistéricas en la Obra de Plutarco (Actas del VII Simposio Español sobre Plutarco, Palma de Mallorca, 2-4 nov. 2000)*, edited by A. Pérez Jiménez and F. Casadesús, pp. 201–210. Madrid: Ediciones Clásicas.

Plett, Heinrich F. (ed.). 1991. *Intertextuality*. Berlin: Walter de Gruyter.

Richardson, Hilda. 1926. "The Myth of Er (Plato, Republic, 616b)." *The Classical Quarterly* 20: 113-133. https://doi.org/10.1017/S0009838800024861

Roig Lanzillotta, Lautaro. 2012. "Plutarch at the Crossroads of Religion and Philosophy." In *Plutarch in the Religious and Philosophical Discourse of Late Antiquity*, edited by L. Roig Lanzillotta & I. Muñoz Gallarte, pp. 1–21. Leiden: Brill. https://doi.org/10.1163/9789004236851_002

Roig Lanzillotta, Lautaro. 2020. "Mito y Revelación en Plutarco: o de cómo el conocimiento divino alcanza a los hombres." In *Mythologica Plutarchea. Estudio sobre los mitos en Plutarco*, edited by Josep Clua pp. 327–350. Madrid: Ediciones Clásicas.

Roig Lanzillotta, Lautaro. Forthcoming. *The Ideal of the Real: Plato's Myths, Gnosticism, and the Historical Jesus*.

Teodorsson, Sven-Tage. 2010. "Plutarch's Interpretation of Plato's Cosmology: Plausible Exegesis or Misinterpretation." In *Gods, Daimones, Rituals, Myths and History of Religions in Plutarch's Works*, edited by L. van der Stockt, F.B. Titchener, H.G. Ingenkamp and A. Pérez Jiménez, pp. 419-435. Málaga: Málaga University Press.

Thayer H.S. 1988. "The Myth of Er." *History of Philosophy Quarterly* 5(4) (Plato issue; Oct.): 369-384.

Vernière, Yvonne. 1977. *Symboles et Mythes dans la pensée de Plutarque. Essai d'interprétation philosophique et religieuse des Moralia*. Paris: Les Belles Lettres.

– 7 –

Religion as a Meaning System

ANJA VISSER

In this chapter, I will examine the meaning system approach to the psychological study of religion. This cognitive psychological approach has been gaining popularity in the psychological study of religion during the past decade, particularly in studies on the role that religion plays in the emotional or psychological well-being of people with a physical illness. Whereas the psychodynamic approach to the psychology of religion (Muthert, Chapter 9, this volume) focuses largely on subconscious, relational and emotional processes of religion, this cognitive approach focuses on largely conscious, individual, and thought processes.

Cognitive approaches in psychology are interested in how we consciously or subconsciously process and interpret the information that reaches our nervous system through our senses, how this interpretation guides our experience of and beliefs about ourselves and the world around us, and how we act upon these experiences and beliefs. One important idea in the cognitive approach to psychology is summarized by the well-known saying: *We see the world not as it is, but as we are.* In other words, our perceptions of and responses to the world are not based on an objective observation of the world around us, but on our interpretation of the world. This interpretation is guided by a constellation of norms, values, beliefs, memories, and attitudes, which has been shaped by our personal experiences and by processes of socialization (what we have been taught through our culture, society, community and family). This constellation of ideas and experiences is often referred to as a "life view", "world view" or a "meaning system". Here, I will use the term "meaning system", because (a) it indicates the function of the constellation of ideas

---

Keywords: religion, spirituality, meaning system, psychology, well-being

and experiences, instead of just describing its content, and (b) this term has been gaining popularity in recent studies on this subject.

On a daily basis, a single person possesses or engages with many different meaning systems on different levels – those of cultures, of subgroups and of one's personal history – that impact their behaviours in varying degrees. The notion or concept of meaning systems is, thus, not unique to psychology, but also occurs in many of the other social sciences, such as sociology, anthropology and political sciences (authors often cited in meaning system literature are, for example, the sociologist Émile Durkheim, the cultural anthropologist Clifford Geertz, and the philosopher/psychologist William James).

In the psychological sense, so on the level of the individual, meaning systems enable a person to experience a degree of continuity in their life by shaping their identity and sense of self, to interpret incoming information from the senses and thereby shaping their worldview and view of the transcendent, and to respond to this interpretation with thoughts, feelings and actions, shaping their behaviour (Paloutzian and Park 2013). In other words, when we develop a meaning system, we develop expectations about ourselves and the world around us. These expectations help us to prepare for events and situations, to ensure that we can quickly and adequately respond to them. Whenever a person encounters a new situation, this is interpreted in light of the existing meaning system. This so-called "appraisal" of the situation guides how the person responds to it, both emotionally and behaviourally (Arnold 1960; Lazarus and Folkman 1987). When the situation does not fit the existing meaning system, expectations about, for example, the ways of the world or one's own abilities are violated and the person will experience a certain degree of emotional discomfort or distress. To alleviate these negative feelings (in other words, to cope with them), the person will search for ways to realign the two levels of meaning. This can be done in several ways, such as adjusting the initial interpretation of the event (so-called "re-appraisal", or "assimilation"), shifting focus to other goals that are part of the meaning system so the event has less impact on what the person finds important, or adjusting the basic beliefs or goals that are part of the meaning system (so called "accommodation") (Park 2010). One of these responses could be to correct our behaviour if it violates expectations of ourselves or others, so that we can maintain our self-image and the social cohesion (Epstein 1985). All of these processes operate both at the conscious level and at the subconscious level.

Approaching religion as a meaning system can help us to understand how religious beliefs, practices and experiences can be both a cause of and a solution to distress. In this chapter, I will first discuss the implications of studying religion as a meaning system for the psychology of religion and then illustrate this approach with research on the relationship between religion and well-being in the context of cancer.

Studying Religion as a Meaning System

Now that we have a sense of what psychology entails and what a meaning system is, let us explore what it means to study religion in a meaning system framework. As indicated, a meaning system is a constellation of norms, values, beliefs, memories and attitudes. Religion – as a universal phenomenon – also includes norms about how we should behave, values of what we should try to accomplish, beliefs about the world and our position in it, memories of thoughts, feelings and acts, and attitudes[1] towards people, things and situations. Thus, it seems to make sense to consider religion to be a meaning system.

However, Silberman (2005) points out that religion is a special kind of meaning system, because it centres around "the sacred" (Pargament 1997) or the "ultimate concern" (Tillich 1957). In addition, religions are one of the few meaning systems that encompass the entire lifespan, offering beliefs, attitudes, norms etc. from the beginning until the end of time and from birth to death (and beyond). It can give meaning and value to everything we experience in our lifetime: time, places, social roles, cultural expressions such as art and music, people such as religious leaders, and objects. In this way, religion acts as an integrating framework for our lives, that shows us what we should try to do and to become and shows us a path by which we can attain this striving (Emmons 1999). It should be noted, however, that this does not have to be a coherent framework.

Consequences for Psychological Research

The meaning system perspective on religion has several far-reaching consequences for how psychologists study this phenomenon, which have not all been resolved. I will briefly discuss some of these here.

---

1. The term "attitude" refers to a mental or emotional position that we take towards something or someone (APA glossary, 13 July 2017). The most basic attitude is the evaluation of something as pleasant or attractive.

There Are as Many Religions as there Are People

Modern-day psychologists like to study human phenomena as universal constructs. This means that they strive for descriptions and explanations of behaviour that apply to as many people as possible, preferably all people, to be able to predict and change that behaviour. In the same way, psychologists of religion have tried to capture religion in a few variables that could describe all denominations. The most common aspects used to study a person's involvement in religion have been service attendance, religious affiliation, personal religious activity such as prayer, reading of holy texts and meditation, belief in a divine power or God, and self-rated level of religiousness (Hill and Hood 1999). To allow for generalization of findings, these aspects have been assessed in broad populations with the use of standardized questionnaires.

However, such a universalist approach disregards the content of religious beliefs, acts and experiences, assuming instead that all religions have some underlying function that does not depend on the content. Regarding religion as a meaning system, on the other hand, implies that content is of vital importance for understanding its function. Both the shared religious (and non-religious) meaning system of the group that the person is a part of and the individual, idiosyncratic meaning system of the person influence their goals, behaviours, and how they interpret their experiences (Silberman 2005). Thus, as Allport stated:

> The subjective religious attitude of every individual is, in both its essential and nonessential features, unlike that of any other individual. The roots of religion are so numerous, the weight of their influence in individual lives so varied, and the forms of rational interpretation so endless, that uniformity of product is impossible.
>
> (Allport 1950: 26)

This does mean that it is much more difficult to study religion as a meaning system with a standardized questionnaire to enable generalization. Instead of (or in addition to) these methods, anthropological research methods are more appropriate in this approach, such as interviews or (participant) observation. With these methods, the function of the beliefs, experiences, and acts can be more fully understood in their context.

Religion is a Process

As indicated above, psychologists interested in the function of religion have for a long time assessed religion with indicators such as frequency of church attendance and religious affiliation. They have then correlated these to, for example, indicators of emotional or psychological well-being[2] to understand if religion influenced these outcomes. However, not only do correlations not represent causations, such findings also do not explain why there might be a relationship between religion and well-being. Mediational analyses have indicated that elements such as social support and a sense of meaning and purpose in life may explain the relationship (Fiorito and Ryan 2007; Steger and Frazier 2005). But these explanations are still limited in helping us to understand how this works; how does religion increase a sense of social support or meaning and purpose, and how does that then enhance emotional or psychological well-being? This limited explanatory power occurs because what is measured is the outcome of a process that religion plays a part in, not the process itself.

Regarding religion as a meaning system draws more attention to the psychological process. The way the person constructs their self-image, worldview and view of the transcendent is influenced by the religious meaning system. Insight into what religious attendance means for the person's sense of self, the world and the transcendent helps us to understand much better why it affects their sense of well-being.

In addition, one of the premises of viewing religion as a meaning system is that its role changes over the lifecycle. This also implies that static indicators of religion, such as religious service attendance do not cut it.

Viewing religion as a meaning system also means that religion itself can change, not only its function in the lives of people (Silberman 2005). Meaning systems are constructed and can, therefore, also be deconstructed and reconstructed. Religion can then no longer be viewed as an independent and universal entity, but as a phenomenon that is part and parcel of our time and our society.

Religion is Reduced to the Cognitive Process of Meaning-Making

A danger of the meaning system approach to religion is that its function is fully reduced to cognitive and conscious meaning-making. Geertz (1973), for example, considers meaning-making to be the most essential

---

2. Emotional well-being, also referred to as hedonic or subjective well-being, refers to a state in which a person experiences satisfaction in life, more positive emotions or moods and less negative emotions or moods (Diener et al. 1999). Psychological well-being, also referred to as eudemonic well-being, refers to a state in which a person experiences growth and human fulfilment (Ryff 1989).

function of religion. Paloutzian and Park (2013: 8) state that "Religion is a hard-to-define, probably inherently unstable subset of the larger need to make meaning ... Efforts to specify this subset in terms of a distinctive, unique feature, such as 'the sacred' are, in our view, misguided."

At some level, these authors have a point. What people consider sacred or of ultimate concern may not be distinctively religious, spiritual or sacred in and of itself, but is mainly just perceived in that way. In other words, the process of sacralization is a process of meaning-making and attribution (Paloutzian and Park 2013). Indeed, as Pargament, Magyar-Russell and Murray-Swank (2005) indicate, even everyday, very secular chores, hobbies or objects can be sacred to a person.

However, to reduce religion's function to only this cognitive process does not do justice to the complexity of religion and its effects on people's lives. As several authors have pointed out, religious meaning is also experienced on a more visceral level, in experiences of connectedness, motivation and (self-)transcendence (Smit 2015; Lans 1996). Of course, these experiences can be a consequence of how we interpret events, such as when we experience a deep connection to nature and a sense of vocation to actively preserve it, because we believe that all life is sacred. However, such a belief can also develop after a deep experience of connectedness or during involvement in preservative work for other reasons. Indeed, research on behaviour change and cognitive dissonance has shown that some beliefs do not precede, but follow behaviour (Metin and Camgoz 2011; Olson and Stone 2014).

Therefore, although it is undeniable that cognitive meaning-making is important in religion and for human functioning, because it allows us to use our experiences and to guide our behaviours, the function of religion goes beyond this conscious process of "making sense". Other approaches to the psychology of religion, such as the psychodynamic approach (Muthert, Chapter 9, this volume), study these affective, relational and subconscious processes in more detail.

Religious Meaning Systems are Not Always Influential

If we assume that the religious meaning system is special because it deals with that which we consider most important in life and it encompasses the entire lifespan and everything in it (Silberman 2005), we would expect that religion always influences our lives as soon as it is present in our meaning system. However, it has become clear that this may not be the case.

There might be two explanations for a lack of influence of a religious meaning system. First, the meaning system may not encompass all aspects of the person's life, thus only affecting some parts of it. In a recent survey of the Dutch population, for example, it was found that only a minority of the Dutch population considers religion to be important in their lives, even though many do still retain some religious beliefs or practices (Bernts and Berghuijs 2016).

Second, even though the religious meaning system may encompass all aspects of the person's life, it still may not be very central to the person's life (Huber 2004). This notion of "centrality" is related to the concept of "faith"; the level of trust in and loyalty to a religion, a deity or an idea (Merriam-Webster dictionary, 13 July 2017). As noted above, religion is just one of the many meaning systems that we engage with to understand the world and to move in it. If the religious meaning system is not very integrated and central in this collection,[3] then it has a lower impact on experiences and behaviours. Several studies on the role of religion in coping with illness have found evidence for this (Dezutter et al. 2010; Schnittker 2001; Wei and Liu 2013).

Example. The Role of Spirituality in Coping with Cancer

To illustrate in more detail how religion can be studied as a meaning system, I will describe a study of myself, Uwland-Sikkema, Garssen, Westerhof and Vingerhoets (Visser et al. 2018; Uwland-Sikkema et al. 2018; Visser et al. 2020). It was during this study that I encountered and came to appreciate the meaning system perspective on religion. The objective of our study was to gain an understanding of how spirituality influenced the emotional well-being of cancer patients who received medical treatment with curative intent, with a view on enhancing spiritual care for these patients.

The primary component of our study was a quantitative study. In this part of the study, 383 cancer patients filled out questionnaires on three occasions: within two months after the cancer diagnosis, six

---

3. Huber (2004) discusses the centrality of religion as part of the personality of the person, instead of as a meaning system. The concept "personality" refers to individual differences in characteristic patterns of thinking, feeling and behaving (APA glossary, 13 July 2017). Such a characteristic pattern of thought, feeling and behaviour may be the consequence of the meaning system, but the meaning system is also shaped by our thoughts, feelings and behaviours. Thus, the distinction between personality and meaning system is not quite clear; it is likely that they interact in intricate ways.

months later and another six months later. Spirituality was defined as "one's striving for and experience of a connection with the essence of life" (Jager Meezenbroek et al. 2012: 142). This connection can be experienced on an interpersonal (with oneself), intrapersonal (with others) or transpersonal level (with nature or something transcendental).

Our choice of definition shows that we regarded spirituality as a universal phenomenon and that we hoped to be able to generalize our conclusions about the relationship between spirituality and well-being to all cancer patients receiving curative medical treatment. Nevertheless, our operationalization of spirituality – through use of the Spiritual Attitude and Involvement List (Jager Meezenbroek et al. 2012) – already included some characteristics of a meaning system in terms of attitudes (trust, acceptance) and values (caring for others). Other aspects of spirituality that we measured were the experiences of meaningfulness, connectedness with nature, transcendent experiences, and spiritual activities.

We also regarded spirituality as a phenomenon distinct from, but related to religion. In line with several other authors (see for example, Dyson, Cobb and Forman 1997; Nolan, Saltmarsh and Leget 2011), we viewed spirituality as reflecting an experiential, individual phenomenon related to the experiences of meaning in life and of connectedness to the sacred (or the essence of life). Religion was viewed as a cognitive-behavioural, collective phenomenon related to beliefs and rituals. Spirituality and religion come together if, for example, a belief in a god and religious practices are accompanied with a sense of meaning in life and connectedness with the object of devotion and the community. Religion and spirituality diverge if, for example, a person experiences meaning and connectedness with the essence of life outside of a religious tradition or if a person holds religious beliefs or engages in religious practices without the experience of meaning or connectedness.

Among others, we examined whether the aspects of spirituality as assessed influenced the strength of the relationship between pain, fatigue and distress, assuming that the spiritual experiences and attitudes would contribute to the patient's ability to cope with these symptoms. We found some indications of such an effect: People who scored high on the spirituality aspects Meaningfulness, Acceptance and Spiritual Activities did not report more distress when their fatigue increased over time, whereas people scoring low on these aspects of spirituality did (Visser et al. 2018). These findings suggest that experiencing life as meaningful, having an accepting attitude to both the negative and positive sides of life or engaging in activities such as meditation or discussing spiritual topics made people feel less anxious or depressed when their fatigue increased. But why exactly?

A Closer Look

To understand better how people experience the role of spirituality in coping with cancer, we conducted interviews with 20 of the participants after they had completed all the questionnaires, approximately one year after they had received the diagnosis. During this narrative interview we asked them to describe how they had experienced the past year, and explored their life view with follow-up and clarification questions about what was important in their life, how they viewed difficulties in life, and what gave them a sense of trust or confidence. We had used purposive sampling for the selection of informants, selecting cases who did not meet our hypothesis that spirituality was associated with higher emotional well-being. These informants, we reasoned, would provide us with the most information about how spirituality and well-being relate.

As a first analytical step, we needed to understand the spirituality of our sample so we could then relate this to how they described its role in coping and well-being. To do this, we examined how the informants described their life view, or in other words, how they described their meaning system. We identified 10 aspects of the meaning systems of our informants: Beliefs or values related to meaning in life, which could be specified in a "mundane" and a "transcendent" form; Beliefs about control, which were divided in an individual and a transcendent form; Self-image; Image of the transcendent; Attitude of trust or acceptance; Attitude towards suffering and death; Beliefs about a future after death; Transformative transcendent experiences.

When examining the relationships between these aspects more closely, we found that the meaning system elements that were not about the transcendent were present among all informants, but the other elements were not. We discovered that there seemed to be four types of meaning systems present within our sample (Uwland-Sikkema et al. 2018).

The first type was named "Omnipresent spirituality". This meaning system contained all 10 elements, but the transcendent elements took centre stage in how the informants described their life view.

The second type of meaning system was named "Accompanying spirituality". This meaning system did not contain all transcendent elements and they were not always central to the person's life view. However, they did seem to play an important role as a foundation for the "mundane" beliefs and attitudes.

The third type of meaning system was named "Enclosed spirituality", because transcendent beliefs, values and attitudes were enclosed within everyday experiences and activities such as experiences of deep connectedness with other people or sudden experiences of awe and beauty.

The fourth type of meaning system was named "Absent spirituality". Although a few meaning system elements with transcendent content were present in the interviews of the people with this meaning system, they did not seem to affect how these informants lived their lives or how they interpreted major life events.

During the second analytical step, we related the elements of the meaning systems and their specific content to how the participants described their emotional well-being during the interviews. We discovered that the meaning system could play three roles: (1) It could be discrepant with the experience of cancer, resulting in negative emotions and feelings such as fear, anger, sadness, depression, disappointment or doubt; (2) it could help to legitimize the occurrence of cancer in terms of comprehensibility or significance,[4] resulting in a sense of peace with the situation because it could be integrated in the person's life story; (3) it could help to maintain focus on continuing that which was important to the person, resulting in a sense of trust towards the future (Visser et al. 2020). Legitimation and continuation were two processes that could help to resolve experienced discrepancies, but also occurred if the participant did not experience any incongruence between having cancer and (elements of) their meaning system. Therefore, these processes seem to be more general adjustment strategies.

When comparing the adjustment process between the different types of meaning systems we had identified earlier, we found that discrepancies occurred across the types, but that the nature of the discrepancies did differ. Perhaps unsurprisingly, the most distressing discrepancies occurred with the meaning system elements that were at the foreground of the types. This is not to say that these were the only discrepancies that manifested themselves within the types, but they were the most impactful.

There were some notable differences in the process of legitimation of the cancer between the types of meaning system. One important difference was that seeking significance occurred more often among the informants with the Omnipresent spirituality meaning system, whereas seeking comprehensibility occurred most often among the informants with the Enclosed spirituality meaning system. This could be explained

---

4. Janoff-Bulman and Frantz (1997) define comprehensibility as an understanding of the causality of an event or whether it makes sense to the person. Meaning as significance is defined by them as the value or impact that the event has for or on the life of the person.

by how they looked at events in life in general; as given opportunities for personal growth or as being fully under personal control.

Another important difference regarding legitimation was that – in contrast to the two types just discussed – no search for legitimation was found among the informants with the meaning systems Accompanying or Absent spirituality. Instead, they described that they quickly accepted the diagnosis as something that can happen to anyone, because it is simply part of life or of the ageing process.

This latter difference was reflected in the outcomes we observed among the participants: The informants with an Omnipresent or Enclosed spirituality meaning system described having come to terms with the experience of cancer and having integrated it into their life story in a positive way, whereas the informants with an Accompanying or Absent spirituality meaning system differed from each other in terms of integration. Some viewed the experience as something they would rather forget about, some viewed it as a positive experience from which they have grown, and some viewed it as more neutral without lasting consequences.

The process of continuation was quite similar between the four types of meaning system, except for the Omnipresent spirituality type. Within the other three types, continuation was centred on "staying positive", either in terms of thinking positively in the case of the Accompanying spirituality type, in terms of trusting in their strength to cope in the case of the Enclosed spirituality type, or in terms of not letting the cancer disrupt daily life in the case of the Absent spirituality type. For the Omnipresent spirituality type, continuation was focused on the experience of connectedness with the transcendent and trusting in its good "intentions".[5] This process differs from that in the other three types, because attention or responsibility is not placed on the individual, but on the transcendent. Both the participants with the Omnipresent and with the Enclosed spirituality meaning system used spiritual activities to strengthen their sense of trust in themselves or the transcendent.

In terms of outcomes of the process of continuation, we noticed that this was closely related to the severity of discrepancy experienced and not so much to the type of meaning system. If the discrepancy manifested itself in a discontinuation of the salient element of the meaning system, it appeared to be much more difficult for the informant to maintain

---

5. The word intentions is placed between quotation marks here, because not all informants viewed the transcendent as something with conscious intentions, but they did all ascribe a certain goal to it. For example, the general sentiment that everything happens for a reason.

or regain their sense of trust towards the future, instead feeling weak, depressed or fearful. If a discrepancy occurred with a different element of the meaning system or no discrepancy occurred, continuation was associated with a positive, confident attitude towards the future.

Lessons Learned

So, what have we learned from this study? First, that the quantitative findings on the relationship between spirituality and distress make sense in light of our more elaborate qualitative investigation of the relationship between the meaning system and psychological and emotional adjustment to cancer. However, the qualitative findings point to multiple pathways by which the elements of spirituality used in the quantitative study influence emotional well-being. For one, in the qualitative study we found that spiritual activities provide distraction, thus directly helping to maintain emotional well-being, but also support the sense of meaning in life and the ability to accept negative life events, an indirect relationship. Second, acceptance may support the experience of meaning, because it ensures that the experience of meaning in life becomes less disrupted due to negative life events. Third, a sense of meaning in life may be both the cause and the consequence of the ability to successfully cope with cancer. After all, we found that a continued sense of meaning in life helps to cope, but coping through seeking meaning can help to strengthen or recover a sense of meaning in life. These interrelationships and cyclical processes are much more difficult to uncover in a quantitative study design.

Second, we learned that the content of the meaning system influences how people cope with cancer and what kinds of problems they encounter that might reduce their ability to cope.

Relatedly, we learned that some generalization across individuals is possible using a meaning system approach, as we were able to distinguish four types of meaning systems. Cautionary notes are appropriate here though, because we studied people under very particular circumstances. Are the differences in the constellation of meaning systems due to differences in the meaning systems as such, or due to some other factor such as coping style, personality, previous life experiences, and so on?

We examined a few of these factors and could not explain the different types of meaning system by either the level of spirituality or religiosity on a validated questionnaire, nor by differences in self-identification as religious, spiritual, neither or both. Neither were their clear differences between the types on questionnaires regarding optimism, social support, or coping style. These findings suggest that differences in the prominence of meaning system elements might actually reflect differences in their cognitive salience – as might be expected of a meaning system – rather than differences in psychological functioning or personality.

What about the differences between the types of meaning system and the coping process that was uncovered? Are the types perhaps an artefact of the coping process and would you find different types when studying people under different circumstances? These are difficult questions to answer. One of the assumptions of the meaning system approach is that when core values or beliefs are threatened by life experiences, distress is most severe (Park 2010; Pargament 2002). This pattern was clearly present in the interviews, so that gives us some confidence to identify these elements as central to the meaning system and that the patterning in differences in the centrality of elements indicates a typology. However, the narrative nature of the interviews allowed our participants to select and order events and experiences in such a way as to convey the message that was important for them to share with this particular person (Ayres 2008; Kohler Riessman 2008). The informants were aware that the purpose of the study was to investigate the relationship between spirituality and coping with cancer and the follow-up questions specifically focused on the life view of the person and how this played a role in their experience. Thus, perhaps we can assume that the meanings that were most prominent in the interviews were also those that were most important to the way the informants had experienced cancer, but we cannot be certain that the same elements will surface when using the same interview with people under different circumstances.

Concluding Remarks

In this chapter, I have discussed a cognitive psychological perspective on the study of religion, wherein religion is treated as a meaning system. I have illustrated this approach with a study on spirituality and coping with cancer.

Studying religion as a meaning system has many advantages for the psychology of religion, because it allows for more nuanced investigations of the influence that religion has on the thoughts, feelings and actions of an individual. However, it is unclear what the repercussions of this approach are. One of the objectives of psychology (of religion) is to enhance the health and well-being of individuals, which requires some degree of generalization and standardization; will this still be possible if we use a meaning system approach? Will it be feasible and cost-effective to provide fully personalized "medicine" for resolving spiritual distress or enhancing the power of religious resources for health and well-being? Moreover, what are we missing when we examine religion in this way? Approaching religion as a meaning system implies an emphasis on cognitive processes; what you do and feel are caused by what you think. The success of mindfulness-based therapies and cognitive therapies – in which people become more aware of their automatic interpretations of what they see, feel and do, and how this affects their sense of well-being –, shows that this idea goes a long way (Sears and Kraus 2009; Carmody et al. 2009; Godfrey et al. 2007). However, studies on fatigue, depression and attribution errors also show that what we feel affects how we think (for example, Kinsinger, Lattie and Mohr 2010; Pullens, De Vries and Roukema 2010). Some theories on embodied cognition go even further, to suggest that little thinking is involved in shaping what we do, but rather that the interaction between the shape and functioning of our bodies and our environment underlies the behaviour that we exhibit (Wilson and Golonka 2013). Thus, perhaps the differences in coping and well-being we've observed between, for example, the people with the Omnipresent spirituality meaning system and the Absent spirituality meaning system are not (just) due to the differences between their meaning systems, but (also) due to differences in how their bodies respond to sensory information and the kinds of sensory information that are available in their environments. This theory offers yet another avenue for investigating why people are religious and how this affects their lives.

About the Author

Anja Visser is assistant professor of spiritual care at the University of Groningen. She specializes in research on the organization and outcomes of spiritual care in healthcare settings. Currently she examines best practices for the integration of spiritual caregivers in primary care and the social domain in the Netherlands (for more information, see https://hdl.handle.net/10411/2P1T3B). She has published various articles on the role spirituality in coping with cancer, on spiritual care, and on research methods in chaplaincy.

References

Allport, G.W. 1950. *The Individual and His Religion*. New York: Macmillan.

Arnold, Magda B. 1960. *Emotion and Personality (Vols. 1 & 2)*. New York: Columbia University Press.

Ayres, Lioness. 2008. "Narrative Interview." In *The Sage Encyclopedia of Qualitative Research Methods*, edited by Lisa M. Given, pp. 545-546. Thousand Oaks, CA: Sage Publications.

Bernts, Ton, and Joantine Berghuijs. 2016. *God in Nederland 1966-2015* [*God in the Netherlands 1966-2015*]. Utrecht: Ten Have.

Carmody, J., R.A. Baer, E.L.B. Lykins and N. Olendzki. 2009. "An Empirical Study of the Mechanisms of Mindfulness in a Mindfulness-Based Stress Reduction Program." *Journal of Clinical Psychology* 65(6): 613-626. https://doi.org/10.1002/jclp.20579

Dezutter, Jessie, Linda A. Robertson, Koen Luyckx, and Dirk Hutsebaut. 2010. "Life Satisfaction in Chronic Pain Patients: The Stress-Buffering Role of the Centrality of Religion." *Journal for the Scientific Study of Religion* 49(3): 507-516. https://doi.org/10.1111/j.1468-5906.2010.01525.x

Diener, Ed, Eunkook M. Suh, Richard E. Lucas and Heidi L. Smith. 1999. "Subjective Well-Being: Three Decades of Progress." *Psychological Bulletin* 125(2): 276-302. https://doi.org/10.1037/0033-2909.125.2.276

Dyson, J.M. Cobb, and D. Forman. 1997. "The Meaning of Spirituality: A Literature Review." *Journal of Advanced Nursing* 26: 1183-1188. https://doi.org/10.1111/j.1365-2648.1997.tb00811.x

Emmons, Robert A. 1999. "Religion in the Psychology of Personality: An Introduction." *Journal of Personality* 67(6): 874-888. https://doi.org/10.1111/1467-6494.00076

Epstein, S. 1985. "The Implications of Cognitive-Experiential Self Theory for Research in Social Psychology and Personality." *Journal of the Theory of Social Behavior* 15(3): 283-310. https://doi.org/10.1111/j.1468-5914.1985.tb00057.x

Fiorito, Basil and Kathleen Ryan. 2007. "Spirituality and Psychological Well-Being: A Mediator-Moderator Study." *Review of Religious Research* 48(4): 341-368.

Geertz, C. 1973. *The Interpretation of Culture*. New York: Basic Books.

Godfrey, E., T. Chalder, L. Ridsdale, P. Seed and J. Ogden. 2007. "Investigating the Active Ingredients of Cognitive Behaviour Therapy and Counselling for Patients with Chronic Fatigue in Primary Care: Developing a New Process Measure to Assess Treatment Fidelity and Predict Outcome." *British Journal of Clinical Psychology* 46(3): 253-272. https://doi.org/10.1348/014466506X147420

Hill, Peter C. and Ralph W. Hood, Jr. 1999. "Affect, Religion, and Unconscious Processes." *Journal of Personality* 67(6): 1015-1046. https://doi.org/10.1111/1467-6494.00081

Huber, Stefan. 2004. "Are Religious Beliefs Relevant in Daily Life?" Paper presented at International Society for Empirical Research in Theology, Bieleveld.

Jager Meezenbroek, Eltica C. de, Bert Garssen, M. van den Berg, Gerwi Tuytel, D. van Dierendonck, Adriaan P. Visser and Wilmar B. Schaufeli. 2012. "Measuring Spirituality as a Universal Human Experience: Development of the Spiritual Attitude and Involvement List (SAIL)." *Journal of Psychosocial Oncology* 30(2): 141–167. https://doi.org/10.1080/07347332.2011.651258

Janoff-Bulman, R., and C.M. Frantz. 1997. "The Impact of Trauma on Meaning: From Meaningless World to Meaningful Life." In *The Transformation of Meaning in Psychological Therapies: Integrating Theory and Practice*, edited by M.J. Power and C.R. Brewin, pp. 91–106. Hoboken, NJ: Wiley.

Kinsinger, Sarah W., Emily Lattie and David C. Mohr. 2010. "Relationship between Depression, Fatigue, Subjective Cognitive Impairment, and Objective Neuropsychological Functioning in Patients with Multiple Sclerosis." *Neuropsychology* 24(5): 573–580. https://doi.org/10.1037/a0019222

Kohler Riessman, Catherine. 2008. "Narrative Analysis." In *The Sage Encyclopedia of Qualitative Research Methods*, edited by Lisa M. Given, 540–566. Thousand Oaks, CA: Sage Publications.

Lans, J. van der. 1996. "Religion as a Meaning System: A Conceptual Model for Research and Counseling." In *Religion, Psychopathology and Coping*, edited by H. Gryzmala-Moszczynska and B. Beit-Hallahmi, pp. 95–105. Amsterdam: Rodopi.

Lazarus, Richard S. and Susan Folkman. 1987. "Transactional Theory and Research on Emotions and Coping." *European Journal of Personality* 1 (May): 141–169. https://doi.org/10.1002/per.2410010304

Metin, Irem, and S.M. Camgoz. 2011. "The Advances in the History of Cognitive Dissonance Theory." *International Journal of Humanities and Social Science* 1(6): 131–136.

Nolan, Steve, Philip Saltmarsh and Carlo Leget. 2011. "Spiritual Care in Palliative Care: Working towards an EAPC Task Force." *European Journal of Palliative Care* 18(2): 86–89.

Olson, James M. and Jeff Stone. 2014. "The Influence of Behavior on Attitudes." In *The Handbook of Attitudes*, edited by Dolores Albarracin, Blair T. Johnson and Mark P. Zanna, pp. 223–272. New York: Psychology Press.

Paloutzian, Raymond F. and Crystal L. Park. 2013. "Recent Progress and Core Issues in the Science of the Psychology of Religion and Spirituality." In *Handbook of the Psychology of Religion and Spirituality*, edited by Raymond F. Paloutzian and Crystal L. Park, 2nd edition, pp. 3–22. New York: Guilford Press.

Pargament, Kenneth I. 1997. *The Psychology of Religion and Coping.* New York: Guilford Press.

Pargament, Kenneth I. 2002. "The Bitter and the Sweet: An Evaluation of the Costs and Benefits of Religiousness." *Psychological Inquiry* 13(3): 168–181. https://doi.org/10.1207/S15327965PLI1303_02

Pargament, K.I., G.M. Magyar-Russell and N.A. Murray-Swank. 2005. "The Sacred and the Search for Significance: Religion as a Unique Process." *Journal of Social Issues* 61: 665–687. https://doi.org/10.1111/j.1540-4560.2005.00426.x

Park, Crystal L. 2010. "Making Sense of the Meaning Literature: An Integrative Review of Meaning Making and Its Effects on Adjustment to Stressful Life Events." *Psychological Bulletin* 136(2): 257–301. https://doi.org/10.1037/a0018301

Pullens, Marleen J.J., Jolanda De Vries and Jan A. Roukema. 2010. "Subjective Cognitive Dysfunction in Breast Cancer Patients: A Systematic Review." *Psycho-oncology* 19(11): 1127–1138. https://doi.org/10.1002/pon.1673

Ryff, Carol D. 1989. "Happiness Is Everything, or Is It? Explorations on the Meaning of Psychological Well-Being." *Journal of Personality and Social Psychology* 57(6): 1069–1081. https://doi.org/10.1037/0022-3514.57.6.1069

Schnittker, Jason. 2001. "When Is Faith Enough? The Effects of Religious Involvement on Depression." *Journal for the Scientific Study of Religion* 40(3): 393–411. https://doi.org/10.1111/0021-8294.00065

Sears, Sharon and Sue Kraus. 2009. "I Think Therefore I Om: Cognitive Distortions and Coping Style as Mediators for the Effects of Mindfulness Meditation on Anxiety, Positive and Negative Affect, and Hope." *Journal of Clinical Psychology* 65(6): 561–573. https://doi.org/10.1002/jclp.20543

Silberman, Israela. 2005. "Religion as a Meaning System: Implications for the New Millennium." *Journal of Social Issues* 61(4): 641–663. https://doi.org/10.1111/j.1540-4560.2005.00425.x

Smit, J. 2015. *Antwoord Geven Op Het Leven Zelf* [*Finding an Answer to Life Itself*]. Delft: Eburon.

Steger, M.F. and P. Frazier. 2005. "Meaning in Life: One Link in the Chain from Religiousness to Well-Being." *Journal of Counseling Psychology* 52: 574–582. https://doi.org/10.1037/0022-0167.52.4.574

Tillich, P. 1957. *Dynamics of Faith.* New York: Harper and Row.

Uwland-Sikkema, Nicoline F., Anja Visser, Gerben J. Westerhof and Bert Garssen. 2018. "How Is Spirituality Part of People's Meaning System?" *Psychology of Religion and Spirituality* 10(2): 157–165. https://doi.org/10.1037/rel0000172

Visser, Anja, Eltica C. de Jager Meezenbroek, and Bert Garssen. 2018. "Does Spirituality Reduce the Impact of Somatic Symptoms on Distress in Cancer

Patients? Cross-Sectional and Longitudinal Findings." *Social Science and Medicine* 214 (August): 57–66. https://doi.org/10.1016/j.socscimed.2018.08.012

Visser, Anja, Nicoline Uwland-Sikkema, Gerben J Westerhof, and Bert Garssen. 2020. "The Role of the Spiritual Meaning System in Coping with Cancer." *Religions* 11(1): 49. https://doi.org/10.3390/rel11010049

Wei, D. and E.Y. Liu. 2013. "Religious Involvement and Depression: Evidence for Curvilinear and Stress Moderating Effects among Young Women in Rural China." *Journal for the Scientific Study of Religion* 52(2): 349–367. https://doi.org/10.1111/jssr.12031

Wilson, Andrew D., and Sabrina Golonka. 2013. "Embodied Cognition Is Not What You Think It Is." *Frontiers in Psychology* 4: article 58. https://doi.org/10.3389/fpsyg.2013.00058

– 8 –

Religion as Attachment

A Psychological Exploration of Relational Dynamics in God Representations

HANNEKE SCHAAP-JONKER

Because I was too afraid to attach myself to people, I have clung to God. At home, I was used to broken promises. But since God isn't able to lie, He wouldn't return to who he had promised to be. ... I can hardly believe that God wants to love me absolutely and unconditionally. It's hard for me to trust that His love will not decrease when I fail. For a long time, I tried to become a "better" child of God. At the moment, it's still difficult not to do my best "to make God happy". I know that I can't earn His love because His grace is sufficient, and that He will never abandon me. However, it's a challenge to me not wanting to "please" Him, just as I have to suppress that tendency by other people.

(Rivkah, 29 years old)

Introduction

To many people in this world, religion is a form of relating to the divine. From a psychological perspective, religious/spiritual relationships can be studied in a way that is analogous to relationships between human beings, also because religion and spirituality build on (early) relational experiences and require specific psychological functions which develop within a relational context.

Keywords: religion, God representation, attachment theory, correspondence, compensation

In this chapter, religion will be studied from attachment theory, a relational approach within psychology, with a focus on relational dynamics in God representations as core aspects of religiousness. First, an overview of attachment theory will be given. Subsequently, the theory of God representations will be described from an attachment approach. Furthermore, two important hypotheses on the function of God representations in the context of attachment will be discussed and illustrated with results of empirical research on God representations. Finally, the strengths and weaknesses of conceptualizing religion as attachment will be discussed.

At the beginning of this chapter, you read a quotation of Rivkah, a young woman with attachment problems. Rivkah's case will illustrate the theory about attachment and God representations, and her God representations and their functions will be discussed at the end of the chapter. In this way, we gain more insight into the origins and functioning of God representations in the context of life history and daily life, and into the relevance of a relational approach of religion. Rivkah has given full consent to publication of the information about her experiences in this volume. To maintain her privacy, identifying information was omitted, which did not significantly alter the content of her case.

Basic Concepts of Attachment Theory

Attachment and Attachment Behaviour

Attachment theory is a relational psychological theory, which states that human beings develop in the context of emotional significant relationships and are fundamentally motivated by them (Bowlby 1982 [1969], 1973, 1980; Hall and Gorman 2003). Already from birth, an infant has the universal need to orient towards the outside world, and participates into interpersonal experiences, being dependent on her/his parents or caregivers (Cassidy 2016; Fonagy, Gergely, Jurist and Target 2002; cf. Mesman, Van IJzendoorn and Sagi-Schwartz 2016; Otto and Keller 2014): the infant has physical and psychological needs, and is dependent on her/his parents for fulfilment of these needs. Parents respond to baby with food, cuddling and holding, and provide love and comfort in this way. As a result, a close emotional bond develops between the "relational baby" and her/his significant primary caregivers, which John Bowlby, the founding father of this theory, has called *attachment* (Bowlby 1982 [1969], 1973, 1980).

Attachment relationships manifest themselves in the strong disposition of the child to seek proximity to and contact with the significant primary caregiver or "attachment figure". This attachment behaviour becomes especially visible in situations when the child is frightened, tired, or ill. In such situations of distress, the attachment figure serves as a safe haven: the child who falls down and has a bleeding knee runs to her/his parent for a plaster and a hug. In addition, the parent serves as a secure base, from which to explore the world and develop new mental and physical skills (Ainsworth 1985; Bowlby 1982 [1969], 1973, 1980; Granqvist 2010). Because of these two important attachment functions, the attachment figure, who is perceived to be stronger and wiser, is unique to the attached person. Hence, the attached person experiences anxiety when being involuntarily separated from the attachment figure, and resists separation – imagine a toddler who is brought to the nursery and starts crying when the parent leaves. Loss of the attachment figure results in grief and mourning.

According to Bowlby (1982 [1969]), the attachment system is active "from the cradle to the grave", and attachment behaviours in later life, for example in romantic pair-bonds during adulthood, are markers of healthy development. Usually, a person develops only one or a few attachment relationships (Bowlby 1982 [1969], 1973, 1980; Ainsworth 1985; Granqvist and Kirkpatrick 2013). Due to emotional and cognitive maturations, the expressions of attachment transform during the life cycle, for example from physical proximity into "felt security", a psychological mode of connectedness (Granqvist 2006, 2010).

Rivkah has not earned this "felt security". In contrast, she developed basic anxiety. Early interpersonal relationships were unsafe and demanding, as she grew up in a family with domestic violence. In addition, she was only loved if she was a "good" child that did not ask anything (such as personal attention) for herself but obeyed and helped her parents with caring for the siblings and housekeeping. Thus, Rivkah was loved conditionally and had to adapt herself to the demands and capricious behaviours of her parents.

Internal Working Models

During early development, the infant learns to internalize the dyadic attachment experiences with significant parental figures. It creates mental representations of repeated patterns of emotional communication between self and others in relationships, which Bowlby termed *internal working models* (IWMs). Thus, IWMs are internal organizations of the sensations, emotions, cognitions, and behaviours which are involved in the child's efforts to maintain "felt security" with a particular attachment figure. By implication, they have both cognitive components (see Bartholomew and Horowitz 1991) and affective-relational components (George and West 1999; cf. Proctor et al. 2009). Once developed, IWMs form the psychic structure that functions as a template or filter for future relational interactions (Bowlby 1982 [1969], 1973, 1980; Hall and Gorman 2003; Hall and Fujikawa 2013). As a form of implicit and not fully conscious memory, IWMs function automatically to a large degree. However, as emotional information is processed on multiple levels, these representations of repeated patterns of relational interaction may also have a more explicit, conscious layer, which can be communicated verbally (Hall and Fujikawa 2013).

IWMs of attachment can be classified on the basis of the positivity of the models of self and other and the accompanying dimensions of anxiety and avoidance, which define four models of attachment or *attachment styles*. When the model of self is positive, indicating that the self is lovable and worthy, and the model of the other is positive, then anxiety and avoidance are low, and the individual is *securely* attached. When the model of self is negative ("I am bad/worthless/incompetent/..."), while the model of the other is positive, anxiety becomes high, in combination with low avoidance, which results in a *preoccupied* attachment style. These IWMs may be expressed in clinging or claiming behaviour ("I cannot survive without you").

Rivkah's narrative reflects this preoccupied attachment style when she tells that she has clung to God. Feeling inferior and bad, she has developed a negative model of self, which enables her to remain loyal to her parents ("I deserve it") and to maintain the benevolence of others and the world (cf. Janoff-Bulman 1992). Positive models of others (often a result of idealization) in combination with negative models of self (resulting from devaluation) brings the benefit of safety and security, as Fairbairn (1952: 66-67) describes that "It is better to be a sinner in a world ruled by God than to live in a world ruled by the Devil" as "a sinner in a world ruled by God may be bad; but there is always a certain sense of security to be derived from the fact that the world around is good and God is in His heaven and All is Right in the world!; and in any case there is always a hope of redemption".

A positive self-model in combination with a negative model of the other, indicating that the other is unreliable, not responsive, and unsafe, results in a dismissive or avoidant attachment style, with low anxiety and high avoidance. At an explicit level, those who are attached in an avoidant way tend to stress their personal strength ("I get by on my own") in combination with idealized representations of others, which are not linked with concrete examples or memories ("My father was always very helpful"). A negative model of self that is combined with a negative model of others means that the individual is caught between high anxiety and high avoidance. These dynamics characterize a fearful attachment style that often results from traumatic experiences, abuse and neglect (Bartholomew 1990; Bartholomew and Horowitz 1991; Granqvist and Kirkpatrick 2013; Priel and Besser 2001). Sixty to seventy per cent of individuals of normal samples have a secure attachment style, while thirty to forty per cent is typified by one of the three insecure attachment styles (Granqvist 2010).

IWMs develop early in life and are quite stable over time and situations. They generalize across relationships and affect (future) relationships such as peer relationships, pair bonds and romantic relationships, for example (cf. Allen and Tan 2016; Feeney 2016; Zeifman and Hazan 2016).

The Caregiving Environment and the Mentalizing Function

A caregiving, responsive environment is essential for attachment security and positive IWMs of self and other, and also for the development of mental functions, such as the capacity for mentalizing and affect regulation.

During early interactions, the caregiver mirrors the affects of the infant by responding to it with facial expressions, voice, and verbal behaviour. Simultaneously, the caregiver treats the new-born baby as a mental agent, unconsciously ascribing a mental state to the infant ("You have to cry? You feel so frightened?"). By these mind-minded interactions with mirroring and affect-regulating behaviour, the infant learns to distinguish its own mental world from both the physical world and the mental world of others, and it learns to understand that mental world (Allen, Fonagy and Bateman 2008: 80–102; Steele and Steele 2008). In this way, it develops the capacity to mentalize, which refers to a mental process of imaginatively perceiving or interpreting one's own or others' behaviour as conjoined with intentional mental states, such as personal reasons, beliefs, feelings, needs and desires (e.g. She slams the door because she is angry). Mentalizing can be described as the capacity to see yourself from the outside and others from the inside, or as the process of holding mind in mind (Allen, Fonagy and Bateman 2008: 1–2). As an aspect of social cognition, it is closely related to the capacity for thinking about thinking, but also to empathy (Baron-Cohen, Lombardo and Tager-Flusberg 2013). The extent to and way in which mentalizing is present or absent differ among people and are context-dependent (Holmes 2006).

During development, the child goes through several modes of mentalizing. It starts with the *teleological mode* of thinking, in which goals are attributed to people and objects, but in close connection to what is observable. "I believe it when I see it" characterizes this mode of thought (Fonagy 2008: 25–26, 38). At the age of two, children think in a *psychic equivalence mode*, equating internal and external and assuming that what they think also exists in reality (think of fantasies about crocodiles under the bed which are experienced as very real). They can see themselves and others as intentional agents, whose prior states of minds and actions can bring about changes in minds and bodies, but they are not yet able to represent mental states independent of physical reality. As a complement to psychic equivalence, children may think in a *pretend mode*, believing that internal states have no implications for the outside world – and these three non-mentalizing modes of experience may also be present during later life, for example in dreaming or in posttraumatic flashbacks (Allen 2006: 17). Traumatic experiences may undermine the mentalizing capacity, which leads to a fixation in or regression to non-mentalizing modes (Allen 2013; Fonagy, Bateman and Luyten 2012). Finally, previous modes of thoughts are integrated into a mentalizing, or reflective mode, in which mental states can be experienced as representations. Inner and outer reality are seen as linked, though differing (Fonagy 2008: 27, 33). The child or adult includes the representation of mind states in its understanding of self and others.

Rivkah's parents were not sensitive to their children's needs, as they both suffered from psychiatric disorders. In fact, the parents did not mind about their children's minds and emotional experiences, which hindered the development of Rivkah's mentalizing function and emotion regulation. Still, she often interprets behaviour and feelings in a psychic equivalence mode. Simultaneously, the unsafe environment at home forced her to overactive pseudo-mentalizing (Bateman and Fonagy 2006: 74), which is characterized by a preoccupation with mental states and a lot of efforts to make inferences about causal relationships between the parent's minds and their behaviour. In this context, she also developed a controlling-caregiving strategy to maintain safety (Allen 2013: 41; Main et al. 2005: 283) ("Dad looks tired, so I have to be quiet and bring his newspaper, to prevent that he becomes angry and will hit me").

Mentalizing is an imaginary activity, in which meaning is constructed on the basis of feelings, thoughts, wishes and expectations, which are not directly observable. It is a form of "grounded imagination", in which the mental, subjective world is separated from objective reality, while simultaneously being anchored in it (Allen 2006: 3–30). Implicitly or explicitly being aware that one's own and another's mental state reflect a certain viewpoint on reality, the mentalizing person develops a "sense of representingness" (Bogdan 2005), knowing that representations of (internal or external) reality are not reality themselves. In a mentalizing mode, an individual is able to reflect on her/his emotions, understanding them while feeling them ('mentalized affectivity"), which is important for recognizing, modulating and expressing emotions (Allen, Fonagy and Bateman 2008: 59; Bateman and Fonagy 2006: 4; Fonagy et al. 2002: 7, 96; Jurist 2005: 426–444). Mentalizing forms a prerequisite for relating and representing, also in the religious domain. It is involved in the capacity for imagination, for transcendence, for symbolizing, empathy, taking perspective, and meaning-making (see also Schaap-Jonker and Corveleyn 2014).

Attachment Theory and Representations of God

Religion as Attachment: God as a Symbolic Attachment Figure

The belief in a personal God with whom believers maintain a personal, interactive relationship often meets the criteria for attachment relationships: love is a central emotion that characterizes the relational space between believer and God. Being stronger and wiser than the individual (even omnipotent and omniscient), God as a symbolic attachment figure serves both as a safe haven and a secure base (Granqvist and Kirkpatrick 2016; Proctor et al. 2009). Empirical studies support the view that people turn to God, for example in prayer, when they face illness, injury, or other negative and distressing life events, when they face separation and loss (death of friends and relatives), and when they have to deal with a difficult life situation (Granqvist and Kirkpatrick 2013; Koenig, King and Carson 2012; Pargament 1997). In addition, believers talk about God "watching over me" and "being by my side", and this secure-base function of religion is also worded in religious literature (Granqvist and Kirkpatrick 2016) and supported by empirical research (e.g. Granqvist, Mikulincer, Gewirtz and Shaver 2012; Hall and Edwards 1996; cf. the distinction that Hvidt et al. 2017 make between "crisis religiosity" and "restful religiosity"). The caregiving, supportive and guiding functions of God representations, fulfilling basic human needs of being seen, loved, and valued, are also reflected in maternal (and, to a lower extent, paternal) functions of God representations. In many empirical studies, God was seen as unconditionally available and present, like the mother, but God's love was also associated with paternal demands, as law, power, and knowledge typified representations of God as well (Vergote 1997: 218-232; cf. more recent research about benevolent and authoritative aspects of God representations, e.g. Johnson, Okun and Cohen 2015; Schaap-Jonker et al. 2017).

God Representations from an Attachment Perspective

God as a symbolic attachment figure is represented by believers (and some authors even state that the God to whom one does not want to attach or believe in is represented too; e.g. Rizzuto 1979). Representational models of God as (divine) "other" and models of self in relation to God form people's God representations, which reflect their God as experienced and believed in personally (in contrast to the "official" God of religious traditions) (Moriarty and Hoffman 2007; Schaap-Jonker 2008). God representations comprise both emotional and cognitive understandings of God, as models of self and other have both affective-relational and cognitive components.

Emotional understandings of God are assumed to reflect subjective experiences of God/the divine (such as experiences that are typified by love, security, anxiety, or distrust) and are developed through the relational, and initially subconscious, process in which IWMs are formed. Parental attachment figures make important contributions to this process (Davis et al. 2013; Hall and Fujikawa 2013; Hoffman 2005; Jones 2007). Thus, early relational interactions with attachment figures are generalized and represented in IWMs, resulting in a specific attachment style (Bartholomew and Horowitz 1991; cf. Davis et al. 2013), and these IWMs guide and integrate an individual's embodied, emotional experiences in relationship with God, usually at an emotional, implicit, and largely nonverbal level, outside of conscious awareness (Davis et al. 2013; Granqvist, Mikulincer, Gewirtz and Shaver 2012; Hall and Fujikawa 2013).

Cognitive understandings of God are based on what people learn about God in propositional terms, which is related to the doctrines that are taught and found within the family and the (local) religious culture (e.g. God as the ground of being; cf. Zahl and Gibson 2012). The internalization of beliefs and doctrines on God occurs in an attachment context, with IWMs guiding the internalization process, which means that people learn about God in interpretative and selective ways (Aletti 2005; Schaap-Jonker 2008). By implication, the more belief-laden cognitive understandings of God, as forms of explicit memory, are related to the more affect-laden emotional understandings of God. Consequently, there is no such thing as one uniform and consistent God representation. Instead, God representations are multi-dimensional processes, as emotional and cognitive understandings of God/the divine are dynamically interrelated and influence each other mutually. Diverse internal and external contextual factors activate different aspects of God representations, both on explicit and implicit levels of awareness (Schaap-Jonker et al. 2008, 2017; Zahl and Gibson 2012).

God Representations and Attachment Styles

Not only are there parallels between religion and attachment relationships, religion and spirituality also capitalize on the operation of the attachment system, making use of its vital psychological functions and processes such as IWMs and the capacity for mentalizing (Granqvist and Kirkpatrick 2013). Hence, God representations differ according to various styles of attachment to God. Proctor and colleagues (2009) have defined the God representations that typify different styles of attachment to God and tested them empirically.

Secure attachment to God is associated with perceptions of God as available, caring, supportive, and responsive to a person's needs, especially in times of distress, when comfort or protection is sought. Corresponding models of self involve self-worth and self-appreciation, understandings of being loved by God, and feeling confident and comfortable in exploring inner and outer world (Proctor et al. 2009; Granqvist and Kirkpatrick 2013).

Insecure anxious/preoccupied attachment to God may involve models of God as inconsistently available or responsive, which is reflected in feelings of uncertainty about one's own worth in the models of self. These IWMs may find expression in deeply emotional, clinging and all-consuming responses to God (cf. Granqvist and Kirkpatrick 2013). Rivkah's case is an example of this style of attachment to God. In case of *insecure, dismissive* attachment to God, God may be represented and experienced as the distant, withdrawn, or abandoning other, especially during times when strength or support are needed. Subsequently, models of God may be perceived as being disinterested and lacking relevance for the individual, not one to be relied on in times of need. Accompanying models of self may range from devaluing oneself, being not worth anything, to defensive self-confidence and autonomy, in which no other is needed. Proctor and colleagues (2009) do not provide descriptions of the representational models of self and God that characterize the *insecure fearful* attachment style. However, it may be assumed that God models involve threat and/or neglect and disinterest, with fearful self-models of devaluation and self-condemnation. Furthermore, these fearful/disorganized IWMs may be characterized by dissociation (Granqvist and Kirkpatrick 2013).

God Representations and Models of Mentalizing

God representations can not only be examined and classified according to IWMs and attachment styles, but also in relation to different modes of mentalizing.

In non-mentalizing modes, God representations are experienced as coinciding with who God really is, and/or are equated with divine reality (see also Muthert's contribution in this volume and her discussion of Ogden's modes of being). People with a *teleological mode* of thinking are focused on God's actions and interventions in their own reality and analyse situations in terms of cause and effect. Specific events are attributed to God's interventions, and God's will is deduced from successive situations. For example, when a person has planned to go to a festival, but falls ill, then the teleological conclusion is that God does not want her to go to the festival – although God's intentions and motivations for this intervention are unclear (cf. Drewes 2011).

Rivkah has also had a period in her life during which she experienced God in a teleological way. In that time, she felt lonely and prayed to God that He should send somebody to visit her or to call her. When nothing happened, she concluded that God also wanted her to be alone.

In the mode of *psychic equivalence*, an individual's own feelings or thoughts are equated to God's feelings and thoughts ("I feel that God is angry at me, so He *is* really angry"; cf. Drewes 2011).

Rivkah's feeling of being not good enough in relationship to God leads to the belief that she is not good enough in God's eyes to be loved without preconditions.

In the *pretend* mode, God is experienced as passive, not responding, and far away, because inner and outer reality are kept apart, and people often feel a void inside (cf. Stålsett et al. 2010).

Only in a *mentalizing* mode, God is experienced personally, as a God who sees, knows, thinks, has intentions, purposes and feelings, and is able to see us externally and internally (Merkur 2013: 169; Rizzuto 2002). Mentalizing individuals keep God's mind in mind, for example when they pray (see Schjoedt, Stødkilde-Jørgensen, Geertz and Roepstorff 2009; cf. Schaap-Jonker and Corveleyn 2014), and interpret God's actions as results of his intentions. The more the mentalizing function has been developed, the more complex God representations are, and the more the individual can experience ambivalence or contradictions in relationship with God. Furthermore, the capacity to mentalize is a necessary prerequisite for experiencing a "sense of representingness" (Bogdan 2005) in relation to God, which means that God representations are viewed and experienced as representations with a symbolic and referential nature, which do not coincide with who God "really" is (Rizzuto 2017; Schaap-Jonker 2011).

Functions of God Representations: Correspondence and Compensation

As we have seen, God representations differ according to various attachment styles and diverse modes of mentalizing. However, how do people use these representations of God? How do they function in the context of their psychological and spiritual well-being?

Within psychology of religion, two opposing hypotheses have been formulated about how individual differences in attachment may relate to religion and spirituality in general and God representations in particular.

According to the *correspondence hypothesis*, individual differences in religiousness and experiences of God correspond to and reflect differences in attachment styles, attachment history and IWMs (Kirkpatrick 2005; cf. Granqvist and Kirkpatrick 2016). Individuals with secure IWMs of self and other perceive God as supportive and experience emotions of love, closeness, trust and security in relationship with God, while those with insecure attachment styles view God as punitive, rigid, distant, passive, unreliable or fear-provoking (see above). Many studies on God representations and mental health support this correspondence pathway (e.g. Braam et al. 2014; Goodman and Manierre 2008; Schaap-Jonker et al. 2002; Van Vliet et al. in press). In addition to *IWM correspondence*, there is evidence for *socialized correspondence*, as secure attachment facilitates religious socialization: those who have warm and sensitive caregivers and feel attachment security tend to adopt their parents" religion and internalize similar religious beliefs, values and behaviours. In contrast, those who are insecurely attached are less likely to embrace their parents" belief systems and religious norms (Granqvist and Hagekull 1999; Granqvist 2002a, 2002b). The mediating mechanism between attachment security and social correspondence seems the acquisition of epistemic trust, which is the capacity to trust others as a source of knowledge about the world. In the context of religious socialization, epistemic trust is reflected in the child's willingness to consider their parents" communication of religious knowledge as trustworthy and relevant to the self (cf. Fonagy, Luyten and Allison 2015; Fonagy, Luyten, Allison and Campbell 2016: 780, 793).

The *compensation hypothesis* posits that insecurely attached individuals develop an attachment relationship with God as a substitute for inadequate and disappointing human attachment figures (Kirkpatrick 2005). For example, when an individual has learned that nobody can be trusted, the divine Other may be the exception to that rule. Different subtypes of compensation can be distinguished. The first subtype is labelled *explicit religious compensation,* which means that individuals with insecure attachment styles tend to show higher levels of religiousness than those who are securely attached, being more involved in religious practices and reporting a stronger belief in God, for instance (e.g. Granqvist 2002b). The second subtype focuses on *emotional compensation*: God as a substitute attachment figure fulfils an affect regulating function, providing feelings of security and safety that were missed, which may happen during times of crisis, or over time (variant: longitudinal compensation) (Granqvist 2002a). Another variant of emotional compensation is *religious change conversion*, which refers to the findings that sudden conversions and religious changes are used to regulate emotional turmoil. Interestingly, Hall and colleagues (2009) argue that emotional compensation actually reflects the insecure IWMs at a motivational level, as underlying insecure attachment dynamics motivate the compensating attachment relationship with God.

Empirical Studies on Corresponding and Compensating God Representations

Various studies support the compensating function of God representations. For example, individuals who experienced a break in romantic relationships reported an increased importance of their relationship with God, and this increase was prospectively predicted by high scores on parental insensitivity (Granqvist and Hagekull 2003). Experimental studies from a social psychological perspective also show that feeling powerless and uncertain, which leads to anxious arousal, is positively associated with beliefs in a God who has control and is confident (e.g. Kay, Gaucher, McGregor and Nash 2010). In addition, sudden converts scored higher on a scale which taps distress-regulating aspects of attachment relationships with God, and they also scored higher on parental insensitivity than non-converts or individuals who reported a more gradual change in religiousness (Granqvist, Mikulincer and Shaver 2010). Furthermore, results of a qualitative Dutch study on representations of God of women who survived incest support the longitudinal emotional compensation, as negatively valenced experiences with God during the time of the sexual violence were changed into more positive representations of God over time for a considerable number of the abused women (Balk-Van Rossum 2017).

The correspondence function of God representations is also supported by empirical research. For example, a loving and non-distant God representation, reflecting IWM correspondence, was related to earned attachment security with the mother (Granqvist 2002b: 95). Furthermore, anxiety and avoidance in attachment to God seem to be associated with anxiety and avoidance in close interpersonal relationships (Beck and McDonald 2004; see for an overview of more empirical research that test the correspondence and compensation hypotheses Granqvist and Kirkpatrick 2013, 2016).

In a recent study among psychiatric patients and persons without any psychiatric diagnosis, both correspondence and compensation of God representations were found. The God representation profile of patients with a borderline personality organization, which indicates structural personality pathology, combines high levels of anxiety, anger and ruling/punishing perceptions of God with low levels of positive feelings, supportive actions and passivity of God (Schaap-Jonker et al. 2017; Van der Velde et al. in press). This type of God representation represents borderline patients" experiences of a negatively valenced, threatening and punishing God, who is unreliable and wrathful (cf. Gravitt 2011; Goodman and Manierre 2008). Thus, on the level of IWMs, insecure models of self, that are typical of borderline patients, were associated with insecure models of God, which points to correspondence. On the contrary, a positively valenced type of God representation, in which high levels of positive feelings towards God were combined with supportive and ruling perceptions of God, was only found among non-patients and the relatively more stable psychiatric patients, but not among patients with structural personality pathology. Although the latter did report some positive feelings towards God, negative feelings and experiencing distance in relation to God were dominant. Interestingly, more positive feelings towards God were associated with an increase of psychological distress among these patients with structural personality pathology. This could be interpreted as an indication of the search for a safe haven, which resembles the compensation hypothesis (Van der Velde et al. 2021).

The Function of God Representations in Rivkah's Case

When Rivkah's report of her God representations is analysed from an attachment perspective, both the corresponding and compensating functions are found in her narrative. First, she tells how God is totally different from human beings: while people are unreliable and break their promises, God is the only trustworthy and faithful one. Thus, God as a substitute attachment figure compensates the shortcomings and mistakes of Rivkah's family, functioning as a safe haven. Secondly, Rivkah tells that relying on God's unconditional love is difficult to her. She links love to being good or behaving well (or even perfectly): love must be earned. By implication, it would be logical to Rivkah that God's love decreases when she makes mistakes. These findings point to correspondence: Rivkah's insecure internal working models filter her perceptions of God and affect her behaviour towards God; her preoccupied attachment style motivates clinging behaviour towards God.

To explain that God representations have both a corresponding and compensating function at the same time, the distinction between explicit and implicit knowledge (or explicit and implicit memory systems) could be helpful. At an explicit, more rational level, positively valenced aspects of Rivkah's God representations compensate for her insecure human attachment. However, at an implicit level, largely outside conscious awareness, unsafe aspects of her God representations correspond to the more affective knowledge of how to be with an attachment figure, which is reflected in Rivkah's internal working models (Hall et al. 2009; Maltby and Hall 2012); in Rivkah's case, these IWMs demonstrate themselves in the tendency to please. While telling her story, Rivkah makes her implicit sense that God loves her only conditionally explicit, which shows that her implicit and explicit memory systems have become disintegrated in an attempt to cope with the non-responsive, non-caregiving environment; this disintegration leads to a discrepancy between explicit and implicit aspects of her God representations (cf. Maltby and Hall 2012). Hence, Rivkah's explicit God representations only compensate the felt insecurity to a limited degree; this compensation does not solve or repair the insecurity on the level of internal working models. To gain more positive models of self, new relational experiences are needed (Moriarty 2006; cf. Lyons-Ruth et al. 1998; Moriarty and Davis 2012).

Discussion and Conclusions

In this chapter, we studied religion from the perspective of attachment theory and explored relational dynamics in God representations. In this way, we linked the study of religious beliefs, experiences and practices to a well-established conceptual framework in psychology, which has a solid basis in empirical research, with clarification of neuropsychological mechanisms. As a result, more insight is gained into the links between individuals" perceived relationships with God and their relational styles, modes of thinking, and experiences in early interactions with parents or significant caregivers (cf. Granqvist and Kirkpatrick 2013). Furthermore, attachment theory not only explains why and how people relate to God and why they embrace certain forms of spirituality in terms of psychological origins and development, but also explicates the psychological functions of religious representations and relationships in their current context (which cannot be detached from their past context). Attention to both implicit and explicit forms of knowing and relating has added value in the study of religion and God representations, as we move beyond visible behaviour or conscious cognitions to processes, which have a more automatic nature and are yet highly influential. In this context, the focus of attachment theory on real-life interaction may also be regarded as a limitation, as there is less attention to internal fantasies, (unconscious) imaginative activities, and distortions which result from defence mechanisms (Rizzuto 2006; cf. Fonagy, Luyten, Allison and Campbell 2016: 780).

Conceptualizations of attachment theory fit monotheistic religions with an emphasis on the relationship between the believer and God/the divine. However, is attachment theory an appropriate hermeneutic instrument for the study of non-traditional and/or non-Western forms of religion and spirituality? Diverse authors point to the role of attachment-related processes in non-monotheistic forms of religion and spirituality. For example, the Buddhistic prayer "I take refuge in the Buddha, the Dharma, and the Sangha" reflects the notions of safe haven and a secure base. In addition, personal teachers and a local religious community may serve the same psychological functions (Augustyn et al. 2017; Mikulincer and Shaver 2007: 248; cf. Shaver et al. 2007). In Hindu monotheism, relational spirituality is also found, as the relationship between a child and her/his parent or a lover to the beloved is one of the forms of relationship between worshippers who follow the path of devotion and God in his form of Rama or Krsna (Augustyn et al. 2017). Furthermore, Granqvist and colleagues (2005, 2009) have found indirect links between attachment and New Age spirituality and mystical experiences: although these "alternative" forms of spirituality are not directly captured by an attachment framework, they are related to disorganized attachment through the mediating pathway of an inclination to experience alterations in consciousness. More research is needed in this context (Granqvist 2010), also to detect cross-cultural patterns and cultural variations in the attachment functions of God representations (cf. Mesman, Van IJzendoorn and Sagi-Schwartz 2016; Otto and Keller 2014).

Of course, attachment theory does not offer a comprehensive theory of religion or spirituality; other psychological mechanisms and systems (but also sociological, political, cultural, theological ones, for example) are needed to explain other aspects of religious/spiritual beliefs, experiences and behaviours. To answer questions such as why people take part in rituals or offer sacrifices, why religions promote specific moral and ethical guidelines or commandments, why some forms of religion are related to prejudice, authoritarianism or violence, and why and how religions function as meaning-making systems, God representations should not only be perceived and studied as attachment figures, but also as social exchange partners (who could offer some benefits in exchange for specific behaviours or sacrifices) as dominant competitor (who asks submission to avoid punishment), or as exponents or reflections of basic human needs, for example (Granqvist and Kirkpatrick 2013; Reiss 2016). Nevertheless, the religion as attachment model enriches the approach of religion between relations by highlighting the roles of early relationships in the form and function of religion and spirituality, the implicit filter of IWMs through which current experiences are filtered, also in relation to God/the divine, and the functions of religion and spirituality for obtaining or maintaining psychic equilibrium and well-being.

About the Author

Hanneke Schaap-Jonker is endowed professor in clinical psychology of religion at the Vrije Universiteit Amsterdam and rector of the Centre for Research and Innovation of Christian Mental Health Care in the Netherlands. As psychologist and theologian, her research interests include God representations and mental health, religion and suicidality, and the interactions between religious factors and psychotherapy. Her current research focuses on self-compassion, religion and mental health. Her second dissertation in 2018 focused on God representations and mental health. Her 2019 inaugural address outlined the contours of a contemporary clinical psychology of religion with a focus on recovery, hope and compassion.

References

Ainsworth, M.D.S. 1985. "Attachments across the Life-span." *Bulletin of the New York Academy of Medicine* 61: 792–812.

Aletti, M. 2005. "Religion as an Illusion: Prospects for and Problems with a Psychoanalytic Model." *Archive for the Psychology of Religion* 27: 1–18. https://doi.org/10.1163/008467206774355367

Allen, J.G. 2006. "Mentalizing in Practice." In *Handbook of Mentalization-Based Treatment*, edited by J.G. Allen and Peter Fonagy, pp. 3–30. Chichester: John Wiley & Sons. https://doi.org/10.1002/9780470712986

Allen, J.G. 2013. *Restoring Mentalizing in Attachment Relationships: Treating Trauma with Plain Old Therapy.* Washington, DC: American Psychiatric Publishing.

Allen, J.G., P. Fonagy and A.W. Bateman. 2008. *Mentalizing in Clinical Practice.* Washington/London: American Psychiatric Publishing.

Allen, J.P. and J.S. Tan. 2016. "The Multiple Facets of Attachment in Adolescence." In *Handbook of Attachment: Theory, Research, and Clinical Applications*, 3rd edition, edited by J. Cassidy and P.R. Shaver, pp. 399–415. New York/London: Guilford Press.

Augustyn, B.D., T.W. Hall, D.C. Wang and P.C. Hill. 2017. "Relational Spirituality: An Attachment-Based Model of Spiritual Development and Psychological Well-being." *Psychology of Religion and Spirituality* 9: 197–208. https://doi.org/10.1037/rel0000100

Balk-Van Rossum, A.W. 2017. "De rol van godsbeelden in de levensverhalen van vrouwen met een incestervaring" ["God Images and their Role in the Life Stories of Female Incest Survivors"]. Doctoral dissertation, retrievable from https://research.vu.nl/ws/portalfiles/portal/41929593

Baron-Cohen, S., M. Lombardo and H. Tager-Flusberg. 2013. *Understanding Other Minds: Perspectives from Developmental Cognitive Neuroscience*, 3rd edition. Oxford: Oxford University Press. https://doi.org/10.1093/acprof:oso/9780199692972.001.0001

Bartholomew, K. 1990. "Avoidance of Intimacy: An Attachment Perspective." *Journal of Social and Personal Relationships* 7(2): 147–178. https://doi.org/10.1177/0265407590072001

Bartholomew, K. and L.M. Horowitz. 1991. "Attachment Styles among Young Adults: A Test of a Four-Category Model." *Journal of Personality and Social Psychology* 61: 226–244. https://doi.org/10.1037/0022-3514.61.2.226

Bateman, A. and P. Fonagy. 2006. *Mentalization Based Treatment for Borderline Personality Disorder. A Practical Guide.* Oxford: Oxford University Press. https://doi.org/10.1093/med/9780198570905.001.0001

Beck, R. and A. McDonald. 2004. "Attachment to God: The Attachment to God Inventory, Tests of Working Model Correspondence, and an Exploration of Faith Group Differences." *Journal of Psychology and Theology* 32: 92–103. https://doi.org/10.1177/009164710403200202

Bogdan, R.J. 2005. "Why Self-ascriptions Are Difficult and Develop Late." In *Other Minds: How Humans Bridge the Divide between Self and Others*, edited by B.F. Malle and S.D Hodges, pp. 190–206. New York: Guilford Press.

Bowlby, J. 1982 [1969]. *Attachment and Loss, Vol. 1: Attachment*. New York: Basic Books.

Bowlby, J. 1973. *Attachment and Loss, Vol. 2: Separation: Anxiety and Anger*. New York: Basic Books.

Bowlby, J. 1980. *Attachment and Loss, Vol. 3. Loss: Sadness and Depression*. New York: Basic Books.

Braam, A.W., H. Schaap-Jonker, M.H. Van der Horst, B. Steunenberg, A.T.F. Beekman, W. van Tilburg and D.J.H. Deeg. 2014. "Twelve-Year History of Late-Life Depression and Subsequent Feelings to God." *American Journal for Geriatric Psychiatry* 22(11): 1272–1281. https://doi.org/10.1016/j.jagp.2013.04.016

Cassidy, J. 2016. "The Nature of the Child's Ties." In *Handbook of Attachment: Theory, Research, and Clinical Applications*, 3rd edition, edited by J. Cassidy and P.R. Shaver, pp. 3–24. New York/London: Guilford Press.

Davis, E.B., G.L. Moriarty and J.C. Mauch. 2013. "God Images and God Concepts: Definitions, Development, and Dynamics." *Psychology of Religion and Spirituality* 5: 51–60. https://doi.org/10.1037/a0029289

Drewes, A. 2011. "Hij en ik: Denken over mensen met een borderline persoonlijkheidsstoornis die denken over God" ["He and I: Thinking about Persons with a Borderline Personality Disorder Who Think about God"]. *Psyche en Geloof* 22(4): 226–232.

Fairbairn, W.R.D. 1952. "The Repression and Return of Bad Objects (with Special References to the 'War Neuroses')". *Psychoanalytic studies of the personality*, 59–81. London: Routledge & Kegan Paul.

Feeney, J.A. 2016. "Adult Romantic Attachment: Developments in the Study of Couple Relationships." In *Handbook of Attachment: Theory, Research, and Clinical Applications*, 3rd edition, edited by J. Cassidy and P.R. Shaver, pp. 435–463. New York: Guilford Press.

Fonagy, P. 2008. "The Mentalization-Focused Approach to Social Development." In *Mentalization: Theoretical Considerations, Research Findings and Clinical Implications*, edited by F.N. Busch, pp. 3–56. New York: Analytic Press.

Fonagy, P., A.W. Bateman and P. Luyten. 2012. "Introduction and Overview." In *Handbook of Mentalizing in Mental Health Practice*, edited by A.W. Bateman and P. Fonagy, pp. 13–16. Arlington: American Psychiatric Publishing.

Fonagy, P., G. Gergely, E. Jurist and M. Target. 2002. *Affect Regulation, Mentalization, and the Development of the Self*. New York: Other Press.

Fonagy, P., P. Luyten and E. Allison. 2015. "Epistemic Petrification and the Restoration of Epistemic Trust: A New Conceptualization of Borderline Personality Disorder and its Psychosocial Treatment." *Journal of Personality Disorders* 29: 575–609. https://doi.org/10.1521/pedi.2015.29.5.575

Fonagy, P., P. Luyten, E. Allison and C. Campbell. 2016. "Reconciling Psychoanalytic Ideas with Attachment Theory." In *Handbook of Attachment: Theory, Research, and Clinical Applications*, 3rd edition, edited by J. Cassidy and P.R. Shaver, pp. 780–804. New York/London: Guilford Press.

George, C. and M. West. 1999. "Developmental vs. Social Personality Models of Adult Attachment and Mental Ill Health." *British Journal of Medical Psychology* 72: 285–303. https://doi.org/10.1348/000711299159998

Goodman, G. and A. Manierre. 2008. "Representations of God Uncovered in a Spirituality Group of Borderline Inpatients." *International Journal of Group Psychotherapy* 58: 1–15. https://doi.org/10.1521/ijgp.2008.58.1.1

Granqvist, P. 2002a. "Attachment and Religiosity in Adolescence: Cross-sectional and Longitudinal Evaluations." *Personality and Social Psychology Bulletin* 28: 260–270. https://doi.org/10.1177/0146167202282011

Granqvist, P. 2002b. "Attachment and Religion: An Integrative Framework." Uppsala: Acta Universitatis Upsaliensis. Doctoral dissertation, retrievable from https://uu.diva-portal.org/smash/get/diva2:161469/FULLTEXT01.pdf

Granqvist, P. 2006. "On the Relation between Secular and Divine Relationships: An Emerging Attachment Perspective and a Critique of the Depth Approaches." *The International Journal for the Psychology of Religion* 16: 1–18. https://doi.org/10.1207/s15327582ijpr1601_1

Granqvist, P. 2010. "Religion as Attachment: The Godin Award Lecture." *Archive for the Psychology of Religion* 32: 5–24. https://doi.org/10.1163/157361210X487177

Granqvist, P., and B. Hagekull. 1999. "Religiousness and Perceived Childhood Attachment: Profiling Socialized Correspondence and Emotional Compensation." *Journal for the Scientific Study of Religion* 38: 254–273. https://doi.org/10.2307/1387793

Granqvist, P., and B. Hagekull. 2003. "Longitudinal Predictions of Religious Change in Adolescence: Contributions from the Interaction of Attachment and Relationship Status." *Journal of Social and Personal Relationships* 20(6): 793-817. https://doi.org/10.1177/0265407503206005

Granqvist, P. and L.A. Kirkpatrick. 2013. "Religion, Spirituality, and Attachment." In *APA Handbook of Psychology, Religion and Spirituality. Volume 1*, edited by K.I. Pargament, J.J. Exline and J.W. Jones, pp. 139-155. Washington, DC: APA. https://doi.org/10.1037/14045-007

Granqvist, P. and L.A. Kirkpatrick. 2016. "Attachment and Religious Representations and Behavior." In *Handbook of Attachment: Theory, Research, and Clinical Applications*, 3rd edition, edited by J. Cassidy and P.R. Shaver, pp. 917-940. New York: Guilford Press.

Granqvist, P., M. Fransson and B. Hagekull. 2009. "Disorganized Attachment, Absorption, and New Age Spirituality - A Mediational Model." *Attachment and Human Development* 11: 385-403. https://doi.org/10.1080/14616730903016995

Granqvist, P., M. Fredrikson, P. Unge, A. Hagenfeldt, S. Valind, D. Larhammar and M. Larsson. 2005. "Sensed Presence and Mystical Experiences Are Predicted by Suggestibility, not by the Application of Weak Complex Transcranial Magnetic Fields." *Neuroscience Letters* 379: 1-6. https://doi.org/10.1016/j.neulet.2004.10.057

Granqvist, P., M. Mikulincer and P.R. Shaver. 2010. "Religion as Attachment: Normative Processes and Individual Differences." *Personality and Social Psychology Review* 14: 49-59. https://doi.org/10.1177/1088868309348618

Granqvist, P., M. Mikulincer, V. Gewirtz and P.R. Shaver. 2012. "Experimental Findings on God as an Attachment Figure: Normative Processes and Moderating Effects of Internal Working Models." *Journal of Personality and Social Psychology* 103: 804-818. https://doi.org/10.1037/a0029344

Gravitt, W.J. 2011. "God's Ruthless Embrace: Religious Belief in Three Women with Borderline Personality Disorder." *Issues in Mental Health Nursing* 32(5): 301-17. https://doi.org/10.3109/01612840.2010.558234

Hall, T.W. 2003. "Relational Spirituality: Implications of the Convergence of Attachment Theory, Interpersonal Neurobiology and Emotional Information Processing." *Newsletter Psychology of Religion* 28: 1-12.

Hall, T.W. and K.J. Edwards. 2002. "The Spiritual Assessment Inventory: A Theistic Model and Measure for Assessing Spiritual Development." *Journal for the Scientific Study of Religion* 41: 341-357. https://doi.org/10.1111/1468-5906.00121

Hall, T.W. and A. Fujikawa. 2013. "God Image and the Sacred." In *APA Handbook of Psychology, Religion and Spirituality*, edited by K.I. Pargament, J.J. Exline and J.W. Jones, pp. 277-292. Washington, DC: APA. https://doi.org/10.1037/14045-015

Hall, T.W., A. Fujikawa, S.R. Halcrow and P. Hill. 2009. "Attachment to God and Implicit Spirituality: Clarifying Correspondence and Compensation Model." *Journal of Psychology and Theology* 37: 27–244. https://doi.org/10.1177/009164710903700401

Hall, T.W. and M. Gorman. 2003. "Relational Spirituality: Implications of the Convergence of Attachment Theory, Interpersonal Neurobiology, and Emotional Information Processing." *Psychology of Religion Newsletter* 28: 1–12.

Hoffman, L. 2005. "A Developmental Perspective on the God Image." In *Spirituality and Psychological Health*, edited by R.H. Cox, B. Ervin-Cox and L. Hoffman, pp. 129–147. Colorado Springs, CO: Colorado School of Professional Psychology Press.

Holmes, J. 2006. "Mentalizing from a Psychoanalytic Perspective: What's New?" In *Handbook of Mentalization-Based Treatment*, edited by J.G. Allen and P. Fonagy, pp. 31–49. Chichester: John Wiley & Sons. https://doi.org/10.1002/9780470712986.ch2

Hvidt, N.C., D. Hvidtjørn, K. Christensen, J.B. Nielsen and J. Søndergaard. 2017. "Faith Moves Mountains – Mountains Move Faith: Two Opposite Epidemiological Forces in Research on Religion and Health." *Journal of Religion and Health* 56: 294–304. https://doi.org/10.1007/s10943-016-0300-1

Janoff-Bulman, R. 1992. *Shattered Assumptions*. New York: Free Press.

Johnson, K.A., M.A. Okun and A.B. Cohen. 2015. "The Mind of the Lord: Measuring Authoritarian and Benevolent God Representations." *Psychology of Religion and Spirituality* 7: 227–238. https://doi.org/10.1037/rel0000011

Jones, J.W. 2007. Psychodynamic Theories of the Evolution of the God Image. In *The God image Handbook for Spiritual Counseling and Psychotherapy: Research, Theory, and Practice*, edited by G.L. Moriarty and L. Hoffman, pp. 33–55. Binghamton, NY: Haworth Press.

Jurist, E.L. 2005. "Mentalized Affectivity." *Psychoanalytic Psychology* 22: 426–444. https://doi.org/10.1037/0736-9735.22.3.426

Kay, A.C., D. Gaucher, I. McGregor and K. Nash. 2010. "Religious Belief as Compensatory Control." *Personality and Social Psychology Review* 14: 37–48. https://doi.org/10.1177/1088868309353750

Kirkpatrick, L.A. 2005. *Attachment, Evolution, and the Psychology of Religion*. New York: Guilford.

Koenig, H.G., D.E. King and V.B. Carson. 2012. *Handbook of Religion and Health*, 2nd edition. Oxford/New York: Oxford University Press.

Lyons-Ruth, K., N. Bruschweiler-Stern, A.M. Harrison, A.C. Morgan, J.P. Nahum, L. Sander, D.N. Stern and E.Z. Tronick. 1998. "Implicit Relational Knowing:

Its Role in Development and psychoanalytic treatment." *Infant Mental Health Journal* 19: 282-291. https://doi.org/10.1002/(SICI)1097-0355(199823)19:3<282::AID-IMHJ3>3.0.CO;2-O

Main, M., Hesse, E. and Kaplan, N. 2005. "Predictability of Attachment Behavior and Representational Processes at 1, 6, and 19 Years of Age: The Berkeley Longitudinal Study." In *Attachment from Infancy to Adulthood: The Major Longitudinal Studies*, edited by K.E. Grossmann, K. Grossmann and E. Waters, pp. 245-304. New York: Guilford Publications.

Maltby, L.E. and T.W. Hall. 2012. "Trauma, Attachment, and Spirituality: A Case Study." *Journal of Psychology and Theology* 40(4): 302-312. https://doi.org/10.1177/009164711204000405

Merkur, D. 2013. *Relating to God: Clinical Psychoanalysis, Spirituality, and Theism.* Lanham, Maryland: Jason Aronson Inc. Publishers.

Mesman, J., M.H. Van IJzendoorn and A. Sagi-Schwartz. 2016. "Cross-cultural Patterns of Attachment: Universal and Contextual Dimensions." In *Handbook of attachment: Theory, research, and clinical applications*, 3rd edition, edited by J. Cassidy and P.R. Shaver, pp. 852-877. New York: Guilford.

Mikulincer, M. and P.R. Shaver. 2007. *Attachment in Adulthood: Structure, Dynamics, and Change.* New York: Guilford Press.

Moriarty, G. 2006. *Pastoral Care of Depression: Helping Clients Heal their Relationship with God.* New York: Haworth Press.

Moriarty, G.L. and E.B. Davis. 2012. "Client God Images: Theory, Research, and Clinical Practice." In *The Psychology of Religion and Spirituality for Clinicians: Using Research in your Practice*, edited by K. O'Grady, E. Worthington, Jr., and J. Aten, pp. 131-160. New York: Routledge.

Moriarty, G.L. and L. Hoffman. 2007. "Introduction and Overview." In *The God Image Handbook for Spiritual Counseling and Psychotherapy: Research, Theory, and Practice*, edited by G.L. Moriarty and L. Hoffman, pp. 1-9. Binghamton, NY: Haworth.

Otto, H. and H. Keller. 2014. *Different Faces of Attachment: Cultural Variations on a Universal Human Need.* Cambridge: Cambridge University Press. https://doi.org/10.1017/CBO9781139226684

Pargament, K.I. 1997. *The Psychology of Religion and Coping: Theory, Research, Practice.* New York: Guilford Press.

Priel B. and A. Besser. 2001. "Bridging the Gap between Attachment and Object Relations Theories: A Study of the Transition to Motherhood." *British Journal of Medical Psychology* 74: 85-100. https://doi.org/10.1348/000711201160821

Proctor, M.T., M. Miner, L. Mclean, S. Devenish and B. Ghobary Bonab. 2009. "Exploring Christians' Explicit Attachment to God Representations: The Development of a Template for Assessing Attachment to God Experiences." *Journal of Psychology and Theology* 37(4): 245–264.
https://doi.org/10.1177/009164710903700402

Reiss, S. 2016. *The 16 Strivings for God: The New Psychology of Religious Experiences.* Macon, Georgia: Mercer University Press.

Rizzuto, A.M. 1979. *The Birth of the Living God*. Chicago, IL: University of Chicago Press.

Rizzuto, A.M. 2002. "Believing and Personal and Religious Beliefs: Psychoanalytic Considerations." *Psychoanalysis and Contemporary Thought* 25: 433–464.

Rizzuto, A.M. 2006. "Discussion of Granqvist's Article on 'The Relation between Secular and Divine Relationships: An Emerging Attachment Perspective and a Critique of the "Depth" Approaches'." *International Journal for the Psychology of Religion* 16: 19–28.
https://doi.org/10.1207/s15327582ijpr1601_2

Rizzuto, A.M. 2017. "Discussion of the Contribution of Stålsett, Engedal and Austad on 'The Persecuting God and the Crucified Self'." In *Ana-Maria Rizzuto and the Psychoanalysis of Religion: The Road to the Living God*, edited by M.J. Reineke and D.M. Goodman, pp. 79–84. Lanham: Lexington Books.

Schaap-Jonker, H. 2008. *Before the Face of God: An Interdisciplinary Study of the Meaning of the Sermon and the Hearer's God Image, Personality and Affective State*. Zürich, Switzerland: LIT Verlag.

Schaap-Jonker, H. 2011. "Gehechtheid, mentaliseren en Godsrepresentaties" ["Attachment, Mentalizing, and God Representations"]. *Psyche en Geloof* 22(4): 226–232.

Schaap-Jonker, H. and J. Corveleyn. 2014. "Mentalizing and Religion: A Promising Combination for Psychology of Religion, Illustrated by the Case of Prayer." *Archive for the Psychology of Religion* 36: 1–20.
https://doi.org/10.1163/15736121-12341292

Schaap-Jonker, H., E.H.M. Eurelings-Bontekoe, P. Verhagen, P and H. Zock. 2002. "Image of God and Personality Pathology: An Exploratory Study among Psychiatric Patients." *Mental Health, Religion and Culture* 5(1): 55–71.
https://doi.org/10.1080/13674670110112712

Schaap-Jonker, H., E.H.M. Eurelings-Bontekoe, H. Zock and E.R. Jonker. 2008. "Development and Validation of the Dutch Questionnaire God Image." *Mental Health, Religion and Culture* 11: 501–515.
https://doi.org/10.1080/13674670701581967

Schaap-Jonker, H., N. van der Velde, E.H.M. Eurelings-Bontekoe and J.M.T. Corveleyn. 2017. "Types of God Representations and Mental Health:

A Person-Oriented Approach." *International Journal for the Psychology of Religion* 27: 199–214. https://doi.org/10.1080/10508619.2017.1382119

Schjoedt, U., H. Stødkilde-Jørgensen, A.W. Geertz, A. Roepstorff. 2009. "Highly Religious Participants Recruit Areas of Social Cognition." *Social Cognitive and Affective Neuroscience* 4: 199–207. https://doi.org/10.1093/scan/nsn050

Shaver, P.R., S. Lavy, C. Saron and M. Mikulincer. 2007. "Social Foundations of the Capacity for Mindfulness: An Attachment Perspective." *Psychological Inquiry* 18(4): 264–271. https://doi.org/10.1080/10478400701598389

Stålsett, G., L.G. Engedal and A. Austad. 2010. "The Persecuting God and the Crucified Self: The Case of Olav and the Transformation of His Pathological Self-Image." *Pragmatic Case Studies in Psychotherapy* 6: 49–100. https://doi.org/10.14713/pcsp.v6i2.1024

Steele, H. and M. Steele. 2008. "On the Origins of Reflective Functioning." In *Mentalization: Theoretical Considerations, Research Findings and Clinical Implications*, edited by F.N. Busch, pp. 133–158. New York: The Analytic Press.

Van der Velde, N., Schaap-Jonker, H., Eurelings-Bontekoe, E.H.M. and Corveleyn, J.M.T. 2021. God Representation Types Are Associated With Levels of Personality Organization and Christian Religious Orthodox Culture. *Journal of Nervous and Mental Disease*. https://doi.org/10.1097/NMD.0000000000001363

Van Vliet, N.K., Schaap-Jonker, H., Jongkind, M., Van der Velde, N. and Van den Brink, A. 2018. De relatie tussen godsrepresentaties en suïcidaliteit bij christelijke patiënten met een depressieve stoornis [The relation between God representation and suicidality in Christian patients with major depressive disorder]. *Tijdschrift voor Psychiatrie* 8: 511–520.

Vergote, A. 1997. *Religion, Belief and Unbelief: A Psychological Study*. Leuven: Leuven University Press.

Zahl, B.P. and N.J.S. Gibson. 2012. "God Representations, Attachment to God and Satisfaction with Life: A Comparison of Doctrinal and Experiential Representations of God in Christian Young Adults." *The International Journal for the Psychology of Religion* 22: 216–230. https://doi.org/10.1080/10508619.2012.670027

Zeifman, D.M. and C. Hazan. 2016. "Pair Bonds as Attachments: Mounting Evidence in Support of Bowlby's Hypothesis." In *Handbook of Attachment: Theory, Research, and Clinical Applications*, 3rd edition, edited by J. Cassidy and P.R. Shaver, pp. 416–434. London: Guilford Press.

– 9 –

Bridging Inner and Outer Worlds

A Psychodynamic Approach to Meaningful Mourning

HANNEKE MUTHERT

Meaningful Mourning: An Introduction

Every summer Geertje (48) has a very difficult time; she feels physically so listless, numb and literally heavy that she can accomplish very little. For weeks she lies in bed and hardly sees anyone. Then, after a slow recovery, she forgets what she has gone through until Spring comes into view again. People around Geertje insist on her seeing a general practitioner or psychologist or at least trying medication. She did try antidepressants once, but being convinced that she is not depressed, she is against medication. A friend who keeps an eye on Geertje, told her that it struck her that after another "heavy" period, Geertje had "survived June again". The word "survival" touches Geertje. Gradually she has come to realize that her physical reactions are related to the loss of her stillborn baby after 32 weeks of pregnancy, now more than 20 years ago. "Then I could not even think about it," she says. "Only now, after all these years, I can be sad in a safe environment." Taking the advice of a friend, she contacted a spiritual caretaker. During one of her conversations with this professional about the loss of her child, Geertje was overwhelmed with emotions when she told her counsellor about a melody that recently had sprung to her mind and kept singing in her head. As she hummed it, the spiritual caretaker recognized a liturgical song in the melody about a God who sees people and takes care of them before they are born (Oosterhuis and

---

Keywords: mourning, religious meaning, modes of being, spiritual care

Oomen 1996).¹ That image moves Geertje. The situation in which she gave birth to her stillborn child was such that she had to be strong. Her family members treated her very harshly and did not show compassion. In their view, there should have been no baby in the first place. Therefore, Geertje felt extremely lonely and thrown back on herself. But this song tells a different story ...²

The consoling effect of the religious meaning of the song that Geertje carries in her head, a meaning that thus far she had been unaware of, in addition to the social support she now receives, helps Geertje to look differently at the child she lost more than twenty years ago. What exactly makes a religious interpretation of what happened to her and her baby back then so crucial to her now? Why was this interpretation not possible before? These are the kind of questions that interest me as a psychologist of religion with a specialization in spiritual care. My research interests concern the psychological dimensions of meaning-making processes in mourning and the role that religion may play in such processes.

Being confronted with loss and having to come to terms with that is an unavoidable part of life. I therefore consider mourning over one's losses in life a normal process. In this chapter I focus on bereavement after death in particular but this theory is applicable to a broad range of losses. Mourning basically entails learning how to live with loss both in a practical way in one's everyday life, but also learning how to integrate the experience of loss in a meaningful way in one's life story (Muthert 2007). Mourning can sometimes be quite complicated, however, to the extent of people getting stuck in the process. Therefore, we need a theoretical framework that addresses the question of how individuals mourn, in order to enhance our understanding of the development of individual psychological abilities and limitations in relation to coping with loss.

In this chapter, I suggest to combine so-called constructional models of mourning (Attig 2010, 2001; Neimeyer et al. 2011), with object relational theory (Ogden 2000, 2005; Melzer 2008) to develop a more adequate theoretical framework and model to work with in counselling. The first perspective emphasizes an active construction of reality; the second adds the impact of important attachment relationships during the construction of these representations of reality. My main argument is that intra-psychic models to understand mourning or effectively

---

1. Dutch verse: "Omdat Gij het zijt, groter dan ons hart, die mij hebt gezien, eer ik werd geboren." See Psalms 139.15-16.
2. This is a depersonalized vignette discussed at expert meetings of senior spiritual carers (including the author), "Train the trainer, spiritual autobiography" in 2016-2017.

support mourning people do not suffice. Not only may individuals with different temperaments respond very differently to "similar" losses, but depending on one's specific personal situation and on the cultural context in which one is embedded the impact of particular kinds of loss can vary greatly. This is illustrated in the vignette above; now that her social circumstances have improved, Geertje's mourning process has also changed and she is now able to find consolation in the songs from the religious community that she belongs to. Her case study illustrates that the socio-cultural context that people live in and relate to always plays a role in mourning. Therefore, building on several scholars in the field of psychodynamic psychology, the point I want to make in this chapter is that how people relate psychologically not only to the object of mourning but also to their environment in the event of loss deserves more attention both in the academic study of mourning processes and in effective counselling. Moreover, the dimension of meaning-making, including religious meaning-making should be taken into account (Winnicott 1969; Mooij 2002; Muthert and Schaap-Jonker 2015). In current theorization and counselling, psychological and social theories about mourning often remain unconnected. Whereas most psychologists tend to focus on intra-personal processes, I would argue that insights into how different socio-cultural circumstances inform the sources that people draw on to make sense of loss in their lives (Leader 2008) are at least as important.

By explicitly linking an intra-psychic model to the social-cultural context, this chapter aims to clarify the relationship between people's inner and outer worlds in the context of mourning. On a theoretical level I will connect psychological and social aspects of mourning by concentrating on religious meaning that can be experienced in what Winnicott has coined "the space in between" (cf. Winnicott 1971; Bion 1965, 1970). My argument also ties in with current counselling literature and political care policies, in which there is a growing interest in spiritual meaning making when dealing with recovery, palliative care, coping and prevention (Boevink 2017; Leget et al. 2010; Huber et al. 2016; ZonMw 2016). As in theorization, in literature on counselling and health policies a person's ability to adapt is often stressed without taken into account changeable contextual factors. To remedy this one-sidedness I suggest that we explore the meaning of grief from a psychological perspective that explicitly includes both people's inner and outer worlds.

Besides theory, counselling is therefore an important dimension in my research. The analysis of case studies of people's mourning processes enhances our insights into how people attribute meaning to their grief, as well as shedding light on effective and less effective counselling. My specific focus in studying counselling practices concerns the field of spiritual care. Theorization and practical interventions in spiritual care concentrate on meaning-making processes. For my own research, this means that I focus on case studies in which mourners get stuck in the process of making sense of their loss and have turned to a professional spiritual caregiver for help. The underlying idea is, however, that studying case studies of problematic grieving can also help to get a clearer picture of mourning processes that do not require professional support.

Outline

In what follows, I will address the question of how a psychodynamic vision of mourning that is based on different modes of being can contribute to a better understanding of variations in mourning behaviour and (religious) meaning-making in everyday life. I will do so by examining first of all which psychodynamic concepts underlie the current psychological mourning models and how these concepts relate to (religious) meaning-making. I will explore where these mourning models offer room for meaning-making processes and what additional psychodynamic knowledge is needed. Next, I will present Thomas Ogden's theory on different modes of being to explain how a diversity of responses to loss can be understood by using his model. Finally, I will address the relationships between intra-psychic grief capacities and social grief reactions. I will link Ogden's model to the theory of his colleague psychoanalyst Darian Leader. In doing so, the various ways in which relationships between the psychological inner world and the social outer world of a grieving person can take shape will come into view, as well as the role of meaning-making in these relationships. Although religion potentially fits in well with all the three modes of being, a good match is not obvious in all cases. In the concluding section of the chapter I will reflect on how the theoretical framework I suggest can be put into practice and what its limitations are. Throughout the chapter, Geertje's case study will be used to illustrate my argument.

Core concepts Concerning Meaning in Mourning Theories

According to object relational scholars, mourning is a fundamental relational capacity (Ogden 1989, 2000, 2005; Bion 1962a, 1962b, 1965, 1967, 1970; Melzer 2008). This means that the so-called "subject-object relation" is at the heart and not the mourning person or "subject" as such, nor the lost "object". The popularity of this approach is reflected in current mourning theories (Attig 2010; Neimeyer 2001; Neimeyer et al. 2011). Whereas earlier models understood mourning predominantly in terms of *decathexis*, that is, the loosening of the ties between the mourning subject and the deceased, nowadays the idea of *renewal of this particular relation* dominates.

In the Freudian line of thinking about *decathexis* (Freud 1917), mourning is a complex and exhausting activity. It includes retrieving the libidinal investments that the ego or mourning person put into the object that is now lost. To put it simply: growth demands investing energy into other persons, ideas and activities. By doing so, one increases room for reality at the expense of purely egotistical wishes and desires. If people, ideas, activities or expectations that are "charged with energy" die, disappear or become less important, one needs to withdraw this energy and reinvest it elsewhere. This fundamental idea of loosening ties with the lost object is reflected in various phase-based mourning models. As a consequence, proper mourning behaviour is considered to consist of withdrawing the investment correctly,[3] ultimately resulting in acceptance.[4] In the former century when these models dominated, the emphasis was on literally creating distance: children were therefore often kept away from dead people and from funerals,[5] for instance, and stillborn children were directly separated from their parents in order to prevent the development of attachment relationships. Looking at Geertje's experience from this perspective, we can observe that for a long period in her life "good" mourning activity was missing. No distance was created at all, and the energy invested in her baby was completely blocked and therefore not available for reinvestment. Years later, the mourning process apparently changed, but still there seemed to be no acceptance.

Leaving behind the *decathexis* perspective, we nowadays look at mourning from the opposite position: the idea of "continuing bonds" (Klass et al. 1996; Hagman 2001). In this perspective, continuation of the relation between the bereft subject and the object lost by transforming it in a specific way becomes central in the mourning activity. Since the lost object is no longer physically present, effective mourning is placed in

---

3. As an example of this proper behaviour people used Kübler-Ross's phases of moving from denial and isolation to anger and eventually sadness (Kübler-Ross 1969).
4. For critical reflections on the various phases and task based mourning models, see Neimeyer (2001), Neimeyer et al. (2011), De Mönnink (2017) and Muthert (2007: 47–50).
5. Many 50–60- or 70-year-old carers and volunteers appoint this practice when they recall the grieving habits of their youth at workshops on loss and longing for (mental) health workers (Muthert et al. 2008).

the light of what supports the mourning subject to redesign the relationship with whom was lost. As a consequence, meaning-making comes into the picture by focusing on the significance of the lost to the subject and how this significance can somehow be preserved in a different form. In this approach, the construction of personal stories are put centre stage. Taking this perspective, it becomes clear that no two concrete processes of mourning are ever the same. This is precisely why transformation and meaning-making are the core concepts in today's more widely used constructionist mourning models.

Relearning the World

One of these models is the *relearning the world* model by the philosopher Thomas Attig (2001, 2010). Attig assumes that every loss causes chaos and that this chaos is hard to endure. To gain insight into people's efforts to control this chaos, Attig distinguishes three processes that mutually influence each other. First, people who experience chaos search for meaning in their specific situation. Secondly, they seek recognition from others for their unique story. Finally, there is the question of more or less acknowledging this experience or event as a loss. All three processes together lead to providing "an answer" to what a specific loss means for a certain person in their specific context (Muthert 2012: 61-69).

Such "answers" are not merely cognitive, but are emotional, physical, cognitive/intellectual, spiritual, social, behavioural and psychological. Therefore, a holistic approach is required to grasp the mourning process. Precisely because the whole person is involved in responding to loss, this individual activity is central to the *relearning the world* model. What I find particularly helpful in Attig's model is that he emphasizes the importance of the context of the mourning person by identifying four interconnected worlds; the physical world delimits which answers are possible. The social world indicates which of these answers are more or less accepted in a specific environment. The world of the self provides insight into which answers the mourner finds easy or more difficult to digest. The world of the person or object lost pertain to answers that are or should be abandoned. Finally, this whole procedure of "answering" is conceived of as a dynamic and continuous process without a necessary end. Attig's approach acknowledges that depending on the circumstances, responses to loss can change over and over again, whereby personal vulnerabilities and contextual options define the limits and inform one's ever evolving biography (Muthert 2007).

For an illustration of such a dynamic process we return to Geertje's story. In retrospect, we could describe Geertje's different responses to the loss of her baby as somewhat speculative: "They said the baby should not be there, so it did not happen", "I'm absent for a while and when I return, I do not look back", "I survived the month of June but … my baby did not'", "I believe God saw me and my baby back then and there", "God and people do see me. Meanwhile the grief over my lost child is still there as well as the tragedy of what happened all those years."

Attig's model lists many factors that can be translated into useful recommendations in counselling (Muthert et al. 2008). However, within this framework the extent to which a loss affects a person is not always visible from the outside. To remedy this, I consider adding De Mönnink's (2001) various layers of experience to the model as valuable. In De Mönnink's view, people experience loss on different levels; on the level the facts, on the level of meaning and on what he calls the level of "existential design". The latter combines having a sense of self-control, of self-worth, of justice and of hope for the future. As I have argued elsewhere, in my view a sense of belonging should be added to this existential design (Muthert 2012: 63). Distinguishing these different layers alerts mourning researchers and counsellors to the fact that people's stories about loss consist of different levels and that all these levels should be listened to in order to understand their personal mourning processes.

Summing up, current theorists on mourning criticize older mourning models for the strong normative link they suggest between "good" mourning and the extent to which one should actually let go of the mourned object over time. It is now acknowledged that in fact, mourning is a much more complex activity than the idea of having to "let go" suggests. New constructionist mourning models see the transformation of the relationship of the mourner with the lost as the core task, in which the importance of personal meaning-making is emphatically emphasized.

I would argue, however, that even the constructionist models cannot adequately explain the big variety in grief reactions that can be observed in people that mourn; people show an enormous creativity in formulating answers, even in mentally very difficult circumstances (Muthert 2012, 2007). How to assess the value and efficacy of these answers to handle loss does not become directly apparent in Attig's model. More specifically problematic in my view is that in Attig's *relearning the world model* religious "answers" do not differ substantially from other kinds of "answers". Nor does it become clear which factors influence the dynamics between different "answers" in the story of one and the same person. In the next section, I will therefore demonstrate that psychodynamic mourning concepts have a greater potential to explain differences in intra- and interpersonal dynamics of formulating "answers" to experiences of loss.

Different Modes of Being in Relation to Meaning-Making

The object relational school in psychology focuses on relations between subject and object. Definitions of what constitutes a human subject vary. Following Verhaeghe, I understand human identity as the continuous dynamic between the body and other, social dimensions of the self (Verhaeghe 2012). The "I" in this conception is no fixed entity. Human identity moves between autonomy and identification, that is, the wish to be connected to others, to belong to a group. This movement between the desire to be independent and the desire to be embedded in meaningful relationships with others is necessarily characterized by tensions. From a psychodynamic point of view one can state that the human subject *is* that field of tension (Thys 2018: 100). This implies that relations between subjects are by definition also dynamic.

Differences between various kinds of relationships that people engage in can be explained by looking at three overarching psychological organizational structures. Each structure defines a subject's psychological capacities. These capacities, also called functions, influence concrete subject-object relations. This refers, for example, to Hanneke Schaap's discussion about "mentalizing" elsewhere in this volume. If a person cannot mentalize, they cannot imagine what their behaviour means to others. This hinders their developing relationships to others. Each organizational structure has also its own defence mechanisms. For example, if sensory impressions dominate, reactions are quite different then when extensive reflection dominates. Other relevant characteristics in respect to my subject are different basis fears and several ways of using symbols (for example, using symbolic equivalence or symbols as referring to something else) (Muthert and Schaap-Jonker 2015).

Thomas Ogden calls these psychological organizational structures "modes of being" (Ogden 1986, 1994: 34–39; Raguse 1994: 213–216). He conceives of these "modes of being" as "different dimensions of experience", indicating that although the three modes can be distinguished, they are also interconnected. This interconnectedness implies that a person usually does not operate from one mode only. On the contrary, in order to function healthily, all three modes are of value, according to Ogden. "The subject is not located in any given position, but in a space (tension) created by the dialectical interplay of the different dimensions of experience" (Ogden 1994: 48). However, at a certain moment within a specific relationship one mode of being will always dominate. In the following subsections, I will first present the different modes. I will refrain from using and explaining the various terms that Ogden uses to refer to the modes, as this would require much more explanatory text on psychodynamic theory. I will therefore refer to the modes by simply calling them mode 1, 2 or 3. Next I will discuss how the three modes of being connect to mourning.

Table 9.1. Modes of being as internal organizational structures

Features	Modes of being		
	Mode 1	Mode 2	Mode 3
"Self-image"	No (dominant) "self"	"Self" as object	"Self" as subject and object
Organizing principle	Sensory sensations	Partial-objects (Splitting)	Whole objects (Repression)
Basic fear	"To deflate"	Destruction of "the good"	To be abandoned
Mode of symbolizing	Presymbolic	Symbolic equivalence	Use of symbols
	"It is"	"It is what it is"	"It is as if…"

Mode 1

Mode 1 provides much of the "sensory floor" of experience, as Ogden (1994: 144) puts it. Central in this mode is the body with its sensory perceptions, whereby feeling with the skin is leading. Sensing that things are hard, soft, hot, cold, wet or dry by rubbing, pinching, caressing, for example, is linked in the literature to the early interactions between primary carer(s) and the young child. Being the largest organ of the human body, the skin remains a very important sense throughout one's life. As an intermediary, this outer layer of a person is in constant contact with the outside world. The main psychological function of the skin is that it is able to "contain" many sensations and experiences (long) before it is even able to connect words or meaning to them. Ogden argues that as long as the body is able to store sensory experiences, fear of disintegration (Ogden 1994, 2009) or deflation (Van Bouwel 2003) cannot prevail. Key terms of sensory experiences that make up mode 1 are rhythm, proximity, continuity and boundaries. These first-mode-experiences prepare a person to develop feelings of safety, comfort, connectedness and security (Dehing 1998; Van Bouwel 2003: 126-128; Calsius et al. 2016; Kinet et al. 2015).

Mode 2

In the second mode the self exists predominantly as object (Ogden 1986: 41-66). This means that there is no personal awareness of having experiences. Thoughts and feelings are simply there. More precisely, there are no feelings or thoughts, but rather a continuous flow of "raw sensory data". The organizational core principle that characterizes mode 2 focuses on distinguishing what is threatening from what is harmless. The two must absolutely not come into contact with each other to prevent the good from being destroyed by the bad. A person is equipped with defence mechanisms to establish this radical and immediate separation of love and hatred, good and bad. For example, the subject can magically and omnipotently think away a hating object to the extent of removing the object from experience. Another strategy is to project one's own fear onto another person, who becomes the "container" of that fear. All this is done without interpretation. General meaning is automatically attached, feeding the experience with vitality (Ogden 1994: 141-144). When the good manages to survive, the subject experiences control and is no longer completely at the mercy of fear. By surviving threats through distinguishing the good from the bad, important psychological functions are prepared for a more personal way of assigning meaning.

Mode 3

In mode 3, danger is no longer experienced as totally destructive. Good and bad can be tolerated to exist side by side in one's experience. Gradually the self and others are experienced as complete persons. In the event of a threat, one is aware of distance between the threat and their own person. Increasingly, they experience that there is room to think about what is happening, to assign meaning to it and finally to respond appropriately. Whereas in the event of indigestible fears and threats in mode two, "containers" are automatically searched for outside the self, now space is found inside the self. As a result, relating to others changes. The subject is no longer entirely dependent on other people's potential to cope with fear and threat, but can be more independent. Thus the human subjectivity expands with the help of all kinds of interconnected psychological developments. As Ogden puts it, the subject develops:

"an enhanced capacity for self-object differentiation, the development of the capacity for symbol formation, increased capacities for affective modulation, reality testing, and memory" (Ogden 1986: 71-72) next to biological maturational factors.

Meaning in Modes of Being

According to Ogden's model of three modes of being, learning to endure new or difficult events is fundamentally connected to a person's relationships with others and to meaning-making. If an experience arouses too much fear and if physical reassurance fails (mode 1), one needs the second mode to deal with that threat. The whole of raw sensory data generating the fear is then projected onto another person (mode 2). Young children are therefore dependent on their primary carers; older children or adults turn more broadly to reliable others. The person they turn to ideally shows how to live with this particular danger by interpreting and labelling it. In doing so, the other person sends the message that the difficult and fear-generating initial situation can be handled. Being able to identify with this message, the subject can create meaning. Once a person knows how to link meaning to what is happening, one can really speak of "experiencing" (Ogden 1994: 81; Bion 1962a). If this whole process repeats itself often enough, the subject is eventually capable to give meaning to potential threats within the self (mode 3). People are confronted with events that are potentially too threatening at any age. They usually tend to appeal to a person in their environment who can act as a "container" of that fear who is capable of handling it. If, however, good examples are absent, the opportunity to give meaning to what is happening to one is also lacking. When Geertje lost her baby, for example, she was unable to meaningfully share the raw loss of her child with other people because they took the stance that her baby should never have been there in the first place. Summing up, to arrive at meaningful interpretations, sufficient distance between self and sensory experiences is required, which the subject can only acquire with the help of others. Only Ogden's third mode offers this space between "I and others". The space between "I and others" in the third mode of being is alternatively referred to in psychology as the "transitional space" (Winnicott 1953, 1971) or the "mentalizing capacity" (Allen et al. 2008; Muthert and Schaap-Jonker 2015). Supporters of these concepts usually emphasize the development of an independent self. In my view, the space between I and others should not be narrowly understood to relate to separation or individuation only. After all, by distinguishing themselves from others, people simultaneously learn to relate to those others. Precisely because relating to others is a crucial factor in meaning-making, in my view both theorists and counsellors who focus on mourning should therefore pay more attention to the growing relational capacity between I and others in this third mode than most tend to do presently. Returning to Geertje, for example, it becomes clear that she could only begin to confront or reflect on her loss once her context offered her a safe space. Only in relation to external persons and religious sources that provide appropriate gestures, forms and words, the capacity to make meaning of what happened to her grew in Geertje.

What does that imply for making sense of loss? Because space and meaning are crucial factors in relating to others and developing a narrative sense of self, the third mode appears as the most mature psychological structure (Klein 1958). Ogden indeed stresses the great variety of psychological functions within the third mode. At the same time, however, he disputes a purely development-oriented conception of the modes and underlines their constant interaction. In my view the three modes can be conceived of as the corners of a triangle, which represents the inner space in which the dynamic self moves. In this representation, alternating between all three functions rather than unilinear development towards mode three loses it normative connotation of signifying regression. Indeed, only when a subject gets stuck in one of the three poles, Ogden speaks of pathology. What I find particularly valuable in this model is that it implies that relational dimensions of meaning-making play a role in all three modes. Besides the verbal or symbolic attribution of meaning (mode 3), one could think of a sensory/physical dimension (mode 1) and a dimension of distinguishing between good and evil; moral sense (mode 2). Conceiving of the inner space thus helps to see how religion can be of significance within all these modes. By explicitly linking the model of the three modes of being to mourning, we take the theorization about mourning one step further.

Different Modes of Being in Relation to Mourning

Ogden (2000) describes mourning as a capacity and experience that is situated in the third mode of being; in order to mourn, it is necessary that one can experience continuity between past and present. Only when one realizes that behaviour in the past has consequences for the present and perhaps also for the future, one can be persuaded to repair what went wrong or adapt one's behaviour. Acknowledging that one's actions can be inappropriate and that others also have power over oneself, affects one's sense of control in the sense of having to admit that there are always things in our lives that are beyond our own control. Feelings of dependence (Winnicott 1953; Niers 2017) must therefore be tolerated, as must strong feelings of sadness. Ogden sees this as the capacity to mourn. When the "I" can connect meaning to the complexity of feelings, activities and physical sensations when suffering loss, Ogden speaks of experiences of mourning.

Creating new meaning is a crucial dimension of such experiences (Ogden 2000: 65-66). A clear example can be derived from novelist David Grossman's *Falling Out of Time* (2014) about parents who lose their child. Grossman knows how to give words to an experience that other bereaved people recognize while at the same time showing new ways of expressing such experiences. His novel does not prescribe how to mourn when a child is lost, but offers space, which in turn offers solace. Other creative examples with the power to console mentioned by Ogden are new memories, stories, dreams or poems. He concludes that: "What one makes in the process of mourning ... is far less important than the experience of making it" (Ogden 2000: 66).

The art of mourning is thus connected with the creation of something new, which brings with it a lively feeling that paradoxically stems from the experience of loss and death (Ogden 2000: 65). However, situations of loss can be so extreme that the capacity to mourn falls short and the mourner cannot but seek recourse to other modes of being. The healing sense of creative mourning in these cases is absent. The mourner has insufficient distance to what happens and attaches no meaning to the experience. As a result, feelings of deadness and emptiness dominate. In these situations, therapeutic interventions should focus on restoring relationships (De Kroon and Verplancke 2017). However demanding the conditions may be, efforts to maintain or re-establish relationships with the outside world are necessary in supporting the capacity to mourn. The issue that remains to be addressed here is how social support can take shape in relation to each of the three modes of being.

Effective Mourning Matches between Social Aspects and Different Modes

On the basis of the above, we can conclude that all modes of being are fundamentally helpful in responding to loss. While the mourning capacity is most developed in the third mode, some losses cannot be handled so that the mourner must rely on objects outside the self. A scholar who has moved beyond intra-psychic models to look at the more psychosocial dimension of mourning is the psychoanalyst Darian Leader (2008). Leader outlines a historical development from public to more individual mourning since the First World War. The enormous numbers of deaths in the Great War hampered farewell rituals that focused on individuals and were often collectively organized. After the war, collective rituals declined and personal mourning became the norm. Leader convincingly argues, however, that we may have underestimated the importance of public mourning. People need the examples of others that show that one does not necessarily completely fall victim to mourning. Put in the words of a psychodynamic perspective one could argue that symbolic mourning examples or frames help the grieving self to identify with their own mourning. It is therefore that professional mourners or funeral professionals play a crucial role in mourning rituals. By "playing" their role within a recognized form, they provide the space in which one's own mourning becomes possible. Like Ogden, Leader therefore also sees an important role for writers or artists in public expressions of mourning. These expressions provide forms for experiences that could not come to the surface and be shared without them.

I would argue that religion is very well suited to take on a similar function (also see: Westerink 2017). Religious rituals for example, show a great "containing" potential (Jongsma-Tieleman 1996). Connecting Leader's theory (Leader 2008: 60–99) to that of Ogden (1986, 1994, 2000), it becomes clear that the kind of support for mourning that Leader points to differs per mode. Again, Geertje's case study can be used to illustrate how this may work. Mode 1 is about physical mourning reactions. When this mode dominates, only periodic mourning reactions are visible. This can be recognized in Geertje's story who, for years experiences physical complaints that she cannot place every time during the season in which her baby died. Her body acts as a "carrier of memory" with all kinds of sensations of listlessness; Geertje feels "heavy and dead". Getting recognition and social attention are supportive for her in this situation. As the effect of the words of her friend who shared her observations about the pattern in Geertje's physical pain illustrates, it is necessary for significant others in the environment of the grieving person to recognize their physical responses, before the mourning person can do so themselves. In the second mode of being loss is experienced as a potential threat, which becomes visible to the outside world through isolation, idealization or anger. This can be also recognized in the case of Geertje, who withdraws from everyday life for a number of weeks or months each year. When fear associated with loss emerges, it is considered a threat and all efforts are aimed at thinking it away. For many years, Geertje could not mourn the loss of her baby, because her environment judged that the baby should not have been conceived. Suggesting that one cannot lose what should not have been there in the first place precludes mourning over what happened. The supportive community that Geertje presently finds herself in, on the other hand, acts as a witness to what has been happening to her. Her friends take care of her because they see that something is wrong and they also make an effort in finding a suitable form to express it. They do this concretely by their repeated attempts to stay close to Geertje when she is having a hard time. Ultimately, they also help her by putting how she feels it into words, as in the "You survived June again" observation. Once in the third mode of being, Geertje can recognize the loss and experience her mourning self, she undertakes numerous attempts to capture that loss in words or images so that it can be lived with. What is of particular interest in my argument about the power of religion in mourning, is that, with the support of her spiritual caretaker, Geertje realized that religion can help her find ways to tell her story; she realizes that the religious song that has been singing in her head provides a sense of consolation. The supportive attitude of the spiritual care giver and other significant persons in Geertje's social context recognize these attempts and provide her with creative examples. Religion, in other words, provides Geertje with images that she understands very differently now that she can experience her loss as a loss. She no longer believes that she was alone at the time; God must have been near. It is just that at the time she was not able to see this. This transformation in Geertje's self-narrative does not suddenly make up for everything. But while her loss remains painful, it does change her perspective on the meaning of what happened to her. In the end, what she could perceive only as a threat is transformed and she experiences her new way of thinking and her relationship to the lost baby as meaningful (see Table 2 for an overview).

Table 9.2. Mourning matches between internal modes of being and social aspects

	Mode 1	Mode 2	Mode 3
"Visible" signs of grief	periodic mourning reactions (physical expression)	withdrawal, isolation and idealization, anger	efforts to transform own mourning using mourning dialogue
Supportive mourning behaviour in the public domain	social awareness and attention	available (symbolic) witnesses	recognition of subjective bereavement processes and available creative mourning models

Religion as a Cultural "Container'

I return to my initial question. How does a psychodynamic vision of mourning, based on different modes of being, contribute to a better understanding of variations in mourning behaviour and (religious) meaning making in everyday life? A well-known statement about mourning attributed to Rabbi Baal Shem Tov (1698–1760) summarizes the theoretical insights I discussed above: *"Forgetfulness leads to exile while remembrance is the secret of redemption."* When a person's response to loss corresponds to the first part of this statement – "forgetfulness leads to exile" – periodic grief reactions, idealization, isolation and anger characterize their mourning, while the capacity to transform images or words is lacking; they do not understand their loss. Responses in the category "remembrance is the secret of redemption" on the other hand are characterized by personal creativity in dialogue with the specific mourning models at hand in the cultural context that the bereaved is embedded in. Both types of mourning are common and neither is fixed; people can move back and forth between the two. The latter turns out to be more effective to come to terms with loss and is therefore the healthier option; people who can creatively transform their relationship to loss to make meaning of what happened feel alive instead of being defined by their loss and feeling empty and powerless.

In some situations, a person confronted with loss is too vulnerable to experience the space between themselves and others and lacks the capacity to create meaning. In such cases mourning requires physical action and a supportive environment as adequate social responses so that mourners are not obliged to immediately turn their suffering into a success story. Religion here can come in the form of a community of fellow-believers who support the grieving person. In situations where the mourner does recognize that good and bad coexist, then religion has a lot to offer as a source for the mourner to transform their relationship to the deceased and create meaning. For all three different modes of being, then, religion offer potential support in mourning by providing rituals, social support and an abundance of strong images, stories, songs, art and materials to draw on. In this sense, alongside art, philosophy or science, religion is one of the cultural sources, which generates potentially meaningful mourning models (Winnicott 1971).

Mourning Theory in Practice

The potential of cultural sources to offer vitalization in relation to mourning is one of the main points of argumentation in this chapter; cultural sources, among which religion, offer continuity, space and meaning by adequately integrating good and evil, among other things. The theoretical framework presented in this chapter can be applied at various levels. I will restrict myself here to one-on-one counselling, in which applying the theory to practice consists of three steps. In case that the current response to loss is seen as problematic by the mourner, first, the spiritual caregiver asks what the response to loss means exactly for the mourning person. Next, an assessment is made of how the grieving person relates not only to their loss but also to important others in their lives. On the basis of these first two steps, the spiritual caregiver examines which intervention if most suitable to help the client in coming to terms with their loss. In Geertje's case, the counsellor recognized her longing for witnesses and for symbolic forms to help her shape her loss more effectively. In addition to the song already mentioned, biblical images of a God who catches people when they fall (Deuteronomy 32.11) and holds them in his hand also proved to be valuable to help Geertje make sense of her loss. These images provided alternatives to the original experience of rejection that she had suffered. By letting God and others witness her story and support her in her search for a new response to her loss, Geertje experiences grief but she also feels alive. One may wonder why Geertje did not experience religion as supportive before. Although religious sources were present, they did not fit in well with her specific second mode needs at the time. This illustrates that religion does not offer a number of metaphors that do good by default. Metaphorical images only work when the third mode of being is dominant. It was precisely support and witnesses that were previously lacking in Geertje's life. Therefore, her response was one of forgetting. But what was forgotten became a heavy weight. Geertje's case study illustrates that it is therefore crucial to recognize which forms of support match with which modes of being of a person who suffers loss. It draws our attention to the fact that, while religion meets the conditions of sufficient playfulness and also offers room for ambivalence and can therefore function very well as a "container" in the western cultural context (Westerink 2017), social awareness of and attention to physical grief as well as the courage to witness suffering are also necessary conditions for assisting people who suffer loss.

Discussion

Besides the possibilities that the theoretical model I have presented in this chapter has to offer, it also has its limitations. It does not, for instance, provide static truths about mourning in the sense of identifying certain subsequent phases or task-based prescriptions. This openness is productive in allowing specific personalized assessments and interventions, but it is also demanding on the counsellor; it requires an ongoing reflective attitude and a constant playfulness in relation to people's various "answers" to loss (mode 3). Recognizing the different modes in oneself and others is crucial for effective counselling. Regarding the process of meaning-making, the counsellor must have an eye for first, second and third mode signifiers, and avoid prioritizing the most mature third form. Such an attitude is not obvious in the western cultural context, which is, among others, strongly characterized by a discourse of the individual as independent agent and being fully responsible for their own lives, a discourse about "winners and losers" that corresponds with the second mode of being (cf. Hermsen 2017; Johannisson 2010; Dehue 2014; Verhaeghe 2012; De Wachter 2012). This discourse diminishes the space or scope for mourning in the third mode and is accompanied by an increase of people suffering depression, burnout and feelings of emptiness. Another complication concerns the models" emphasis on invisible inner processes. This contrasts with the popularity of observable facts and objective knowledge through numerical transparency.

A second limitation concerns the internal standard of the model itself, which characterizes the third mode as the most mature and healthy. This leaves less room for playfulness than suggested. Besides, what this model describes as healthy capacities may be different in other than western cultural contexts. Maturity and health are culturally informed concepts. Finally, while the concepts of "subject" here understood as the person suffering loss, and "object", here the deceased are central to the model, variations exist within psychodynamic thinking as to what actually constitutes a subject and object and what characterizes subject – object relations. These alternative views will emphasize other conceptions or psychological functions that lead to other counselling models.

About the Author

Hanneke Muthert is professor of psychology of religion and spiritual care at the Faculty of Theology and Religious Studies, University of Groningen. Her current research projects focus on (1) disaster chaplaincy, (2) meaningful work and (3) psychopathology, religion and good spiritual care practices. The overarching theme is characterized by how to support people in diverse care contexts (home, healthcare, work) to live their daily lives coping with significant losses and longings. In relation to an observed lack of common language sharing existential issues, she elaborates on the idea of concrete practice places in the near future. For publications see www.rug.nl/staff/j.k.muthert/research.

References

Allen, J.G., Peter Fonagy and Anthony. W. Bateman. 2008. *Mentalizing in Clinical Practice*. Washington, DC: American Psychiatric Publishing.

Attig, T. 2010. *How We Grieve: Relearning the World*, 2nd edition. Oxford: Oxford University Press.

Attig, T. 2001. "Relearning the World: Making and Finding New Meanings." In *Meaning Reconstruction and the Experience of Loss*, edited by R.A. Neimeyer, pp. 33–54. Washington, DC: American Psychological Association. https://doi.org/10.1037/10397-002

Bion, W.R. 1962a. *Learning from Experience*. London: Heinemann.

Bion, W.R. 1962b. "A Theory of Thinking." *International Journal of Psycho-Analysis* 43: parts 4–5.

Bion, W.R. 1965. *Transformations*. London: Heinemann.

Bion, W.R. 1967. *Second Thoughts*. London: Heinemann.

Bion, W.R. 1970. *Attention and Interpretation*. London: Heinemann.

Boevink, W. 2017. *HEE! Over Herstel, Empowerment en Ervaringsdeskundigheid in de psychiatrie*. Utrecht: Trimbos-instituut.

Calsius, J., J. De Bie, R. Hertogen and R. Meesen. 2016. "Touching the Lived Body in Patients with Medically Unexpected Symptoms: How an Integration of Hands-On Bodywork and Body Awareness in Psychotherapy May Help People with Alexithymia." *Frontiers in Psychology* 7: 153. https://doi.org/10.3389/fpsyg.2016.00253

Dehing, J. 1998. "Over gelijkheid en verschillendheid – Van primordiale identiteit tot discriminerend bewustzijn." In *Een bundel intense duisternis: Psychoanalytische opstellen rond W.R. Bion*, edited by J. Dehing, pp. 111–163. Apeldoorn: Garant.

Dehue, T. 2014. *Betere mensen: Over gezondheid als keuze en koopwaar*. Amsterdam: Uitgeverij Augustus.

De Kroon, J. and T. Verplancke. 2017. "Als in een zwarte spiegel: Over het syndroom van Cotard." *Tijdschrift voor Psychoanalyse* 23(2): 105–115.

De Mönnink, H. 2017. *Verlieskunde: Methodisch kompas voor de beroepspraktijk*. Houten: Bohn Stafleu van Loghum.

De Wachter, D. 2012. *Borderline Times: Het einde van de normaliteit*. Tielt: Uitgeverij LannooCampus.

Freud, S. 1917. "Trauer und melancholie." *Internationale Zeitschrift für Ärztliche Psychoanalyse* 4: 288–301.

Grossman, D. 2014. *Falling Out of Time*, translated by Jessica Cohen. New York: Vintage Books.

Hagman, G. 2001. "Beyond Decathexis: Toward a New Psychoanalytic Understanding and Treatment of Mourning." In *Meaning Reconstruction and the Experience of Loss*, edited by R.A. Neimeyer, pp. 13–31. Washington, DC: American Psychological Association. https://doi.org/10.1037/10397-001

Hermsen, J.J. 2017. *Melancholie van de onrust*. Amsterdam-Antwerpen: Uitgeverij De Arbeiderspers.

Huber, M., M. van Vliet, M. Giezenberg, B. Winkens, Y. Heerkens, P.C. Dagnelie, J.A. Knottnerus. 2016. "Towards a 'Patient-Centred' Operationalisation of the New Dynamic Concept of Health: A Mixed Methods Study." *British Medical Journal* 5: 1–12. https://doi.org/10.1136/bmjopen-2015-010091

Johannisson, K. 2010. *De kamers van de melancholie: Over angst, verveling en depressie*. Translated by E. van der Heijden en W. Jongeneel. Amsterdam: Ambo/Anthos.

Jongsma-Tieleman, N. 1996. *Godsdienst als speelruimte voor verbeelding: Een godsdienstpsychologische studie*. Kampen: Uitgeverij Kok.

Kinet, M., K. Vuylsteke Vanfleteren, S. Houpermans. (eds). 2015. *Als het lichaam spreekt*. Apeldoorn: Garant.

Klass, D., P.R. Silverman, S.L. Nickman (eds). 1996. *Continuous Bonds: New Understandings of Grief*. New York: Routledge.

Klein, M. 1958. "On the Development of Mental Functioning." In *Envy and Gratitude and Other Works, 1946-1963: The Writings of Melanie Klein Volume III* (1975): 236–246. New York: The Free Press.

Kübler-Ross, E. 1969. *On Death and Dying*. New York: Macmillan.

Leader, D. 2008. *The New Black: Mourning, Melancholia and Depression*. London: Penguin Books.

Leget C., T. Staps, J. van de Geer, C. Mur-Arnoldi, M. Wulp, H. Jochemsen. 2010. "Richtlijn Spirituele zorg." Retrieved from www.oncoline.nl/spirituele-zorg (accessed 25 June 2018).

Melzer, D. 2008 (1978). *The Kleinian Development*. London: Karnac Books.

Mooij, A. 2002. *Psychoanalytisch gedachtegoed: Een modern perspectief*. Amsterdam: Boom.

Muthert, H. 2007. *Verlies en Verlangen: Verliesverwerking bij schizofrenie*. Assen: Van Gorcum.

Muthert, H. 2012. *Ruimte voor verlies: Geestelijke verzorging in de psychiatrie*. KSGV 2-80. Tilburg: KSGV.

Muthert, H., J.H. Diephuis, H.E. Luijten and C.J. Slooff. 2008. "Verliesverwerking bij psychotische stoornissen. Verlangen naar betekenis: Achtergrond, theoretisch kader en een traininginstrument (reader en workshops) voor hulpverleners." In *Complicaties bij de behandeling van mensen met een psychose*, edited by C.J. Slooff, F. Withaar and M. van der Gaag, pp. 145-260. Kenniscentrum schizofrenie No. 6. The Hague: Schizofrenie stichting – Kenniscentrum voor zorg en beleid.

Muthert, H. and Schaap-Jonker. 2015. "Verbeeldingskracht als denkmodus- over trauma, kunst en zoeken naar zin." *Psyche en geloof* 26(1): 49-61.

Neimeyer, R.A. (ed.). 2001. *Meaning Reconstruction and the Experience of Loss*. Washington, DC: American Psychological Association. https://doi.org/10.1037/10397-000

Neimeyer, R.A., D. Harris, H. Winokeur and G. Thornton (eds). 2011. *Grief and Bereavement in Contemporary Society: Bridging Research and Practice*. New York: Routledge. https://doi.org/10.4324/9780203840863

Niers, P. 2017. "Narcisme in de Nederlandse psychoanalyse." *Tijdschrift voor psychoanalyse* 23(1): 42-55.

Ogden, T.H. 1986. *The Matrix of the Mind: Object relations and the psychoanalytic Dialogue*. London: Karnac Books.

Ogden, T.H. 1989. *The Primitive Edge of Experience*. London: Karnac Books.

Ogden, T.H. 1994. *Subjects of Analysis*. London: Karnac Books.

Ogden, T.H. 2000. "Borges and the Art of Mourning." *Psychoanalytic Dialogues* 10(1): 65-88. https://doi.org/10.1080/10481881009348522

Ogden, T.H. 2005. *This Art of Psychoanalysis: Dreaming Undreamt Dreams and Interrupted Cries*. London: Routledge.

Ogden, T.H. 2009. *Rediscovering Psychoanalysis: Thinking and Dreaming, Learning and Forgetting*. London: Routledge.

Oosterhuis, H. and A. Oomen. 1996. "Groter dan ons hart." *Gezangen voor Liturgie* 488: 465-468.

Raguse, H. 1994. *Der Raum des Textes. Elemente einer transdisziplinären theologischen Hermeneutik*. Stuttgart: Kohlhammer.

Thys, M. 2018. "Onontkoombaar en ongrijpbaar." *Tijdschrift voor Psychoanalyse* 24(2): 99–112.

Van Bouwel, L. 2003. "Van een projectiescherm naar een mentale ruimte: residentiële psychotherapie met jonge psychotische patiënten." In *Spreken en Gesproken Worden. Psychoanalyse en Psychosen*, edited by J. Smet, L. Van Bouwel, and R. Vandenborre, pp. 119–144. Leuven: Garant.

Verhaeghe, P. 2012. *Identiteit*. Amsterdam: De Bezige Bij.

Westerink, H. 2017. *Lust en onbehagen*. Amsterdam: Uitgeverij Sjibbolet.

Winnicott, D.W. 1969. "The Use of an Object and Relating through Identifications." In *Playing and Reality*, D.W. Winnicott (1971): 86–94. London: Tavistock Publications.

Winnicott, D.W. 1971. *Playing and Reality*. London: Tavistock Publications.

Winnicott, D.W. 1953. "Transitional Objects and Transitional Phenomena: A Study of the First Not-Me Possession." *International Journal of Psychoanalysis* 34: 89–97.

ZonMw. 2016. "ZonMw-signalement over Zingeving in Zorg. De mens centraal." Retrieved from https://publicaties.zonmw.nl/fileadmin/zonmw/documenten/Corporate/ZonMw_zingeving_herdruk_totaal.pdf.

– 10 –

Dilemmas in Participant Observation in Religious Contexts

KIM KNIBBE

Introduction

Increasingly, participant observation is employed in religious studies. This method owes much to the discipline of anthropology, but also to the more qualitative approaches developed in sociology. Within the field of religious studies, recent decades have seen a shift from a predominantly "history of religions" approach to a focus on the study of "lived religion" (McGuire 2008; Nyhagen 2017; Orsi 2013).

Participant observation, unsurprisingly, involves both observation and participation. But how you observe, and how you participate, and crucially, to what extent, is open to variation and interpretation. Much of this variation is due to differences in setting and context, as well as what role you are allocated or carve out for yourself in a particular context. Taking the most straightforward kind of research in a religious context as a point of departure, namely a church congregation, there are choices that will influence what you will observe and how you participate. Do you volunteer to pour coffee? Or do you join the choir? Do you help out with the children's service, or do you stick to attending the main service? Furthermore, there are issues to do with your own fixed positions (gender, race, age) that will influence how you have access to a context, where and how you can participate. In this chapter, I will not address these issues, since these are discussed in any good handbook on ethnographic research methods and qualitative research methods (Denzin and

---

Keywords: participant observation, ethnography, religious practice, research ethics, not participating

Lincoln 2005; Knibbe 2015; Denzin 2003). Rather, this chapter focuses on the specific challenges that may occur when doing research in contexts that involve an understanding of the world that may be at odds with your own. Participation, then, may open up many more complex issues than we might think at first. How do you participate in praying, if you think there is no God? Does it make sense to join in anyway? What kind of knowledge might you obtain if you do participate? How do you respond when people pray over you or aim to convert you? Or when a medium tells you she has a message for you from your deceased grandmother? Where and how do you draw the line in participation?

In the following, I will discuss some of the dilemmas that participant observation in a religious context may involve by describing the contexts in which I carried out fieldwork. This will allow me to explicate all the minute decisions that may go into (not) participating, as well as the kinds of knowledge we may gain through this practice, even when we decide not to participate. Furthermore, especially in doing research in religious contexts, becoming a good researcher also means that one has to develop one's ability to reflect on the issues that might come up through your involvement in a context that very often is designed to address you on an existential level, but to which you may come "merely" as a researcher.

Belief or Practice?

In the introduction of this book, we addressed the problem of belief when studying religion: does one take the position, *a priori*, that religious beliefs are false, as Lett proposes (methodological atheism)? Or do we leave room for the possibility that there might be "more", as Ninian Smart (2015) proposes (methodological agnosticism)? Or do we go along with the suggestion that being a believer might actually enable us some kind of special insight into religion, as Evans Pritchard and Victor Turner seem to suggest? In any case, doing fieldwork in a religious context may challenge you epistemologically (how do I know what I know, do I know in the same way as others do?) and ontologically (what exists?).

Epistemologically, you may be told, as I have been told many times by religious and spiritual practitioners, that it is no use interviewing them, you must experience it. In other words, they do not believe you can gain any valuable insight by talking to them, you must *do* like them to understand what it's about. So, basically, my interlocutors questioned my methodology and suggested full participation and learning to experience what they experienced as the best avenue; whereas I would not immediately agree that experiencing would be the best way to understand what they are doing. So this creates a stalemate even before the research actually starts. Similarly (as also happened to me), born-again Christians may insist that it is no use asking for which bible texts underpin certain practices, because if you have not been baptized in the spirit you will not be able to understand the text: becoming born-again is the precondition to developing knowledge.

Ontologically, you may be challenged by references to beings you don't think exist, yet in participating in a religious context, you may join in activities that do presuppose the existence of that which you may think does not exist and find that somehow, through doing this, the possible existence of these entities suddenly becomes much more plausible (so is this the "experiencing" then, does this create a specific kind of knowledge after all, like spiritual practitioners say?). Or, alternatively, you may feel like a fraud every time you participate and the practices continue not to make sense to you, so how can you then understand why people do this? In carrying out participant observation, there is the underlying assumption that fieldworkers will experience a "thinning" of the membrane that separates different worlds, as Ewing and Harding suggest (Harding 1987; Ewing 1994). And this is exactly what fieldwork is in fact aimed at: to uncover how the world makes sense from the point of view of your interlocutors.[1]

In the following, I will depart from this observation of the thinning of the membrane, but take it out of the quite "intellectual" realm of belief, into the embodied realm of religious practice, focusing on how religious contexts may not only invite and expect bodily participation, but also address the sense in ways that are unavoidable, and effective. Intellectually, it might not be such a big step outside of your own comfort zone to consider the possibility that a God may exist who interferes with your life, when in your daily life you don't consider that a possibility. After all, as academics and students we entertain different or even opposite points of view all the time. However, to actually participate, physically, in religious practices and rituals that address beings and realms that you normally do not address might be a different matter altogether.

Between the fall of 1999 and winter of 2002, I carried out fieldwork in the Netherlands in several contexts where spiritual practitioners

---

1. Harding also refers to the problem of doing fieldwork with what she calls "the repugnant other": groups that in your own intellectual and social environment are considered too horrible to be legitimate research subjects, and who may hold points of view that you find morally and ethically objectionable. This lies outside the scope of this chapter, but see Harding and Howell for a discussion of these topics (Harding 1991; Howell 2007).

congregate. As a student, I carried out research where for half a year I attended the "healing services" of the Dutch medium Jomanda, and later, for my PhD research, I participated for more than a year in a "spiritual society" where members aimed to practise their psychic and healing abilities, as well as in a Catholic pastoral centre characterized by a very liberal interpretation of Catholicism. In the following section, I will first introduce the setting, and then tease out which issues arose there.

Spiritual Healing and Paranormal Practices

At the entrance of the big hall (which can host several hundred people), my entrance ticket is checked and I receive a card which is energetically charged. While looking for a seat, electronic music starts playing, a slow melody in a minor key. People grab each other's hands, and sing along: "we are all together now, to get the power of the light, let us all hold hands and go inside …". My hands are grabbed, and I sway along (uncomfortably). Jomanda enters the stage while the song is repeated, singing into the microphone, dressed in a long blue gown wearing gold-strapped sandals. When the song fades away, several people have fallen onto the floor, sometimes shouting and writhing uncontrollably, and ushers hurry to stand guard, ensuring that nobody touches them. Many people have their eyes closed, some are crying. Jomanda intones: "everything that happens here, is meant to be. You will never receive more than you can handle". She encourages people to formulate a wish, something they are hoping for.

After this opening, the healing service develops along several parallel tracks: she invites particular people to lie down on the stretchers that are set out on the podium. While they are lying there, she walks into the audience to address individual people with a message. Every now and then, she will invite everyone who has a particular complaint (such as a headache, or cancer, or anxiety) to stand. The idea is that while people are lying down on the stretcher, or standing, they are being worked on by "the other side". Potentially, since she is a medium, everyone in the room might be subjected to such a treatment. She tells everyone not to be surprised to experience a sensation of paralysis, or being engulfed by emotion, falling down, or swaying back and forth, and warns people not to touch anyone who exhibits such involuntary behaviours. As people told me during interviews, touch by a human while you are being treated by the other side is experienced as searing pain, a burning sensation.

At the time that Jomanda rose to fame, her healing-services were often discussed with outrage by the highbrow media in the Netherlands.

"Medieval", quackery and swindler were the accusations levelled at her. These highbrow media acted surprised, as if they couldn't believe that such things were occurring in this day and age (namely, the mid-1990s, which in their view was modern and free of such practices). Yet, what happens during these healing-services, is a magnification and elaboration of a set of practices that many people engage in that might include mediumistic healing on a smaller scale, but also tarot card reading, aura reading, astrology, finding your spirit animal and all sorts of other practices. These practices are not medieval, but arose and developed mostly since the nineteenth century, first in elite circles, but have now become more widely practised, although usually outside of the mainstream. In the spiritual society I participated in, people gathered together once a month for various activities: sometimes a healer or aura-reader visited, these evenings were always quite full with people who might only attend once. Other evenings were members only, and involved discussing and practising particular skills: dream interpretation, tarot-card reading, family constellation enactment, sound healing.

Many of the practices and behaviours in these circles went against my own common sense understanding of what exists and what is possible in the world, let alone received scientific understandings. Gradually, I realized that I was not alone in that: many visitors to the healing services of Jomanda and to the spiritual society were actually also quite sceptical. Common to both of these settings was an emphasis on efficacy: people were invited to check whether things worked for them, and freely expressed when things did not "work" for them. A difference between many others, however, and myself is that I came for research, and was not necessarily interested in efficacy. However, I trained myself to be more interested in efficacy. Let me explain why.

In preparing for this research, I employed an understanding of participant observation that was strongly influenced by phenomenological anthropology. Phenomenological anthropology concerns itself with how people perceive the world with all their senses, through practical engagement with the world. Rather than view culture and religion as abstract systems of signs and symbols, phenomenological anthropology understands them as embodied realities that are always already meaningful in particular ways to people. To understand how people in a particular setting (including religious settings) understand the world, it is therefore important that the researcher submits him or herself to at least some of the same routines, physical settings, movements, food and food preparation techniques, bodily disciplines and mental techniques that make up the world that he or she enters. The researcher thus has to become an apprentice of the people s/he is aiming to understand,

and let herself be taught to do things correctly, understand and perceive things correctly, taste and prepare food correctly and so on. Important to mention here is the notion of "bracketing", taken from phenomenology, which means that as a researcher, one suspends judgment about the "reality" of the phenomena one studies. It involves a suspension of disbelief, a conscious choice not to let your mind immediately deconstruct what is presented to you to conform to your preconceived ideas about how the world works.

So, I suspended judgment, but also oriented myself more fully to the question of efficacy and apprenticed myself in practical ways. In the case of Jomanda, this implied that I joined in the singing, held hands, that I mentally held a question or problem in mind when she asked me to do so, that I came forward for a "thumbprint" when she asked a particular group (such as those with a headache, if I happened to fall into that category) to come forward. This, of course, also meant bracketing my discomfort with these practices, and the way they made me feel more than a little ridiculous. It also meant that when people showed me pictures of their "scars", which were taken to be proof that the "other side" had operated them, I did not immediately deconstruct what I saw on the picture to be the result of, for example, sitting in a particular position for a while with creased clothes. In the context of the spiritual society, it meant that I joined in meditations where people asked the divine light to come into their bodies. Although one cannot assume that one will experience the exact same thing, this mimeticism (bodily awareness of the other in oneself) accomplishes a reciprocity of viewpoints, and therefore an intersubjective basis for understanding that goes beyond an intellectual exchange of views (Jackson 1989: 130).

Indeed, I would argue that pursuing participation as an embodied practice was quite important to being able to sift through the ways that people navigated away from their own initial scepticism: not through an intellectual process of becoming convinced of the reality of "the other side", auras, spirits etc., but rather through an experiential process that was focused on evidence, that followed from their own participation and "trying out" of things, people's own evaluations of the efficacy of certain practices and interpretations. Many times, I was drawn into conversations about aura pictures, or the interpretation of a tarot card, and saw how particular bodily sensations, sudden "intuitions" and thoughts, images that popped into someone's mind, became part of the process of interpretation in ways that I would not have understood if I had not learnt to pay attention to those things myself, if I had never turned my attention inwards when asked to do so, or imagined light flowing through my body. On some occasions, I had experienced quite extraordinary things and had long-running discussions about what these experiences might mean. Most importantly, I had learned that it is not so much the literal meaning of a sign, the colour of an aura, or a message that is important. Rather, it is the way such a sign could move people from one, sometimes rather hopeless, fixed or bleak outlook on life, into a whole new way of experiencing their life and the possibilities in it. Exactly because people were sceptical, an unexpected sign or message that at first did not make sense but then suddenly "clicked" became all the more convincing of the central underlying premise that was the aim of all these practices: that there is a spiritual world, and that the beings on the other side care for you, guide you and want the best for you (Knibbe 2012; Knibbe, van der Meulen and Versteeg 2012; Knibbe and Versteeg 2008).

So how did all this affect me personally? Did I come away assuming those things as well, having successfully apprenticed myself as I had set out to do? Yes and no. As I have explained elsewhere, I became proficient at experiencing the world in a meaningful way, as imbued with spiritual guidance and in some ways convinced that indeed, there is particular reason why certain things happen in our life. Yet in the end I chose, consciously, to step out of this world, move away from these practices and the meaning they embody. Fieldwork is not without consequences, also for the fieldworker. Which brings me to my next theme: *not* participating. There are, in every sort of fieldwork, moments when a researcher will not want to participate, however dedicated one is.

Not Participating

While participating can give one many insights into a particular context that goes beyond the intellectual and semantic, *not* participating can be equally illuminating, although in perhaps confusing ways. Participating in the context of Jomanda is quite a clearly demarcated event. The healing services lasted for about 2½ hours, and then everyone went home. I conducted interviews for a maximum of 2½ hours and then went home. I lived in Amsterdam, while the healing services and interviews took place all over the country. There was very little that I did not participate in while the research was ongoing. In sum, although the practices of this setting stretched my sense of the real, it did not give rise to occasions where I thought it truly dangerous (to my sanity or otherwise) to participate. However, in the case of the spiritual society, and spiritual practices in other settings (paranormal markets, private consultations and courses), participation created a denser network of movement and connections across a much smaller area focused on the south of Limburg. I met the same people again and again, and when talking to one person, we sometimes talked about other people we knew in common. So that also meant people got to know me better as well: whatever I revealed about my own family history, for example. I had family in the region, some people knew my aunt, who was a family doctor, and told me things about her spiritual development (that she had gold in her aura, for example, very special). They told me things about myself quite frequently, about my aura, my weaknesses and future path in life. So what I did as a fieldworker could not be separated so easily from who I was as a person in the rest of my life. Mostly, I did not find this too complicated, I simply noted things down, asked further questions to clarify what people meant, thanked them for flattering descriptions and shut up thoughtfully when they were unflattering. Although these kinds of comments and observations could be unsettling and I might have to think through how to interpret them, they did not hold me back from participating. However, there were several occasions where my family history did cause moments of non-participation.

In a way that at the time I was not fully prepared to admit, my own upbringing and family history had informed my choice of topic: I was doing research in the South of Limburg where I had grown up, a Catholic region, as part of a non-Catholic nuclear family but connected to an extended family that was very much moulded by Catholicism: my grandfather had been in a convent during the interbellum, which he had kept a secret from most of his children. He had already made his eternal vows. When he broke these vows, he was excommunicated and he had to stay out of public sight for a while. Somehow, a friendly priest in another diocese agreed to celebrate the marriage between him and my grandmother despite this, and they had nine children, honouring, despite my grandmother's frequent exhaustion, the Catholic injunction not to use contraceptives. My mother, in contrast, decisively broke with the church and sent us to a Waldorf school, based on the spiritual teachings of Rudolf Steiner. Meanwhile, many of her older brothers and sisters raised their children (my cousins) Catholic. Growing up then, I had been both observer and participant, both part and apart from my cultural surroundings, as well as part of a sub-culture where people pursued spiritual insights within a wider setting that was largely hostile to these practices and ideas.

While I did not mind the ways people discussed me and my spiritual development, nor did I mind very much to play with different interpretations of things that happened during healing or mediumistic sessions, or after drawing a particular tarot card, I did shy away whenever a medium told me they had a message from my grandmother for me. On some occasions, I could not refuse to hear the message. Both times, this was a channelled message and everybody in the closed setting where the medium performed received a message and a personal tape recording of the message afterwards to listen to it again. The message coming from her was quite general (that she was looking out for me) so I was not unduly rattled. However, my grandmother had made herself known on another occasion in a way that was harder to ignore. (The following recaptures an incident described and analysed more fully in Knibbe 2020).

During my fieldwork I attended mostly small group sessions. However, I also occasionally attended mass. Usually, I would not participate in taking communion except during small celebrations where the priests knew me, and knew I was not a baptized Catholic but offered me communion regardless. Once, during the celebration of a mass, a priest (whom I knew and liked) walked into the crowd to offer communion. When he offered me the communion, I refused, my throat literally closed up. At that moment, I could not explain why I felt so conflicted, I had after all participated during smaller more private communions, with these same priests present. In the 2020 article, I explain this by referring to the process through which I became aware of the ways the communion had been used to force women to submit to their husbands sexually and to bear more children than they actually wanted. This was enforced through detailed questioning during confession, yearly visits by the chaplain or parish priest. If a woman indicated that she wanted to limit the number of children or asked whether she had to submit to her husband against her own wishes, she was not granted absolution, unless she promised to resume "normal marital relations": nothing should get in the way of conception. If one did not get absolution, one could not receive communion. So women who wanted to be able to keep their head high in their community submitted. Including my grandmother, who had tried, unsuccessfully, to miscarry when she was pregnant with the fifth. And then had four more children after that fifth child.

This knowledge, so personal and close to me, informed my bodily reaction to the offer of the communion during mass: I could not. The public character of the communion, and the public character of the possibility that one might be refused communion, was key to this. Thus; rather than submit to the symbolic order in which this possibility was embedded, I refused, almost involuntarily. I did not participate.

Reflections

In this chapter, I have put forward a view on participation as embodied practice. Thus, participation is not just a matter of tagging along to create more opportunities for observation. Rather, it implies a view of religion, culture and ritual as embodied practices that require that the researcher is ready to apprentice herself to learn to become a reasonably competent participant in this context. Although I did not consciously assume a "belief" in the reality of "the other side" guiding us, I came to understand on a physical level how one could become convinced of this reality, and how it made as much sense, if not more, as assuming that there is no such thing as "the other side". To put it into more difficult words: through learning different epistemologies (ways of acquiring knowledge), I was able to apprehend other ontologies (notions about what exists and the nature of things). However, what I learned could only serve as a starting point for creating a better understanding: one should never generalize one's own experiences.

Let me explain this through a concrete example: The first few times that I attended healing services, I was really quite bored and could not see the appeal. It was certainly not entertainment, the way some newspapers had disparagingly described it. It was too long, too chaotic and did not make sense in any way to the observer. It did not really engage the senses in a pleasing way. Reviewing my notes afterwards, I felt that I did not understand at all what happened there. Yet many participants of Jomanda's healing services told us that they could already feel themselves entering another state of consciousness as soon as they heard the opening tones of the "song of light", the music played at the beginning of every healing service. Others told us that they sensed the "other side" starting their work immediately when the music started. Indeed, I observed that several participants collapsed onto the floor or were fixed by paralysis even before Jomanda came on stage. As I became a more frequent visitor, the song of light became a cue to turn my attention inwards and start observing myself for any sign that something might be about to happen. This way of participating, I noticed, made the sessions much less boring and chaotic, but rather full of potential significance where the unexpected could be expected to occur, in the form of dozens of small miracles, not only through what one could observe in oneself, but also through Jomanda's encouragement to look for evidence in other ways: scratches on a wedding ring that people would put under their chairs, colours appearing around Jomanda's hands with special significance, spots on a photograph of a loved one.

It was this understanding of the healing services as full of potential significance that enabled me to make sense of what people told me during interviews, and to be attentive to the specific ways the very "boring" messages that people received could become entwined with their personal biography and narrative, charging their life with significance even in those cases where physical healing was far away. So I did not use my own experiences (this is possible through the genre of auto-ethnography), but simply used the embodied skills I had learned and the sensations these skills produce to be able to navigate what people were telling me and reinforce the intersubjective understanding one aims for in interviewing and interpreting interview.

Yet, as I have also outlined, I did not always participate, and I would never advise anyone to participate at all costs. To begin with, I was perhaps more ready than the average researcher to risk my own sense of what is real and what is not. Some anthropologists argue that one should be ready to take these risks (Castro, Pedersen and Holbraad 2014). After all, how can one do proper research if one assumes a priori that the people one studies have nothing of worth to say about the world? I would argue that it is important to consciously think about what one is willing to risk, as well as reflect on what one is not willing to risk. Both are equally instructive about the boundaries between the researcher and the research setting. However, I would not advocate that one should in all cases take these risks.

Indeed, the reason why one does not want to cross this boundary can be enlightening, although not in a simple way. It needs more analysis. In the case where I refused the communion, does my refusal mean that that all those people who did participate in communion agreed with the symbolic universe that I was refusing, where women were forced to submit sexually and have children against their will? Certainly not. Many of those present would be horrified if I put this to them as a statement. The symbolic universe they submitted to was theologically centred on a God of love, who freely gave his life and became the miracle of the resurrection, the notion that even in the midst of death, life will persist. On a more practical level, they submitted to a ritual order to reconnect them with past generations, how they had been raised, and the notion that one should be in a state of grace.

So how can we understand this? As a researcher, I had made certain connections between current ritual practices and in particular the ways they can be used to exclude particular groups of people. Others did not make these connections, at least not in this setting. In other settings in the same region, priests had been known to explicitly instruct specific groups not to come forward for communion; divorcees, those who had engaged in sex before marriage (and had not confessed this), homosexuals and so forth. This use of the sacraments was generally regarded as an outrage. The chapel where this incident took place was known to be served by quite liberal priests, who did not agree with using the sacrament as a weapon. I knew this. Yet, the public character of the communion and the ambiguity of the ritual act, with its potential to exclude people, led me to my involuntary protest.

In conclusion, in participant observation we need to be critical of the knowledge we gain and the conclusions we draw from this knowledge. Both participating and the moments when one does not participate can be illuminating entry-points. Meanwhile, it is important to avoid the pitfall of generalizing one's own experience (see also Berger's critical discussion of Renato Rosaldo's famous article on finally being able to understand "the headhunter's rage" when grieving for the death of his wife, Michelle Rosaldo; Berger 2010). In addition, it is important to note that one should not give in to the temptation to assume that "believers" or those who practice religion, are as totalizing in inhabiting their world as they may appear to be (Coleman 2015). Often, religious practice constitutes a "partial culture", in which people engage some of the time, but not all of the time.

Concluding Remarks

Many people who have carried out participant observation in religious contexts have written about the dilemmas that may arise. I have described some of these dilemmas and the questions and avenues of investigation these may open up in the context of spiritualism and Catholicism. There are many more dilemmas, of which some of the more obvious ones have to do with attempts at converting the researcher. This is something that is almost impossible to avoid if one does research among "born again" Christians. However, even in those deeply uncomfortable and sometimes intimidating moments, something can be learned, about the techniques of persuasion (Harding), ideas about texts and the embodiment of the holy spirit, but also about the ethics of the context in which one participates. The way out of such a conversion attempt is blocked in every way or populated by demons. So what happens after the researcher refuses? Is he or she shunned? In most cases, this does not happen, which again teaches us something about religious contexts in terms of their everyday ethics and social dynamics.

Doing research in a religious context can be one of the most challenging things you will ever do, confronting you in a practical way with issues, dilemmas and questions that are usually confined to the libraries of philosophers in the setting of everyday life. The underlying issues regarding epistemology and ontology are subject to ongoing debates both in anthropology and in religious studies, conducted under the headings of phenomenological anthropology, the ontological turn in anthropology, and the lived religion approach in religious studies.

About the Author

Kim Knibbe is associate professor of anthropology and sociology of religion at Groningen University. She is currently directing the project "Sexuality, Religion and Secularism" with Rachel Spronk (funded by NWO). Previous research focused on Catholicism and spirituality in the Netherlands and on Nigerian Pentecostalism in Europe and the Netherlands. She has also published a series of theoretical and methodological reflections on studying religion. Her most recent co-edited books and special issues are *Secular Societies, Spiritual Selves?* (with Anna Fedele, 2020) and *Theorizing Lived Religion* (with Helena Kupari, Journal of Contemporary Religion, 2020).

References

Berger, Peter. 2010. "Assessing the Relevance and Effects of 'Key Emotional Episodes' for the Fieldwork Process." In *Anthropological Fieldwork: A Relational Process*, edited by D. Spencer and J. Davies, pp. 119–143. Newcastle upon Tyne: Cambridge Scholars Publishing.

Castro, Eduardo Viveiros de, Morten Axel Pedersen and Martin Holbraad. 2014. "The Politics of Ontology: Anthropological Positions." Retrieved from http://culanth.org/fieldsights/462-the-politics-of-ontology-anthropological-positions.

Coleman, Simon. 2015. "Borderlands: Ethics, Ethnography, and 'Repugnant' Christianity." *HAU: Journal of Ethnographic Theory* 5(2): 275–300. https://doi.org/10.14318/hau5.2.016

Denzin, Norman K. 2003. *Strategies of Qualitative Inquiry*. Thousand Oaks, CA: Sage.

Denzin, Norman K. and Yvonna S. Lincoln. 2005. *The Sage Handbook of Qualitative Research*. Thousand Oaks, CA: SAGE.

Ewing, Katherine P. 1994. "Dreams from a Saint: Anthropological Atheism and the Temptation to Believe." *American Anthropologist* 96(3): 571–583. https://doi.org/10.1525/aa.1994.96.3.02a00080

Harding, Susan. 1987. "Convicted by the Holy Spirit: The Rhetoric of Fundamental Baptist Conversion." *American Ethnologist* 14(1): 167-181. https://doi.org/10.1525/ae.1987.14.1.02a00100

Harding, Susan. 1991. "Representing Fundamentalism: The Problem of the Repugnant Cultural Other." *Social Research* 58(2): 373-393.

Howell, Brian M. 2007. "The Repugnant Cultural Other Speaks Back: Christian Identity as Ethnographic 'standpoint'." *Anthropological Theory* 7(4): 371-391. https://doi.org/10.1177/1463499607083426

Jackson, Michael. 1989. *Paths toward a Clearing; Radical Empiricism and Ethnographic Inquiry*. Bloomington, IN: Indiana University Press.

Knibbe, Kim E. 2012. "An Ethnography of a Medium and Her Followers: How Learning Takes Place in the Context of Jomanda." In *Meister Und Schüler in Geschichte Und Gegenwart: Von Religionen Der Antike Bis Zur Modernen Esoterik*, edited by Almut Barbara Renger, pp. 383-398. Göttingen: V&R unipress.

Knibbe, Kim E. 2015. "Qualitative Research." In *Vocabulary for the Study of Religion*, edited by Robert A. Segal and Kocku von Stuckrad, pp. 170-172. Leiden: Brill.

Knibbe, Kim E. 2020. "Is Critique Possible in the Study of Lived Religion? Anthropological and Feminist Reflections." *Journal of Contemporary Religion* 35(2): 251-68. https://doi.org/10.1080/13537903.2020.1759904

Knibbe, Kim Esther and Peter Versteeg. 2008. "Assessing Phenomenology in Anthropology." *Critique of Anthropology* 28(1): 47-62. https://doi.org/10.1177/0308275X07086557

Knibbe, Kim Esther, Marten van der Meulen, and Peter Versteeg. 2012. "Why Participation Matters to Understand Ritual Experience." *Fieldwork in Religion* 6(2): 104-119. https://doi.org/10.1558/firn.v6i2.104

McGuire, Meredith B. 2008. *Lived Religion: Faith and Practice in Everyday Life*. Oxford: Oxford University Press.

Nyhagen, Line. 2017. "The Lived Religion Approach in the Sociology of Religion and Its Implications for Secular Feminist Analyses of Religion." *Social Compass* 64(4): 495-511. https://doi.org/10.1177/0037768617727482

Orsi, Robert A. 2013. *Between Heaven and Earth: The Religious Worlds People Make and the Scholars Who Study Them*. Princeton, NJ: Princeton University Press.

Smart, Ninian. 2015. *The Science of Religion and the Sociology of Knowledge: Some Methodological Questions*. Princeton, NJ: Princeton University Press. https://doi.org/10.1515/9781400868889

Away from the Centre

On the Edges and Adjacencies of Religious Forms

SIMON COLEMAN

Introduction: Recognizing Religion

Even those of us who live in supposedly secular societies remain surrounded by religious forms – physical, verbal, and behavioural – that signify the continuing visibility of sacred traditions and institutions. These forms range from "ambient" features of our environment (Engelke 2013), including religious buildings that occupy prime locations in many cityscapes (Oliphant 2015), to actions that push more overtly into the public sphere, such as civic prayers, processions, or even protests. Nor are such forms necessarily created by religious practitioners themselves: for instance, loaded depictions of Muslim or Christian "fanaticism" regularly feed the news cycles of national broadcasting networks as well as the volatile commentaries of social media.

Under these discursive conditions, where representations of religious activity are so easily diffused to and debated within varied and overlapping publics, both believers and sceptics benefit from characterizing religion in essentialist terms: it is rendered a distinct, recognizable "thing," which can then be either promoted or opposed.[1] For anthropologists, who generally try to study religion without participating in such bifurcating

---

1. I do not address here the distinctions, common nowadays in popular discourse, between the "religious" and the "spiritual".

Keywords: adjacency, aesthetics, articulation, coherence, insider-outsider, ritualization

ideological battles, the question of how to deal with religion as "object" remains complex and troubling. In recent years, a cleavage has emerged between those scholars who take a cognitive approach (Salazar 2010), which often implies that religion is hard-wired into our mental apparatus as a consequence or side-effect of human evolution, and those who imply that myriad social constructions of religious practice – including its absence – are possible within human communities. It has become something of an intellectual reflex in recent years among socio-cultural anthropologists to invoke Talal Asad's scepticism towards the idea of ever providing a "definitive" definition of religion, as expressed most clearly in his critique of what he sees as Clifford Geertz's (1973) focus on meaning (famously expressed as symbols, moods, and motivations), which for Asad merely supports the assumptions of "modern essentialist theologians" (Asad 1983: 237). Instead, Asad emphasizes the idea that any given definition of religion will always reflect, and be limited to, the prevailing historical and political conditions of its production. In his view, current anthropological understandings and approaches to religion are likely to be situated within assumptions about searching for coherence that have roots in certain manifestations of Christian thought itself (Asad 1983: 29; see also Tomlinson and Engelke 2006: 3).

This chapter will question how we as scholars often understand coherence and consistency in religion. But I begin by noting that neither extreme essentialism nor equally obdurate nominalism will take us very far in studies of religion. Furthermore, whichever stance we take, we should acknowledge that to propose that religion is *inherently* harder to comprehend ethnographically than, say, politics or economics, is to provide it with a privileged and indeed somewhat essentialized place in our own analytical schemas – one that sees "religion" (implying here an underlying human phenomenon that somehow cross-cuts different faiths) as inhabiting a realm of set-apart experience that can only be grasped from some putative and stable "insider's" position.[2] This argument can be made about *any* aspect of culture, not just putative interactions with spirits or the divine.

Yet, despite our definitional and analytical scruples we must somehow, and however provisionally, highlight and demarcate our religious

---

2. Some of what I have to say in this chapter will have relevance to discussions of phenomenology (for a clear exposition of this method and theory in anthropology, see Knibbe and Versteeg 2008). While I am sympathetic to the broadly phenomenological argument (or at least aim) that anthropology as a discipline must avoid translating religion into categories remote from religious experience, I am also concerned to avoid the idea of religion as constituting a realm inherently beyond all categories of experience of the religious "outsider".

objects – or salient forms – of study as part of the process of rendering them available to being viewed and investigated. Our scholarly descriptions of such forms emerge out of establishing contexts of interpretation and analysis that are problematic and provisional fictions, but necessary ones (compare Dilley 1999), and they also rely to some extent, though certainly not fully, on informants" own verbalized reports. Another challenge is that ethnography itself – a word that means not just collecting data but also *writing* about it – contains an inherent descriptive bias towards generalization. We are likely to be much more cautious nowadays than E.E. Evans-Pritchard was in referring to how "the Nuer think" or what "the Azande say", just as ethnography as an innocent or transparent mode of description is no longer assumed (e.g. Marcus and Fischer 1986; Geertz 1988). Nonetheless, we are still for the most part oriented towards emphasizing the clearly discernible and patterned, the overtly organized, and the "continuous" (Robbins 2007) character of what we study, including religious practices. Even when viewed as mere epiphenomena of deeper political or economic forces, religious ideologies or practices are generally presented in systemic or semi-systemic terms, as embodied by Jean and John Comaroff's (2000) suggestive linkage of "occult economies" with the emergence of "millennial" religious movements of the late twentieth century.

While we should not conflate religion with ritual, the latter has played a highly significant role for anthropologists in making religion "legible" and accessible as an object of study and indeed writing. Even in post-modern times, we still draw quite frequently on that part of our Durkheimian inheritance that focuses on centripetal tendencies and recognizable forms of human sociality, and are likely to fix much of our attention on people being overtly and self-consciously religious – praying, sermonizing, sacrificing, and so on. Rupert Stasch has recently referred to the ways in which "anthropological work has converged toward a theory" that notes how ritual contains "unusual density" of "representational relations", with the result that "a ritual event is characterized by the exceptional quantity and vividness of the general types that are felt as present in its concrete particulars" (Stasch 2011: 159).

Anthropologists can claim that their approach to ritual – and religion in general – has taken us beyond merely normative understandings of informants" practices. However, our avoidance of the purely normative has not precluded us from focusing on that which is clearly reproducible, standing out in stark cultural relief. In the search for religious phenomena that are construable, Birgit Meyer's discussion of "sensational forms" shows how the seemingly transcendent can become recognizable primarily for informants, but also presumably for analysts. Her approach involves perceiving such forms as:

> relatively fixed, authorized modes of invoking, and organizing access to the transcendental, creating and sustaining links between religious practitioners in the context of particular religious organizations. Sensational forms are transmitted and shared, they involve religious practitioners in particular practices of worship and play a central role in forming religious subjects. Collective rituals are prime examples of sensational forms, in that they address and involve participants in a specific manner and induce particular feelings.
>
> (Meyer 2012: 16)

A corollary of Meyer's position (ibid.: 19–20) is that it involves a broadening out of aesthetics to link with an Aristotelian notion of *aisthesis*, understood as organizing a *total* sensory experience of the world. Despite the relative emphasis on authorized ritual, the approach indicates the intriguing possibilities of going beyond marked religious actions per se, since the question remains of how certain forms might involve participants away from the church or temple – beyond overt religious centres. To put the point another way, we might ask how "formal" do "forms" need to be for us to discern their religious effects and indeed affects? Or, to adopt Stasch's terms, how "dense" and "vivid" must they be in their concrete particularities?

In this chapter, I reflect on what happens when we also attempt to locate, and recognize, religious activity that is located in behaviours far from the ideals of dense, reproducible, collective – and often set apart – social action. There are various ways in which we might characterize such distancing from conventional religious forms – forms that are neither "elementary" in a Durkheimian sense of highlighting the "essential" in religion, nor spectacularly "sensational" if we take the latter to imply fixed and authorized means to access the transcendent. I am interested in what happens when we pay more ethnographic attention to what I call "edges" and "adjacencies" of religious forms. While the idea of the edge implies the sense of an interface with the outside as well as the notion of the "outer limits" of a phenomenon, adjacency suggests parallelism and proximity between apparently distinct phenomena, including the possibility of mutual influence between them.

Using these terms opens up a number of further issues. In characterizing an "edge" we are also by implication defining a "centre", potentially suggesting both a hierarchy of value and the assumption that such distinctions are permanent. I do not deny that religious groups or ideological formations regularly define areas of more marked activity, often attributing them higher spiritual status. However, my point is to look more closely at what happens away from such areas – examining fuzzier forms that are no doubt still influenced by them, and yet are more inchoately and diffusely expressed. In addition, what actually constitutes a centre or an edge may sometimes depend upon the particular and evanescent circumstances of the moment.

I argue that "edges" can be as important sociologically as "centres": not merely in the sense implied by Mary Douglas (1966) that boundaries define identity and thus retain potency, but also because much of religious life is spent on the fringes or penumbras of overt, intense, and/or authorized pious experience. To try to understand what it means to be a "Pentecostalist" or a "Catholic" it is sometimes necessary to observe such experience at times and in places that are *not* religiously marked – or not obviously religious at all. In this sense I agree with João Pina-Cabral and Frances Pine's assertion that looking on the margins of religion is less about a perverse focus on "odd" behaviour, and more about appreciating how religion, among many other things, often "inhabits the margins of other socio-cultural areas" (Pina-Cabral and Pine 2008: 3). My argument also resonates with Catherine Bell's well-known emphasis on ritualization rather than ritual per se, implying that "ritual activities be removed from their isolated position as special paradigmatic acts and restored to the context of social activity in general (Bell 1992: 7); though while Bell notes how ritualization draws attention to certain actions, privileging them in relation to the quotidian (ibid.: 74), I want to explore the sometimes scarcely discernible and not always attention-grabbing ways in which religious "orientation" (I hesitate it to call it commitment) may be evoked through actions that resist obvious forms of coherence or discernibility.

One methodological implication of my argument is simply a reinforcement of the classic ethnographic method of "hanging out" with informants, observing as many areas of their lives as possible, but the banality of such an assertion is mitigated by the observation that this is a strategy that is nowadays in frequent danger of being sidelined: it is much more difficult to achieve in many of the contemporary conditions of ethnographic fieldwork on religion, especially in large-scale urban areas, where we gain primary access to informants at times when they are gathered explicitly to "be religious" in mosques, church meetings, or prayer groups. Another implication involves a plea to look more closely at forms of religious expression that are far from exemplary – not odd *per se*, but perhaps expressing diffuseness, incompetence, partiality, disengagement, inconsistency, ambivalence, indifference – and to regard them as potentially just as significant and indeed constitutive of religious behaviour as more obviously committed, proficient, and authorized forms of piously inclined behaviour. I do not mean here so much a reiteration of work on apparent "failures" in performance (e.g. Hüsken 2007), but rather an appreciation of the fact that so much activity on the part of believers is inevitably and chronically an approximation, translation, hint, or even reversal of more authorized forms. Just because something is non-exemplary, that does not mean it is not sociologically significant, or indeed just as much a product of how a religion is characteristically manifested as, say, a sermon. Indeed, marginal behaviour can even take place within and help to constitute the space and time of the explicitly in-gathered assembly, as core participants are frequently conjoined with a more motley assortment of attendees, who may or may not wish – or know how – to be involved in authorized forms of worship; or even as a core participant retreats at times to the margins.

In the following, I refer briefly to two recent analyses that highlight the complex relationships between centres and edges of religious engagement that I am discussing, illustrating their spatial, temporal, and social dimensions. I then provide a short ethnographic depiction of an example of "edgy" religious commitment that is drawn from my own observation and experience.

Saliencies and Structurations

In an article drawing on fieldwork among Christians based in and around Damascus in 2005, Andreas Bandak (2012) discusses what happens when he joins informants in celebrating the Feast of the Holy Cross. Significantly, Bandak starts his analysis of the ethnographic event not in church but in a car, journeying out of the city to a holy site with his friend Nabil – a young man who sings in a choir, wears a cross around his neck, and often describes himself as a Catholic. Despite embodying and displaying such apparent "forms" of conventional and pious religious attachment, what Nabil demonstrates to Bandak throughout the event is a far less coherent bundle of "meanings, feelings, sensations, thoughts and identities" (ibid.: 536) that vary in terms of duration and intensity – flitting from talking of miracles as well as praying in church to exalting sexual relations between Christians and Muslims, praising the security then being offered to the Christian minority by the Syrian regime, and even denying his own identity as a believer.

Should we as ethnographers pick through this mish-mash of positions in order to render consistent and convincing Nabil's stance as a pious believer, privileging his engagement with the ritual and symbolic densities of his faith? Doing so would help descriptive coherence; but it would also flatten out the shifting orientations, temporalities, and framings of the evening's experience. In my terms, Bandak's analysis reveals various religious edges and adjacencies through which to comprehend Nabil's participation in the Feast, alongside conventional liturgical activity. One edge is that between the car journey and the entry into church: perhaps initially understood as separating secular from sacred time, though such a division – if assumed to be static and impermeable – misses much that is significant about Nabil's life as a Christian, which seems to take place as much in vehicles as it does in places of divine service. During the evening, the edge between these activities not only divides but also conjoins them, rendering them partially complementary, constituting a religious "event" that begins well before entering the church. Another edge is between professed belief and disbelief – both positions capable of being rhetorically adopted by Nabil within a very short space of time, so that locating the border between the two also indexes religious stances that are unlikely to be random, but are nonetheless highly fluid. Furthermore, again thinking of the evening as a whole, we might think of pious language as juxtaposed with discussions of both transgressive sexual conquest and state security – the latter two illustrating the crossing and the firming of boundaries respectively, venturing into sexual politics and *realpolitik*, but also embodying framings of religiously-inflected identity quite as much as prayer does.

To see Nabil's shifts as problematic inconsistencies or flawed beliefs is to misunderstand the chronically unstable, or at least oscillatory, formation of such subjectivity (see also Coleman 2014). Bandak uses a metaphor of foregrounding and backgrounding to indicate questions of saliency at any given ethnographic moment (see also Bandak and Jørgensen 2012), and notes that these can occur consciously or subconsciously. Emergent through such contexts of shifting encounters and performance frames, Christianity plays into what Bandak (2012) calls "tonalities of immediacy": ways in which religious subjects take up different positions within a relatively short timespan, which may include overt ritual and non-ritual action as well as blends between the two. Tonality – a term derived from music theory – indicates the background against which melodies can be played, and the point is not only that apt performance requires the learning of tonalities, but also that the latter can function as bundles or open structurations (more open than conventional forms of habitus), enabling and constituting movements between different forms of ritual and ideological commitment, "making shifts of orientation between different positions possible" (Bandak and Jørgensen 2012: 537), while "making some motifs [temporarily] recede as others gain saliency" (ibid.).

Bandak uses Deleuzian imagery to evoke the sense of the constant making and remaking of ritual form, as well as of interactions between cultural foregrounds and backgrounds (Deleuze 2006). Broadly comparable theoretical impulses are behind other recent work that looks not at Christianity but at Islam – though part of my and these authors" intentions is also to extend understandings of what might come under the purview of these religions. In their introduction to *Articulating Islam*, Magnus Marsden and Konstantinos Retsikas (2013: 1) emphasize "the varying ways in which Islam is deeply yet also diffusely embedded in everyday experience; sometimes being of central significance and at other times less important to people's lives", and I note their acknowledgement of the complementarities rather than necessary oppositions between the "deep" and the "diffuse" in the experience of religious commitment – in effect allowing "density" to retreat (at times) to the sidelines.

While Bandak uses an aesthetic metaphor to capture his approach, Marsden and Retsikas experiment with parallels that are more explicitly systemic and even architectural in quality, though retaining a tensility that resonates with the inherent flexibility of Bandak's tonality. One of their key concepts is described as follows (Marsden and Retsikas 2013: 2): "Systematicity refers to the efforts required and undertaken by Muslims to evoke Islam in the midst of particular historical and social contingencies" – and my reading of this analysis is that tracing such efforts should be a matter of ethnographic observation, rather than being based on common assumptions scholars might have of which connections are likely to be significant. Islam is therefore experienced and constituted by informants and ethnographers through various registers, which in turn point to another key concept, that of "articulation", which broadly describes the active though not always conscious transformation of Islam, as (following Cantwell-Smith 1962) religion is understood to be "continuously produced" precisely by means of its "enmeshment" with other aspects of social life (ibid.: 3). An important entailment of such an approach is that, among the multiple possible identifications involving being Muslim, none is taken to be inherently primary (ibid.: 25).

Neither "tonality" nor the workings of "systematicity" imply that identifying oneself with a religious faith is purely random or merely contingent upon the social imperatives of the moment: obviously forms of adherence and expectation can be learned, and are also subject to institutional forms of reproduction. However, both analytical frameworks indicate the temporalities (and tonalities, and tensilities) of commitment and adherence, their different registers and densities but also different forms, while indicating how religious saliences come into play in framing religious orientations that shift over time, altering as background and foregrounds shift, with or without the intentions of "believers" being involved. Both approaches show how being Christian or Muslim involves much more than conventional forms of attendance in a church or mosque: both density and diffuseness of commitment might occur in religious or apparently secular places and situations. I want therefore to indicate how attention to shifting edges and adjacencies has informed my own fieldwork by briefly introducing an informant who initially forced me to reflect on such issues.

Miriam: Within and Between Religious Worlds

I first met Miriam[3] in the 1980s, when I had just begun to carry out my PhD fieldwork in two Christian congregations in Uppsala, Sweden: an older and well-established Pentecostal church and its new rival, a brash and neo-Pentecostal ministry called the Word of Life (Coleman 2000). Actually, Miriam almost scared the life out of me in my very first fieldwork experience at a service in the Pentecostal church when she confirmed the worst nightmare of many an ethnographer in such circles by marching across to me and, in the hearing of many others in the room, asking bluntly (but benignly) who I was and whether I was born again. I was rescued by the fact that in fact the service was still going on, so that other congregants asked her to hush while we listened to the closing words of the pastor.

Over time, Miriam and I talked under more relaxed circumstances, especially when we realized that we were both attending services at the local Pentecostal Church but also at the Word of Life. Like many other Pentecostals who occasionally attended the newer group, she saw the Word of Lifers' forms of worship as closely akin to those of the older church, but speeded up, more urgent, and therefore indexing a desire to engage in revival that she still saw as an important part of her ritual life. But my real ethnographic revelation came when Miriam and I went home to have lunch in her apartment after a Sunday morning service at the Pentecostal church. I was struck not only by her elegant furniture and beautifully ordered home but also by the numerous Russian Orthodox icons adorning the dark walls. Miriam – who on the way to her apartment had been discussing that day's sermon in the Pentecostal church with some enthusiasm – explained without any obvious embarrassment that the icons represented an important dimension of her religious and ritual life. She had inherited them from family (who were not, I believe,

---

3. A pseudonym.

Pentecostalists themselves) and thus felt surrounded and protected by loved ones as she moved around the apartment.

As I left Miriam's apartment that day I wondered how her icons could "fit" with a Pentecostal or indeed a neo-Pentecostal sensibility, the aesthetic and theological coherence that I had assumed would exist among believers, especially those who regularly and publicly (and, as far as I could tell, sincerely) professed their Bible-based, spirit-filled credentials. Was Miriam to be seen as "odd"? But in fact, she was hardly alone among Word of Life as well as Pentecostal supporters in what appeared from one vantage-point to be the incoherence of her ritual and aesthetic life, even if there were not many others who had Orthodox icons in their homes. In subsequent years I have also come to compare what I saw in Miriam's apartment with observations made by others. In his book *Visual Piety*, for instance, David Morgan (1998: 153) contrasts research indicating that Protestants in the US expressed contempt for religious imagery with his own findings that many were in fact quite fond of such images. Similarly, work on a charismatic church in Stockholm by Jessica Moberg (2013: 117) has carried out some fascinating explorations of how material pieties include conventional participation in services but also the use of yoga, the deployment of prayers from the Liturgy of the hours, and so on.

Such findings are picking up contrasts between public worship and private homes; but they are also suggesting the varieties of religious forms and aesthesis that go into the construction of religious subjects whose orientations are chronically framed and reframed through temporal, spatial, and social circumstances. As I have described her, Miriam was something of a *bricoleur*, moving with some regularity between different religious practices and material affordances. Such complexities of engagement would not have been visible to any ethnographer who restricted their observations to noting her enthusiastic engagement in services held at either the Pentecostal church or the rival Word of Life. We should not impose a facile consistency on to her "total" spiritual life, but rather see how the latter was made up of formations where saliencies, foregrounds and backgrounds, edges and adjacencies, shifted as she moved through her day. At the Pentecostal church and the Word of Life Miriam prayed in a focused and frequently intense fashion, incorporating tongues and body movements, often collectively coordinated and choreographed, and directed towards the stage. The densities of such experiences contrasted with her engagement with the icons in her home. She did not pray in front of such images, but incorporated them into the background of her life as "ambient" and diffuse presences – much as a person's family might be experienced as an easily taken-for-granted and yet highly significant dimension of one's life: "sensational" in terms of engaging the body, if decidedly "unsensational" in relation to conscious and public ritual engagement.

These varied features of Miriam's spirituality may or may not have articulated with each other. Certainly, her participation in both the Pentecostal Church and the Word of Life seemed to draw out the ways in which the newer group injected a fresh feeling of intensity, speed, and commitment into semiotic forms (tongues, prayer, body movements) that were broadly shared between the two congregations. Meanwhile the icons acted as what one might call "media of adjacency," permitting a degree of mutual reinforcement between two presences – those of sacred figures and of family. Marsden and Retsikas (2013) might therefore describe such a relationship as a form of enmeshment. And, to take the possibilities of articulation to their logical extremes, we might even conceive of the possibility of the Russian icons leading Miriam to a closer and Pentecostal-like relationship with Jesus – not by acting as they would in an Orthodox Church, but by reminding her of the virtues and comforts of intimacy itself, as made available in a familial relationship but also through being in touch with a deeply personal saviour. In any case, I do not think we can see the density and direction of collective Pentecostal prayer as being by definition more important to Miriam's religious subjectivity than the more diffuse and ambient images dotted around her home.

Inside-Out?

I conclude by pointing out one further implication of my argument. I have been questioning the idea that the definable spiritual centre of a given "believer" should be seen as internally consistent (see also Schielke 2009) or that we should focus as ethnographers on dense, easily recognized forms of the religious life. The religious informants discussed here – most notably Nabil and Miriam, but also the numerous cases mentioned in Marsden and Retsikas's volume – move across many different contexts of experience and activity even in the course of a single day. As noted, such mobility can make the "hanging out" type of fieldwork difficult, but I also suggest that the diversity and variety of informants' "systematizing" and "articulating," which take in ostensibly sacred and secular contexts and numerous aesthetic forms, may also lend a curious advantage to the contemporary ethnographer. For in situations where informants" frames of reference take so many and varied forms, the idea of a stable and firm division between believer and non-believer, or informant and anthropologist, also begins to break down, especially in situations where other cultural referents may be broadly shared. Even as foreground and background may shift their mutual positioning, so may conceptions of insiderhood and outsiderhood.

Thus, to suggest that the interpretative frames and practices of construal of many informants are fundamentally different from those of the ethnographer because of the constant and consistent possession of a mysterious yet substantive thing called "belief" begs at least as many questions as it answers. Although I do not think my answer would have satisfied her, I could perhaps have answered to Miriam, when she first asked whether I was "born again," that in all likelihood we shared much in common in our understanding and experience of religious forms: an appreciation of the ebb and flow of worship, an engagement in images and their connections with other forms of sociality, an understanding that spiritual experience could take place in the home quite as much as in the church. In other words, comprehension of what anthropologists call religion involves appreciation of aesthetic affinities that apparently have little to do with a firm stance of belief, but everything to do with forms of participation and commitment whose sensibilities, tonalities and tensilities we have only begun to discern.

About the Author

Simon Coleman is Chancellor Jackman Professor at the Department for the Study of Religion, University of Toronto. His research interests include pilgrimage, Pentecostalism, cathedrals, ritual, and religious infrastructures. He has carried out fieldwork in Sweden, the UK, and Nigeria. Recent books include *The Anthropology of Global Pentecostalism and Evangelicalism* (NYU Press, 2015, co-edited with Rosalind Hackett) and *Pilgrimage and Political Economy* (Berghahn, 2018, co-edited with John Eade). His latest book, *Powers of Pilgrimage: Religion in a World of Motion*, is being published by New York University Press in December 2021.

References

Asad, Talal. 1983. "Anthropological Conceptions of Religion: Reflections on Geertz." *Journal of the Royal Anthropological Institute* 18(2): 237–259. https://doi.org/10.2307/2801433

Bandak, Andreas. 2012. "Problems of Belief: Tonalities of Immediacy among Christians of Damascus." *Ethnos* 77(4): 535–555. https://doi.org/10.1080/00141844.2012.728024

Bandak, Andreas and Jonas Jørgensen. 2012. "Foregrounds and Backgrounds – Ventures in the Anthropology of Christianity." *Ethnos* 77(4): 447–458. https://doi.org/10.1080/00141844.2011.619662

Bell, Catherine. 1992. *Ritual Theory, Ritual Practice*. Oxford: Oxford University Press.

Cantwell-Smith, Wilfred. 1962. *The Meaning and End of Religion*. Minneapolis, MN: Fortress Press.

Coleman, Simon. 2000. *The Globalisation of Charismatic Christianity: Spreading the Gospel of Prosperity*. Cambridge: Cambridge University Press.

Coleman, Simon. 2014. "Pilgrimage as Trope for an Anthropology of Christianity." *Current Anthropology* 55(10): 281–291. https://doi.org/10.1086/677766

Comaroff, Jean and John Comaroff. 2000. "Millennial Capitalism: First Thoughts on a Second Coming." *Public Culture* 12(2): 291–343. https://doi.org/10.1215/08992363-12-2-291

Deleuze, Gilles. 2006. *The Fold*. New York and London: Continuum.

Dilley, Roy. 1999. *The Problem of Context*. Oxford: Berghahn.

Douglas, Mary. 1966. *Purity and Danger: An Analysis of Concepts of Pollution and Taboo*. London: Routledge.

Engelke, Matthew. 2013. *God's Agents Biblical Publicity in Contemporary England*. Berkeley, CA: University of California Press. https://doi.org/10.1525/california/9780520280465.001.0001

Geertz, Clifford. 1973. *The Interpretation of Cultures: Selected Essays*. New York: Basic Books.

Geertz, Clifford. 1988. *Works and Lives: The Anthropologist as Author*. Stanford, CA: Stanford University Press.

Hüsken, Ute (ed.). 2007. *When Rituals Go Wrong: Mistakes, Failure, and the Dynamics of Ritual*. Leiden: Brill. https://doi.org/10.1163/ej.9789004158115.i-377

Knibbe, Kim and Peter Versteeg. 2008. "Assessing Phenomenology in Anthropology." *Critique of Anthropology* 28(1): 47–62. https://doi.org/10.1177/0308275X07086557

Marcus, George and Michael Fischer. 1986. *Anthropology as Cultural Critique: An Experimental Moment in the Human Sciences*. Chicago, IL: University of Chicago Press.

Marsden, Magnus and Konstantinos Retsikas. 2013. "Introduction." In *Articulating Islam: Anthropological Approaches to Muslim Worlds*, edited by Magnus Marsden and Konstantinos Retsikas, pp. 1–31. Heidelberg: Springer. https://doi.org/10.1007/978-94-007-4267-3_1

Meyer, Birgit. 2012. "Religious Sensations: Media, Aesthetics and the Study of Contemporary Religion." In *Religion, Media and Culture: A Reader*, edited by Gordon Lynch, Jolyon Mitchell and Anna Strhan, pp. 159–170. London: Routledge.

Moberg, Jessica. 2013. "Piety, Intimacy and Mobility: A Case Study of Charismatic Christianity in Present-Day Stockholm." PhD thesis, Södertörns högskola.

Morgan, David. 1998. *Visual Piety: A History and Theory of Popular Religious Images*. Berkeley, CA: University of California Press.

Oliphant, Elayne. 2015. "Beyond Blasphemy or Devotion: Art, the Secular, and Catholicism in Paris." *Journal of the Royal Anthropological Institute* 21(2): 352–373. https://doi.org/10.1111/1467-9655.12210

Pina-Cabral, João and Frances Pine. 2008. "On the Margins: An Introduction." In *On the Margins of Religion*, edited by Frances Pine and João Pina-Cabral, pp. 1–10. Oxford: Berghahn.

Robbins, Joel. 2007. "Continuity Thinking and the Problem of Christian Culture." *Current Anthropology* 48(1): 5–38. https://doi.org/10.1086/508690

Salazar, Carles. 2010. "Anthropology and the Cognitive Science of Religion. A Critical Assessment." *Religion and Society* 1: 44–56. https://doi.org/10.3167/arrs.2010.010104

Schielke, Samuli. 2009. "Being Good in Ramadan: Ambivalence, Fragmentation, and the Moral Self in the Lives of Young Egyptians." *Journal of the Royal Anthropological Institute* 15(1): 24–40. https://doi.org/10.1111/j.1467-9655.2009.01540.x

Stasch, Rupert. 2011. "Ritual and Oratory Revisited: The Semiotics of Effective Action." *Annual Review of Anthropology* 40: 159–174. https://doi.org/10.1146/annurev-anthro-081309-145623

Tomlinson, Matt and Engelke, Matthew. 2006. "Meaning, Anthropology, Christianity." In *The Limits of Meaning: Case Studies in the Anthropology of Christianity*, edited by Matthew Engelke and Matt Tomlinson, pp. 1–37. Oxford: Berghahn.

– 12 –

The Importation and Generation of the Religious and the Sacred in Political Song

JORAM TARUSARIRA

Introduction

This chapter argues that texture, meaning and understanding of the religious and/or the sacred are not cast in stone but a result of practices, discourses and narratives weaved around that which is defined as such. Practices, narratives and discourses created by political songs that are meant to coordinate and mobilize political support in Zimbabwe, created a numinous vision and version of Zimbabwe that was to be delivered by then President Mugabe who was said to be "anointed" to guide his followers and deliver them from the land of Egypt (coloniality) to the promised land (independence and sovereignty). I demonstrate that political songs imported and generated the religious and/or the sacred from existing religious traditions into the political sphere, thus are a concrete example to show that to study "religion" is not to study a "thing" in itself, but how particular ideas (and discourses) of "religion" are practised and operationalized in various contexts. In contributing to the scientific study of religion, the dynamic of importing and generating the religious and/or sacred demonstrates that the meaning and understanding of the religious and/or sacred do not have an existence in and by themselves; they are not givens, but a result of practices, discourses and narratives. Numerous factors such as history, context, culture, ideology inter alia influence the conception, thus what is religious and/or sacred at every turn is socio-centric, relational or between relations. What is

---

Keywords: songs; practices, narratives and discourses; theodicy; religious/sacred/spiritual; Zimbabwe

not perceived as religious and/or sacred at one moment can be made so at another and vice-versa. This chapter uses the intersection of religion and politics, which is a case of religion in the public domain.

Religion in the Public Domain

For the most part, when discussing the relationship between religion and the public domain, the tendency is to consider the direct input of established religious motifs into the public square. We consider the social infrastructure that religion provides in, for instance, antislavery, temperance, pacifism, and civil rights (Beckford 2001). There is less focus on the other way around, that is, teasing out the religious, sacred or spiritual in seemingly non-religious, sacred or spiritual discourses and practices. Deploying religious songs, this chapter argues that there can be a religious, sacred and spiritual quality in entities, phenomena or situations that are perceived as non-religious, and this has implications for the quality or texture of actions that emanate therefrom. Thus, I echo the sentiments of Demerath and Schmitt (1998: 390), that "seemingly nonreligious" movements for change in civil rights, gender relations, the environment, and welfare "are religious at their edges, if not their core".

Because the categories "spirituality" and "religious" are often used in the religio-political discourse in Zimbabwe interchangeably, and I am subsuming spirituality under religion in this chapter, it is in order to briefly comment on them. These terms are important for this chapter because they both refer to levels of meaning and significance which go beyond the surface appearance of everyday realities. They both point to the possibility that ostensibly routine, taken-for-granted, matter-of-fact phenomena may conceal deeper or higher levels of reality. Spiritual insights convey a sense of the ultimate significance of things. Thus the "spiritual", defined in this way, shades off into the "religious". While religious embraces spirituality, it adds the implication that supernatural, superhuman or super-empirical powers are responsible for the ultimate significance of everything. This accounts both for the requirement that they should be worshipped or venerated and for the belief that the truth about their intentions is contained in revelations, relics, scriptures, artefacts, hierophanies, and so forth. The most important sociological implication of the differences between the two terms is that the "religious" provides a better basis for the development of communities of believers subject to control by authoritative knowledge and religious specialists. Nevertheless, communities of believers invariably provide opportunities for the cultivation of spiritual interests in the context of preaching, prayer, worship, and pastoral activities (Beckford 2001: 240). In addition to the importation of religion into the public realm and bringing one's own religious values and beliefs into the public domain, which is often the focus, this chapter will also accentuate how the religious and/or the sacred can be generated in the public domain.

Some discourses and practices give rise to spiritual and religious associations when actors detect a sense of the sacred or the ultimate in their ideology, sentiments, or collective actions. The term "sacred" signifies phenomena which, from a religious or spiritual point of view, are infused with such power and significance that they command strong reverence or fear. The sense of the sacred may be linked to feelings of optimism, or at least hope, that good will ultimately triumph over evil. The character of participants" spiritual experiences varies with each movement's ideology or its claims about the causes of problems and the preconditions for their solution (Antze 1976; Rice 1994). Transcending problems can be seen as a form of transcendence revealing sacred power (Jacobs 1990). Transcendental experiences may also be attributed to the "collective effervescence" (Durkheim 1915; Mellor and Shilling 1997) accompanying selfless immersion in a movement's enthusiastic activities and celebration of its unity of purpose. There is a spiritual excitement stimulated by the occasional embodied celebrations of collective identity and purpose that occur among people involved in collective action. It is also common for ecological movement activists not only to pepper their language with religious terms such as "the sacred", "sacrilege", "profanation", and "redemption", but infuse deep commitment to the cause. The religious and/or the sacred can, thus be constructed via different media, which include songs.

Songs as Constructors of Religious/Sacred Narratives

Songs can narrate a story; thus, when they do so, they become narrative constructors. In conflict situations, narratives provide an orientation to a society or a group, justify actions, make a group feel it needs security, present a positive idea of the group, present the victimhood of the group, delegitimize the opponent, instil patriotism, build unity, and call for peace (Bar-Tal and Salomon 2006). This narrative framework espouses a religious, sacred and transcendental character because, as I noted above, the sense of the sacred can be found in feelings of optimism, or at least hope, that good will ultimately triumph over evil, a movement's ideology or its claims about the causes of problems and the preconditions for their solution (Antze 1976; Rice 1994) and transcending problems can be seen as a form of transcendence revealing sacred power (Jacobs 1990). Transcendental experiences may also be attributed to the "collective effervescence" (Durkheim 1915; Mellor and Shilling 1997) accompanying selfless immersion in a movement's enthusiastic activities and celebration of its unity of purpose. A closer analysis of the quality of political narratives during contestation for political power shows that they address the aforementioned. They give a sense and feeling of optimism, hope and the feeling that evil will be triumphed, and give causes of problems a religious or sacred origin, even if this means being the devil and narratives give the feeling that transcending problems can be a revelation of the power of the sacred. Durkheim defines religion as a system of unified beliefs and practices relative to sacred things, that is to say, things set apart and forbidden – beliefs and practices which unite into one single moral community called a church, all those who adhere to them (Durkheim 1915: 47). Cognizant of the limitations of functional definitions (see the Introduction to this volume), chief being that there is a danger of making everything qualify as religious, narratives, especially during time of conflict, set things (communities included) apart as representations of the sacred and a moral code of what is to be done or not is also articulated. They do this through the articulation of particular ideologies and beliefs about the conflict and the other, meant to satisfy the quest for cognitive, emotional and moral meaning. The narratives therefore stress the importance of a moral community and of the sanctity and moral regulation for social cohesion (Smith 2003: 27). This is a case of generating the sacred from what is seemingly not religious or sacred, resulting in what is known as political religion. When narratives become shared, they can influence action, which can generate collective effervescence (see Durkheim 1915). The feelings of awe, optimism, hope, triumph and collective effervescence generate a numinous aura around the narrative.

Songs evoke emotions, create a common sense of belonging and communicate dogmas effectively (Chitando 2002). They have an inherent ability to evoke powerful emotional responses in listeners (Koelsch 2010: 131). Evoked emotions impact and enhance the subjective experience of other sensory stimuli and music causes the release of oxytocin which is critical to generation of trust and affiliation (Baumgartner, Lutz, Schmidt and Jancke 2006: 151; Missig, Ayers, Schulkin and Rosen 2010: 2607). In line with the argument of this chapter, Cross asserts that "music is not only sonic, embodied and interactive; it is bound to its contexts of occurrence in ways that enable it to derive meaning from and interactively confer meaning on, the experiential contexts in which it occurs" (Cross 2003: 108). Music elicits inexplicable emotions of joy, awe and ecstasy, while increasing trust, empathy and cooperation among participants. When music is embedded in the ordinary or imports or generates religious rituals, it transforms the ordinary into the extraordinary thereby creating or laying a foundation for the creation of the sacred.

Since narratives are meant to supply meaning for life within a group context, and songs are part of the technology of constructing the meaning, it follows that songs, in existential or ontological terms, have a theodical function, here understood as provision of answers to questions of ultimate meaning (Gerth and Mills 1946: 271ff; Campbell 2007: 166; 2010: 738–757). Meaning can be provided at three levels – cognitive, emotional and moral. At the cognitive level meaning is provided by explaining why things are as they are. Since it is not enough to know "what is" but also what the people are meant to feel about this picture of life and the universe presented to them – whether to be awestruck, amazed or fearful, or hopeful, joyous or welcoming, meaning can be supplied at the emotional level, thereby offering guidance on what to feel and under what circumstances. Meanings provided influence how people think and feel, as well as how they should act in the world. Narratives as meanings guide people on what it is that "they should think, how they should feel, on what basis they should judge others as well as themselves, together with what actions they ought to perform to attain salvation, peace or enlightenment" (Campbell 2007: 167). They seek to provide a coherent, credible, visionary and morally satisfying comprehensive meaning system (Campbell 2007, 2010: 741). The resultant effect of theodicy is a sense of the sacred. Causes of problems are given a religious or sacred origin, often the devil or evil and the theodical narratives give the feeling that transcending problems is a revelation of the power of the sacred. The religious or sacred quality makes whatever action is decided upon become more forceful than would simple provision of information and explanation of events or situations.

Narratives become theodicies, the very moment they answer and explain existential questions. They account for the *who, what, why, how, when* and *where* of situations in the course of addressing questions of ultimate meaning. These elements give the narrative force and help make it not only memorable but also sacred. The "ideal type" of national narrative during political contestation is structured according to the following format, which is replete with sacred and religious connotations, by importation and/or generation (see Auerbach 2010):

- *Who?* There are messiahs, heroes, heroines and martyrs of the narrative and this person or persons personify the entire national entity as

it is or as it should be. This or these heroes and/or heroines, can also symbolize the suffering of the people and its continuing sacrifice.
- Under the *what* element, the victory of "our" side is told and this victory could be miraculous or religious in nature. It is here that the existential question is asked and answered. If not about victory it will tell of how "we" were defeated by murderous people who did so with no justification.
- The *why* dimension deals with why a group undertakes what it does. In the context of conflict, for instance, each side will attribute its good deeds – peace initiatives, release of prisoners, etc. – to internal factors such as the pursuit of its own inherent sense of peace and justice, while negative acts – the killing of children, terrorist attacks, targeted killings, etc. – will be attributed to external factors and usually to the enemy, as it is the enemy, in its wickedness and aggression, that forced them to act this way out of self-defence.
- The *how* dimension speaks to the manner in which an injustice happened or a group says it happened and how that explanation contributes to why a group thinks it is justified to act in the way it does.

The who, what, why, when, where and how are always contextual and when songs construct the religious and/or the sacred narratives, they do this not within a vacuum, but a particular context. The context of the song under study is Zimbabwe's socio-economic and political milieu.

The Context of the Song: Zimbabwe's Socio-economic and Political Milieu

Zimbabwe's postcolonial traumatic experiences such as the Ndebele tribe massacre in the 1980s, violent and chaotic land reform since 1999, intense conflict and violence, and unprecedented socio-economic and political upheaval characterizes the context within which the song "Nora" under study in this chapter is located. Zimbabwe attained independence in 1980 after a protracted war of liberation against British rule. Save for the Matabeleland massacre, in which at least 20,000 people were killed by the ruling regime in the early 1980s, Zimbabwe performed well on the development front. The 1990s, however, were characterized by a declining economy against the global economic liberalization. Zimbabwe adopted the Economic Structural Adjustment Programme (ESAP) from international financial institutions in 1990 (Bond and Manyanya 2002: 17). This programme led to increased suffering of the ordinary person, loss of jobs, reduced incomes, and the crumbling of social services. Consequently, people began to distance themselves from the government. The decline of workers" incomes led to a series of nationwide strikes by the labour movement. A civic organization, National Constitutional Assembly (NCA), closely linked to the Zimbabwe Congress Trade Unions (ZCTU) – even overlapping in leadership – began to link governance crises to the constitution. It argued that the Lancaster House Constitution, that was signed on 21 December 1979, ending the liberation struggle and directly leading to the creation and recognition of the Republic of Zimbabwe, was defective and had outlived its usefulness (Masunungure 2004). It resolved to spearhead the crafting of a new national constitution. Campaigns were held nationwide and this forced the government to set up its own constitutional commission (CC) in 1999. The people articulated what they wanted to the CC which, under the guidance of the ruling regime, did not consider people's contributions. The NCA successfully mobilized the people to reject the government-sponsored constitution and demand a people-driven constitution. At the ZCTU's National Working People's Convention in February 1999, a new labour-based political party Movement for Democratic Change (MDC) was formed (Raftopoulos 2004; Masunungure 2004). Since independence in 1980 the MDC has posed an unprecedented threat to the ruling party, the Zimbabwe African National Union – Patriotic Front (ZANU PF).

The constitutional referendum was carried out in February 2000 and the results were a clear defeat for Mugabe. 55 per cent of the voters rejected the government-sponsored draft constitution. This was the first government defeat since 1980 and it posed a threat in elections that were following. As ZANU PF faced the threat of mass democracy, a construction of narratives ensued via numerous avenues including songs. The system used crude propaganda, violence and intimidation to indoctrinate youth into thinking that their own impunity and abuse of power was part of the struggle to protect ZANU PF and Zimbabwe from foreign influence (Smith 2003). ZANU PF and Zimbabwe were thus set apart, thereby becoming a representation of the sacred, with specific things forbidden, uniting people into a new kind of church. ZANU PF and Zimbabwe became objects separated and venerated, with specific marks of differentiation such as flags, anthems and other public symbols. War veterans, unemployed manipulated youths and party cadres violently invaded commercial farms across the country under the Third Chimurenga (Third Liberation) struggle project after the first resistance to colonization in the late 1890s and the second in the 1950s. It is uncontested that the local people had been evicted from productive land in the 1890s and this continued to the 1960s. Faced with growing opposition the land issue was incorporated into the nationalist agenda and used as a political tool (Sachikonye 2004). The farmers" workers, mostly of Malawi and Zambian origin, were accused of conniving with their white employers to destroy ZANU PF. Their farmhouses were set on fire by the invaders, occupants attacked with sticks, knobkerries, pick handles and pieces of hose pipes. The majority of people supported the land reform programme but reservations lie in the chaotic and violent mode in which it was carried out.

In the rural areas ZANU PF youths and war veterans convened meetings where huge crowds sang and danced to revolutionary songs in support of ZANU PF whose resultant effect was collective effervescence. Suspected members of the MDC were beaten and forced to renounce their membership. These meetings were also platforms for political education from the party cadres, under the principle which is expressed as we will later see, in the song "Nora" which goes as follows: "*Toraika vanhu vakadai; Dzidzisai gwara reZANU*" ("Take such people and teach them the doctrine of the party"). In towns, the party thugs were terrorizing people in high density suburbs, attacking all suspected MDC supporters, and abducting them for torture. The communities were instigated against each other according to which political party one supported (Sachikonye 2004). This instability resulted in dwindling support for the ruling regime, which then resorted to full-blown propaganda. Songs such as *Nora* became instruments to raise a political consciousness that was sympathetic to the ruling party.

Enter Political Songs – the Song "Nora"

The song "Nora" was composed for the ruling party ZANU PF, by the late national Commissar and Elections Director, Elliot Manyika. This song is selected for this chapter because it is one of the "hit" songs played using the public address system during political rallies. It is played as entertainment for the people at the political rallies. The people sing and dance along because they now know the lyrics by heart since the song is often played on state television, especially during election campaign periods. Table 12.1 shows the lyrics of the song in the Shona language and translated into English, out of which I will distil the importation and generation of the religious and/or sacred.

Table 12.1. Lyrics of "Nora".

In the Shona language	English translation
Zvinoda vakashinga Moyo savaMugabe	One has to be resilient like Mr Mugabe
Kune vamwe vakapanduka	Others have sold out or rebelled
Nepamusana pekuda mari	Because of the love for money
Kune vamwe vakapanduka nepamusana pekusafunga	Others have rebelled because they do not think
Toraika vanhu vakadai	Gather these people
Dzidzisai gwara reZanu	Teach them the doctrine of the party
Viva ZANU, Zanu ndeyeropa	Viva ZANU, ZANU is a party of blood
Viva Zanu, Zanu Ndeyekushupika	ZANU is about sacrifice
Darwin kune magamba. Akafira iyoyi Zimbabwe	In Mt Darwin there are heroes, who died for this country Zimbabwe
kuGwanda kune magamba akafira iyoyi Zimbabwe	In Gwanda there are heroes, who died for this country Zimbabwe
kwaMutare kune Magamba akafira iyoyi Zimbabwe	In Mutare there are heroes, who died for this country Zimbabwe
Buruwayo kune magamba, akafira iyoyi Zimbabwe	In Bulawayo there are heroes, who died for this country Zimbabwe
Masvingo kune magamba akafira iyoyi Zimbabwe	In Masvingo there are heroes, who died for this country Zimbabwe
KuGweru kune magamba akafira iyoyi Zimbabwe	In Gweru there are heroes, who died for this country Zimbabwe
kwaMutoko kune magambaakafira iyoyi Zimbabwe	In Mutoko there are heroes, who died for this country Zimbabwe
Bindura kune magamba akafira iyoyi Zimbabwe	In Bindura there are heroes, who died for this country Zimbabwe
Ku Chinhoyi kune magamba akafira iyoyi Zimbabwe	In Chinhoyi there are heroes, who died for this country Zimbabwe
Viva Zanu Kugara musango taneta	Viva ZANU, we are tired of staying in the bushes
Viva Zanu ndeyekushupika	ZANU is about struggle
Viva Zanu ndeyeropa	ZANU is about sacrifice
Viva Zanu kugara musango kushupika	Viva ZANU, staying in the bushes is a struggle

The Religious and the Sacred in Political Song

In the introduction to this chapter, I indicated that I will a deploy a political song as a concrete example to show that to study religion is not to study a thing in itself, but rather how particular ideas (discourses) of "religion" are practised and operationalized in various contexts. In the following section, I distil the religious and/or sacred from the song "Nora".

The Religious/Sacred in the Political "Nora"

In contrast to Mugabe, opposition politicians are characterized as traitors who rebel and sell out because of the love for money (*"kune vamwe vakapanduka nepamusana pekuda mari"* ["Others have sold out because of the love for money"]) and stupidity (*"Kune vamwe vakapanduka nepamusana pekusafunga"* ["others have sold out because they do not think"]). The traitors are said to have sold out or are selling out to the Western countries, erstwhile colonizers, for pieces of silver (money), actions reminiscent of Judas Iscariot in the Bible. The metaphor of Judas Iscariot is forceful in Zimbabwe where at least 80 per cent of the population of about 13 million people say they are Christians. Traitors and sellouts are supposed to be taught the doctrine of the party, commonly known as *"gwara remusangano"* ("guidelines of the party"), which is espoused in the party's manifesto and constitution. (*"Toraika vanhu vakadai, dzidzisai gwara reZanu"* ["Teach these people the doctrine of the party"]). The party's manifesto and constitution can be allegorized to the sacred scriptures. They have to be taught the doctrine of the party as is the case in teaching doctrine to the non-believers in some religious traditions.

The song "Nora" refers to ZANU PF as a party of the struggle and its members, the living and the dead, as the epitome of sacrifice (*"Viva Zanu ndeyekushupika, Viva Zanu ndeyeropa"* ["Zanu is about struggle, Zanu is about sacrifice"]). The language of sacrifice is replete with religious and sacred connotations as it is linked to the ultimate price the fighters were prepared to pay for the ancestral land, with others losing life (*"kune magamba akafira iyoyi Zimbabwe"* ["there are heroes who died for the country Zimbabwe"]) and limb in the process. Sacrifice is a motif that is connected to ultimate commitment and selfless offer of oneself for what is of utmost value. Mugabe and the other heroes are viewed as messiahs (*"Zvinoda vakashinga Moyo savaMugabe"* ["One has to be as resilient as Mr Mugabe"]). Heroes and messiahs are seen as "authentic" – pure, true, pristine, original. In the song "Nora", the mention of Mr Mugabe's sacrifice as well as that of the heroes and heroines demonstrates that they are the epitome of authenticity, which according to Smith (2003: 38) is the equivalent of holiness as it is understood in traditional religions.

The distinction between the authentic and the false or inauthentic carries the same emotional freight as the division between the sacred and the profane. And just as the sacred things are set apart as representations of the sacred and forbidden in Durkheimian terms, so authentic objects and persons are separated and venerated openly or tacitly as representations of the sacred. Heroes provide models of conduct and they are to be emulated. What is important is not the fact of their heroism and genius, but the virtues and qualities they embody and the message of hope they proclaim (Smith 2003: 41). The dead heroes (*"kune magamba akafira iyoyi Zimbabwe"* ["there are heroes, who died for this country Zimbabwe"]) who sacrificed their lives complete the image of the sacred motif of the entire process of the liberation struggle. In the song, the aspect of sacrifice of the heroes is repeated in the same way to drill the message. Their blood, which was spilt, is perceived as the water that nourishes the struggle to this day in the same way the blood of Jesus nourishes the Christian faith. In African religions, the dead provide the sacred umbrella to the living and they are at the centre of the fortune/misfortune complex. To succeed in liberating Zimbabwe from the colonizers as well as to safeguard the hard-won independence requires the blessing of the heroes and in political matters, the glorious dead liberation war heroes have that responsibility of safeguarding the nation. They are the guardians of the land (Schoffeleers 1979) and the authors of the sacred history of the land called Zimbabwe. The song thus addresses the living to act in accordance with and in honour of the dead, thus, keeping faith with the dead.

As Chitando and I have written elsewhere (Chitando and Tarusarira 2017), to Zimbabwean nationalists, the territory of Zimbabwe represents something that is more than the soil: it is "holy land" for which precious blood has been and should be shed. Woe to those who overlook this heavily spiritual "truth"! In the Zimbabwean context, if one swears with the dead who lie buried in the soil (for example, swearing by their late mother: *"ndinopika namai vangu varere pachuru or ndinopika nevari pasi"* ["I swear by my mother who lies buried on the anthill or I swear by those under the soil"]) during a conflict, that signals that the person is ready to do the worst. The conflict has been escalated and sacralized by reference to the dead who are united with the soil. It is now a cosmic war (Juergensmeyer 2000). Mugabe has often made such acts of speech, swearing by Nehanda and Kaguvi, the spirit mediums who provided the religious support and guidance to the liberation war fighters in Zimbabwe, especially during the second liberation struggle. When he would say this, violence would break out like a whirlwind, because the dead are not to be joked with or about and questions of the land are existential, thus sacred.

The fast-track land reform programme is a case in point. Mugabe articulated an appealing indigenous theology of the land. He urged the "sons and daughters of the land" not to compromise on land because the land had not been reclaimed cheaply: the sacred blood of the ancestors and combatants had been shed in the armed struggle for it to be recovered. According to Mugabe:

> Our perspective on the land reform programme derives from our struggle for sovereign independence, and the compelling fact that the last and decisive seven years of that struggle took an armed form that demanded of us the precious and ultimate price of our blood. We died and suffered for our land. We suffered for sovereignty over natural resources of which land, *ivhu/umhlabati*, is the most important.
>
> (Mugabe 2001: 109)

The quest to recover the stolen ancestral land was a sacred duty, which had to be obeyed, even if it meant violence had to be perpetrated. In leading the taking back of the land, Mugabe was alleged to be obeying ancestral oracles (see Mukonyora 2011: 137; Chitando and Tarusarira 2017).

The song "Nora" proceeds to note that the liberation fighters are tired of staying in the bushes ("*Viva Zanu Kugara musango taneta*" ["Viva ZANU we are tired of staying in the bushes"]). The liberation struggle was a guerrilla warfare fought from the bushes. The liberation fighters are moving from the bushes or wilderness back to ancestral homeland, which they left to join the liberation struggle ("*Viva Zanu kugara musango kushupika*" ["Viva ZANU staying in the bushes is a struggle"]). They want to die and be buried in their homeland alongside the graves of their kith and kin. Home is a special territory that is sanctified and set apart (Smith 2003: 131). It is a place of rest and protection, where the ancestors watch over the living descendants. In the Shona religion in Zimbabwe, it is not uncommon to hear people in urban areas, including those in the diaspora, say "*Kana ndikafa ndinofanira kunovigwa kumatongo kumusha kwangu kunova kwakasara rukuvhute rwangu*" ("When I die, I would like to be buried at my traditional homestead because that is where my umbilical cord is buried"). The idea is that when a child is born, his or her umbilical cord is buried in the soil around the homestead, signifying connection with the soil, where one is founded and where his or her ancestors lie buried. Where one's umbilical cord is buried is therefore his or her roots and that has sacred significance.

From a Christian perspective, the journey from the bushes back home can be allegorized to the exodus of Israel from Egypt, the wandering in the wilderness of Sinai, and the entrance into Canaan, which constitute one of the greatest of the Old Testament types (symbols) of the Christian salvation. Canaan is a land full of honey and milk, as is expected in a liberated Zimbabwe. The liberation struggle was a journey at two levels: first the liberation fighters travelled long journeys, including outside the country to train as fighters and fought in different parts of the country far away from their own homes. Second, the process of fighting the liberation war is a journey in itself towards salvation or liberation from the colonizers. Notable in the preceding is that African religion and Christianity intersect to justify actions undertaken. Not only is the religious and/or secular identifiable in what we might call overt religious language and motifs as we know them from established religions. It is also detectable in the theodical function of the song.

The Theodical Function of the Song "Nora"

The song "Nora" has a theodical function, which creates a sense of the sacred through meanings and explanations that provide or evoke feelings of optimism, or hope, that good will ultimately triumph over evil (Antze 1976; Rice 1994). It further give causes of problems a religious or sacred origin, even if this means being the devil and narratives give the feeling that transcending problems can be a revelation of the power of the sacred. This song gives an optimism that lies in the fact that it is possible to be a sovereign country free from the reigns of colonial oppressions. This is not an easy process, but one that requires the resilience such as that of the leader Mr Mugabe (*"zvinoda vakashinga moyo savaMugabe"* ["One has to be as resilient as Mr Mugabe"]), who was the epitome of rootedness and authentic messiahs, heroes and heroines who are resilient and this depiction presents him as almost superhuman and part of the cosmic order. The authentic is the irreplaceable and fundamental, and authenticity is the new religious sanctity that the political has transmuted into (Smith 2003: 40). Transcending coloniality and neo-colonialism can be perceived as a revelation of the power of the sacred. Mugabe often referred to his long life and career in politics as a consequence of God's intervention (Tarusarira 2016).

The song addresses the five Ws and H – *who, what, when, where, why* and *how* – which provide a unity and coherence based on a logical relationship among these five elements, and gives the narrative force and helps make it not only memorable but also one with sacred aura. It addresses, first, the *who*. The liberation fighters fought for the country called Zimbabwe and anyone who does not identify with or subscribe to their perspective of the history of the country is a devil and sellout, a Judas Iscariot. Secondly, it addresses the *what*. The liberation struggle is the foundational myth of the country and nation called Zimbabwe. Thirdly it engages with the *when*. The struggle against colonialism (Chimurenga) in Zimbabwe is often divided into two phases. The first phase is the Ndebele and Shona resistance against the British South Africa Company which led the colonial enterprise in the early 1890s, while the second phase was begun in the 1960s and continued until the late 1970s. When an event took place is a mythical point in time that links what happened "in those days" to these times. For parties in a conflict, time undergoes a process of "collapse" (time collapse – the past and the present are brought into close proximity) in which "the interpretations, fantasies and feelings about a past shared trauma commingle with those pertaining to a current situation" (Volkan 1997: 35). The case of linking third Chimurenga (liberation struggle) to the first and second is an illustrative example in the case of Zimbabwe. The gap between these periods ceases to make sense. What matters most is what happened. Fourthly, the song addresses the *where*. The liberation war was fought from various locations across the country as well as outside Zimbabwean borders. That is why the song mentions various locations in Zimbabwe (Darwin, Mutare, Buruwayo, Masvingo, Gweru, Mutoko, Bindura, Chinhoyi) as places where dead liberation war fighters lie buried for those who got the privilege of burial. As for others, they were never seen again and are assumed to be dead. Outside the borders of Zimbabwe, places like Chimoio and Nyadzonia camps in Mozambique, where liberation fighters were bombed to death, remain key markers of "holy" places, the Calvary, where liberation fighters sacrificed their lives for the sake of the freedom of the generality of Zimbabweans. Where an event took place is, thus, not a meaningless geographical point; rather it is a "place of legend" charged with historic and religious connotations. No wonder Chimoio memorial camp in Mozambique, where at least 3000 liberation war fighters were bombed to death in 1977, remains an epic of the ultimate sacrifice during the liberation struggle of Zimbabwe. The dispute over names of places echoes the dispute over the link between the place and those who fight for and over it while making use of the national narratives that have come to be tied to this place. No wonder following attainment of independence many African countries took new names for the countries (for example Rhodesia became Zimbabwe) as well as for the streets. It can be distilled from the preceding account that the religious and/or the sacred quality is embedded in the narrative by way of importation of religion or generation of the sacred. The extent to which the song as a narrative import and generates the religious and the sacred respectively is determined by its context. Fifthly, the song addresses the *why*, which is that the country was colonized and it needed to be liberated. Lastly, it engages with *how* the war was fought. It was a guerrilla warfare fought in the bushes, involving a lot of struggles and sacrifices.

The song "Nora", like other political songs, praised Zimbabwe's then President Robert Mugabe and his ZANU PF regime. This song was belted out during ritualistic campaign political rallies. When music is embedded in political or religious rituals, it transforms the ordinary into the extraordinary thereby laying the foundation for the creation of the sacred. It is therefore not surprising that in Zimbabwean politics religious songs have been imported into the political discourse (Chitando 2002). The deployment of music through musical galas and the musical jingles was not only for mere entertainment but also a central part of the indoctrinating fundamentalist nationalist project of ZANU PF, whose ideology, characterized by the vision and version of Zimbabwe to be delivered by the "hero and political legend" President Mugabe, had become an apocalyptic knowledge disposed towards subject formation. Apocalyptic power and knowledge relations produce apocalyptic subjects even within nations.

Those subjected to ZANU PF indoctrination become dependent on that ideology, because it provides them with the answers that satisfy their desire for cognitive, emotional and moral meaning especially during conflict times when the natural order or normalcy is disturbed. Whether the explanation of the meaning is based on true facts or not is neither here nor there at this point. What is important is to provide answers that people can live with. No wonder Judith Butler (1997) points out that "Power is not simply what we oppose but also, in a strong sense, what we depend on for our existence and what we harbor and preserve in the beings that we are" (ibid.: 2). Subjection also results in an ambivalent situation in which the subject develops "passionate attachment" to his or her own subordination. This formulation helps clarify why members even of a democratic society are so susceptible to compliance with power relations that subordinate them, and it is clearly integral to a fundamentalist mindset. The narrative produced by political songs creates a fundamentalist mind and the articulated impact of music dovetails with the characteristics of religious fundamentalism. All these fundamentalist initiatives had emotional and psychological functions. Thus, huge loudspeakers that belt out nationalistic music have become a common feature of ZANU PF's political rituals, with party enthusiasts dancing.

Those deploying political rituals capitalize on the fact that "politics is not merely about material interest, but also producing and using symbols. It is through symbols that people give meaning to their lives; full understanding of political allegiances. The power of the ritual stems from its psychological underpinnings. A ritual also serves to link the individual to society" (Kertzer 1988: 10). To understand how the various activities described above, undertaken by the ZANU PF, are fundamentalist and subsequently tools for subject formation, we need to understand that participation in the ritual, for example going through all the right protocol, behaviours, sitting arrangements, speeches, song and dance and dressing (think party campaign regalia) in everyday politics, at rallies and musical bashes "involves physiological stimuli, the arousal of emotions. Rituals work through the senses to structure our sense of reality and our understanding of the world around us" (ibid.). These rituals in themselves do not only import religion but also generate the sacred.

Conclusion

Using the case of political songs, this chapter has demonstrated that the meaning and conception of religion and/the sacred is consequent of relations. The focus on the song is normally on its ability to evoke powerful emotional responses in listeners, impact and enhance the subjective experience of other sensory stimuli, and the release of oxytocin which is critical to generation of trust and affiliation. In addition to this, this chapter has indicated that latent in the song is a spiritual and sacred quality, if the song is not already a religious one imported into the public sphere. The chapter engaged with the seemingly religious as well as the not-seemingly religious elements in the song "Nora" to argue that songs can import as well as generate a religious and/or sacred quality. Elements such as teaching opposition members the "doctrine" of the party, that ZANU is a party of blood and sacrifice, and that there are heroes who died to liberate the country espouse a religious and/or sacred quality. From a functional perspective, the song is theodical. It provides answers to questions of ultimate meaning in contexts of instability. These questions centre around the who, what, when, why, where and how. The song "Nora" plays this role with regard to the contestation for political power in Zimbabwe. It, thus emerges, as I pointed out from the outset, that the meaning and conception of the religious and/sacred is not ontological (has not existence in and by itself), but epistemological (a construction out of discourses and narratives). Religion is not a reality waiting to be discovered but a result of the discourses and narratives particular actors and institutions weave around that which is attached religious and/or sacred value, using a particular language, which reflects their subjectivities and interests. It is therefore plausible to argue that the proffered definitions of religion tell us more about those offering them, than that which they claim to be telling us about, in this case religion.

About the Author

Joram Tarusarira is assistant professor of religion, conflict and peacebuilding and the director of the Centre for Religion, Conflict and Globalisation at the University of Groningen, the Netherlands. He has expertise in religion, conflict, peacebuilding and reconciliation; religion and politics; and religion and climate conflicts. His recent publications include *Religion and Human Security in Africa* (2020, co-edited with E. Chitando).

References

Antze, P. 1976. "The Role of Ideologies in Peer Psychotherapy Organizations: Some Theoretical Considerations and Three Case Studies." *Journal of Applied Behavioral Science* 12(3): 323–346. https://doi.org/10.1177/002188637601200306

Auerbach, Yehudith. 2010. "National Narratives in a Conflict of Identity." In *Barriers to Peace in the Israeli-Palestinian Conflict*, edited by Yaacov Bar-Siman-Tov, pp. 99–134. Jerusalem: The Jerusalem Institute for Israel Studies.

Bar-Tal, D. and G. Salomon. 2006. "Israeli-Jewish Narratives of the Israeli-Palestinian Conflict: Evolution, Contents, Functions, and Consequences." In *Israeli and Palestinian Narratives of Conflict: History's Double Helix*, edited by R.I. Rotberg, pp. 19–46. Bloomington, IN: Indiana University Press.

Baumgartner, T., K. Lutz, C.F. Schmidt and L. Jancke. 2006. "The Emotional Power of Music: How Music Enhances the Feeling of Affective Pictures." *Brain Research* 1075: 151–164. https://doi.org/10.1016/j.brainres.2005.12.065

Beckford, James, A. 2001. Social Movements as Free-floating Religious Phenomena. In *The Blackwell's Companion to Sociology of Religion*, edited by R.K. Fenn, pp. 229–248. Oxford: Blackwell. https://doi.org/10.1111/b.9780631212416.2001.00015.x

Bond, Patrick and Masimba Manyanya. 2002. *Zimbabwe's Plunge: Exhausted Nationalism, Neoliberalism and the Search for Social Justice*. Harare: Weaver Press.

Butler, Judith. 1988. "Performative Acts and Gender Constitution: An Essay in Phenomenology and Feminist Theory." *Theatre Journal* 40(4): 519–531. https://doi.org/10.2307/3207893

Butler, Judith. 1997. *The Psychic Life of Power: Theories in Subjection*. Stanford, CA: Stanford University Press.

Campbell, Collin. 2007. *The Easternization of the West: A Thematic Account of Cultural Change in the Modern Era*. Boulder, CO: Paradigm.

Campbell, Collin. 2010. "The Easternization of the West: Or How the West Was Lost", *Asian Journal of Social Science* 38: 738–757. https://doi.org/10.1163/156853110X522911

Chitando, Ezra. 2002. "Down with the Devil, Forward with Christ! A Study of the Interface between Religious and Political Discourses in Zimbabwe." *African Sociological Review* 6(1): 1–16. https://doi.org/10.4314/asr.v6i1.23200

Chitando, E. and J. Tarusarira. 2017. "The Deployment of a 'Sacred Song' in Violence in Zimbabwe: The Case of the Song 'Zimbabwe Ndeye Ropa Ramadzibaba' (Zimbabwe Was/Is Born of the Blood of the Fathers/Ancestors) in Zimbabwean Politics." *Journal for the Study of Religion* 30(1): 5–25. https://doi.org/10.17159/2413-3027/2017/v30n1a1

Cross, I. 2003. "Music as a Biocultural Phenomenon: The Neurosciences and Music." *Annals of the New York Academy of Sciences* 999(1): 106–111. https://doi.org/10.1196/annals.1284.010

Demerath, N.J. III and T. Schmitt. 1998. "Transcending Sacred and Secular: Mutual Benefits in Analysing Religious and Nonreligious Organization." In *Sacred Companies: Organizational Aspects of Religion and Religious Aspects of Organizations*, edited by N.J. Demerath, Peter Dobkin Hall, Terry Schmitt, Rhys H. Williams, pp. 381–400. New York: Oxford University Press.

Durkheim, É. 1915. *The Elementary Forms of the Religious Life*, translated by J.W. Swain. London: George, Allen & Unwin. https://doi.org/10.1097/00000446-191609000-00024

Gerth, H.H. and C. Wright Mills. 1946. *From Max Weber: Essays in Sociology*. New York: Oxford University Press.

Jacobs, J. 1990. "Women-Centered Healing Rites." In *In Gods We Trust: New Patterns of Religious Pluralism in America*, edited by T. Robbins and D. Anthony, pp. 373–383. New Brunswick, NJ: Transaction.

Juergensmeyer, Mark. 2000. *Terror in the Mind of God: The Global Rise of Religious Violence*. Berkeley, CA: University of California Press.

Kertzer, David. I. 1988. *The Power of Rites: Ritual, Politics, and Power*. New Haven, CT: Yale University Press.

Koelsch, Stefan. 2010. "Towards a Neural Basis of Music-evoked Emotions." *Trends in Cognitive Science* 14: 131–137. https://doi.org/10.1016/j.tics.2010.01.002

Masunungure, Eldred. 2004. "Travails of Opposition Politics in Zimbabwe since Independence." In *Zimbabwe: The Past is the Future*, edited by D. Harold-Barry, pp. 147–192. Harare: Weaver Press.

Mellor, P. and Shilling, C. 1997. *Re-Forming the Body: Religion, Community and Modernity*. London: Sage.

Missig, G., L.W. Ayers, J. Schulkin and J.B. Rosen. 2010. "Oxytocin Reduces Background Anxiety in a Fear-Potentiated Startle Paradigm." *Neuropsychopharmacology* 20: 858–865. https://doi.org/10.1038/npp.2010.155

Mugabe, Robert Gabriel. 2001. *Inside the Third Chimurenga: Our Land is Our Prosperity*. Harare: Department of Information and Publicity, Office of the President and Cabinet.

Mukonyora, Isabel. 2011. "Religion, Politics, and Gender in Zimbabwe: The Masowe Apostles and Chimurenga Religion." In *Displacing the State: Religion and Conflict in Neoliberal Africa*, edited by J.H. Smith and R.I.J. Hackett, pp. 136–159. Notre Dame, IN: University of Notre Dame Press.

Raftopoulos, Brian. 2004. "Nation, Race and History in Zimbabwean Politics." In *Zimbabwe: Injustice and Political Reconciliation*, edited by B. Raftopoulos and T. Savage, pp. 160–175. Cape Town: Institute for Justice and Reconciliation.

Rice, J.S. 1994. "The Therapeutic God: Transcendence and Identity in Two Twelve-Step Quasi-Religions." In *Between Sacred and Secular: Research and Theory on Quasi-Religion*, edited by A.L. Greil and T. Robbins, pp. 151–164. Greenwich, CT: JAI Press.

Sachikonye, Lloyd M. 2004. "Land Reform and Farm Workers." In *Zimbabwe: The Past is the Future*, edited by D. Harold-Barry, pp. 69–76. Harare: Weaver Press.

Schoffeleers, Matthew, 1979. *Guardians of the Land: Essays on Central African Territorial Cults*. Gweru: Mambo Press.

Smith, Antony. D. 2003. *Chosen Peoples: Sacred Sources of National Identity*. Oxford: Oxford University Press.

Tarusarira, J. 2016. *Reconciliation and Religio-political Non-conformism in Zimbabwe*. London: Routledge. https://doi.org/10.4324/9781315603940

Volkan, Vamik. 1997. *Bloodlines: From Ethnic Pride to Ethnic Terrorism*. New York: Farrar, Straus and Giroux.

– 13 –

Comparing Notes

The Anthropological Approach to the Study of Islam in Europe

MARJO BUITELAAR

Introduction

A few years ago, a friend of mine felt that her life had somehow come to a standstill. After her youngest child had moved out, she realized how stale her marriage had become. Workwise, she had a good position that paid well, but lately she had begun to wonder about the purpose of it all. To get in touch with what she really wanted in life, she decided to take a sabbatical and walk the pilgrimage route to Santiago de Compostela.

About the same time, Nilgün, a Turkish-Dutch participant in my current Hajj research, found herself in a similar situation: having divorced early in her marriage, her focus had always been on working hard to provide for her children. The crown on her work had been the recent wedding of her eldest son. Soon afterwards, however, she found herself drained of all energy and staring into emptiness. A friend suggested she take a break: "Why not join the mosque group that's going on Umra, the voluntary pilgrimage to Mecca?" Initially, Nilgün dismissed the idea, considering the cost an insurmountable obstacle. The more she allowed herself to dream about it, however, the stronger her desire to visit Mecca grew. Not just to have a break, she hastened to explain during our interview; what she had longed most for, was to stand in front of the

---

Keywords: deconstructing the "Muslim Other", Islam as foreground/background presence, everyday religion, intersectionality, ethnography

Ka'ba to pray for the well-being of her children, and to thank the Lord for the strength He'd given her to raise them as a single mum. In short, Nilgün felt Mecca pulling her towards itself like a magnet and eventually could not resist: she sold her golden bangles, and some family members stepped in to help her pay for the journey.

What struck me in Nilgün's story was how for this deeply religious woman, the pilgrimage to Mecca, for Muslims the holiest city on earth, was so closely intertwined with her daily concerns, such as the well-being of her children and herself. Her religiosity is obviously shaped not only by authoritative Islamic beliefs and practices, but also by those related to other dimensions of her life, in this specific instance particularly her position as a single mother. Nilgün's story illustrates the argument I want to make in this chapter about the significance of the anthropological approach to study Islam as "lived religion". In this approach, the focus is on the embeddedness of religion in people's daily life-worlds and the active and creative ways in which individuals appropriate authoritative beliefs and practices as they grapple with the complexities of everyday life.

The second argument I wish to make is that besides the academic relevance of studying what religion actually means to people "on the ground", the anthropological production of knowledge also serves an important societal interest, particularly in relation to the issue of cultural diversity. To introduce this line of argumentation, let me return to Nilgün once more.

As a token of my gratitude to Nilgün for sharing her pilgrimage stories with me, at the end of our interview sessions I gave her the catalogue of the Hajj exhibition at the National Museum of Ethnology in Leiden (cf. Mols 2013). Flipping through the pages she expressed surprise: How could it be that in the Netherlands, where so many people think of Islam in negative terms, a museum should care to host an exhibition on what Nilgün called "the beauty of Islam"?!

A few months later, I saw Nilgün's surprise more or less mirrored by that of a Dutch journalist who interviewed me about the then upcoming Hajj for a news show of RTL, a national Dutch television broadcasting company. One of the rites I described was the *wuquf*, consisting in the pilgrims standing at Mount Arafat to contemplate their lives and ask God forgiveness for their wrongdoings. The *wuquf* inspires many pilgrims to decide to make a fresh start and lead a more meaningful life upon return home. "Gee", the interviewer exclaimed in response to my explanation of the *wuquf*, "I had no idea Islam could be like that. This sounds all pretty spiritual, kind of like what you hear people say who go to Santiago de Compostela!"

Unfortunately, this particular dialogue between the interviewer and myself did not make it into the broadcast. The reason I mention it here, is that the mirror image of Nilgün's surprise and that of the journalist points to a gap; a gap between what western non-Muslims often think Islam is about on the one hand – namely politics, oppression and violence – and, on the other hand, what Islam actually means in the everyday lives of most Muslims – a source of consolation, inspiration, strength. The second argument I want to make in this chapter is that as Islam and the West are increasingly pitted against each other in popular European discourse, it is precisely this gap that makes anthropological knowledge production about the meanings of Islam in everyday social existence of utmost importance. I will start by reflecting on the dominant discourse in the West concerning Muslims and Islam and its effect on religious studies, and then turn to elaborate on how the anthropological approach to the study of Islam can contribute to a more productive debate in which "selfing" and "othering" is replaced by comparing notes in the sense of recognizing commonalities and taking this common ground as a point of departure to discuss differences.

Islam, Conflict and Globalization

Globalization and the further integration and expansion of the European Union have changed the life-worlds of Europeans significantly over the past decades. These processes went hand in hand with a growing presence and, above all, an increased visibility of Muslim citizens in the public domain. These simultaneous trends, exacerbated by a refugee crisis and by violent attacks by perpetrators who claim to act in the name of Islam, have resulted in Muslims becoming the focus of public anxiety.

In the dominant public discourse, Islam is mostly portrayed as a static and monolithic religion that is intrinsically incompatible with modernity and Western values. Also, Islamic scriptures like the Qur'an and the Hadith, the sayings of the prophet Muhammad, tend to be assumed to determine all dimensions of Muslim life. Thus, people of Muslim backgrounds are reduced to their "Muslimness" (Brubaker 2013). They are viewed as Muslims only, rather than being recognized as multi-dimensional individuals whose life-worlds and daily concerns overlap significantly with fellow citizens of non-Muslim backgrounds. To put it differently, in the dominant discourse Muslims are represented as "the other"; the "them" who do not belong to "us". Vice versa, exclusivist Muslim discourses in which non-Muslims are being othered also exist, for example in representations of non-Muslims as being promiscuous or otherwise lacking morals.

As a result of such exclusivist discourses, commonalities in how people of Muslim and other backgrounds tackle everyday life concerns are easily obscured. The surprise expressed by the journalist whom I referred to in the opening section of this chapter illustrates this. The journalist was struck by the fact that certain parallels that can be drawn between the practices and meanings of Muslim pilgrimage to Mecca and those of pilgrims who go to Santiago de Compostela. While it is largely known in the Netherlands that people who embark on the Camino de Santiago do not necessarily do so for religious motives only, the idea that Muslims may similarly have additional or other than religious motives to perform the pilgrimage to Mecca does not readily occur to many non-Muslims.

In policy-making the unease about Muslim presence in Europe is reflected in a strong focus on security issues and the integration of Muslims (cf. Sunier 2014). Not surprisingly, societal demand for information about Islam has increased tremendously over the past two decades. For scholars in Islam studies, this raises the question of how we can best cater for such demands. What are the most productive ways to contribute to public debates about contemporary Islam? Also, how do societal interests in religious studies relate to the academic study of religion?

The past decade has shown an upsurge of studies on Muslim radicalization and terrorism, often conducted by experts in political science and international relations. I therefore welcome recent trends at departments of religious studies to create centres of expertise in religion and conflict, such as the Centre for Religion, Conflict and Globalization at my own Faculty of Theology and Religious Studies at the University of Groningen (www.rug.nl/research/centre-for-religious-studies/religion-conflict-globalization/?lang=en). Taking a religious studies perspective as their starting point, researchers affiliated to these centres produce knowledge and provide policy advice that offer more nuanced understandings of "religion" and its relations to politics and society than political scientists outside the field of religious studies tend to produce. As religious studies scholars, then, we have a big responsibility to contribute to knowledge production about religion and conflict.

There is a danger, however, in the trend that can be observed in academic research in response to such public demand. Reflecting on the state of the art in the anthropology of Islam in Europe in a recent overview, the anthropologist Nadia Fadil argues convincingly that as a result of the present dominance of a societal discourse on Islam as a violent religion, and the related demand for research findings that can be worked into state policies of governance, the anthropology of Islam in

Europe is caught in an epistemological impasse. This deadlock is a consequence of the historical Orientalist discourse that continues to inform the dominant popular European frame in which Muslim citizens are presented as the abject "Other". One of the tensions caused by this frame revolves around the challenge to deconstruct representations of a binary opposition between a Western "us" and a Muslim "other", while simultaneously acknowledging the specificity of the religious experiences of European Muslim citizens. For anthropological scholarship on Islam in Europe this is reflected in the double bind researchers are confronted with when seeking to "account for the distinctiveness of ethical subjectivity of Muslims, while at the same time downplaying it" (Fadil 2019: 118). While acknowledging that being affected by a discourse in which integration into European society is the yardstick that demarcates the distinction between the "good" Muslim and the "bad" Muslim cannot be avoided by researchers on Islam in Europe (nor by European Muslim citizens, for that matter), the main argument that I wish to make in this chapter is that in order fully to grasp the rich and varied meanings of what Muslims identify as "religious" in their lives, it is vital that besides situations in which religion is foregrounded, we should also investigate circumstances in which religion is only a background presence.

The Anthropological Approach to Islam

This, in my view, is where the unique contribution of the anthropological approach to the study of contemporary Islam comes in: through long term participation in the lives of the people we study, by observing them as they try to make sense of the puzzles of everyday life, and by engaging with them far more extensively through small-talk than by means of formal interviews, ethnographers learn how religious understandings and practices are embedded in people's wider life-worlds (cf. Blok 1978; Jansen and Driessen 2013). Through participant observation, ethnographers gain insights in how religious concerns intertwine with other motivations, and how believers may foreground religion in some settings, and leave it unaddressed in others. In the remainder of this chapter, I will argue that the ethnographic mapping of the contextual presence of Islam in the everyday lives of Muslims is of crucial importance in the study of contemporary Islam for both academic and societal reasons.

Marjo Buitelaar

Ethnographic Accounts of Religion and Everyday Life

Ethnographic research not only provides us with insights in the wide variety of ways in which the Islamic scriptures are appropriated in practice – thus serving academic interests – but ethnographic accounts also challenge the assumed gap between Muslims and non-Muslims that characterizes public anxiety about Islam in Europe – thus serving societal interests. Ethnographic accounts of the experiences of individuals of Muslim backgrounds as they try to make sense of everyday social existence take us beyond specifically Muslim understandings, yet without glossing over them (cf. Rasanayagam 2013: 116–117). By telling stories about how people tackle the kind of everyday concerns we all have to deal with, ethnographers render the lives of their research participants intelligible to others, thus allowing people of different backgrounds to find common ground and take what they share as a point of departure to discuss their differences. In other words, the ethnography of everyday life-worlds produces the kind of knowledge that invites people to compare notes (cf. Orsi 2005).

Ethnographic accounts of people's daily concerns also contest the assumption in the public discourse that Islam determines all dimensions of Muslims lives. The problem of this assumption is that it presupposes the existence of a cultural essence; it implies a view of culture as a kind of mould that keeps producing identical copies (cf. Baumann 1999: 25). Contrary to this static conception of culture, anthropologists understand culture as time-sensitive, open-ended models of historically embodied traditions, that are continuously adjusted in the practice of everyday life (cf. Marsden and Retsikas 2013: 14). Anthropologists therefore study culture not only as a force that shapes people's daily life-worlds, but also as a resource that people draw on to address their everyday concerns and to make sense of their experiences.

The Cultural Toolkit Approach

One could conceive of culture as providing people with a "toolkit" that contains various kinds of tools to interpret and act upon the world (cf. Swidler 2001: 104–106). Cultural toolkits come with a socially transmitted body of knowledge and views that functions as a kind of "instruction manual" on how to use those tools. Some guidelines are articulated explicitly, while others "go without saying"; we incorporate them by observing others apply them.

Rather than strictly following the rules, in the practice of everyday life people improvise upon established ways of doing and seeing things. In doing so, they are active contributors to the innovation of tools and their use. Over time, as changing circumstances create new issues to be tackled, people may invent new tools or adopt instruments from other people's cultural toolkits. Gradually, some older tools fall in disuse and are thrown out of the toolkit. Alternatively, they simply end up at the bottom, maybe disappearing from collective memory altogether, or making a come-back to serve new purposes, as the renewed popularity of the pilgrimage to Santiago de Compostela illustrates (cf. Roseman 2004).

Not all cultural tools are equally valued by those who share similar toolkits, nor does everybody have equal access to tools. For most Muslims, for example, the pilgrimage to Mecca is beyond reach because of their gender, their financial situation, health issues, or, as of recently, because of the quota system that allows only a small number of applicants to be issued with hajj-visa (cf. Bianchi 2004: 11). Moreover, there is often no consensus among people who have similar toolkits concerning the issue of which tools should be used how to tackle a specific situation. Take, for example, package tours to Mecca that include safaris on quads in the Saudi desert. Such overly touristic activities are frowned upon by many Muslims (Buitelaar 2017). Particularly among older Muslims the pilgrimage to Mecca is conceived of as an act of penitence and obedience; it is the fulfilment of one's last religious duty in preparation to meet one's Creator (Haq and Jackson 2009; McLoughlin 2009). Quad safaris obviously have no place in such conceptions. This example illustrates that the use of cultural toolkits is always open to contestation and innovation. Therefore, while Islamic scriptures may provide a "script" to lead a morally good life, the ways Muslims interpret and enact that script is shaped by the wider cultural context in which they are embedded (cf. Jeldtoft 2013). Moreover, Islam is not the only moral register that informs Muslims' life-worlds. In the course of everyday life, people engage in a number of different socio-cultural settings, each with their own frames of reference and value systems (Zigon 2009). To complicate matters, people's views and practices are not only informed by the local contexts they physically inhabit, but also include imagined and enacted global connections (Appadurai 1996). The world of commercial media, for instance, strongly promotes exactly the kind of consumerist life-style that creates a market for package tours to Mecca that include quad rides (cf. Haenni 2011; Aziz 2001).

Marjo Buitelaar

The Intersectionality Approach

The overlapping and intersecting settings and imaginaries that inform people's life-worlds result in a hodgepodge of tools to tackle the complexity of everyday social existence. Not everybody is equally well equipped to cope with such complexities and, again, not everybody has equal access to specific tools; a person is never Muslim only, but also gendered, young or old, rich or poor, of specific ethnic and educational backgrounds, and so on and so forth. These various identity categories intersect to locate a person's position in society, their access to specific resources, and their outlook on life. Therefore, social identifications such as gender, class, religion, ethnicity, do not simply "add up" but intertwine and mutually constitute each other (Phoenix 2006).

Being a Muslim, for example, only comes in the modality of being a Muslim woman or man of a specific age and ethnic background. The intersectionality approach therefore entails first of all reflecting on how the researcher's own positionality informs their presuppositions about the people they study, and, secondly, exploring what different insights "asking the other question" may produce (Davis 2014: 22–24). If we study the beliefs and practices of Muslims, for example, this means trying to forget for a moment about the Muslim dimension of the stories of our research participants to do an exercise in telling the story of these beliefs and practices from another identity marker or position they have in society, such as people with lower class migrant backgrounds. In the case of Nilgün, for example, the woman presented in the introduction to this chapter, telling her pilgrimage story from her position as a single mother provides relevant insights in the nature of her piety.

Comparison of the narratives produced by looking through different lenses produces richer accounts of the complexity of people's lives and the multiple factors that contribute to how their views and practices are informed by various cultural discourses and their being positioned in different sets of power structures simultaneously. Also, exactly because individuals are no automatons that simply act out scripts, but active contributors to the cultural contexts they are embedded in, a more constructivist strand within the intersectionality approach focuses on how they creatively employ their agency to act within and upon the structures that define their life-worlds (Prins 2006). Therefore, rather than a priori privileging a decontextualized "Muslimness", the meaning of Islam in the lives of Muslims is more productively explored by taking an intersectionality approach to tease out the complex and often contradictory ways in which various frames of reference and different sets of power relations simultaneously inform their life-worlds and personal agency (cf. Schielke and Debevec 2012).

Taking intersectionality seriously implies that as researchers we should avoid a one-sided focus on how Islam is invoked in situations where people close ranks and take a public stance to defend their interests either *as* Muslims or *against* Muslims. To assess the scope and import of diverging habits and value systems in the everyday routines of living together as citizens of different backgrounds, settings where Islam's presence is less foregrounded must also be taken into account. One reason for this is that precisely since everyday life is complex and full of ambiguities, in their daily practices people do not always manage to live up to high moral standards quite as much as they think or say they do when reflecting on those standards on a meta-level. This is often overlooked in debates about the compatibility or incompatibility of so-called "Western" and "Islamic" norms and values.

Moreover, as I mentioned earlier, in their daily routines people navigate multiple socio-cultural scenarios. As they move between different settings, they improvise upon and negotiate between different moral registers (cf. Schielke 2010). Several ethnographic studies have demonstrated, for example, that the social ethics of women involved in Islamic revivalist movements are not only informed by principles that they derive from authoritative interpretations of Islamic sources, but also include liberal political concepts such as democracy, rights and equality (e.g. Fadil 2008; Jouili 2015; Hafez 2011).

Studying Islam as a Foreground and as a Background Presence

While obviously not all research into contemporary Islam focuses on conflicts, there is a strong tendency in Islam studies to concentrate on situations where Muslim actors or those who interpret their practices foreground what they conceive of as "the religious". To capture the contextual meaning of Islam in people's everyday lives, we must, however, equally study settings in which religion is only a casual or background presence. Take, for example, a statement by Malika, a Moroccan-Dutch woman whom I interviewed as part of my life story project (cf. Buitelaar 2009, 2014). After pondering my question what being Muslim meant to her, her first response was: "Well, I don't drive my car as a Muslim, for instance." Nevertheless, later in the interview Malika mentioned that listening to Qur'an recitation while driving home after a long working day helps her to unwind. Depending on her mood, however, she may equally opt for a Leonard Cohen album.

The detail about Malika's switching between the Qur'an and Leonard Cohen to reduce stress, illustrates that if we move away from an over-emphatic research focus on specifically religious matters to explore Islam as a background presence in the everyday mundane practices of Muslims, distinctions between "us" and "them" become more fuzzy. An even more powerful example concerns the public expressions of shared grief by Dutch football fans over the fate of Ajax midfielder Abdelhaq (or "Appie") Nouri, who lay in a coma for years and suffers serious brain damage after collapsing during a football match in 2017.

Shortly after the fateful match, thousands of fans from all walks of life gathered at Nouri's home in Amsterdam to pay respect to him and his family. It was obviously Nouri's "being one of us" as an Ajax player that enabled people to identify so strongly with what he and his family were going through. The family itself inserted their Muslim identity as a self-evident element in sharing their grief with the crowd. Nouri's father, for example, asked people to pray for his son. Interestingly, in media coverage of the event, the family's religiosity was neither foregrounded nor ignored. For example, a particularly strong "bonding" image appeared of a young blond Ajax fan shaking hands with Nouri's sister who wears the kind of cape-like covering that is often associated with an orthodox religious style. Other images showed #StayStrongAppie banners that fans put up, all of which having the Ajax logo and colours, one of them including a $du^c\hat{a}$', a supplication prayer in Arabic.

Pertinent to my argument here is the "normalizing" effect of the casual or background presence of Islam in these images. This demonstrates the power of shared, immediate experiences – in this case shared grief over Nouri's tragic fate – to acknowledge both commonalities and differences. In turn, this acknowledgement enables productive communication and interaction that crosscuts diverse ways of being in the world. In other words: it is concrete shared experiences that create common ground and space for "comparing notes". Comparing notes in the sense of opening up to the perspectives of others and scrutinizing our own in order to recognize, assess and learn from both commonalities and specificities.

Concluding Remarks: Comparing Notes in a Globalized World

The argument that I wished to make in this chapter can be summed up by stating that the overall contribution of anthropology to the study of contemporary Islam that I deem most valuable for both for academic and societal reasons concerns the issue of how in specific settings being Muslim intersects with other social identifications and positions to inform Muslims' views and practices as they try to make sense of their daily lives. To take this intersectionality approach seriously, I propose to study not only topics in which Islam takes centre stage but to also investigate topics in which Islam is only a background presence.

If we want the knowledge thus produced to be effectively applied to contribute to public debates about Islam, this means that we not only take seriously the intersecting identifications and positions of Muslims, but equally those of other actors in the debate. Conducting participant observation in situations that take them out of our own comfort zones provides anthropologists of religion with a thorough training in de-exceptionalizing others and, to some extent, becoming strangers to themselves. Ideally, in today's globalized world, such trainings should be part of educational programmes in good citizenship in all schools. But learning to look through an anthropological lens is not the same as becoming an anthropologist. Even ethnographers, who have been equipped to voluntarily tackle the unfamiliar in situations of their own choosing, will acknowledge that this is not always easy and can cause anxiety. In contrast to ethnographers who voluntarily seek the unfamiliar, for most people whose life-worlds are directly affected by Islam's growing presence in contemporary Europe, confrontation with the unfamiliar was not their own choice, nor have they been professionally trained to handle cross-cultural encounters. The very real experiences of uncertainty and anxiety in the daily lives of "ordinary" people that come with globalization must be taken into account in our research on the dynamics of Islam's presence in Europe and the ways encounters between Muslim and non-Muslim European citizens inform the beliefs and practices of all actors involved.

Therefore, the most valuable contribution that the anthropological approach can make to the public debate about Islam in Europe is to tell stories that undermine those spread by actors who tap into feelings of anxiety and oversimplify the complexities of both societal issues and people's multiple identifications and positions in society by scapegoating a specific category of citizens for all societal wrongs. Since framing multi-dimensional people of Muslim backgrounds as "the Muslim other" is the main feature in such discourses of exclusion, ethnographic counter-narratives can demonstrate the fluidity and fuzziness of distinctions between "us" and "them" by producing analytical descriptions of the contextual presence of Islam in Muslims' everyday lives and how

Marjo Buitelaar

these relate to both shared and different concerns of other European citizens.

About the Author

Marjo Buitelaar is professor of contemporary Islam from an anthropological perspective at the University of Groningen. Her research interests concern Islam in everyday life and narrative identity construction in a post-migration context. Buitelaar is presently programme-leader of a research project on "Modern Articulations of Pilgrimage to Mecca" (NWO grant 360-25-150). Her most recent co-edited books in English are *Religious Voices in Self-Narratives* (2013), *Hajj, Global Interactions through Pilgrimage* (2015) and *Muslim Women's Pilgrimage to Mecca and Beyond. Reconfiguring Gender, Religion and Mobility* (2021).

References

Appadurai, Arjun. 1996. *Modernity at Large. Cultural Dimensions of Globalization.* Minneapolis, MN: University of Minnesota Press.

Aziz, Heba. 2001. "The Journey: An Overview of Tourism and Travel in the Arab Islamic Context." In *Tourism and the Less Developed World: Issues and Case Studies*, edited by D. Harrison, pp. 151–159. Wallingford: CABI. https://doi.org/10.1079/9780851994338.0151

Baumann, Gerd. 1999. *The Multicultural Riddle. Rethinking National, Ethnic and Religious Identities.* London: Routledge.

Bianchi, Robert. 2004. *Guests of God: Pilgrimage and Politics in the Islamic World.* Oxford: Oxford University Press. https://doi.org/10.1093/0195171071.003.0004

Blok, Anton. 1978. "Participerende waarneming." In *Antropologische Perspectieven*, pp. 19–46. Muiderberg: Coutinho.

Brubaker, Rogers. 2013. "Categories of Analysis and Categories of Practice: A Note on the Study of Muslims in European Countries of Immigration." *Ethnic and Racial Studies* 36(1): 1–8. https://doi.org/10.1080/01419870.2012.729674

Buitelaar, Marjo. 2009. *Van Huis uit Marokkaans. Levensverhalen van Hoogopgeleide Migrantendochters.* Amsterdam: Bulaaq.

Buitelaar, Marjo. 2014. "Dialogical Constructions of a Muslim Self through Life Story Telling." In *Religious Stories We Live By: Narrative Approaches in Theology and Religious Studies*, edited by R. Ganzevoort, Ch. Hermans, and A. Korte, pp. 143–155. Leiden: Brill. https://doi.org/10.1163/9789004264069_012

Buitelaar, Marjo. 2017. "Moved by Mecca: The Meanings of the Hajj for Present Day Dutch Muslims." In *Muslim Pilgrimage in Europe*, edited by Ingvild Flaskerud and Richard Natvig, pp. 29-42. London: Routledge. https://doi.org/10.4324/9781315597089-2

Davis, Kathy. 2014. "Intersectionality as Critical Methodology." In *Writing Academic Texts Differently: Intersectional Feminist Methodology and the Playful Art of Writing*, edited by Nina Lykke, pp. 17-29. New York: Routledge.

Fadil, Nadia. 2008. "Submitting to God, Submitting to the Self: Secular and Religious Trajectories of Second Generation Maghrebi in Belgium." Doctoral dissertation, Catholic University of Leuven.

Fadil, Nadia. 2019. "The Anthropology of Islam in Europe: A Double Epistemological Impasse." *Annual Review of Anthropology* 48: 17-132. https://doi.org/10.1146/annurev-anthro-102218-011353

Haenni, Patrick. 2011. "La consommation n'a pas d'odeur ... Quelques réflexions sur le religieux en culture de masse." *Social Compass* 58(3): 316-322. https://doi.org/10.1177/0037768611412140

Hafez, Sherine. 2011. *An Islam of Her Own: Reconsidering Religion and Secularism in Women's Islamic Movements*. New York: New York University Press. https://doi.org/10.18574/nyu/9780814773031.001.0001

Haq, Farooq and John Jackson. 2009. "Spiritual Journey to *Hajj*: Australian and Pakistani Experience and Expectations." *Journal of Management, Spirituality and Religion* 6(2): 141-156. https://doi.org/10.1080/14766080902815155

Jansen, Willy and Henk Driessen. 2013. "The Hard Work of Small Talk in Ethnographic Fieldwork." *Journal of Anthropological Research* 69(2): 249-263. https://doi.org/10.3998/jar.0521004.0069.205

Jeldtoft, Nadia. 2013. "Spirituality and Emotions: Making a Room of One's Own." In *Everyday Lived Islam in Europe*, edited by N. Dessing, N. Jeldtoft, J. Nielsen and L. Woodhead, pp. 85-100. Farnham: Ashgate.

Jouili, Jeanette. 2015. *Pious Practice and Secular Constraints: Women in the Islamic Revival in Europe*. Stanford, CA: Stanford University Press. https://doi.org/10.1515/9780804794893

Marsden, Magnus and Konstantinos Retsikas. 2013. "Introduction." In *Articulating Islam: Anthropological Approaches to Muslim Worlds*, edited by M. Marsden and K. Retsikas, pp. 1-31. Dordrecht: Springer. https://doi.org/10.1007/978-94-007-4267-3_1

McLoughlin, Séan. 2009. "Holy Places, Contested Spaces: British-Pakistani Accounts of Pilgrimage to Makkah and Madinah." In *Muslims in Britain: Identities, Places and Landscapes*, edited by R. Gale and P. Hopkins, pp. 132-149. Edinburgh: Edinburgh University Press. https://doi.org/10.3366/edinburgh/9780748625871.003.0008

Mols, Luit. 2013. *Verlangen naar Mekka: De hadj in Honderd Voorwerpen*. Leiden: Rijksmuseum Volkenkunde te Leiden.

Orsi, Robert. 2005. *Between Heaven and Earth: The Religious Worlds People Make and the Scholars Who Study Them*. Princeton, NJ: Princeton University Press. https://doi.org/10.1515/9781400849659

Phoenix, Ann. 2006. "Editorial Intersectionality." *European Journal of Women's Studies* 13(3): 187–92. https://doi.org/10.1177/1350506806065751

Prins, Baukje. 2006. "Narrative Accounts of Origins: A Blind Spot in the Intersectional approach?" *European Journal of Women's Studies* 13(3): 277–290. https://doi.org/10.1177/1350506806065757

Rasanayagam, Johan. 2013. "Beyond Islam: Tradition and the Intelligibility of Experience." In: *Articulating Islam: Anthropological Approaches to Muslim Worlds*, edited by M. Marsden and K. Retsikas, pp. 101–118. Dordrecht: Springer. https://doi.org/10.1007/978-94-007-4267-3_5

Roseman, Sharon. 2004. "Santiago de Compostela in the Year 2000: From Religious Center to European City of Culture." In *Intersecting Journeys: The Anthropology of Pilgrimage and Tourism*, edited by E. Badone and S. Roseman, pp. 68–88. Urbana, IL: University of Illinois Press.

Schielke, Samuli. 2010. *Second Thoughts about the Anthropology of Islam, or How to Make Sense of Grand Schemes in Everyday Life*. ZMO Working Papers 2. Berlin: ZMO.

Schielke, Samuli and Liza Debevec. 2012. "Introduction." In *Ordinary Lives and Grand Schemes. An Anthropology of Everyday Religion*, edited by S. Schielke and L. Debevec, pp. 2–16. New York, Oxford: Berghahn Books.

Sunier, Thijl. 2014. "Domesticating Islam: Exploring Academic Knowledge Production on Islam and Muslims in European Societies." *Ethnic and Racial Studies* 37(6): 1138–1155. https://doi.org/10.1080/01419870.2012.753151

Swidler, Ann. 2001. *Talk of Love. How Culture Matters*. Chicago, IL: University of Chicago Press. https://doi.org/10.7208/chicago/9780226230665.001.0001

Zigon, Jarrett. 2009. "Within a Range of Possibilities: Morality and Ethics in Social Life." *Ethnos* 74(2): 251–276. https://doi.org/10.1080/00141840902940492

– 14 –

Configurations of Values

PETER BERGER

> What ought to be compared is not religion, but the general configuration of values, which in all cases but one is coterminous with religion.
> (Dumont 1970: 33)

"Relation" is perhaps the single most important word with reference to approaches associated with structural anthropology. Informed by structural linguistics, such approaches assume that meaning is always constituted in a relational way. In order to know what "blue" is in any particular culture or language, for example, one needs to know all the other colour dimensions that are acknowledged and distinguished in the given case. Another consequence of this is that such approaches assume some kind of abstract totality, system or whole in contrast to actual and partial realizations of such systems. This chapter deals with relationships between ideas and it will become apparent below that the concept of value already implies such relationships.

Ideas enable human beings to organize the diversity of their perception of the world around them (social and otherwise); they constitute worldviews. Because of that function, as pointed out in the introduction to this volume, ideas have a relatively high degree of durability. Otherwise, sustained attempts of meaning-making would be difficult, if not impossible. Moreover, as they are provided by culture, ideas have a conventional character and are shared. Ideas would also be without consequence if they did not translate into implicit or explicit rules and if they did not inform people's actual behaviour. But ideas do all this and as such anthropologists and historians (among others) consider the study

---

Keywords: Louis Dumont, structural anthropology, values, hierarchy, ideology, cultural change

of ideas as important in their attempt to understand culture, politics, history, and certainly religion.

Above, I have presented properties of ideas as if there were agreement or certainty about these issues. But these are in fact the big questions that this chapter is concerned with. What are ideas? How are ideas related and do they really constitute "systems"? If ideas are so enduring, how do they change? How are ideas related to action, and vice versa? Ideas are all around us but we do not have direct access to people's minds. Thus ideas cannot be collected like shells on a beach but can only be inferred, from behaviour, texts and objects. But how can we properly identify ideas and find out which ideas are more important than others for a given community? I have also stated above that ideas are shared, but they are not all shared equally by all members of a community. So how do we account for this? I cannot hope to deal with any of these issues thoroughly here, but I will attempt to make a start for students who are interested in these questions.

The chapter will first give a very brief outline of the development of this approach and how it evolved in different directions. In the following section I will start by introducing the work of Louis Dumont, the most important scholar in the anthropological study of value, by first discussing his views on comparison. Subsequently, I will summarize the main analytical concepts and illustrate them by examples. In the final section I deal with the issue of transformation of systems of ideas and values before emphasizing, in the conclusion, a few points as to why this approach has something to offer for students of religion.

From "Symbolic Classification" to "Values"

For the discipline of socio-cultural anthropology, which is the concern of this chapter, Emile Durkheim and Marcel Mauss's seminal work *Primitive Classification* provided the starting point for the discussion. This essay (Durkheim and Mauss 1963 [1903]) anticipates many of the arguments of Durkheim's later work *Elementary Forms of Religious Life* (1995 [1912]), in particular with regard to the origin of ideas or "collective representations". Durkheim uses the term "collective representations" to indicate that the categories of thought, the ideas referred to above, are social in a twofold way. They originate in society in the sense that ideas are generated, reproduced and also modified as a consequence of collective activities, ritual action having an important place in this regard. A certain settlement pattern, for example, gives rise to categories of space specific to that community. Moreover, these collective representations also refer back to society, as they express "the various aspects of the social being" (Durkheim 1995: 441; Lukes 1992: 6–8). A classic, ethnographically informed example is the classification of time among the Nuer as described by Evans-Pritchard. "Ecological time" is derived from social action in relation to cattle: "time is to them a relation between activities" (Evans-Pritchard 1940: 100). "Structural time" is much more abstract and a reflection of the relationship between ancestors and the living. Thus, the way the Nuer collectively organize their economic and social life gives rise to these ideas that are at the same time about Nuer economy and social structure.

No matter how fancy they might appear to an outside observer, ideas are thus very real as they result from and refer back to social action and "collective forces," as Durkheim would have it. Another crucial dimension relevant to the present discussion is the notion of transfiguration (Durkheim 1974: 95, 86f; Hatch 1973: 177f). Cultural ideas (as collective representations might also be called) are not a direct reflection of objective reality, but are always already transformed and mediated. The Nuer representations of time mentioned above do not reflect any objective property of time. The ecological conditions and changing seasons do not directly result in categories of "ecological time" but the latter refer to collective activities motivated by such general conditions. Surely we "see time" when we notice how flowers wither or how people are born and die, but the socially generated ideas about these phenomena do two things: they add fixity to fleeting sensations (vide durability of ideas) and they add meaning and value. Let me give an example from my own research. The ethnic group I have done most fieldwork with are the Gadaba, an indigenous ("Adivasi") community in highland Central India.[1] I will refer to them throughout this chapter. For this community, the idea of "seniority" is crucial. This is not just an acknowledgement of the natural fact of age but a cultural assessment that grants higher status to those who are relatively older, such as an older brother, but is extended from this domain to organize different kinds of people, food, relationships, places or deities.

The ideas of Durkheim and other members of his group have been hugely influential both within France and beyond. The above-mentioned Evans-Pritchard, in particular, introduced their work to the UK and for

---

1. For a short general overview of this ethnic group see Berger (2019), for a brief synthesis of their rituals and religious system see Berger (2017) and for a comprehensive description and analysis see my monograph Berger (2015) (note: I barely use the word "religion" in my book on religion).

several generations up to the present-day anthropologists at Oxford and Cambridge (and elsewhere) have applied and developed their ideas further (see the work of Mary Douglas, Rodney Needham, Edmund Leach, Stanley Tambiah, Nicholas Allen, Robert Parkin and many others).

In France, Durkheim and Mauss's initial impetus strongly influenced Claude Lévi-Strauss, the name most associated with structuralism. His general aim has been aptly summarized as "seek[ing] structure *in* culture" (Gellner 1981: xxxiii); discovering the ways ideas are connected in human thought processes, in other words the study of "symbolic classification" as it came to be called (Needham 1979). Lévi-Strauss argued on the basis of his research on kinship, classification ('totemism") and mythology that human beings think in contrasts, or binary oppositions. These contrasts are not to be sought on the surface level of empirical phenomena but are rather deep structures that can be unearthed through structural analysis. A myth, for example, has an explicit narrative or story, but its message lies hidden in its structure and is communicated without actors necessarily being aware of it, in much the same way that the structure of music effects certain results in a listener without them knowing how (Lévi-Strauss 1968, 1983).

Lévi-Strauss's work has been crucial for the development of anthropology and was repudiated as much as it was praised. Apart from scholars who viewed Lévi-Strauss's work as an intellectual mind game, several criticisms were particularly relevant, informing the way in which his approach has been developed, namely his disregard for the human agent and actual practice, for relationships of power and for historical processes. This led different scholars to attempt to rectify some of these weaknesses in their own theoretical thinking. Pierre Bourdieu (1990; see McCloud 2012), for example, considered Lévi-Strauss's structure too abstract and far removed from real life. He developed the concept of *habitus*, which locates cultural patterns in bodily practice rather than in intellectual processes alone. He also focused on dimensions of power and economy in symbolic processes (forms of "capital"). Although the American anthropologist Marshall Sahlins shares Bourdieu's interest in practice, he rather conversely showed that there is symbolism in power and the economy, that there is no human domain unmediated by cultural ideas (Sahlins 1976). One of Sahlins's major contributions was to investigate the relationship between cultural structures (systems of ideas) and historical processes, the role events play in the transformations of ideas (see Golub et al. 2016). In the following, I will focus on a third strand in the development of structural anthropology, namely Louis Dumont's theory of value.[2] Unlike Bourdieu, Dumont remained quite close to the theoretical project of Lévi-Strauss (and Durkheim and Mauss). Dumont contributed the concept of value to the structural approach, which entails hierarchy, a relationship between ideas.

Comparison of Ideologies

Strongly influenced by his teacher Marcel Mauss, and in complete contrast to post-colonial arguments about "othering", Dumont regards cultural difference or alterity as something positive, even an epistemological necessity for anthropology as a discipline. Difference is crucial for the possibility of gaining knowledge about other cultures, and consequently also one's own. Anthropological understanding, from this perspective, is generated through difference. As a consequence, comparison lies at the heart of Dumont's endeavour, even "radical comparison" (Dumont 1986: 6; see de Coppet 1992; Dumont 1970; Iteanu and Moya 2015b) as he calls it, the creative confrontation of two different configurations of ideas and values, of two ideologies as a whole. "Ideology" here means "the totality of ideas and values common to a society or a group of people in general" (Dumont 1977: 7; see also Dumont 1994: vii). The comparison is radical because it does not start from given entities for comparison, say comparing "politics" or "religion" in two different societies. How can we assume that these two categories are acknowledged by the society we study or, if they are acknowledged, that they occupy the same semantic spectrum or carry the same meanings, given that meanings are defined in relation to the ideological configuration that a category is a part of (see Hardenberg 2010)? Rather, the entities for comparison result from the confrontation of ideologies, in particular the contrast between the ideology of the observer in relation to the one studied. In Dumont's words:

> our most general rubrics, such as ethics, politics, economics, are not easily applied to other societies ... In the last analysis, in order to truly *understand* we must be able on occasion to ignore this partitioning and to search, in the whole field, for what corresponds on *their* side to what *we* acknowledge, and what corresponds on *our* side to what *they* acknowledge. In other words, we must strive to construct on both sides comparable facts.
> (Dumont 1986: 3, original emphasis)

Thus, what is studied in such a comparison is how ideologies are structured in each case, which ideas and values are prominent, and how

---

2. For a discussion of the theories of Bourdieu, Dumont and Sahlins in relation to the structural analysis of cultural change see Berger and Sahoo (2020: 18–25).

they relate to and are separate from each other. Obviously, this is piecemeal work and never complete. Dumont has likened moving to and fro between sets of ideas and values to a "journey" (Dumont 1994: viii). In that sense, he travelled a good deal. Born in 1911, he had Marcel Mauss as his teacher in the mid-1930s.[3] He was a prisoner of war in Germany during the Second World War and managed during that time to study German and Sanskrit. After the war he again picked up his interest in Indian society, which he studied intensely for many years. The result of these efforts was his book on the Indian caste system and its ideology. *Homo Hierarchicus* (Dumont 1980 [1966]) is the most important (and most contested)[4] contribution to the anthropology of India in the twentieth century. In studying India and especially the significance of hierarchy, he became aware of the necessity of the radical comparison outlined above. Consequently, for the rest of his life until his death in 1998, he studied different dimensions of what he called modern ideology. *Homo Aequalis* (English title: *From Mandeville to Marx*; Dumont 1977) investigates the genesis of the category of "economy" in modern (i.e. Euro-American) ideology. *Essays on Individualism* (Dumont 1986), as the title suggests, studies how the individual has been established as the paramount value, and in his last book, *German Ideology* (Dumont 1994), he discusses German and French configurations of values as two national variants of modern ideology. He has thus worked in many ways as a historian of ideas in his study of ideology. Important here are not the particular arguments in any of these books – I will return to modern ideology in the last section – but the general theory of value that he came to develop in the course of his research. The introductions to the monographs mentioned give a good general overview of this approach and his lecture "On Value" (Dumont 1986: ch. 9; 2013) is probably the most consistent summary of his general ideas, even though, as students regularly point out to me, it is difficult reading.

There is no linear reception history of Dumont's theory of value. One of the first recognitions of the general relevance of Dumont's ideas is represented by the volume *Contexts and Levels: Anthropological Essays on Hierarchy* (Barnes et al. 1985). For a long time, however, the theory was not much discussed outside the circle of close associates (see Barraud and Platenkamp 1990; Barraud et al. 1994), with a few exceptions (Needham

---

3. See Madan (1999) for a biographical essay.
4. His arguments on India in particular have been very critically discussed. See the two symposiums on "Homo Hierarchicus" in *Contributions to Indian Sociology* (Madan 1971) and *The Journal of Asian Studies* (Richards and Nicholas 1976). See also Arjun Appadurai's review article "Is Homo Hierarchicus?" (1986) and Collins (1989). For a critical reading of Dumont's "Essays on Individualism" see Macfarlane (1992-1993).

1987; Robbins 1994; Jolly and Mosko 1994; with regard to the study of religion in general, Strenski 1989), although anthropologists working in all corners of the world had been influenced by Dumont in their ethnographic work. In contrast, Dumont's theory has received a lot of attention over the last ten years (see Berger et al. 2010; Haynes and Hickel 2016; Iteanu and Moya 2015a; Otto and Willerslev 2013a, 2013b; Parkin 2003; Rio and Smedal 2009; Robbins and Siikala 2014a; Strenski 2008).

Value and Hierarchy

Values are an example of what Durkheim called collective representations, categories of thought that transfigure reality. Because they are social in the twofold sense mentioned above, they are also specific to certain groups at a certain point in history. But values are a special kind of representation; while the latter organize the diversity of our perception, the former are also crucial in structuring the set of representations in any particular ideology.[5] Furthermore, in every configuration of representations there is one (perhaps several) that is most important and which often represents the idea of that society as a totality. These paramount or ultimate values have an even more important function in the organization of the ideology as many subordinate ideas and values derive from and are related to this paramount value.

The aspect of added meaning in the process of transfiguration is very explicit in the term "value". However, this does not mean that values are only ideals that people consciously strive for (Durkheim 1974: 93). Values might be explicit and upfront. Often there is a word or an expression in the respective language that represents an important value, such as the value of brotherhood (*bai*) among the Gadaba, to which I will return below. But this need not be the case and values can be implicit, "unperceived" (Dumont 1994: 8), not directly articulated (Barraud et al. 1994: 118) or "unavowed" (Moya 2015). In other words, values may inform people's thought and action independent of and even in spite of what they want to think or do.

The obvious question then is how to identify values. Even though not all values are directly equivalent to specific words, language is clearly crucial in being able to identify values as language is linked to the articulation of worldviews. Furthermore, Sherry B. Ortner (1973: 1339)

---

5. See Robbins (2004: 336, n. 6) for a useful distinction between categories and values that I do not discuss here further. See also Durkheim (1974: 95) on "concepts" versus "ideals of value".

provided indicators with regard to "key symbols" that are also useful for the present purpose. First of all, the people with whom a researcher is working may point out to her what they think of as significant in their culture or religion. Certainly, this is the explicit dimension, mentioned above. Another common indication is that people tend to be positively or negatively emotionally involved with reference to values. Because values are often implicit, asking directly about them during fieldwork usually proves fruitless. For instance, the Gadaba customarily give a young calf as part of the bridewealth. To ask "why" would be pointless because the person asked would most likely simply refer to "tradition" (*niam*). But when I asked a Gadaba if one could bring a young buffalo instead, he reacted very strongly: it would be completely unacceptable and anyone doing so could never show their face again at the weekly market. It was a matter of shame (*laj*) and thus related to values, in this case to values of brotherhood (represented by buffaloes) and affinity (represented by cows) that should not be confused. Another feature that Ortner mentions is the degree of cultural elaboration, to which I will return in the final section. This elaboration can have many different forms: linguistic elaboration, great ceremonial care, economic investment or the time spent on something.

A very important indicator in my view is that things (objects, words, practices, people) referring to values appear in many different empirical situations or contexts. When I started my fieldwork with the Gadaba, I soon realized that a certain kind of sacrificial food (*tsoru*) was of relevance in a variety of different empirical contexts: annual village rituals dedicated to local deities, harvest rituals, death rituals, reconciliation of conflicts, times of "supernatural" distress, myths, references to why a man was blind in one eye and one room in every house was reserved for cooking only this kind of food. Naturally, I looked closer and tried to understand the full implications of this phenomenon. Finally, Ortner (following Durkheim here) mentions restrictions. More restrictions point towards aspects of a culture that people consider important. This is also clearly the case with regard to *tsoru*. In a concrete context of an annual village sacrifice, the following rules apply: those who share *tsoru* with the deity have to be male, married, "earth people" (of the same village clan) and must not have eaten earlier on that day. In other contexts, fewer rules apply, quite clearly because the Gadaba consider these of lesser importance. In addition to the elaboration of restrictions I would like to stress another aspect, namely the question of transgression of these rules. Quite often, actors disregard rules. However, such as in the above-mentioned context of *tsoru* consumption, reaction to transgressions would be strong. Significantly though, actors would not even think of breaking these rules, which they consider divinely inspired and in that sense entirely "natural".

If an ideology consists of a set of ideas and values, one might imagine this as a kind of conceptual latticework, a static grid, like a conceptual dictionary containing all the relevant categories between its covers. But social life is much too dynamic to be adequately interpreted with such a model. Different aspects of Dumont's theory seek to account for and analytically explain the dynamics of ideas and values without letting go of the assumption that these processes are patterned. Two important concepts in this regard are "context" and "level" (see Barnes et al. 1985; Hardenberg 2007). As pointed out above, context refers to an empirical situation, quotidian or spectacular, such as a class at a university, a football match, a demonstration or a presidential inauguration. Levels, on the other hand, refer to dimensions or planes within an ideology and as such cannot be observed directly but only inferred, among other things from the way in which ideas within an ideology relate to each other, as I will point out below. The analytical distinction of levels is important because otherwise we cannot grasp the double relationship of a hierarchical opposition consisting of identity and contrariety between two ideas; this would appear to us instead as a "logical scandal" (Dumont 1986: 227). I will also return to this double relationship shortly.

Dumont assigns three properties to values, the first being encompassment. Here we are at the very heart of what hierarchy means for Dumont. In contrast to a binary opposition described by Lévi-Strauss or Needham (see Dumont 1986: 225f), a value always entails a hierarchical opposition: it is superior to its opposite and includes or contains it. The subordinate idea is encompassed. We may also call this encompassed idea a value if it in turn is able – perhaps in different contexts – to encompass other ideas/values. The superior, encompassing value thus represents a larger whole, a totality and it is precisely the relationship between a whole and a part of that whole that Dumont calls hierarchy.[6] The terms value, hierarchy and encompassment thus refer to and imply each other.

One of the examples Dumont provides for a hierarchical opposition are the right and left hands (Dumont 1986: 228f). The two hands represent not only a binary or distinctive opposition but have a hierarchical relation of encompassment. It is mostly the right hand that is superior to the left, a fact also reflected in the metaphorical use of the right/left contrast in many languages with regard to *right*eousness and morality.

---

6. Dumont gives definitions of hierarchy in many places in his work, the best and most elaborate one, in my view, appearing in the chapter "The Anthropological Community and Ideology" (1986: 227).

But Dumont in particular stresses that the superior hand has a different relation to the whole, the human body, and represents this totality. He gives the example of the Nuer, as described by Evans-Pritchard, where the spear as an extension of the right hand signifies the self (ibid.: 228f). Realizing that the right hand stands for the person, it also makes sense that people greet and seal contracts by shaking their right hands. Because of the hierarchical nature of the opposition between right and left, these categories have a double relation as mentioned above; they are contrasted as opposition, as "right" versus "left", and at the same time, because the right encompasses the left and represents the totality, there is identity, as the left is included in the right. While this may seem contradictory, the distinction of levels enables us to make better sense of this twofold relation. On a superior level the right hand represents the whole and on this level the left is not "visible", as it were, but part of the whole. On a subordinate level the opposition between right and left becomes explicit again (see Dumont 1980: 239f).

As a second example we can return to the Gadaba and their sacrificial food (*tsoru*). This food is usually prepared from the head (plus blood and liver, the "life" of the animal) and is contrasted with the body meat (*lakka'*). The head meat/*tsoru* stands for the whole (the brothers of the founding clan of the village) and encompasses the body meat/*lakka'*. The hierarchical relation is expressed and performed in relation to people, time and space. In one sacrificial context an intermediate category is introduced and the ubiquitous criterion of seniority that I mentioned above is used to express the hierarchical relationship. The "earth people" of the village's founding clan share "senior *tsoru*" (head meat), starting first and sitting right next to the shrine of the deity. Their affines start second and sit a bit further away and share "junior *tsoru*" (neck meat), while all other men of the village (women being excluded in this context) eat *lakka"* (body meat) several hundred metres away from the shrine. In this context we can thus infer from the sacrificial commensal practice the hierarchical relationships between different groups of people. Even among the earth people sharing *tsoru*, not all are equal. The most senior man (in terms of status, not age) among them is the village sacrificer, who represents the village as a totality in all kinds of ritual situations. He sits right next to the shrine and always starts eating first and gets up first when the sacrificial meal is finished. Depending on the level we are considering with regard to this particular context, hierarchical oppositions – sacrificer/other agnates, brothers/affines, earth people/latecomers, men/women – become visible or are hidden as subordinate categories are encompassed.

This example also illustrates the second property of values, namely segmentation. As values are relational entities and not essences, they can branch or subdivide into units *"of the same nature but smaller scale"* (Dumont 1980: 42, original emphasis). Elsewhere, Dumont writes with reference to segmentation: "distinctions are numerous, fluid, flexible, running independently of each other, overlapping or intersecting; they are also variably stressed according to the situation at hand, now coming to the fore and now receding" Dumont (1986: 253). Annual village sacrifices usually articulate the opposition between the senior earth people of the village and all others ('latecomers"), the former eating *tsoru* (head meat), the latter *lakka'* (body meat). In only one particular instance – the most "senior" shrine of the village introduced above – the category of *tsoru* is segmented into "senior *tsoru*" (head, eaten by earth people) and "junior *tsoru*" (neck, eaten by affines). This segmentation is significant as it acknowledges the importance of the affinal element in relation to the earth people representing the village as a totality and elevating the affines above all other (non-Gadaba) "later-comers" resident in the village. This example illustrates both encompassment and segmentation. Let us approach the third property of values by way of a question.

Why does it make a difference to distinguish hierarchical oppositions from distinctive oppositions? The point is that it makes a difference when they are reversed (Dumont 1986: 230). The feature of reversal is the third feature that Dumont points out for values. Such a reversal may occur in the same context or in a different one. For example, one could imagine that the earth people, after having eaten the superior sacrificial food, carry the affines (who have eaten relatively inferior food) on their shoulders back into the village. This would constitute an inversion within the same empirical context, as the earth people are first senior with regard to *tsoru* consumption but then junior as carriers of the affines (the opposite is in fact the case, however, thus confirming the seniority of the earth people). But such inversions of hierarchical oppositions often happen in different contexts. In *Homo Hierarchicus* (1980) Dumont discussed the fourfold classification of the *varna*, mentioned first in ancient Indian texts (Rig Veda). All four categories clearly relate to a whole as they originate in the body of the Cosmic Man (Purusha), who sacrifices himself and thus gives rise to the distinction of the interdependent *varna*. I will only focus here on the two most important ones, the Brahman (sacrificer, custodian of religion) and the Kshatriya (king, representing power and material wealth). Both categories are related in a hierarchical opposition. The Brahman is economically and politically dependent on the king, while the latter is dependent on the Brahman in relation to "religion" (*dharma*, cosmic order). In relation to the value of *dharma* that the Brahman represents and maintains with his sacrifices, the king's goal of *artha* (material interest) is inferior and encompassed. In a particular context, such as an investiture ceremony, the king may be temporarily represented as encompassing the Brahman and the value of *dharma*. Hence, relations between values are not absolute and fixed but dynamic.

Any reversal, Dumont argues, points to distinctions people make within the system of ideas and values, a distinction of different levels. On a superior level within the ideology, the Brahman encompasses the king (and the earth people their affines in the Gadaba example) and represents the totality and unity. On a lower level the Brahman opposes the king and the contrast is stressed. Only this distinction of levels within ideologies enables us, according to Dumont, to avoid seeing a logical scandal – identity and difference at the same time – and allows us to account for different dimensions within an ideology. If the king encompasses the Brahman in any particular context, then this would point to a different and subordinate level in which the value of *artha* is stressed. As I indicated above, a change of relationship between ideas – reversal being one case – points towards distinctions or levels within the system of ideas and values. Such shifts occur in different contexts in a society at any given time. But relationships between ideas and values may change, and do change, as part of a historical process, which is the topic of the final section.

Values in Transformation and Interaction

Although not always acknowledged, most – if not all – of Dumont's work has a diachronic dimension: it concerns the transformation of representations in time. Like his teacher Mauss, Dumont is generally interested in the long-term evolution of ideas, rather than in cultural change that is happening more or less in front of an ethnographer's eyes. But Dumont's theory is valuable for understanding both the long-term and short-term processes of cultural transition. In this final section I will briefly discuss both. Joel Robbins in particular has drawn attention to this aspect of Dumont's theory and has been among the most innovative scholars in developing it further (Robbins 1994, 2004, 2009; Robbins and Siikala 2014b).

With regard to the long-term transformations of ideas, Dumont's distinction between "individualism" and "holism" is crucial. For Dumont, these terms designate the two kinds of ideologies (he calls them, unfortunately in my view, modern and non-modern respectively), each with various variants. While holism is the standard form, individualism is the more recent and "eccentric phenomenon" (Dumont 1970: 31), the ideology of Western modernity (Dumont 1977, 1986, 1994). In non-modern or "traditional" societies, values refer directly to and represent the social dimension of being human. The specific form of collective being that is most important for any particular society is often represented in that society's paramount value, a value that usually represents the idea of that society as a totality. Hence, holistic ideologies are those that value the social whole. The Gadaba, for example, express and manifest their values of brotherhood and affinity with regard to sacrificial performances. The foundation of society in myths and the idea of society as a whole are also related to the constitution of these values through the sacrificial process that always contextually creates a hierarchical distinction as described above. Gadaba actually express their idea of their society as a totality in the formula "twelve brothers, thirteen seats" (*baro bai tero gadi*), in which the totality (twelve) of brothers (*bai*) is complemented by a subordinate affinal element (the additional, thirteenth seat).

The ideas and values of the modern configuration of individualism are, of course, also social in origin, but this particular ideology denies its socialness as it were. As empirical human beings, individuals are a universal phenomenon and every society consists of individuals in that sense. Modern ideology, however, has elevated the individual to a paramount value that subordinates all other ideas and values. This category of the individual was long in the making. Dumont traces the development from early Christianity, via the reformation to the period of enlightenment. This transformation was absolutely fundamental, a "mental revolution" (Dumont 1970: 32) in several ways that I cannot discuss here but only mention briefly.

Modern ideology (Dumont 1994: 6f) considers value as something secondary and voluntary, a dimension that can be added to a world of "facts" that can be scientifically studied on a value-neutral basis. It also separates the subject from the object and transforms what in holistic ideology is a matter of degree into a radical ontological distinction. As a consequence of the individual as a valued autonomous monad (a devaluation of relationships and sociality), elements in modern ideology are disconnected or "atomized" (e.g. Dumont 1970: 32) and while elements are integrated hierarchically in holistic ideologies (e.g. the nested relationships I described with regard to the Gadaba sacrifice), elements in modern ideology are one-dimensionally juxtaposed (Dumont 1986: 262f). In the evolution of individualist ideology, autonomous spheres developed that were hitherto integrated into a hierarchical – and necessarily religious – whole: politics (now merely the field of individuals seeking power), economics (individuals competing for material wealth), and religion (individuals in relation to God). As in every ideology, paramount values have repercussions for the whole system and many other ideas and values derive from them. As such, the value of the individual has many concomitants. Ideas of "equality" and "liberty" derive from the paramount value (see Robbins 1994) as do notions of "class" (individuals with common interests), "property" (what belongs exclusively to the individual) or "nation" (a collection of individuals and a collective individual) (Dumont 1970).

In Dumont's view, these two types of ideology do not monolithically oppose each other but interact (Dumont 1994: ch. 1). Confronted with modern culture as the bearer of individualistic ideology, autochthonous cultures may disappear or reject the dialogue. Most often, however, interaction and "acculturation" (Dumont 1994: 6), a two-way process, take place. As a consequence, individualism and holism are found in hybrid ideological formations where individualism is predominant in some domains, while giving way to holism in others. Robbins and Siikala (2014b: 125) have argued that Dumont's theory of ideologies in interaction actually provides a "distinct approach to globalization".

Apart from long-term transformations of or interactions between ideologies, cultural change can occur very quickly. It can occur in different cultural domains. Let me illustrate this with the Gadaba once again (Berger 2020). As I outlined above, Gadaba place great emphasis on the domain of ritual and sacrificial food. All the key values of brotherhood, affinity and seniority are elaborated and worked out in ritual contexts and thus in relation to the socio-cosmic order or "tradition" (*niam*). In contrast, everyday life is not morally elaborated but left relatively unmarked. Certain actions in everyday life may not be appreciated but they are not assessed in a religious sense. Alcohol consumption, for example, is very common and vital for social and ritual life. However, some Gadaba drink excessively, with severe economic consequences and causing disruption to the domestic life. While this is experienced as a problem, it is not addressed in terms of value. This changed recently among Gadaba converts to a Hindu reform movement, many of whom converted because they suffered from alcohol-related problems. They stress an ascetic lifestyle and abstain from meat and alcohol. It is precisely the quotidian domain that they ethicize in religious terms as they link it to a newly conceived individual spiritual development and the new value of "happiness-peacefulness" (*suk santi*). In this way they articulate the domain of everyday life in a new way, offer a new avenue to conceptualize the "alcohol problem" in religious terms and also offer alternative behavioural patterns to deal with it. This example shows that every configuration of values has certain domains it elaborates and others that it neglects. Consequently, every system of values is enabling in some ways and limiting in others.[7]

Robbins in particular has pointed out the value of Dumont's theory for understanding processes of relatively sudden and radical change and added further analytical flexibility by focusing on the degree of elaboration of values and the different valuation of contexts (Robbins 2007, 2009). If a paramount value is crucial for organizing ideas and values within the ideology, then a shift in paramount values must have repercussions for the configuration as a whole. The Urapmin of Papua New Guinea, where Robbins conducted fieldwork, traditionally had a strong focus on ancestors. Within a short time span, however, they completely converted to Christianity. As individual salvation came to be the paramount value, aspects of the traditional religion contradicted this value and its concurrent assumption of the omnipotence of God. Traditional ideas did not vanish completely, as Robbins argues, but their place in the ideology has changed. The elaboration of traditional ideas related to spirits (*motobil*), for example, has been limited. They may be elaborated as long as they do not contradict dominant values and if they are articulated elaborately, this only occurs in contexts of lesser value. As such, spirits are prominent only in contexts of illness but encompassed by God, who represents the domain of Spirit as a whole (Robbins 2009: 73–74). In addition to Dumont's distinctions between contexts and levels, reversal and segmentation, Robbins has thus further refined the conceptual tools in order to understand complex processes of change from a structural perspective.

Conclusion

Dumont (1986: 237) wrote that "we have at our disposal a word that allows us to consider all sorts of culture and the most diverse estimations of the good without imposing on them our own; we can speak of our values and their values while we could not speak of our good and their good". Indeed, speaking of *our* good turns as quickly into discussing *their* evil as *our* religion leads to *their* superstition. Moreover, there is the problem of defining the realm of religion. Does a certain group of people have religion, and if so, do they have "religion"? Or can a certain

---

7. Another example from India that demonstrates this latter aspect is the conversion of the Sora people from animism to Baptist Christianity, involving both loss and redemption (Vitebsky 2017).

phenomenon legitimately be studied under the umbrella of "religion"? In the epigraph at the beginning of this chapter, Dumont refers to his argument that – like economy and politics – religion only became a separate domain in the evolution of modern ideology. As such, scholars of religion should avoid assuming such an autonomous field among the societies they study. In my opinion the study of values circumvents some of the problems that have been pointed out with reference to the concept of religion (see Introduction and Mason in this volume). If "a hierarchy of ideas is indispensable to social life" (Dumont 1980: 20), such configurations are relevant for any community at any point in history and can thus be studied. Often these ideologies will be closely related to "religion" ('in all cases but one", as Dumont says) but we do not have to bother about whether this is or is not the case.

In a very brief way I have presented here some of Dumont's ideas (including their heritage) that I believe are valuable for the study of religion. As to why his approach is important, in my view three things stand out. First, Dumont offers a methodology to study systems of representations in motion, while maintaining the assumption that these processes are patterned. In contrast to the "elemental approach" (Robbins 2009: 67), which only enumerates items of a culture or religion that have or have not changed (leaving the actual process described as "mixture" or "hybridity" inside a kind of black box), Dumont's tools sketched here allow for a more thorough analysis and understanding. Second, Dumont presents an open theoretical framework. In accordance with his own view of himself as a "craftsman" working on an uncompleted task and his strong emphasis on collaboration and cooperation (Galey 1982: 11), the theory is open for further developments. Dumont's terminology can be improved and refined and new dimensions investigated. His model is also compatible with other approaches, such as Bourdieu's practice theory (Alvi 1999) or the theory of the "event" provided by Marshall Sahlins (Robbins 2004), who also grants structural significance to these apparently erratic phenomena and pays particular attention to interested actors. Effervescent contexts of death may have special importance in this regard (Berger 2016). Finally, the theory can be – and has been – very widely applied, with regard to diverse types of historical or ethnographic data and to all kinds of themes relating to social, religious or political life, from Gadaba sacrificial rituals to the changing values of immigrant communities in Berlin (Toukolehto 2015).

About the Author

Peter Berger (PhD 2004, FU Berlin) is associate professor of Indian religions and the anthropology of religion at the University of Groningen. His areas of interest include the anthropology of religion, indigenous religions (esp. in India), theory and history of anthropology and the anthropology of India. His books include *Feeding, Sharing and Devouring: Ritual and Society in Highland Odisha, India* (De Gruyter, 2015), and he coedited *Godroads: Modalities of Conversion in India* (Cambridge UP, 2020), *Ultimate Ambiguities: Investigating Death and Liminality* (Berghahn, 2016), *The Modern Anthropology of India* (Routledge, 2013) and *The Anthropology of Values* (Pearson, 2010).

References

Alvi, Anjum. 1999. "Bearers of Grief: Death, Women, Gifts, and Kinship in Muslim Punjab." PhD dissertation, Freie Universität Berlin.

Appaduari, Arjun. 1986. "Is Homo Hierarchicus?" *American Anthropologist* 13(4): 745–761. https://doi.org/10.1525/ae.1986.13.4.02a00090

Barnes, Robert H., Daniel D. Coppet and Robert Parkin. 1985. (eds.) *Contexts and Levels: Anthropological Essays on Hierarchy*. Oxford: JASO.

Barraud, Cécile and Josephus D.M. Platenkamp. 1990. "Rituals and the Comparison of Societies." *Bijdragen tot de Taal-, Land- en Volkenkunde* 146(1): 103–23. https://doi.org/10.1163/22134379-90003230

Barraud, Cécile, Daniel de Coppet, André Iteanu and Raymond Jamous. 1994. *Of Relations and the Dead: Four Societies Viewed from the Angle of their Exchanges*. Oxford: Berg.

Berger, Peter. 2015. *Feeding, Sharing, and Devouring: Ritual and Society in Highland Odisha, India*. Berlin: De Gruyter. https://doi.org/10.1515/9781614513636

Berger, Peter. 2016. "Death, Ritual, and Effervescence." *Ultimate Ambiguities: Investigating Death and Liminality*, edited by P. Berger and J. Kroesen, pp. 147–183. New York: Berghahn.

Berger, Peter. 2017. "Feeding, Sharing and Devouring: Alimentary Rituals and Cosmology in Highland Odisha, India." *Highland Odisha: Life and Society Beyond the Coastal World*, edited by B. Pati and U. Skoda, pp. 71–106. New Delhi: Primus.

Berger, Peter. 2019. "Gadaba: Society on the Menu." In *Brill Encyclopedia of the Religions of the Indigenous People of South Asia*, edited by Marine Carrin (editor-in-chief), Jean Jaurès, Michel Boivin, Gérard Toffin,

Centre d'Études Himalayennes, Paul Hockings, Raphaël Rousseleau, Tanka Subba, Harald Lambs-Tyche. Retrieved from http://dx.doi.org/10.1163/2665-9093_BERO_COM_032299.

Berger, Peter. 2020. "Rupture and Resilience of Religion: Dynamics between a Hindu Reform Movement and an Indigenous Religion in Highland Odisha." *Godroads: Modalities of Conversion in India*, edited by P. Berger and Sarbeswar Sahoo, pp. 246–271. New Delhi: Cambridge University Press. https://doi.org/10.1017/9781108781077.012

Berger, Peter, Hardenberg, Roland, Kattner Ellen and Michael Prager (eds). 2010. *The Anthropology of Values: Essays in Honour of Georg Pfeffer*. New Delhi: Pearson.

Berger, Peter and Sarbeswar Sahoo 2020. "Introduction." *Godroads: Modalities of Conversion in India*, edited by P. Berger and Sarbeswar Sahoo, pp. 1–46. New Delhi: Cambridge University Press. https://doi.org/10.1017/9781108781077.002

Bourdieu, Pierre. 1990. *The Logic of Practice*. Cambridge: Polity Press.

Collins, Steven.1989. "Louis Dumont and the Study of Religions." *Religious Studies Review* 15(1): 14–20.

de Coppet, Daniel. 1992. "Comparison, a Universal for Anthropology: From 'Re-presentation' to the Comparison of Hierarchy of Values." In *Conceptualizing Society*, edited by A. Kuper, pp. 59–74. London: Routledge.

Dumont, Louis. 1970. "Religion, Politics, and Society in the Individualistic Universe." *Proceedings of the Royal Anthropological Institute of Great Britain and Ireland* 1970: 31–41. https://doi.org/10.2307/3031738

Dumont, Louis. 1977. *From Mandeville to Marx: The Genesis and Triumph of Economic Ideology*. Chicago, IL: University of Chicago Press.

Dumont, Louis. 1980. *Homo Hierarchicus: The Caste System and its Implications*. Chicago, IL: University of Chicago Press.

Dumont, Louis. 1986. *Essays on Individualism: Modern Ideology in Anthropological Perspective*. Chicago, IL: University of Chicago Press.

Dumont, Louis. 1994. *German Ideology: From France to Germany and Back*. Chicago, IL: University of Chicago Press.

Dumont, Louis. 2013. "On Value." *HAU: Journal of Ethnographic Theory* 3(1): 287–314. https://doi.org/10.14318/hau3.1.028

Durkheim, Émile. 1974 [1911]. "Value Judgements and Judgements of Reality." In *Sociology and Philosophy*, translated by D.F. Pocock, pp. 80–97. New York: The Free Press.

Durkheim, Émile. 1995 [1912]. *The Elementary Forms of Religious Life*, translated by Karen E. Fields. New York: The Free Press.

Durkheim, Émile and Marcel Mauss. 1963 [1903]. *Primitive Classification*, translated and edited by Rodney Needham. London: Cohen & West.

Evans-Pritchard, Edward E. 1940. *The Nuer: A Description of the Modes of Livelihood and Political Institutions of a Nilotic People*. Oxford: Oxford University Press.

Galey, Jean-Claude. 1982. "The Spirit of Apprenticeship in a Master Craftsman." In *Way of Life: King, Householder, Renouncer – Essays in Honour of Louis Dumont*, edited by T.N. Madan, pp. 3–12. New Delhi: Motilal Banarsidass Publishers.

Gellner, Ernest. 1981. "Introduction." In E.E. Evans-Pritchard, *A History of Anthropological Thought*, edited by André Singer, pp. vii–xxxvi. London: Faber and Faber.

Golub, Alex, Daniel Rosenblatt and John D. Kelly (eds). 2016. *A Practice of Anthropology: The Thought and Influence of Marshall Sahlins*. Montreal: McGill-Queens University Press.

Hardenberg, Roland. 2007. "Context and Values: A Discussion of Concepts." In *Periphery and Centre: Studies in Orissan History, Religion and Anthropology*, edited by G. Pfeffer, pp. 153–172. New Delhi: Manohar.

Hardenberg, Roland. 2010. "A Reconsideration of Hinduization and the Caste-Tribe Continuum Model." In *The Anthropology of Values: Essays in Honour of Georg Pfeffer*, edited by P. Berger, R. Hardenberg, E. Kattner and M. Prager, pp. 89–103. New Delhi: Pearson.

Hatch, Elvin. 1973. *Theories of Man & Culture*. New York: Columbia University Press.

Haynes, Naomi and Jason Hickel. 2016. Special issue: "Hierarchy, Value, and the Value of Hierarchy." *Social Analysis* 60(4): 1–133. https://doi.org/10.3167/sa.2016.600401

Iteanu, André and Ismaël Moya. 2015a. Special issue: "Comparison Made Radical: Dumont's Anthropology of Value Today." *HAU: Journal of Ethnographic Theory* 5(1): 113–250. https://doi.org/10.14318/hau5.1.006

Iteanu, André and Ismaël Moya. 2015b "Mister D.: Radical Comparison, Values, and Ethnographic Theory." *HAU: Journal of Ethnographic Theory* 5(1): 113–136. https://doi.org/10.14318/hau5.1.006

Jolly, Margaret and Mark S. Mosko. 1994. Special issue: "Hierarchy." *History and Anthropology* 7(1–4): 1–409. https://doi.org/10.1080/02757206.1994.9960839

Lévi-Strauss, Claude. 1968 "The Structural Study of Myth." In *Structural Anthropology*, pp. 206–231. New York: Penguin.

Lévi-Strauss, Claude. 1983. "Overture." In *The Raw and the Cooked: Mythologiques Volume 1*, pp. 1–34. Chicago, IL: University of Chicago Press.

Lukes, Steven. 1992 [1973]. *Émile Durkheim: His Life and Work: A Historical and Critical Study*. London: Penguin Books.

Macfarlane, Alan. 1992–1993. "Louis Dumont and the Origins of Individualism." *The Cambridge Journal of Anthropology* 16(1): 1–28.

Madan, T.N. 1971. "On the Nature of Caste in India A Review Symposium on Louis Dumont's Homo Hierarchicus." *Contributions to Indian Sociology* 5: 1–81. https://doi.org/10.1177/006996677100500102

Madan, T.N. 1999. "Louis Dumont 1911–1998: A Memoir." *Contributions to Indian Sociology* 33(3): 473–501. https://doi.org/10.1177/006996679903300301

McCloud 2012. "The Possibilities of Change in a World of Constraint: Individual and Social Transformation in the Work of Pierre Bourdieu." *Bulletin for the Study of Religion* 41(1): 2–8. https://doi.org/10.1558/bsor.v41i1.002

Moya, Ismaël. 2015. "Unavowed Value: Economy, Comparison, and Hierarchy in Dakar." *HAU: Journal of Ethnographic Theory* 5(1): 151–172. https://doi.org/10.14318/hau5.1.008

Needham, Rodney. 1979. *Symbolic Classification*. Santa Monica, CA: Goodyear Publishing Company.

Needham, Rodney. 1987. *Counterpoints*. Berkeley, CA: University of California Press.

Ortner, Sherry B. 1973 "On Key Symbols." *American Anthropologist* 75(5): 1338–1346. https://doi.org/10.1525/aa.1973.75.5.02a00100

Otto, Ton and Rane Willerslev. 2013a. Special issue: "Value as Theory, Part I." *HAU: Journal of Ethnographic Theory* 3(1): 1–170. https://doi.org/10.14318/hau3.1.002

Otto, Ton and Rane Willerslev. 2013b. Special issue: "Value as Theory, Part II." *HAU: Journal of Ethnographic Theory* 3(2): 1–160. https://doi.org/10.14318/hau3.2.002

Parkin, Robert. 2003. *Louis Dumont and Hierarchical Opposition*. New York: Berghahn.

Richards, John F. and Ralph W. Nicholas. 1976. "Symposium: The Contributions of Louis Dumont". *The Journal of Asian Studies* 35(4): 579–650. https://doi.org/10.1017/S0021911800080189

Rio, Knut M. and Olaf H. Smedal. 2009. (eds.) *Hierarchy: Persistence and Transformation in Social Formations*. New York: Berghahn.

Robbins, Joel. 1994. "Equality as a Value: Ideology in Dumont, Melanesia and the West." *Social Analysis* 36: 21–70.

Robbins, Joel. 2004. *Becoming Sinners: Christianity and Moral Torment in a Papua New Guinea Society*. Berkeley, CA: University of California Press.

Robbins, Joel. 2007. "Between Reproduction and Freedom: Morality, Value, and Radical Cultural Change." *Ethnos* 72 (3): 293–314. https://doi.org/10.1080/00141840701576919

Robbins, Joel. 2009. "Conversion, Hierarchy, and Cultural Change: Value and Syncretism in the Globalization of Pentecostal and Charismatic Christianity." In *Hierarchy: Persistence and Transformation in Social Formations*, edited by K.M. Rio and O.H. Smedal, pp. 65–88. New York: Berghahn.

Robbins, Joel and Jukka Siikala. 2014a. Special issue on "Dumont, Values, and Contemporary Cultural Change." *Anthropological Theory* 14(2): 121–248. https://doi.org/10.1177/1463499614534059

Robbins, Joel and Jukka Siikala. 2014b. "Hierarchy and Hybridity: Toward a Dumontian approach to Contemporary Cultural Change." *Anthropological Theory* 14(2): 121–132. https://doi.org/10.1177/1463499614534059

Sahlins, Marshall. 1976. *Culture and Practical Reason*. Chicago, IL: University of Chicago Press.

Strenski, Ivan. 1989. "Louis Dumont, Individualism, and Religious Studies." *Religious Studies Review* 15(1): 22–29.

Strenski, Ivan. 2008. *Dumont on Religion: Difference, Comparison, Transgression*. London: Equinox.

Toukolehto, Saara. 2015. "Mothers of the Kiez: Values and Cultural Change in Immigrant Communities in Neukölln, Berlin." MA thesis, University of Helsinki.

Vitebsky, Piers 2017. *Living without the Dead: Loss and Redemption in a Jungle Cosmos*. Chicago, IL: University of Chicago Press.

– 15 –

Epilogue

Studying Religion in Context – Diversity and Commonalities in Approaches

PETER BERGER, MARJO BUITELAAR AND KIM KNIBBE

This book's main objective has been to offer insights into how scholars from different disciplines in the humanities and social sciences approach the study of religion: how do they conceptualize and delineate the object of study, what methodologies do they apply to produce their data, what questions do they ask of the data they work with, and which theories do they engage to explain and interpret their material? Although some of the chapters, such as those by Vanden Auweele and Jedan, contain more meta-level discussions and are thus not focused on making sense of "data", they nevertheless demonstrate the "method" of the philosophy of religion.

Students may have observed that some of these approaches overlap and many may be complementary, whereas others are radically different from each other. As we outlined in the introduction, our explicit intention has not been to provide a cohesive account of how "religion" should be studied. Indeed, as we explained there, the subject matter of "religion" is often delineated in very different ways by different scholars. As demonstrated in the chapters, this results in different kinds of questions, different approaches and different kinds of insights and knowledge.

Some of the more specific overlaps in approaches obviously occur in contributions by authors trained in the same discipline. Yet even these contributions demonstrate a variety of approaches and methodological tools, as illustrated by the contributions from psychologists and anthropologists. At the same time, as we step back to compare all contributions in the volume, we see the differences increase, but the similarities between approaches by authors from different disciplines also stand out more.

There is broad agreement among most authors, for example, about the fact that the primary object of study are the embodied acts of making sense of the world and of one's own place in it, as well as the stories and artefacts related to this. In the contributions from the psychologists in particular, however, this understanding of religion as referring to specific parts of culture is broadened to a more "conceptual" approach that can be applied irrespective of the particular "content" of the symbols and systems of meaning it refers to. This more conceptual approach is also present in Berger's chapter, which shows how an approach that focuses on values can be applied.

In terms of "looking for religion", the historical approach presented by Mason stands out as being most radically inductive – in other words, starting from what the data tells us rather than imposing external categories (such as "religion") on it. Mason asks what these sources can tell him about how the people he studies constructed their world and interacted with each other. In order to formulate well-informed answers to that basic question underlying his research, the historian as interpreter needs both familiarity with the conventions of the people studied – requiring a thorough knowledge of their languages and socio-economic and political circumstances – and an openness to any surprises they might find.

Like Mason's contribution, that of anthropologist Berger also demonstrates that an approach focusing on indigenous configurations of categories and values can dispense with the analytical category of "religion". Indeed, the inductive approach also characterizes the work of anthropologists and many other social scientists. The main difference is that historians study the material traces that human activities have left behind, while social scientists tend to study processes as they unfold. Like historians, they need to know the languages and socio-historical circumstances of the people studied. Therefore, although historians mostly work with historical texts and artefacts and anthropologists deal in addition with the stories, ideas and behaviour of living people, they ask similar questions of these different sources. Anthropologists and historians are concerned with social semantics, patterns and interpretation rather than laws and causal explanation (Cohn 1987; Evans-Pritchard 1950; Geertz 1990). Ethnohistory (e.g. Dirks 1988), an important branch of anthropology, complements ethnographic work with research in local archives and, conversely, some historians call their library and archival research "fieldwork" (Buskens 2016: 19).

Peter Berger, Marjo Buitelaar and Kim Knibbe

Studying social or psychological mechanisms with a view to explaining, generalizing or even predicting, is more the domain of sociologists and psychologists, most of whom employ deductive reasoning on the basis of narrowly defined categories and hypotheses to be tested. However, as we outlined in the introduction, all researchers proceed from some basic assumptions about relationships between the phenomena that they study (e.g. language use or access to sources and social hierarchy) and thus engage in theorizing. In practice, therefore, on a methodological level, the most relevant difference between approaches is the specific balance that a researcher opts for when combining inductive and deductive modes of reasoning for the production and interpretation of data.

What stands out in connecting the various contributions is that, overall, the authors approach the study of religion in terms of what religion "does" or means to people rather than asking what religion "is". Many of the contributors take contextuality as their point of departure – religion as it is understood and "done" in practice by people in a specific social context. The "lived religion" approach, as this perspective is also called within the social sciences, can equally be applied to study how the views and practices of religious specialists "spill over" into domains beyond religious institutions (cf. Knibbe and Kupari 2020). Several contributions address how collectively-held religious ideas relate to practice. Van den Belt, for instance, discusses how, among other things, his research looks at the ways in which specific interpretations of authoritative texts are transmitted through visualization of specifically meaningful narratives in woodcuts.

Taking contextuality as a point of departure also brings to the fore the issue of how people connect what they identify as specifically "religious" to values that feature in other moral registers and cultural discourses that speak to them or that they draw on for orientation in everyday life. As various contributions illustrate, the very distinctions that people make to separate religion from other cultural frameworks can create, reconfirm or collapse boundaries between different groups or categories of people. This illustrates the importance of always being mindful of the ways that "religion as a category" creates facticity at different levels, as we outlined in the introduction. Mason demonstrates how this can be done in hindsight, as in the dominant Christian tradition of reading religion into different groups of inhabitants in the Graeco-Roman world to create a narrative about Judaism as the "mother religion" that gave birth to the "daughter religion" of Christianity. In her contribution, Buitelaar touches upon how this Christian historiography has recently acquired new meanings; claims about the Judeo-Christian heritage of European culture are being made to exclude categories of more recent

European citizens with Muslim backgrounds by reducing them to their "Muslimness". Employing religion as an effective tool for making political claims is also highlighted in Tarusarira's contribution, which argues that the specific religious themes that resonate in a Zimbabwean political song address very basic human fears, needs and desires, thus linking ultimate concerns to practical political matters on the ground, and furnishing the latter with religious connotations.

Studying religion in context thus requires that scholars be ever mindful of the multiple overlapping and intersecting settings and imaginaries that inform people's life-worlds, and how these overlaps and intersections, but also of how disjunctures, affect individual people differently. As Buitelaar notes in her contribution, not everybody is equally well-equipped to cope with such complexities, nor do people have equal access to specific tools; besides being of a specific religious denomination, a religious practitioner is also of a specific gender, age, class, ethnic and educational background. Various social dimensions of identity intersect to locate a person's position in society, their access to specific resources and their outlook on life. Therefore, factors such as gender, age, class, religion, ethnicity, health and education mutually constitute each other in the specific ways that individuals appropriate the religious sources available to them. The usefulness of taking what feminist scholars have coined the "intersectionality approach" (cf. Shields 2008; Brah and Phoenix 2004; Crenshaw 1989) appears in many contributions in this volume, most prominently in the chapters by Coleman, Muthert, Schaap-Jonker and Visser. Also, precisely because everyday life is complex and full of ambiguities, people in their daily practices do not always manage to live up to the high moral standards that they claim to when they themselves or researchers reflect on those standards on a meta-level. In this sense, studying religious doubt or negligence is equally relevant to the study of lived religion as studying faith and religious ardour (cf. Beekers and Kloos 2018).

As well as drawing our attention to the political dimensions of religion, Tarusarira's analysis of a political song also indicates that it is not only the ideas or values being transmitted through the song that make it so powerful, but that the song's sensuous dimensions as it is performed also affect people. Indeed, most contributors to this volume approach religion as an embodied phenomenon, in the sense that religion addresses and works through people's cognitive, sensory and affective capacities. A shared point of departure is that even if some religious traditions have developed systematic and rationalized dogmas and doctrines, they speak to and through the senses to evoke emotions and attitudes through the stories, symbols and rituals that are told, visualized, or otherwise enacted. Religion thus has the capacity to simultaneously enable and discipline people in developing a specific kind of subjectivity and a certain habitus, a set of embodied dispositions acquired or literally incorporated, through which one interprets and acts upon the world by being socialized in a particular socio-cultural environment (cf. Bourdieu 1977). Moreover, as Saba Mahmood (2005) and Charles Hirschkind (2006) argue in their influential studies on participants in Islamic revivalist movements in Egypt, individuals can also actively employ religious practices as "bodily techniques" in acts of deliberate self-fashioning, for example to pursue ethical formation.

The current interest in the body and emotions in the study of religion that also appears in this volume help to correct the bias towards the cognitive content of religion, which, as Vanden Auweele mentions in his contribution to this volume, has long predominated in religious studies, particularly in the philosophy of religion. The "bottom-up" approach that has replaced the "top-down" approach in the philosophy of religion, as addressed by Vanden Auweele and Jedan, therefore parallels a more general trend in the current study of religion to investigate religion as an embodied practice in which cognitive and affective dimensions mutually influence each other as normative scripts are enacted by religious practitioners.

Related to approaching religion as embodied, and thus speaking not only to and through reason but equally engaging the senses and emotions, is the issue of where to "find" religion. The "lived religion" approach adopted by most of the anthropologists in this volume entails not only studying institutional or collective religious views and practices, but also looking beyond these to ask how people appropriate authoritative religious forms and improvise on them in their routines of everyday life. Referring to Birgit Meyer's argument about religion as a "sensational form" that addresses and involves participants in a religious practice in a specific manner and induces particular feelings (Meyer 2012), Coleman in his contribution asks how "formal" such "forms" need to be for us to discern their religious effects and affects. Coleman thus raises another issue that returns in several other contributions as well: the relation between authoritative, collective practices in which religion is "foregrounded" and explicitly set apart from other domains on the one hand, and more personal religious practices and interpretations on the other, which may not be in line with authoritative forms and cannot be separated from other domains in daily life. Coleman suggests that we also study circumstances where religion, to use Buitelaar's words, is a "background presence" that may or may not be explicitly or consciously identified as religious by those who engage in them.

Apart from the already mentioned more ethnographic contributions, the relation between the collective and the personal, and the cognitive and affective dimensions of religion also feature prominently in the contributions that offer psychological perspectives on the study of religion. As a variant on Meyer's focus on the ways that religion addresses the senses and emotions, all three psychological contributions reflect on how psychological processes may in turn shape people's religious interpretations of sensory and emotional experiences. Visser and Muthert do so by addressing how people may draw on religion as a source to make sense of their experiences when coping with loss or illness, while Schaap-Jonker looks at how psychological processes such as attachment to primary caregivers in early life may inform people's conceptions of God. Comparing the three psychological contributions illustrates how adopting an inductive or deductive mode of reasoning does not clearly distinguish perspectives from the humanities and social sciences; different lines of research in both fields combine inductive and deductive modes in different ways. While Visser and Muthert make inferences from the data they have produced, Schaap-Jonker scrutinizes the material she works with to test working hypotheses about the relationship between attachment and religiosity on the basis of indicators that are formulated deductively.

The contextual approach that characterizes many of the contributions to this volume raises one more issue that runs through all the chapters: the actual methods used by scholars. Many of the chapters are based on qualitative research and thus take an inductive approach to researching religion, where concepts and theories do not have to be defined very strictly in advance (although they are present, as we have outlined in the introduction). Qualitative research methods (historical, ethnographic, textual, etc.) are particularly suited to a contextual approach since these are designed to probe complexity. Mason's contribution illustrates how this can be accomplished in a historical approach through close scrutiny of texts and artefacts. The contributions from the anthropologists of religion illustrate the merits of ethnographic research. As Buitelaar argues in her contribution, ethnographers learn how religious understandings and practices are embedded in people's wider life-worlds through long-term participation in the lives of the people studied, by observing them as they try to make sense of the puzzles of everyday life, and by engaging with them far more extensively through a multitude of quotidian conversations than by means of formal interviews. Through participant observation, ethnographers gain insights into how religious concerns are intertwined with other motivations and pursuits, and how religion may be highlighted in some settings and left unaddressed in others.

However, generalizing beyond the narrative accounts of the intricacies of such processes in specific historical or contemporary case studies is a tricky affair, to say the least. As the chapters by Visser and Schaap-Jonker demonstrate, quantitative research methods, such as large surveys, are better suited to discerning macro-scale patterns in how religion intersects with other factors in people's lives. This necessarily implies a deductive approach and requires researchers to strictly define and operationalize their concepts. Visser rightly points out, however, that statistically significant outcomes do not necessarily guarantee validity in the sense of a correspondence between how research participants themselves understand religion and the indicators formulated by the researcher to operationalize the analytical category of religion that is their point of departure.

While scholars using quantitative methods have to be mindful of how their concepts and the ways they formulate their survey questions influence the results of their research, qualitative researchers similarly have to critically reflect on the concepts and categories they use. Furthermore, the contributions by Buitelaar, Coleman and Knibbe in this volume demonstrate the importance of reflecting on the "situatedness" of the researcher: their own positioning and the ways they are positioned by their research participants. While scholars working on texts and artefacts only have to reflect on how their own situatedness informs the assumptions and inferences they make, researchers in research projects involving direct contact with the people studied will need to be mindful of their own feelings and reactions as embodied researchers, as well as of how they are being positioned by their research participants. As Knibbe argues in her contribution, drawing a line to indicate how far we wish – and are allowed – to go when taking part in their lives depends on how we ourselves and the people we work with draw boundaries between self and others. Similarly, as Van den Belt argues in his contribution, validation of our research methods as researchers studying religion is very much a matter of accounting for the ways in which our data collection, analysis and interpretation is informed and limited by our own normative stances and positionality.

As we stated in our introduction, we put together this volume with the aim to elucidate *how* scholars study religion. Although we did not aim for coherence, our shared point of departure is that religion should be studied "in context". As we also outlined in the introduction, to enable conversation and further existing insights into the fascinating phenomena linked to religion, we think it is important to approach the diversity of scholarly work one inevitably encounters with the following questions in mind: what conception or modality of religion is implied, or in other words, how does a particular scholar define their subject matter? What concepts and forms of theorizing are employed? What levels of analysis (categories, rules and/or practices) are addressed through a particular approach? What kinds of insights and new questions does a particular approach generate?

It is our hope that these questions will enable students to orient themselves in approaching the multitude of scholarly approaches congregating around the study of religion, but also to choose and perhaps combine the scholarly approaches most suitable for their own enquiries.

About the Authors

Peter Berger (PhD 2004, FU Berlin) is associate professor of Indian religions and the anthropology of religion at the University of Groningen. His areas of interest include the anthropology of religion, indigenous religions (esp. in India), theory and history of anthropology and the anthropology of India. His books include *Feeding, Sharing and Devouring: Ritual and Society in Highland Odisha, India* (De Gruyter, 2015), and he coedited *Godroads: Modalities of Conversion in India* (Cambridge UP, 2020), *Ultimate Ambiguities: Investigating Death and Liminality* (Berghahn, 2016), *The Modern Anthropology of India* (Routledge, 2013) and *The Anthropology of Values* (Pearson, 2010).

Marjo Buitelaar is professor of Contemporary Islam from an anthropological perspective at the University of Groningen. Her research interests concern Islam in everyday life and narrative identity construction in a post-migration context. Buitelaar is presently programme-leader of a research project on "Modern Articulations of Pilgrimage to Mecca" (NWO grant 360-25-150). Her most recent co-edited books in English are *Religious Voices in Self-Narratives* (2013), *Hajj, Global Interactions through Pilgrimage* (2015) and *Muslim Women's Pilgrimage to Mecca and Beyond. Reconfiguring gender, religion and mobility* (2021).

Kim Knibbe is associate professor of anthropology and sociology of religion at Groningen University. She is currently directing the project "Sexuality, Religion and Secularism" with Rachel Spronk (funded by NWO). Previous research focused on Catholicism and spirituality in the Netherlands and on Nigerian Pentecostalism in Europe and the Netherlands. She has also published a series of theoretical and methodological reflections on studying religion. Her most recent co-edited books and special issues are *Secular Societies, Spiritual Selves?* (with Anna Fedele, 2020) and "Theorizing Lived Religion" (with Helena Kupari, *Journal of Contemporary Religion*, 2020).

References

Beekers, Daan and David Kloos. 2018. *Straying from the Straight Path: How Senses of Failure Invigorate Lived Religion*. Oxford: Berghahn. https://doi.org/10.2307/j.ctvw04jdt

Bourdieu, Pierre. 1977. *Outline of a Theory of Practice*. Cambridge: Cambridge University Press. https://doi.org/10.1017/CBO9780511812507

Brah, Avtar and Ann Phoenix. 2004. "Ain't I a Woman? Revisiting Intersectionality." *Journal of International Women's Studies* 5(3): 75–86.

Buskens, Léon. 2016. "Introduction. Dichotomies, Transformations, and Continuities in the Study of Islam." In *Islamic Studies in the Twenty-first Century: Transformations and Continuities*, edited by Léon Buskens and Annemarie van Sandwijk, pp. 11–27. Amsterdam: Amsterdam University Press. https://doi.org/10.1515/9789048528189

Cohn, Bernard S. 1987. *An Anthropologist among the Historians and Other Essays*. New Delhi: Oxford University Press.

Crenshaw, Kimberlé. 1989. "Demarginalizing the Intersection of Race and Sex: A Black Feminist Critique of Anti-discrimination Doctrine, Feminist Theory and Antiracist Politics." *University of Chicago Legal Forum* 1989(1): 138–67.

Dirks, Nicholas B. 1988. *The Hollow Crown: Ethnohistory of an Indian Kingdom*. Cambridge South Asian Studies, no. 39. Cambridge: Cambridge University Press. https://doi.org/10.1017/CBO9780511557989

Evans-Pritchard, E. E. 1950. "Social Anthropology: Past and Present the Marett Lecture, 1950." *Man* 50: 118–124. https://doi.org/10.2307/2794464

Geertz, Clifford. 1990. "History and Anthropology." *New Literary History* 21(2): 321–335. https://doi.org/10.2307/469255

Hirschkind, Charles. 2006. *The Ethical Soundscape: Cassette Sermons and Islamic Counterpublics*. New York: Columbia University Press.

Knibbe, Kim, and Helena Kupari. 2020. "Theorizing Lived Religion: Introduction." *Journal of Contemporary Religion* 35(2): 157–176. https://doi.org/10.1080/13537903.2020.1759897

Mahmood, Saba. 2005. *The Politics of Piety: the Islamic revival and the feminist subject*. Princeton, NJ: Princeton University Press.

Meyer, Birgit. 2012. "Religious Sensations: Media, Aesthetics and the Study of Contemporary Religion." In *Religion, Media and Culture: A Reader*, edited by Gordon Lynch, Jolyon Mitchell and Anna Strhan, pp. 159–170. London: Routledge.

Shields, Stephanie. 2008. "Gender: An Intersectionality Perspective." *Sex Roles* 59: 301–311. https://doi.org/10.1007/s11199-008-9501-8

Index

academic study of religion (ASR)
   as an approach 1f1, 2
   competing paradigms in 17
acculturation 288
Adiabene 124
Adiabenians 125
adivasi (indigenous people) 277
adjacencies of religious forms
   and Nabil's religious forms
      233–236, 238
   and Miriam's case 236–239
   conceptions of 231
   importance of studying 40, 233,
      234, 238, 239, 299
Aelia Capitolina *see* Jerusalem,
   historical Judaea
affect regulation 172
Africa
   religions of 254
   theory development in
      anthropology in 18
agnostic field 16
aisthesis 231
Ake/Acco, historical Judaea 118
alienated participation 40
Allen, Graham 137
Allen, Nicholas 278
Allport, Gordon 153
Amazonia 18
Annas, Julia 140

ancient clubs/voluntary associations
   36, 121, 122, 125, 126, 129
animism 4, 18
Anselm of Cantebury (Saint) 55, 56
anthropology
   and the inductive approach 297,
      298
   and theory 13, 17, 18, 21, 230
   approach to ritual 230, 231
   comparative method in 18
   comparing history and 297
   competing paradigms in 17–19
   ethnographic method 18, 26,
      29–31, 33, 39, 78, 214, 224, 229,
      230, 232, 235–239, 265, 266, 271
   importance in studying Islam
      262–266
   intersectionality approach in 42,
      268–271, 299
   method of introspection in 18
   methods and methodologies in 18,
      26, 29–31, 33, 39, 40, 214–219
   paradigms in 17–19
   participant observation method
      12, 39, 40, 153, 214–226, 265,
      266, 271, 301, 301
   phenomenological anthropology
      218, 229f2
   structural anthropology 19, 29, 42,
      275, 278, 279, 281, 283–290

Index

anxiety 170, 171, 172, 175, 180
Aquinas, Thomas (Saint)
    Summa Theologiae 55
approaches to the study of religion
    academic study of religion (ASR) 1, 2, 17
    anthropology 17–19, 25, 27, 30, 39–42, 214, 218, 228, 229, 230, 238, 239, 262–271, 275, 289, 290, 297
    cognitive psychological approach 37, 150, 154, 155, 162, 163
    contextual approach 2, 3, 38, 39, 95, 268, 271, 298, 299, 301, 302
    cultural toolkit approach 266, 267
    differences between 2, 3, 22, 25, 54, 97, 100, 101, 103, 107–111, 150, 264, 297, 298
    history 1, 13, 25, 36, 77–79, 103, 105, 107–109, 115, 116, 297
    history of philosophy 72–79, 82–85
    intersectionality approach 42, 268–271, 299
    intertextuality 36, 37, 134–138, 136f5, 146
    meaning system approach 37, 150–163, 297
    philosophy of religion 1, 2, 34, 35, 52, 53–55, 54f1, 67
    psychodynamic theory 39, 150, 155, 194, 195, 198–209
    relational psychological approach 38, 39, 168–172, 174–183, 193–210
    religious studies 2, 3, 35, 71, 79, 95, 96, 100–103, 107–111
    sensational forms approach 230, 231
    similarities 2, 3, 19, 78, 79, 95, 96, 100–103, 107–110, 116, 117, 296–298, 300, 301
    sociology 1, 29, 58, 64, 74, 75, 79, 151, 214
    theology 2, 3, 35, 36, 54, 55, 94–111
Arab people 118

Arad, historical Judaea 118
archetypal theology 97, 98
architextuality 138, 139
Aristotle
    efficient cause 99–101, 109
    final cause 99–101, 109
    formal cause 99, 100, 107
    material cause 98, 99, 100, 107
    Metaphysics V 98
    Physics II 98
articulation 235, 238
Asad, Talal
    and the problem of belief 30
    anthropology of the secular 10
    criticism of 'universal' definitions of religion 10, 36, 229
    on Geertz 10, 30, 65 229
Ascalon, historical Judaea 118, 119, 120
atheistic naturalism 57
Athens, Greece 81
attachment theory
    and God representations 38, 169, 174–183, 301
    and non-traditional forms of religion and spirituality 182, 183
    and non-Western forms of religion and spirituality 182, 183
    attachment styles 171, 172, 175–182
    attachment figure, 38, 170, 174, 175
    limitations of conceptualising of religion as attachment 38, 182, 183
    merits of conceptualising of religion as attachment 30, 182, 183
    nature and function of attachment 169, 170
Attig, Thomas
    criticism of Attig's model 198
    relearning the world model 197
Aurelius, Marcus
    and stoicism 83
    To Himself 83

Index

authenticity 252, 254
avoidance 171, 172, 180
Azande (ethnic group, Africa)
   Evans-Pritchard and the 29, 31, 230
   witchcraft 29, 31
Azotans 118

Baal Shem Tov (Rabbi) 207
Bakhtin, Michail M.
   and intertextuality 135
   theory of literature 135, 135f2, 135f3
Bandak, Andreas
   fieldwork with Christians in Damascus 233–235, 238
   on questions of saliency 234
   'tonalities of immediacy' and Christianity 234
Barnes, Robert H.
   Context and Levels: Anthropological Essays on Hierarchy 280
Barthes, Roland 37, 136
Bavinck, Herman 109
behaviour
   changes of 25
   conception of 22
   how to study 22, 24
   relationship between rules, categories, and 22–25, 276
Bell, Catherine 232
Bellah, Robert 8
belief as method 27–30
Berger, Peter L. 27
Berlin, Germany 60, 62, 121, 290
Berytus, Lebanon 120
Bethlehem, historical Judaea 123
Bevir, Mark 79, 79f10, 80
biblical studies 102
binary oppositions 42, 265, 278, 283, 285
Bindura, Zimbabwe 250, 255
bodily techniques 300
Borges, Jorge Luis 137
Bourdieu, Pierre
   habitus 23, 25, 278
   practice theory 278, 290
Bowlby, John 169, 170
bracketing (See also *epoché*) 219
bricoleur 237
Britain
   evolution paradigm in 19
   rebellion against British rule in India 16
   liberation of Zimbabwe from 247, 255
Buddhism
   and attachment processes 182
   and scholar positioning 30
   and conceptions of religion 5, 54, 60, 74, 115
   in comparative work, 82
Bulawayo/Buruwayo, Zimbabwe 250, 255
Butler, Judith 256

Caesar Divi Nervae Filius Nerva Traianus Optimus Augustus (Emperor Trajan) 126
Camino de Santiago (Way of St. James) 261, 262, 264, 267
Canaan, Southern Levant 254
Caputo, Jack 66
caricature 141, 142f13
Carthage, Tunisia 118
categories
   and meaning 275–279
   changes to 25, 276, 277, 286–290
   function of 24, 276, 277
   how to study 24
   relationship between behaviour, rules, and 22–25, 276
   conceptions of, 24, 276, 277
Catholicism
   and a universal essence of religion 65
   and participant observation, 217, 221, 222, 225
   identity 232, 233
   communion practices and family planning, 222, 224, 225

Index

Celsus 128
Centre for Religion, Conflict, and
    Globalization (Rijksuniversiteit
    Groningen) 264
Chaldean Oracles 143
Chidester, David
    criticism of the category of
        'religion' 4, 6
    Empire of Religion 6
Chimoio, Mozambique 255
Chimurenga (struggle against
    colonialism) 248, 255
Chinhoyi, Zimbabwe 250, 255
Chitando, Ezra 252
Christian aristotelianism 97
Christianity (See also *specific actors,
    institutions, and streams*)
    and philosophy 34, 55, 58–67, 81,
        82, 127
    and the individual 7, 8, 287
    and the study of religion 2, 26, 30,
        71
    and theology 2, 54, 81, 82, 94, 95,
        96, 97, 107, 109, 110
    born-again Christians 33, 216, 225,
        236, 239
    Christian identity 233–236
    Christian imagery in *Nora* 251, 252,
        254
    Christians in Damascus 233, 234
    Christian fundamentalism/
        fanaticism 28, 228
    conceptions of religion and 4–6, 10,
        34, 36, 54, 64–67, 71, 113–115,
        229
    in the Graeco-Roman world 36,
        122, 125–129
    relationship between Judaism and
        36, 113–115, 128, 129, 298
    Urapmin and 289
Cicero, Marcus Tullius
    and stoicism 84
    impact of 'Myth of Er' on 143
    Tusculan Disputations 84
Cilicia, Turkey 118

civil religion 8
Clarke, Samuel 58
Cleanthes 83
Clement of Alexandria
    and Christian criticism of *ethnos*
        allegiance 127
    Exhortations to the Greeks 127
coherence and consistency in religion
    and individual commitment 74, 75
    and Miriam's Pentecostalism
        236–238
    and Nabil's religious forms 233,
        234, 238
    and formal/dense religious forms
        40, 231–236, 300
    religious forms that resist 231–238
    scholarly imposition of 233, 234,
        237
    scholarly understandings of 229,
        238, 239
collective actions 8, 231, 244, 276
collective effervescence 8, 244, 245,
    249
collective forces 277
collective representations (See also
    categories) 24, 252, 276, 277, 281,
    286
Comaroff, Jean 230
Comaroff, John 230
Communism 55
comparing notes 42, 263, 266, 268, 270
comparison
    history and anthropology 297
    modern and ancient religions
        113–115, 117, 118, 121, 231, 297
    religion and art 34, 61
    religion and philosophy 34, 61
    religious studies and theological
        approaches 35, 94–97, 100–104,
        107–111
    radical comparison 279, 280
    theological and historical
        approaches 103, 107–111
compensation hypothesis
    core hypothesis 38, 179

types of compensation 179–181
support for compensation hypothesis in God representations 179–181
comprehensibility 159, 159f4
Confucianism
  and conceptions of religion 115
  and stoicism 82
construction of religious subjects 237
constructional models of mourning
  conception of mourning 196, 197
  combining object-relational theory and 193, 202–206
  criticism of 198
  processes of meaning-making 197, 198
contextuality 298
continuation 142, 142f13
Corpus Hermeticum (Hermes Trismegistus) 143
correspondence hypothesis
  core hypothesis 38, 178
  internal working model (IWM) correspondence 178–181
  socialized correspondence 178, 179
  studies supporting correspondence hypothesis in God representations 180, 181
cosmic war 252
crane vs. skyhook theories 5
Cranach, Lucas 104, 105
Crantor
  On Grief 84
Cross, Ian 245
cultural elaboration 282, 289
cultural toolkit approach
  access to tools 267, 299
  as an approach 266, 267
culture
  and attachment theory 183
  and ideas/values 275–278, 281, 289, 290
  and meaning systems 37, 150, 152
  and mourning 194, 197, 207–209

and philosophy 71–73, 78–84, 87
and the problem of belief 28–31
and unilinear development 4, 7
changes in 267, 286–290
conceptions of 10, 14, 17f5, 22, 25, 218, 223, 266, 267
cultural diversity 41, 42, 262, 270–272, 279
Graeco-Roman culture 117–129
religion and 3, 4, 10, 14, 17, 17f5, 21, 22, 54, 115, 175, 207, 208, 218, 223, 225, 242, 290, 297, 298
three levels of culture 21–25
Cyprus 81
Cyrenaeans 139

Daoism 115
death
  and burial in Zimbabwe 253, 254
  and meaning systems 152, 158
  and mourning 193, 196–198, 205
  and Plutarch and Plato's Myths of the Afterlife 140–144
  and religion 152, 174
  and Stoicism 84, 89
  in *Nora* 250–253, 255, 256, 257
  Shona burial practices, 253, 254
decathexis 196
deductive reasoning 29, 298, 301, 302
Deleuze, Gilles 235
Demerath, Nicholas Jay 243
De Mönnink, Herman 198
Derrida, Jacques 136
dialogic literature 135, 135f2, 135f3
divine transcendence 35, 66, 67
dogmatics (theology) 102
Douglas, Mary 232, 278
Droogers, André 33
duca (supplication prayer) 270
Dumont, Louis 42, 276, 278–290
Durkheim, Émile
  and Dumont 42, 279, 281
  and functionalism 19
  and meaning systems 151
  and structuralism 19, 276–279

Index

and the indigenous peoples of
  Australia 7
and the study of religion 7, 8, 230
collective effervescence 8, 244, 245
collective representations 24, 276,
  281
conception of religion of 7, 7f2, 8,
  245
'Individualism and the
  Intellectuals' 8f3
influence of 277–279
Primitive Classification 276
rules and sanctions for 23
sacredness of the individual 8, 8f3
*The Elementary Forms of the Religious
  Life* 7f2, 276
theory of the elementary forms of
  religious life 7, 231

ectypal theology 97
edges of religious forms
  and centres 231, 232
  and Nabil's religious forms
    233–236, 238
  and the case of Miriam 236–239
  importance of studying 40, 232,
    233, 238, 239, 299
Egypt
  and *ethnē* 119, 120, 128
  as coloniality 41, 242, 254
  exodus of Israel from 254
  Islamic revivalist movements in 300
Egyptians 119, 120, 124, 128
Eliade, Mircea 4, 5, 6, 7, 8
elliptic continuation 145
embodied cognition theory 163
Engelke, Matthew 11, 30
Engels, Friederich 62
England 40, 114f3
enmeshment 235, 238
epistemic trust 179
epoché 26
Erikson, Erik 20
essentialism 2, 3, 95, 228, 229
ethnographic experience 27, 31–34

ethnography
  and the 'edges' and 'adjacencies' of
    religious forms 233–239
  and Evans-Pritchard 26–31, 33, 230
  method of 18, 26, 29–31, 33, 39, 78,
    214, 224, 229, 230, 232, 235–239,
    265, 266, 271
  beyond the researcher's comfort
    zone 216, 219, 221, 222, 225, 226,
    271
  challenge of contemporary
    conditions of 232, 238
  problem of belief in 26–34, 39,
    215–222, 225, 226, 239
  thinning of the membrane
    separating worlds in 33, 95, 216,
    239
ethnohistory 297
ethnos (formative origin group)
  118–129
Europe (See also specific countries,
    religions, and leaders)
  and conceptions of religion 5, 6
  effects of European perceptions
    of Islam 41, 262–265, 270–272,
    298, 299
  European perception of Islam 41,
    262–265, 270–272
eudaimonia (happiness) 81, 84
Evans-Pritchard, Edward Evan 26,
  28–31, 33, 215, 230, 277, 284
evolution 4, 17–20, 26, 100, 229
Ewing, Katherine 20, 32–34, 216
explicit memory 171, 176, 181

Fadil, Nadia 264
Fairbairn, William Ronald Dodds 171
felt security 170, 171, 181
Ferrari, G.R.F. 140
food
  sacrificial food 277, 282–285, 288
football
  and 'effervescence' 8
  grief of Muslim and non-muslim
    fans for Abdelhaq Nouri 41, 270

forgery 141, 141f11
format of 'ideal type' of national narrative in political contestation 246, 247, 254–256
France
    Durkheim and 7, 278
    French sociology of religion 74
    modern ideology in 280
Frazer, James George 26
Freud, Sigmund 20, 196
Fujikawa, Annie 179
functionalism 6, 11, 19
fundamentalism 28, 256

Gadaba 277, 281, 282, 284–288, 290
Gadara, Jordan 120
Gale, Jason
    Stoicism: Full Life Mastery 85
    Stoicism: Introduction to the Stoic Way of Life 85
Garssen, Bert 156
Gaza, historical Judaea 120
Gazans 118
Geertz, Clifford
    and meaning systems 151, 154
    and neutral researcher positionality 27, 30
    Asad's criticism of Geertz' definition of religion 10, 30, 65, 229
    conception of culture 10
    conception of religion 9, 10, 30, 154
Geist (spirit) 61
Genette, Gérard 37, 136–139, 141–146
genos/gens (See *ethnos*)
ger (See *prosēlytos*)
Gerasa, Jordan 120
Germany
    German law concerning defamation of foreign representatives 23, 24
    German Enlightenment 58, 59
    modern ideology in 280
    norms surrounding forms of greetings 23

values of immigrant communities in 290
Giddens, Anthony 25
globalization 42, 263, 264, 270, 271, 288
God
    as an attachment figure 38, 174–183
    attachment processes and functions and representations of 38, 169, 174–183, 301
    cognitive understandings of 175, 176
    emotional understandings of 175, 176
    nature of 2, 55, 56, 67
    proofs for the existence of 55–58, 56f2
    representations of 176, 181
    theology, revelation and a transcendent 34, 94–103, 107–111
    understanding religion from an understanding of God 55
Gomarus, Franciscus 96
Graeco-Roman culture
    and Christianity 36, 122, 125–129
    and Judaism 36, 122–129
    and religion 36, 113–118, 121–126, 129
    ethnos and *polis* in 118–129
grand narratives 34, 35, 66
Granqvist, Pehr 182
Greeks 116, 118, 119, 120
Grossman, David
    Falling Out of Time 204
grounded imagination 174
Gwanda, Zimbabwe 250
Gweru, Zimbabwe 250, 255

habitus 23, 25, 234, 278, 300
Hadith 263
Hajj pilgrimage 261, 262, 267
Halcrow, Sarah R. 179
Hall, Todd W. 179

Index

Harding, Susan 33, 216, 216f1, 225
Hegel, Georg Wilhelm Friedrich
   and the end of religion 61, 62
   comparing religion and art 34, 61
   comparing religion and philosophy 34, 61
   essence of religion 34, 60, 61
   importance of history for understanding religion 52, 60, 61
   self-consciousness of *Geist*/reason 34, 61
hegemony of Western discourse and perspectives
   and conceptions of religion 4-6, 25, 42, 74, 75
   and Islam 206, 207
   and psychological theories 39, 208, 209
   in relation to science 20, 33, 34
   in researcher positioning during ethnography 33
Hellenism/Hellen-ism 115
Henry, Michel 66
Herodotus 115, 116, 124
hetairia. (See *ancient clubs*)
heterodiegetic 143f14
hierarchy (Dumont) 42, 283-287, 290
Hill, Peter C. 179
Hinduism
   and conceptions of religion 5, 54, 60, 115
   artha (material interest) 286
   Brahman (sacrificer, custodian of religion) 285, 286
   caste system 42, 280
   dharma (cosmic order) 182, 285, 286
   Gadaba and 288
   Kshatriya (king, representation of power and material wealth) 285
   Purusha (Cosmic Man) 285
   relational spirituality and attachment theory in monotheistic 182
   Rig Veda 285
   varna 285
Hippos, historical Syria 120
Hirschkind, Charles 300
historia (research/history) 115, 116
history
   and the inductive approach 297, 298
   as an approach 1, 13, 25, 36, 77-79, 103, 105, 107-109, 115, 116, 297
   comparing anthropology and 297
   constructivist historical approach 36
   theological approach as compared with 103, 107-111
history of philosophy
   benefits of engaging with 35, 71, 87-89
   comparative work stimulated by 81-83, 85, 86
   concept of 'lived religion' for a 35, 74-76, 79
   concept of 'tradition' for a 82
   criteria for evaluating findings from a 79, 80
   methodological anachronism of a 76-79
   Smart's 7 dimensions of religion for a 35, 72-74, 79-86
   standard approach in 72-79, 82-85
homodiegetic, 143, 143f14
Hughes, Aaron W. 13
Hume, David 57, 58
Husserl, Edmund 26
hybridity 290
hypertext 137-139, 142f13, 143, 144, 146
hypertextuality 138, 138f7
hypotext 137, 138, 142f13, 144f16

icons (Russian Orthodox) 236, 237, 238
ideas
   and meaning 275-279
   changes to 276, 277, 286-290
   function of 276, 277

Index

nature of 276, 277
relationship between behaviour, rules, and 22–25, 276
relationship between value and 42, 277, 281, 283, 286
see also categories
ideology (Dumont)
Dumont's conception 42, 279–283, 286
  modern ideology (Dumont) 280, 286–290
  non-modern ideology (Dumont) 286–288
  political ideology and religion 242, 244, 256
idolatry 115
Idumaeans 118
Ilongot (ethnic group, Philippines) and Renato Rosaldo 29, 225
  headhunting 29, 225
implicit memory 171, 176, 181
imposition of external categories 76, 78, 297
incolae (See *metics*)
incommensurability of paradigms in the study of religion 17, 19
India
  conversion of Sora from animism to Baptist Christianity 289f7
  Dumont on 277, 280f4, 285
  Gadaba people of 277, 281, 282, 284–288, 290
  interpretation of stomach pain in central 15
  rebellion against British rule in 16
Indigenous Australians 7
individualism (Dumont) 286–288
inductive approach 297, 298
Ingold, Tim 13, 14, 20, 21
insider/outsider problem (see also *problem of belief*) 3, 238, 239
instrumental/secondary causes 99, 100
intention of the woodcut illustrations in Martin Luther's catechism 105–107

interaction 288
intermodal 145f18
internal working models (IWMs) 38, 170–172, 175–183
intersectionality approach
  benefits of an 42, 268–271, 299
  intersectional identities 268, 269, 271, 299
  nature of 268, 269
  researcher presuppositions and 269
intertext 37, 134, 135, 135f1
intertextualité 135f4
intertextuality
  and Plato and Plutarch's myths of the Afterlife 37, 139–146
  as an approach 36, 37, 134–138, 136f5, 146
  Genette's approach to 37, 137–146
  progressive approach to 136, 137
  traditionalist approach to 136, 137
intertextuality (Genette) 137, 138
intramodal 145f18
intra-psychic model
  insufficiency of 193, 194, 204
  linking social-cultural context and 193, 194
Islam
  academic study of 264, 265, 269
  and articulation 235
  and cultural diversity 41, 42, 205, 206, 208–212
  and systematicity 235
  and the intersectionality approach 209–211 268–271
  as lived religion 41, 262–272 269
  conceptions of 235, 236, 262–266, 271, 272
  density and diffuseness of Islam in everyday experience 235, 236, 265–272
  dichotomy of Muslim and Western non-Muslim conceptions of 262–264, 298, 299

Index

effects of European perceptions of 41, 262–265, 270–272, 298, 299
as an entanglement of the religious and non-religious 41, 235, 236, 262, 266–272
ethnography and 266, 269–272
importance of studying background presence of 41, 42, 265–272
increasing pitting in discourse of the West against 41, 263–265, 271
Muslim identity 235, 236, 267
terrorism, radicalization, and fanaticism in 41, 228, 263, 264
Islam Studies 264, 269
interpretive tradition 10

Jaffa, historical Judaea 118
James, William 151
Jerusalem, historical Judaea 114, 118, 120–126, 128
Jomanda (Johanna Wilhelmina Petronella Damman) 217–220, 223
Josephus, Titus Flavius
Antiquities of the Jews 124
discussion of Jews-Judaeans as an *ethnos* 120, 122, 124, 127
Judaea 114, 119–121, 124, 126, 128
Judaeans 36, 114, 119–129
Judaism
as a religion 113–115, 123–125
conceptions of Jews-Judaeans in the ancient world 36, 122–129
conversion to 122–125
Jews-Judaeans as an *ethnos* 36, 119–129
relationship between Christianity and 36, 113–115, 128, 129, 298
Juda-ism 36, 115
Julianus, Flavius Claudius 128

Ka'ba 262
Kaliningrad/Königsberg, Germany 58

Kant, Immanuel
essence of religion 34, 52, 58–60
proofs for the existence of God 55–56, 56f2
religion and morality for 34, 52, 59, 60
Kapic, Kelly M. 96
Kearney, Michael
immersive experience of studied worldview 31–33
Kearney, Richard 66
Kierkegaard, Søren 62
kinship
affinity 282, 284–288
bai (brotherhood) 281, 282, 287, 288
Lévi-Strauss on 278
Kirkpatrick, Lee 38
Kristeva, Julia 37, 135, 135f2, 135f4, 136, 136f5
Kuhn, Thomas 16, 17

ladder of development 4
'land issue' in Zimbabwe 249, 253
lateral participation 40
Latour, Bruno 16
Leach, Edmund 278
Leader, Darian
importance of public expressions of mourning 205
linking Ogden and 195, 205
theory of mourning 204–206
Leiden, Netherlands 262
Leontopolis, Egypt 123
Lett, James 27, 28, 33, 215
levels of analysis
as a navigation tool 3, 22, 25, 303
how to study the levels 22–24
in theological contributions to religious research 107–111
relationship between the levels 22–25
the three levels 22–25, 303
levels of meaning
cognitive 246, 256

Index

emotional 246, 256
moral 246, 256
Lévi-Strauss, Claude
   and binary oppositions 42, 278, 283
   and Bourdieu 278, 279
   and Dumont 42, 279, 283
   and Durkheim 278
   and Mauss 278
   and structuralism 278
   function of myths according to 141, 278
   human thought patterns for 18, 278
Lewis, Thomas A. 70f1, 88
Limburg, Netherlands 220, 221
literary theory 136
lived philosophy 76, 76f5, 79, 80f11, 85, 88
lived religion 26, 35, 74, 75, 79, 87, 214, 226, 262, 298–300
Locke, John 58
logical scandal 283, 286
logos (reason/speech) 63, 96, 142
Luther, Martin
   Deutscher Catechismus 35, 103–106
   Enchiridion 104
   Kleiner Catechismus 35, 104–106
   Short Form of the Ten Commandments, the Creed, and the Lord's Prayer 106
Lutheran Protestantism 36, 97, 106, 107

McCutcheon, Russell 4, 5,
McGuire, Meredith B. 74, 75
MacIntyre, Alasdair 82, 82f13
Macrobius Ambrosius Theodosius 143
Magyar-Russell, Gina M. 155
Mahmood, Saba 300
Malawi 249
Marion, Jean-Luc 66
Marsden, Magnus
   Articulating Islam 235, 238
   articulation 235, 238

enmeshment 235, 238
systematicity 235
Martyr, Justin
   Dialogue with Trypho – a Jew 114
Marx, Karl 55, 62
Maslow, Abraham 20
Masuzawa, Tomoko
   criticism of the category of religion 4, 5, 6
   The Invention of World Religion, or, how European Universalism was Preserved in the Language of Pluralism 5
Masvingo, Zimbabwe 250, 255
Matabeleland massacre 247
Matabeleland, Zimbabwe 247
Mauss, Marcel 276, 278–280, 286
meaning system (See also *Study of religion/spirituality as a meaning system*)
   centrality of a meaning system 156, 158
   conception in the study of religion 37, 150–152
   encompassment 155, 156
   experiences beyond meaning system causing emotional distress 37, 151, 159–162
   function of a 37, 150–155, 159
   influence of a religious 155, 156
   methods for realignment of novel experiences and 37, 151, 159–162
   relationship between socialisation, personal experience and 37, 150, 151
Mecca, Saudi Arabia 261, 262, 264, 267
media of adjacency 238
media turn 11, 12
Melanchthon, Philip
   and the goal of the woodcut illustrations 105–109
   and the production of the woodcut illustrations 104–105

Index

choice of biblical stories for woodcut illustrations 104–107, 298
on Christian obedience and disobedience to divine law 105–107
Instructions for the Visitors of Parish Pastors 106
mentalized affectivity 174
mentalizing
 function in the religious domain 174, 177, 178
 nature of 172–174, 199, 202
 teleological mode 173, 138
 pretend mode 173, 138
 psychic equivalence mode 173, 138
 reflective/mentalizing mode 173, 174, 177, 178
metatextuality 138, 139
metics 120
methodological agnosticism 27, 39, 94, 110, 215
methodological atheism 27, 39, 94, 110, 215
methodological ludism 33
methodological theism 39, 215
methods and methodologies for studying religion 1, 2, 7, 13, 17–20, 27, 29–31, 39, 40, 43, 70, 73–75, 79, 86, 95, 96, 101–103, 107–109, 115, 116, 134–139, 153, 214, 215, 218, 219, 232, 290, 296, 301, 302
mētropolis (mother-polis) 36, 120, 123
Mexico
 witchcraft in 31, 32
Meyer, Birgit
 and the media turn 11, 12
 'sensational forms' approach 230, 231, 300, 301
Moabites 123
Moberg, Jessica 237
modes of being
 and meaning-making 199–208

fit between religion and the modes of being in mourning 39, 195, 203, 204–208
 mode 1 200–207
 mode 2 200–209
 mode 3 200–204, 206–209
 mourning capabilities of 39, 203–209
monotheistic traditions 4, 182
Morgan, David
 and the media turn 11
 Visual Piety 237
motobil (spirits) 289
mourning
 as essentially relational 39, 195–198, 203
 as making meaning/sense of loss 39, 197, 198, 203, 204
 conceptions of 193, 195–197, 203, 204
 decathexis-based understanding of relational changes in 196, 198
 fit between religion and the modes of being in 39, 195, 203, 204–208
 importance of socio-cultural context in 39, 194, 197, 204–209
 meaning-making in 197, 202–207, 301
 modern understanding of relational changes in 195–198
 mourning capabilities of religion 193, 205–208
 mourning capabilities of the three modes of being 39, 203–209
 theories of 193–206, 209
 value of focusing on relational space in 39, 202, 203
Movement for Democratic Change (MDC) 248
Mozambique 255
Mt. Darwin, Zimbabwe 250, 255
Mugabe, Robert
 and *Nora* 40, 242, 250–256
 utilisation of the importance of land in Zimbabwe by 253

316

Muhammad (Prophet) 263
Murray-Swank, Nichole A. 155
music
    and its context 245, 246
    creative power of 245, 246, 256
Muslim 'other' 263, 265, 271
Mutare, Zimbabwe 250, 255
Mutoko, Zimbabwe 250, 255
mystic experiences and attachment theory 182, 183
mythos 63, 142

Nag Hammadi Library 143
narratives
    and collective effervescence 244, 245
    and morality 245, 246, 256
    and songs 244–247, 254–256
    as meanings 245, 246, 256
    functions of 244–246
    political narratives 245–247, 256
    religious, sacred, and transcendental character in 40, 41, 244–247
    theodical narratives 246, 247, 254–257
narrativization 145
National Constitutional Assembly (NCA) 248
natural theology 54, 55
Ndebele 247, 255
Needham, Rodney 22f8, 278, 283
neo-evolutionism 19
neo-Pentecostalism 236, 237
Netherlands
    Dutch law against blasphemy 24
    Dutch media and spiritual healing services 217, 218, 223
    Dutch spiritual healing services 217–219, 220, 223
    Dutch spiritual society 217–219
    dichotomy of Muslim and non-Muslim conceptions of Islam in 262, 263
    importance of religion for the Dutch 156
    liberal Catholic pastoral centre in 217, 222, 225
    norms surrounding forms of greetings 23
    problem of belief and spiritual identifying individuals in 40, 216–224
    study of God representations of female incest survivors in the 180
New Age spirituality 182
niam (tradition) 282, 288
Nietzsche, Friederich 52, 57, 65
nominalism 229
Nora (Zimbabwean political song)
    actions prescribed in 252
    and its context 247–249, 251–254
    and the theme of land 252, 253
    as a theodicy for Zimbabwe 41, 254–257, 299
    Christian imagery in 242, 251, 252, 254, 255
    colonialism as represented in 251, 252, 254–256
    how it represents Robert Mugabe as religious/sacred 40, 41, 242, 250–254, 256
    how it represents ZANU-PF as religious/sacred 40, 250, 251, 256, 257
    how it sets apart Robert Mugabe 40, 41, 242, 250–254, 256
    how it sets apart ZANU-PF 40, 250, 251, 256, 257
    what it indicates about what is defined as religious/sacred 40, 41, 242, 257, 258
normativity in the humanities 74, 87, 88, 88f14, 97, 102, 107–111, 230, 302
norms *see* rules 22f9
Nouri, Abdelhaq 41, 270

Index

Nuer (ethnic group, Africa) 29, 30, 230, 277, 284
Nyadzonia, Mozambique 255

object-relational theory
  combining constructional models of mourning and 193, 202–206
  conception of human subject 199, 202, 203, 209
  conception of mourning 195, 196, 198, 203, 204
  processes of meaning-making 197, 201–204, 302
Ogden, Thomas
  conception of mourning 203, 204
  importance of public expressions of mourning by creatives 204
  linking Leader and 195, 205, 206
  nature of modes 199, 200, 203
  modes of being's mourning capabilities 203–209
  three modes of being 199–209
oratio obliqua 142
Ortner, Sherry B. 281, 282

paganism 5, 115
Pakistan 32
Paloutzian, Raymond F. 155
Papua New Guinea
  cultural change among the Urapmin 289
  theory development in anthropology in 18
paradigm(s) (See also *incommensurability of paradigms in the study of religion*)
  copresence of 19
  in anthropology 17–19
  in the academic study of religion (ASR) 17
  in psychology 19, 20
  Kuhnian paradigms 16, 17
  neo-evolutionist 19
  of evolution 17–20, 26
  of function/functionalist 19, 20
  of meaning 19
  of power 19, 30
  paradigm shifts 16–20
  revivals of 19
  structuralist 19
  world religions paradigm 5, 9
paratextuality 138, 139
Pargament, Kenneth I. 155
Parkin Robert 278
parity argument 76–79, 76f7
Park, Crystal L. 155
partial culture 225
participant observation
  and epistemological challenges 215, 216, 226
  and ontological challenges 215, 216, 226
  and participation involving conflicting worldviews 12, 39, 167–225, 302
  as a method 12, 39, 40, 153, 214–226, 265, 266, 271, 301, 302
  as embodied practice 216–225
  attention to efficacy in 218–220
  beyond the researcher's comfort zone 216, 219, 221, 222, 225, 226, 271
  bracketing in 26, 219
  factors to be aware of in 223–225
  learning other epistemologies to apprehend other ontologies in 223
  not participating in 220–222, 224, 225, 302
  thinning of the membrane separating worlds in 33, 95, 216, 239
  willingness to risk one's ontology in 224
Paul the Apostle 125–127
Pentecostalism
  Pentecostal beliefs and practices and Russian Orthodox icons 237, 238
  Pentecostals in Sweden 40, 236, 238

Pergamum, Turkey 121
Persians 116, 124
phase-based mourning models 196, 196f3, 209
phenomenological anthropology 218, 226, 229f2
Philo of Alexandria, 120, 122, 124, 127
philosophy
   comparative 82
   disciplines of 53
   nature of philosophical thought 51, 53
   shift from thinking unity to thinking difference in 51, 66
philosophy as an art of living 76f5, 83
Philosophy in History: Essays in the Historiography of Philosophy (Rorty, Schneewind, and Skinner) 77, 79
philosophy of religion (see also individual philosophers and movements)
   analytic 52
   and the end of religion 61, 62
   and the proofs for the existence of God 55–58, 56f2
   and religion as universal and/or timeless 34, 52, 54, 58–65
   as an approach to the study of religion 1, 2, 34, 35, 52, 53–55, 54f1, 67
   bias toward cognition 64, 65, 67, 300
   comparing religion and art 34, 61
   comparing religion and philosophy 34, 61
   continental 51, 52, 54
   essence of religion and postmodern 34, 35, 66, 67
   essence of religion for Hegel 34, 60, 61
   essence of religion for Kant 34, 52, 58–60
   essence of religion for Schelling 34, 62–64

Phoenicians 118, 120
Pigliucci, Massimo
   How to be a Stoic 85
Pina-Cabral, João 232
Pindar 128
Pine, Frances 232
Plantinga, Alvin 109
Plato
   Apology 142
   function of myths for 73, 141, 142
   Gorgias 142
   'Myth of Er' 37, 140–143, 145, 146
   Phaedo 142
   Phaedrus 43, 142
   Republic 140–142, 146
Plato and Plutarch's myths of the Afterlife 139–146
Platonism 139
Pliny the Elder 122
Pliny the Younger 126, 128
Plutarch of Chaeronea 37, 138–146
polis 118–123, 125–127, 129, 146
political religion 245, 299
political theology 54
polytheistic traditions
   and the Stoics 82, 83
   nature of gods in 2
   Schelling, development of language and 63, 64
Pontus-Bithynia, Turkey 126
Popper, Karl 21
Porphyry of Tyre 128
positionality 27, 30, 36, 40, 94, 95, 101, 110, 268, 302
positivism 27, 28, 30, 94
postmodern philosophy 34, 35, 66, 67
practical theology 102
primitive religion/societies 4, 5, 7, 27, 29
Prince, Gerald 137
problem of belief
   and methodological agnosticism 27, 39, 94, 110, 215
   and methodological atheism 27, 39, 94, 110, 215

Index

and methodological theism 27–30, 39, 215
and participation as embodied practice 40, 216, 218–220, 222–225
belief as method 27–30
ethnographic experience 27, 31–34
position of neutrality 26, 27, 31, 32
positionality 27, 30, 36, 40, 94, 95, 101, 110, 268, 302
positivism 27, 28, 30, 94
researcher religiosity/non-religiosity and the study of religion 3, 12, 26–34, 39, 214–226, 239, 302
prosēlytos ('religious' convert) 123
Protestantism
  and norms of religion and religious commitment 74, 75, 76f5, 87
  bias toward cognition 65
proximate final cause 100, 101, 103
pseudo-mentalizing 173
Pseudo-Skylax 118
psychodynamic theory
  as an approach to the study of mourning 39, 150, 155, 194, 195, 198–209
  conception of the human subject 199, 209
  fit between religion and the modes of being in mourning 39, 195, 203, 204–208
  importance of symbolic mourning examples on the 205–208
  limitations of the model 209
  modes of being 39, 195, 199–209
  modes of being and their mourning capabilities 39, 203–209
  mourning capabilities of religion on the 193, 205–208
psychological approaches to the study of religion
  and cognitive approaches 37, 150, 154, 155, 162, 163

and modes of reasoning 298, 301
  and psychodynamic approaches 39, 150, 155, 194, 195, 198–209
  and relational approaches 38, 39, 168–172, 174–183, 193–210
  and the study of religion as a meaning system 37, 150–163, 297
psychological organisational structures 199, 200
psychological well-being 150, 154, 154f2

qualitative research methods 38, 39, 74, 79, 86, 161, 180, 214, 301, 302
quantitative research methods 38, 74, 79, 86, 156, 161, 302
Qur'an 263
questions of ultimate meaning 41, 100, 102, 110, 246, 257, 299

rational theology 54
reality effects 5, 6
reflexivity in psychology 16
relationality 136
relational psychological approaches to religion
  as an approach 38, 39, 168–172, 174–183, 193–210
  God representations and attachment processes and functions 38, 169, 174–183, 301
  limitations of a relational approach 39, 209
  limitations of conceptualising of religion as attachment 38, 182, 183
  merits of a relational approach 39, 203
  merits of conceptualising of religion as attachment 38, 182, 183
relational space
  conception of 39

Index

value for psychologists of religion of exploring 39
value in studying bereavement of focusing on relational space 39, 203
religio 114
religion
and culture 3, 4, 10, 14, 17, 17f5, 21, 22, 54, 115, 175, 207, 208, 218, 223, 225, 242, 290, 297, 298
and Dumont's theory of value 42, 43, 275, 276, 287–290
and media 242–246
and ritual 8, 40, 60, 64–67, 72, 100, 101, 121–123, 157, 205, 230–234, 229, 300
and the sacred 4, 7, 8, 40, 41, 152, 155, 242–245
as a socio-cultural phenomenon 3, 54, 57, 58, 67, 242
as an embodied phenomenon 72, 216, 218, 223, 297, 299, 300
as conflicting with science 4, 7, 27, 28, 33, 34, 117, 207
as relation 2, 21, 52, 242, 257
as understood/studied in context 2, 3, 11, 21, 30, 299, 302
as universal 4, 5, 34, 52, 54, 63, 64, 65, 152–154
categorical approach to defining 4, 5, 6, 10, 11
Christianity and conceptions of 4–6, 10, 34, 36, 54, 64–67, 71, 113–115, 229
comparing modern and ancient 113–115, 117, 118, 121, 231, 297
conceptions of 3–12, 29, 34, 35, 40, 41, 54, 55, 58–67, 71, 72, 95, 152–157, 162, 163, 218, 223, 228–230, 235, 242–244, 257, 258, 264, 265, 289, 290, 296–300, 302, 303
conceptual approach to defining 6–12, 297

criticisms of the category of 4–6, 114, 115
development of language and 34, 64
disbelief in 28, 33, 95, 219, 234, 238, 239, 299
distinguishing ideologies, spiritualities, and 9, 156, 157, 243, 244
divide between non-religious spheres and 5, 10, 11, 118, 121, 242–244, 289, 290, 298, 299, 301, 302
function of 7, 8, 59, 151–154, 298
importance of studying religion as a background presence 41, 42, 232, 233–237, 263–265, 269–272, 300
in the public domain 242–247, 256, 257, 299
problem of defining 4–6, 9–11, 54, 114, 115, 228, 229, 245, 289, 302
reality of the category of 5, 6, 11, 113–115, 117, 118, 242, 251, 298
scholarly focus on coherent and consistent 229, 230, 233, 234, 237, 238, 239
substantive approaches to defining 4–7, 9–12
sui generis 5, 17, 17f5
religion vécue 74
religious commitment and adherence
and Protestantism 74, 75
density in 230, 232–235, 237, 238
diffuseness in 231–235, 237
density and diffuseness in 233–237, 262, 265–270, 271, 272
temporalities of 234, 235
religious forms 231, 232, 233, 237, 238, 239, 300
religious meaning-making 154, 155, 193–195, 206–208, 301
religious studies
as an approach to the history of philosophy 70–73, 75–87

321

Index

as an approach to the study of religion 2, 3, 35, 71, 79, 95, 96, 100-103, 107-111
as compared with theology 35, 94-97, 100-103, 107-111
benefits of engaging with the history of philosophy for 35, 71, 87-89
policy advice on religion and conflict in 264
relativist perspectivism 66
research questions 1, 2, 5, 14, 17-19, 25, 34, 35, 40, 43, 51, 52, 54, 58, 67, 72-75, 78, 83, 85, 86, 88, 100-105, 108, 109, 117, 136, 137, 183, 193, 195, 207, 219, 225, 226, 229, 231, 234, 238, 239, 264, 268, 276, 281, 282, 296, 297, 302, 303
researcher
  positioning 26-34, 36, 39, 40, 94, 95, 101, 103, 108, 110, 214, 215, 185, 268, 302
  presuppositions of the 30, 36, 39, 40, 52, 101, 108-110, 268, 302
Retsikas, Konstantinos
  Articulating Islam 235, 238
  articulation 235, 238
  enmeshment 235, 238
  systematicity 235
Richardson, Hilda 140
Riffaterre, Michael 136
ritual
  and collective representations 276
  and mourning 204, 207
  and participant observation 216-219, 221-225
  and philosophy 60, 64-67, 73, 83, 122
  and religion 8, 40, 60, 64-67, 72, 100, 101, 121-123, 157, 205, 230-234, 229, 300
  and sensational forms 230, 231, 237, 238, 300
  and the Gadaba 282, 284-288, 290

contexts of ritual density and commitment 40, 230-232, 237, 238
function of 257
music and 246, 256, 257
political ritual 256, 257
ritual practices as exclusionary 224, 225
ritualization 6, 232
Robbins, Joel 42, 286, 288-290
Robertson-Smith, William 26
Romans 81, 114, 118- 120, 122, 124-128
Rome, Italy 118, 124
Rosaldo, Renato 29, 225
Rosenberg, Alex 17
rules
  changes to 24, 25
  deviance from 22, 23
  function of 22, 24
  how to determine/study 23, 24
  implicit and explicit 23
  relationship between behaviour, categories, and 22-25, 276
  sanctions and 23, 24
Russian Orthodox Church 236, 238
Russians 135

sacralization 6, 8, 12, 155
the sacred
  and action 246
  and discourses and practices 40, 41, 242, 243, 244, 252, 257, 258
  and narratives 40, 41, 244-247
  and 'Nora' 40, 41, 251, 252, 254-257
  and songs 40, 41, 242, 244-246, 257
  and religion 4, 7, 8, 40, 41, 152, 155, 242-245
  and spirituality 157, 244
  and the secular 228, 234, 238, 242, 243
  and transcending problems 244-246, 254
  as generated in the public domain 242-247, 256, 257

conceptions of 4, 7, 8, 40, 41, 152, 155, 242, 244, 257, 258
  in Durkheim's sense 7, 8, 244, 252
  in Eliade's sense 4, 7, 9
  sacralization 6, 8, 12, 155
sacredness of the individual 8, 8f3, 287
sacred-profane distinction 4, 7, 8, 252
sacrifice in the ancient world 121
Sahlins, Marshall 19, 25, 278, 290
Samaritanism/Samaritan-ism 115
Santiago de Compostela Spain 261, 262, 264, 267
Sarapta, Lebanon 118, 119
Saussure, Ferdinand de 135
Saxony, German 106
Schelling, Friedrich Wilhelm Joseph
  against the Hegelians 52, 62
  and Christ as a potential reunifier of all people 34, 64
  development of language and divergence of religions for 34, 63, 64
  essence of religion 34, 62–64
  first all-encompassing God as that which unites all people 34, 63
  on mythology, philosophy, poetry, and revelation 63, 64
Schmidt, Wilhelm (Pater) 28
Schmitt, Terry 243
scholasticism 94, 97–101, 107, 110
Schopenhauer, Arthur 52, 57
science
  as conflicting with religion 4, 7, 27, 28, 33, 34, 117, 207
  hegemony/privileged place of 20, 66
  rationality and, 20, 27, 28
Scythians 124
Scythopolis, historical Judaea 120
secta (group/faction) 127
secular/secularism
  and the sacred 228, 234, 238, 242, 243
  as a challenge to religion 7
  interdependence of religion and 10, 11, 71, 72
  religion in contexts of 228, 234–236, 238, 243, 244, 254
  study of the 10, 11
  'systematizing' and 'articulating' in contexts of 238
Seneca, Lucius Annaeus 84
sensational forms 230, 231, 237, 238, 300
sense of representingness 178
sermo de Deo (discourse about God/God-talk) 96, 111
shell categories 36, 117
Shona (ethnic group, Africa) 249, 253, 255
Shona religion 253, 254
Sidon, Lebanon 120
Sidonians 118
Siikala, Jukka 288
Sikhism 5
Silberman, Israela 152
Sinai, Egypt 198
Smart, Ninian
  Dimensions of the Sacred 9
  conception of religion 9, 35, 72
  methodological agnosticism 27, 215
  on normativity in religious studies 88f14
  seven dimensions of religion 9, 35, 72, 72f2, 72f3, 73, 74, 79, 81, 82, 83, 84, 85, 86
Smith, Antony 252
Smith, Jonathon Z.
  Imagining Religion 5
  on the category of religion 4, 5, 11
Sparta 119
Spartans 124
spiritual healing services
  Dutch media reaction to 217, 218, 223
  experiences of attendees at 217–220, 223, 224

Index

healing services in the
    Netherlands 217–219, 220, 223
  history of 218
  practices and processes of 217–220
  scepticism of visitors and efficacy
    218–220
spiritual societies
  practices and processes of 217–220
  scepticism of visitors and efficacy
    218–220
spirituality
  and the emotional well-being of
    cancer patients 156–162
  and the sacred 157, 244
  conceptions of 157, 243, 244
  distinguishing religion and 9, 157,
    243
society
  conceptions of 8, 17f5, 22
  distinguishing between culture
    and 22
  relationship between religion and
    7, 8, 22
  sui generis 17f5
  symbols and 7, 8
  three levels of society 22
sociology
  and deductive reasoning 298
  and Durkheim 7, 8, 42
  and lived religion 74, 75, 214, 300
  and meaning systems 151
  as an approach to the study of
    religion 1, 2, 29, 58, 64, 74, 75,
    79, 151, 214, 300
  civil religion 8
  interpretive tradition in 10
  sociological significance of edges
    and approximations 232, 233,
    299
Socrates 140, 142, 144, 146
songs
  abilities of 245, 246, 256, 257, 299
  and context 247, 249
  narratives and 244–247, 254–257

theodical function of 246, 247,
    254–257
Sora (ethnic group, India) 289f7
South Africa 6
Stasch, Rupert 230, 231
Steiner, Rudolph 221
Stengs, Irene 11
Stockholm, Sweden 237
Stoic Six Pack (Anon.) 85
stoicism 35, 71, 80–87
structural anthropology 19, 29, 42,
    275, 278, 279, 281, 283–290
study of religion/spirituality as
    a meaning system (see also
    meaning system)
  as an approach 37, 150–163, 297
  cognitive psychological approach
    to the 37, 150, 154, 155, 162, 163
  conception of a meaning system in
    37, 150–152
  limitations of approach 38,
    153–156, 162, 163
  merits of approach 38, 153, 154,
    162, 163
  quantitative research vs.
    qualitative research in the 38,
    161, 162
  role of religion/spirituality in
    causing/solving distress 37, 151,
    157–163
stylistic imitation 141
Sufism 32
suk santi (happiness-peacefulness) 288
Sweden
  material pieties in a charismatic
    church in 237
  pentecostals in 40, 236, 237, 238
symbols
  and religion 7, 8, 9, 60, 61, 64, 65,
    218, 229, 297, 299
  function of 7, 8
  in culture as opposed to in religion
    10
  politics and 257

Syria 118–120, 233
Syrians 120, 122, 128
systematic theology 54, 66, 102, 107
systematicity 235, 238

Tacitus, Publius Cornelius 128
Tambiah, Stanley 278
terror management theory 14
text 134, 135, 135f1
Thayer H. S. 140
The Daily Stoic (Holiday and Hanselman) 85
theism 57
theodicy
    and Plutarch and Plato's myths of the Afterlife 141, 143, 144, 146
    and narratives, 246, 247
    and the sacred 246, 254
    conceptions of 41, 246
    Nora as a 41, 254–257, 299
theologia crucis 67
theologia gloriae 67
theologia viatorum (pilgrim theology) 98, 101, 102
theology
    and Aristotle's four causes 98–101, 107, 109, 110
    and philosophy 54–57, 60, 100
    as an approach to the study of religion 2, 3, 35, 36, 54, 55, 94–111
    historical approach as compared with the approach of 103, 107–111
    religious studies approach as compared with 35, 94–97, 100–103, 107–111
    need for reflection on researcher presuppositions in 36, 94, 103, 108–111, 302
    revelation, divine transcendence, and 35, 95–98, 100–103, 107–110
theological contributions on an epistemological level of analysis 36, 109–111
theological contributions on a material level of analysis 35, 107, 108, 110
theological contributions on a methodological level of analysis 35, 36, 108–110
theory
    anthropology and 13, 17, 18, 21, 230
    as a non-solitary activity 14, 15, 20
    as a practice and/or an ongoing process of argumentation 13, 14, 15, 20, 21
    conceptions of it 13, 14, 15, 20
    distinguishing method from 13
    history and 13
    impact of social embeddedness and/or theorizer's perspective on 15, 16, 30
    important features of academic 20, 21
    need for 13, 14, 21, 298
    philosophy and 13
    psychology and 14
    radical self-reflection and 21, 30
    relationship between data and 18, 19, 20
    who can theorize 15, 16, 20
Tertullian of Carthage 127
thiasos (See *ancient clubs*)
Third Chimurenga (third liberation) 248, 255
Thum, Veronika 104
time 120, 152, 255, 277
time collapse 255
Toland, John 58
tonalities of immediacy 234
tonality 234, 235
totemism 7, 278
transcendent experiences and collective effervescence 244
transfocalization 144, 144f15, 146
transitional space 202
transmodalization 145, 145f18

Index

transmotivation 144, 144f16, 145
transvocalization 144, 144f15
transposition 136f4, 136f5, 138, 139, 139f10, 145
transtextuality 138, 138f6, 139
triple mediation 6
Turner, Victor 30, 215
Tylor, Edward B.
  and Christianity 26
  and Durkheim 7
  conception of religion 3, 4, 6, 7, 9
  cross-cultural analysis 7
  method of introspection 18
  science-religion relationship for 4
  unilinear development 18
types of spirituality-based meaning systems
  absent spirituality 159–163,
  accompanying spirituality 158–162
  enclosed spirituality 158–162
  omnipresent spirituality 158–163
Tyre, Lebanon 118–120
Tyrians 118, 119

ultimate concern 152, 155, 299
ultimate final cause 100, 101, 109
ultimate significance 243, 244, 246
Umra (voluntary pilgrimage to Mecca) 261
Ungeheure (monstrosity) 61
uniformitarian view 18
unilinear development 4, 18, 203
United States 237
Uppsala, Sweden 236
Urapmin (ethnic group, Papua New Guinea) 289
Uwland-Sikkema, Nicoline F. 156

values
  and processes of change 42, 286–290
  and globalization 42, 288
  conceptions of 279, 281–283

Dumont's theory of 42, 276, 279–290, 297
Dumont's theory of value according to Robbins 42, 286–289
  identifying 281–283
  indicators of 291–283, 288, 289
  kinds of 281
  paramount values 281, 287–289
  properties of 283–286
  relationship between hierarchy and 42, 283–287
  relationship between ideas and 42, 277, 281, 283, 286
  study of religion and Dumont's theory of value 42, 43, 275, 276, 287–290
Verhaeghe, Paul 199

Weber, Max 10, 22
Webster, John 97
Westerhof, Gerben J. 156
White, Leslie 19
Winnicott, Donald 14, 194
witchcraft
  and Evans-Pritchard 29, 31, 33
  forms of Azande 29, 31
  forms of Mexican 31, 32
  theory of 32
Wittenberg, Germany 104
Wittgenstein, Ludwig 71
Wohlrab-Sahr, Monika 10
woodcut illustrations in Martin Luther's Catechisms 35, 103–108
Woolgar, Steve 16
world religions 5, 9, 114, 115
wuquf 262

Zambians 249
ZANU-PF *see* Zimbabwe African National Union – Patriotic Front
ZCTU *see* Zimbabwe Congress Trade Unions
Zeno of Elea 81

Index

Zimbabwe
    as represented in 'Nora' 40, 41, 242, 250–257
    importance of land in 248, 249, 252, 253
    importance of the dead in 251, 252
    socio-economic and political milieu of 247–249
Zimbabwe African National Union – Patriotic Front (ZANU-PF)
    actions against the threat of mass democracy by 248, 249
    indoctrination and propaganda tactics of 242, 248, 249, 256, 257
    and *Nora* 40, 249–253, 256, 257
    and the Movement for Democratic Change 248
Zimbabwe Congress Trade Unions (ZCTU) 248

www.ingramcontent.com/pod-product-compliance
Lightning Source LLC
Chambersburg PA
CBHW050837230426
43667CB00012B/2035